Driving Modern Business Intelligence Architecture for Operational Efficiency

Abdelraouf Ishtaiwi
University of Petra, Jordan

Ahmad Al-Qerem
Zarqa University, Jordan

Mohammad Al Khaldy
University of Petra, Jordan

Mohammad Alauthman
University of Petra, Jordan

IGI Global
Scientific Publishing
Publishing Tomorrow's Research Today

Vice President of Editorial	Melissa Wagner
Director of Acquisitions	Mikaela Felty
Director of Book Development	Jocelynn Hessler
Production Manager	Mike Brehm
Cover Design	Jose Rosado

Published in the United States of America by
IGI Global Scientific Publishing
701 East Chocolate Avenue
Hershey, PA, 17033, USA
Tel: 717-533-8845
Fax: 717-533-7115
Website: https://www.igi-global.com E-mail: cust@igi-global.com

Library of Congress Cataloging-in-Publication Data

Names: Ishtaiwi, Abdelraouf, 1975- editor | Al-Qerem, Ahmad, 1975- editor | Al Khaldy, Mohammad, 1978- editor | Alauthman, Mohammad, 1979- editor
Title: Driving modern business intelligence architecture for operational efficiency / edited by: Abdelraouf Ishtaiwi, Ahmad Al-Qerem, Mohammad Al Khaldy, Mohammad Alauthman.
Description: Hershey, PA : IGI Global Scientific Publishing, [2026] | Includes bibliographical references and index. | Summary: "This book assists both the theoretical and practical understanding of current Business Intelligence (BI) architectures"-- Provided by publisher.
Identifiers: LCCN 2025013359 (print) | LCCN 2025013360 (ebook) | ISBN 9798337321257 hardcover | ISBN 9798337321264 paperback | ISBN 9798337321271 ebook
Subjects: LCSH: Business intelligence | Organizational effectiveness
Classification: LCC HD38.7 .D75 2025 (print) | LCC HD38.7 (ebook) | DDC 658.4/72--dc23/eng/20250929
LC record available at https://lccn.loc.gov/2025013359
LC ebook record available at https://lccn.loc.gov/2025013360

British Cataloguing in Publication Data
A Cataloguing in Publication record for this book is available from the British Library.

Table of Contents

Detailed Table of Contents

The chapter discuses the application of business intelligence and artificial intelligence in promoting organisational competitiveness. This is a review of 40 journal articles. The review showed that business intelligence and artificial intelligence are effective in supporting organisational competitive and innovative strategies. However, challenges that hinder the adoption and implementation of these technologies include lack of knowledge or expertise, lack of trust, ethical concerns, inadequate and outdated infrastructure and limited funding. The review then recommended extensive educational programmes and capital investments in business intelligence solutions. The review further recommended further research into the adoption and implementation of these technologies among business organisations.

In the dynamic landscape of the commercial vehicle industry, the integration of data analytics and business intelligence has emerged as a pivotal force in revolutionizing logistics operations. This abstract explores the transformative impact of advanced analytics on optimizing supply chain processes, increasing operational efficiency, and fostering strategic decision-making within the context of commercial vehicle logistics. Big data analytics enables companies to gain actionable insights into their supply chain, facilitating real-time tracking, route optimization. Business intelligence tools play a crucial role in converting raw data into meaningful information, empowering stakeholders to make informed decisions. This strategic approach allows for agile responses to market fluctuations, demand variations, and regulatory changes. Provides a comprehensive overview of the transformative potential of data

container orchestration frameworks like KubeEdge, organizations can process data locally, reduce bandwidth usage, and maintain operational continuity even under network disruption. The chapter also introduces hybrid edge-cloud models that support tiered data processing, model lifecycle management, synchronization, and unified security frameworks.

Mohammad Al Khaldy, University of Petra, Amman, Jordan
Ala Hamarsheh, Computer Science, Faculty of Information Technology, Arab American University, Jenin, Palestine

The acceleration of digital transformation initiatives has intensified organizational demands for immediate, actionable insights from vast data streams. Traditional business intelligence architectures often struggle to fulfill these requirements due to inherent latency constraints and batch-oriented processing paradigms. This chapter addresses the critical gap between conventional analytics approaches and contemporary business requirements by proposing a comprehensive framework for implementing real-time analytics pipelines within business intelligence architectures. Through systematic analysis of architectural components, data engineering methodologies, stream processing frameworks, and visualization approaches, we establish a structured implementation pathway for organizations. Findings demonstrate that successful real-time analytics deployments require deliberate architectural choices that balance latency requirements with analytical depth while addressing organizational readiness dimensions.

Manish Kumar, L.N. Mishra College of Business Management, Muzaffarpur, India

The integration of Artificial Intelligence (AI) into Business Intelligence (BI) is transforming data-driven decision-making by enhancing predictive capabilities, automating analytics, and boosting efficiency. This chapter examines AI's role in modern BI, focusing on machine learning (ML), deep learning, and natural language processing (NLP) as key enablers. AI-powered BI enhances real-time data processing, enables predictive modeling, and helps organizations anticipate trends, optimize strategies, and mitigate risks. A comparative analysis highlights AI's improvements in accuracy, speed, and scalability over traditional BI. Real-world applications in finance, healthcare, and retail demonstrate AI’s impact in generating actionable insights. The chapter also explores challenges like data quality, algorithmic bias, and

Preface

INTRODUCTION

In today's era of digital transformation, Business Intelligence (BI) architectures have evolved into strategic assets that grant organizations the competitive edge necessary to thrive. Modern enterprises face the daunting challenge of harnessing vast volumes of diverse data—complex, fast-moving, and often beyond the scope of traditional analytical systems. Current-generation BI systems integrate cutting-edge technologies such as artificial intelligence, big data analytics, and cloud computing to transform raw information into actionable intelligence, enabling informed, knowledge-based decision-making.

Over the years, BI architectures have undergone substantial transformation, delivering both advancements and new challenges in commodification, deployment, and scalability. Critical issues now extend beyond technical design to encompass organizational behaviors and strategic management considerations. These include the intricacies of data management frameworks, distributed processing, enterprise systems integration, and the diverse patterns of adoption across industries. Addressing these complexities requires a multidisciplinary approach that blends technical innovation with strategic foresight.

Driving Modern Business Intelligence Architecture for Operational Efficiency seeks to advance both the theoretical and practical understanding of contemporary BI architectures. The aim of this volume is to bring together state-of-the-art research that examines how architectural decisions influence operational efficiency and decision support in modern organizations. Contributions in this book will explore emerging BI frameworks, methodological innovations, and empirical case studies that offer deep insights into the design, implementation, and utilization of BI systems.

We have invited contributions from a wide range of perspectives—spanning theoretical explorations, technological developments, methodological approaches to architectural implementation, and real-world case studies. By uniting these diverse viewpoints, the volume aspires to provide a holistic understanding of BI architecture that benefits both academia and industry.

This book is designed to serve multiple audiences:

- Academics and Researchers will find it a valuable resource for advancing theoretical exploration and empirical inquiry into BI architecture, methods, and applications.
- Industry Professionals, including IT architects, data analysts, BI developers, and enterprise system designers, will gain practical insights, methodological guidance, and real-world case evidence to design effective BI solutions.
- Business Leaders and Decision-Makers will discover strategies for leveraging BI systems to drive operational efficiency, competitive advantage, and informed strategic investment.
- Students and Educators will be able to use the book as an advanced resource in data science, business analytics, and information systems programs.
- Policy Makers and Consultants will benefit from a clearer understanding of how BI architectures can be leveraged to boost organizational productivity and foster innovation in digital transformation initiatives.

By addressing the varied needs of these audiences, this volume functions as both an authoritative reference and a practical handbook. Our ultimate goal is to help organizations unlock the full potential of modern BI architectures, enabling them to harness heterogeneous data, improve decision-making, and achieve sustainable success in an increasingly data-driven world.

ORGANIZATION OF THE BOOK

In *Chapter 1*, the authors explore the intersection of Business Intelligence (BI) and Artificial Intelligence (AI) as key enablers of organizational competitiveness. Drawing from a comprehensive review of forty journal articles, this work demonstrates how these technologies strengthen both competitive positioning and innovative strategies. At the same time, it surfaces the practical barriers—ranging from skill shortages and ethical concerns to infrastructure gaps and funding constraints—that hinder adoption. The chapter concludes with a call for robust educational programs, increased capital investment, and expanded research to support effective implementation.

Chapter 2 turns attention to the commercial vehicle industry, where data analytics and BI are reshaping logistics. By harnessing big data for real-time tracking, route optimization, and agile decision-making, organizations can better navigate market fluctuations, regulatory demands, and evolving customer needs. The authors highlight how these tools transform raw data into actionable insights, positioning BI and analytics as indispensable assets for operational efficiency in complex logistics ecosystems.

In *Chapter 3*, the focus shifts to designing scalable BI architectures that bridge technological innovation with organizational needs. The discussion emphasizes adaptive frameworks capable of sustaining evolving analytics capabilities while ensuring interoperability and agility. Evidence from practice shows that such architectures deliver faster reporting cycles, reduced latency, and improved operational oversight—demonstrating the strategic importance of scalability in data-driven enterprises.

Chapter 4 explores the frontier of *Edge Intelligence*, moving BI processing closer to data sources for latency-sensitive, real-time analytics. As IoT adoption grows, industries such as healthcare, manufacturing, and retail increasingly rely on decentralized analytics to meet performance, privacy, and compliance demands. The chapter examines hybrid edge-cloud models, lightweight machine learning deployment, and unified security frameworks that together enable operational continuity even in challenging network environments.

The growing demand for immediacy in analytics is addressed in *Chapter 5*, which proposes an implementation framework for real-time analytics pipelines within BI architectures. By detailing architectural choices, data engineering methods, stream processing technologies, and visualization approaches, the authors demonstrate how to balance latency reduction with analytical depth. This chapter provides both strategic and technical pathways for organizations seeking to modernize their analytics capabilities.

Chapter 6 investigates the integration of AI into BI for predictive decision-making. Through machine learning, deep learning, and natural language processing, AI-enhanced BI enables organizations to forecast trends, optimize strategies, and mitigate risks. Comparative analyses and case studies in finance, healthcare, and retail illustrate gains in accuracy, speed, and scalability, while also addressing challenges such as data quality and algorithmic bias.

In *Chapter 7*, BI architectures are applied to Moodle-based e-learning systems to improve both operational efficiency and educational outcomes. The authors present a conceptual model combining data warehousing, predictive analytics, and personalized dashboards with the modular capabilities of Moodle. Use cases span student performance prediction, clustering, recommender systems, and real-time interventions, with attention given to infrastructure challenges, faculty engagement, and data integrity.

Chapter 8 examines BI's integration into Quality Assurance (QA) processes, transforming QA from reactive assessment to proactive, data-driven improvement.

Drawing on case studies in healthcare, SaaS, and e-commerce, the chapter addresses the technical, organizational, and cultural factors that influence successful integration. The emphasis on aligning QA metrics with broader business outcomes underscores BI's role in elevating software quality as a strategic imperative.

The synergy of AI, machine learning, and BI is the subject of *Chapter 9*, where the authors detail how advanced analytics uncover patterns in structured and unstructured data, automate processes, and support intuitive, self-service data exploration. With benefits spanning resource optimization, risk management, and customer experience enhancement, the chapter also cautions that strategic adoption is necessary to fully realize value in an increasingly data-saturated environment.

Chapter 10 offers case studies from manufacturing and logistics to illustrate BI-driven process automation. Through predictive analytics, real-time dashboards, and connected platforms, organizations achieve improvements in forecasting accuracy, delivery timeliness, labor allocation, and equipment utilization. The authors provide a framework for designing and implementing automation initiatives that align with lean operational goals.

Finally, *Chapter 11* addresses security within BI architectures through the combined application of zero trust frameworks and predictive analytics. The discussion underscores the inadequacy of traditional perimeter-based models against today's sophisticated threats, advocating for adaptive authentication, anomaly detection, and granular access controls. Predictive models play a crucial role in anticipating and mitigating breaches, ensuring the integrity of data-driven decision-making in complex enterprise environments.

CONCLUSION

As the chapters in this volume collectively demonstrate, modern Business Intelligence architectures are no longer static systems but dynamic ecosystems—deeply intertwined with emerging technologies, organizational strategies, and sector-specific challenges. From AI-driven predictive analytics to edge-enabled real-time processing, and from scalable design frameworks to integrated applications in logistics, manufacturing, education, and security, the contributions here reveal both the extraordinary potential and the intricate complexities of contemporary BI systems.

A recurring theme across these works is the recognition that technical innovation must be matched with organizational readiness, cultural adaptation, and strategic investment. The transformative power of BI lies not only in its ability to process vast, diverse datasets, but also in its capacity to inform agile, evidence-based decision-making that sustains competitive advantage. Yet, realizing this potential demands overcoming significant barriers—ranging from infrastructure limitations and data governance challenges to ethical concerns and evolving security threats.

This collection aims to equip readers—whether they are academics, industry professionals, business leaders, policy makers, or students—with a nuanced understanding of the architectural choices, implementation strategies, and future trends shaping the BI landscape. By bringing together diverse perspectives, methodologies, and case studies, the volume offers both a theoretical foundation and a practical guide for navigating the next era of Business Intelligence.

In closing, *Driving Modern Business Intelligence Architecture for Operational Efficiency* stands as both a reflection of current advances and a springboard for future inquiry. It is our hope that the insights contained within will inspire continued innovation, foster informed decision-making, and contribute to the evolution of BI architectures that are not only operationally efficient, but also resilient, ethical, and adaptable to the ever-changing demands of the digital age.

Chapter 1
Business Intelligence and Artificial Intelligence for Organisational Competitiveness

Elisha Mupaikwa
https://orcid.org/0000-0002-0313-7139
National University of Science and Technology, Zimbabwe

ABSTRACT

The chapter discuses the application of business intelligence and artificial intelligence in promoting organisational competitiveness. This is a review of 40 journal articles. The review showed that business intelligence and artificial intelligence are effective in supporting organisational competitive and innovative strategies. However, challenges that hinder the adoption and implementation of these technologies include lack of knowledge or expertise, lack of trust, ethical concerns, inadequate and outdated infrastructure and limited funding. The review then recommended extensive educational programmes and capital investments in business intelligence solutions. The review further recommended further research into the adoption and implementation of these technologies among business organisations.

INTRODUCTION

Organizational competitiveness has been studied using a variety of frameworks. These frameworks have recently demonstrated that artificial intelligence and data analytics have become important facilitators of company competitiveness, but new technical advancements have also opened up new avenues for business intelligence

DOI: 10.4018/979-8-3373-2125-7.ch001

and competitiveness. Thus, the combination of these technologies promises to offer countless opportunities to boost business enterprises' competitiveness. Being a low-cost producer, concentrating on market niches and segmentations, and utilizing technology are just a few of the competitive strategies that organizations have historically employed. When incorporated into these competitive strategies, artificial intelligence(AI) and business intelligence (BI) hold the potential to open up countless opportunities for businesses. As a result, it requires that studies on integration strategies be taken into account. In examining organisational competitiveness, the internet and the web's advancements have been acknowledged to be vital cogs for attaining organisational competitiveness. The internet and the web's rapid technological advancements have broken down geographical boundaries to businesses, necessitating an increase in organizational competitiveness. For many organizations, these developments have also made information and market access easier. Because of this competitive climate, businesses, especially smaller businesses in emerging nations, have been increasingly encouraged to invest in competitive strategies. The dynamic nature of the competitive environment in which many organizations operate means that their tactics for competitiveness are constantly changing. Deep technological breakthroughs in systems, software, and applications have been the focus of the globalization era, and according to Parada et al. (2015), businesses that operate in international marketplaces face difficulties on both a local and global level unless they adopt and adapt to these technological developments of the digital environment. This is also because businesses in this environment are committed to maintaining profitability and worldwide competitiveness while negotiating a complex web of internal and external demands (Aljawarneh, 2024). On the outside, they negotiate the shifting landscape of growing regional and international rivalry and swift technical advancement. As such, organizations must improve customer service, reduce expenses, and maximize efficiency internally while maintaining their competitive advantage (Zheng et al., 2023). Maintaining long-term advantages, therefore, requires fostering competitive strategies in areas such as quality, pricing, agility, customer response, and innovation (Yusuf et al., 2022). The recognition of the relevance of competitive strategies and innovations has strengthed R&D In many organizations, whose primary purpose is to secure the sustainability of the organization and to combat competition in a setting where threats from competitors are common.

Many organizations have resorted to new technologies like BI, which is frequently powered by artificial intelligence and big data analytics, to become more competitive. These technologies allow them to make use of the limitless amounts of data that are available to them. Though few scholars have looked into how BI and AI may be integrated into organizational competitiveness, from available literature, these technologies have enhanced decision-making and increased organizational competitiveness. The literature has extensively documented BI as a tool that can support business advancement by improving decision-making processes, which in turn can improve firm performance and business value (BV) (Paradza and Daramola, 2021). To maintain long-term profitability and sustainability, business organizations must make appropriate decisions in the highly competitive and dynamic modern business environment (El-Haddadeh et al., 2021). To produce strategic information, BI makes it possible to crunch and analyze enormous amounts of organizational data. BI has emerged as a result of the expansion of AI technology, which has led to the transformation of information techniques to optimize business operations and decisions (Chen and Lin, 2021). Therefore, the chapter aims to shed light on how BI can incorporate AI, as well as how big data and data analytics principles can be incorporated into competitive strategies for businesses. It is hoped that by combining data analytics, AI, and BI, organizations will be able to investigate these technologies and improve their competitiveness. BI systems combine operational and historical data with analytical tools to provide business planners and decision-makers with competitive and critical information. The goal of BI is to improve the quality and timeliness of data so that managers may better understand how their organization compares to its competitors. BI tools and technologies, for instance, can be used to analyze changes in market share, consumer behaviour and spending patterns, customer preferences, corporate capabilities, and market conditions (Bharadiya, 2023). This chapter, therefore, first provides the context of BI and its supportive infrastructure and how various BI technologies may be used to enhance organisational competitiveness. The chapter also discusses Porter's forces model and how it has been used to study the competitiveness of organisations.

Background

Organizations have begun to make use of the growing use of Big Data and developing technologies in recent years to evaluate and obtain important insights related to decision-making processes. To provide enterprises with useful and actionable intelligence, the practice of competitive intelligence (CI) involves keeping an eye on rivals (Ranjan and Foropon, 2021). In this sense, one of the many important elements of effectively guiding CI and eventually incorporating such important insights into CI strategies is the ability to utilize and unlock the potential of big data tools and methodologies. The competitiveness of commercial organizations has thus been greatly aided by digital technology in a variety of forms, including executive information systems, management information systems, decision support systems, and process control systems. Senior managers can now make informed decisions about information technology investments and create strategies to combat competitive rivalry in environments that are marked by strong supplier and buyer bargaining power, threats from substitute products, and new entrants into traditional markets. These technologies and information systems have also harnessed the powerful power of AI and data analytics to process large volumes of data. Porter's five forces model is the source of these variables used to examine an organization's competitiveness Competitiveness has become essential to the survival and development of industrial firms in an increasingly international market. Porter (1990) defined competitiveness as a company's capacity to continuously outperform its competitors in terms of price, quality, and innovation, establishing and maintaining a competitive edge in the marketplace. Even while competitiveness is important, many industrial businesses struggle to manage and improve their competitive position (Abdiqaxarovich, 2023). Another method for examining organizational competitiveness is the value chain model, which has been used by some organizations as a result of the incorporation of IT tools into essential applications. According to Dunning (2019), competitiveness is the capacity of an organization to acquire and preserve a competitive edge by providing its clients with better value. Competitiveness is especially crucial in the industrial sector since it fosters innovation, productivity, and sustainable growth, all of which eventually support a country's total economic development. According to Grant (2019), cost-effectiveness, product quality, innovation, and market positioning are some of the elements that affect competitiveness. These elements support a business's capacity to stand out from rivals, draw in and keep clients, and succeed over the long haul in the marketplace. Because companies with a significant competitive edge are better able to invest in new technologies, adjust to shifting market conditions, and maintain a solid financial performance, Porter (1991) highlights the close relationship between competitiveness and sustainable growth.

The comparison of business competitiveness and technological advancement has become critical in the big data environment. This is because, compared to earlier times, the storing of vast amounts of data is made possible by technological advancements. In this environment, companies can get information from clients as well as rival companies, which aids in their differentiation. This information is regarded as an asset that can be used to gain a competitive edge, contingent on each company's skills. Information systems, such as business intelligence, help a firm implement its plan and make it stronger so that it may stand out in its industry (Ragazou et al., 2023). Numerous research that has looked into organizational competitiveness are included in the literature. The uses of data analytics have also been examined in other recent studies, which have acknowledged that modern organizations today function in a large data environment that is beyond the handling and processing capabilities of older systems. Artificial intelligence technologies have been characterized in the literature as one of the main foundations for processing complicated data requirements of organizations in the management of such data. BI technologies have emerged as a result of the merging of data analytics and AI technology. Both small and medium-sized firms are using BI solutions, which are growing in popularity. From tactical to strategic, they are used to support a range of business decisions. BI can be viewed as both a safeguard for businesses and a set of tools and best practices that let senior executives access, evaluate, and turn company data into information that helps them make quick decisions (Ragazou et al., 2023). The crucial role that business intelligence (BI) plays in influencing corporate decision-making has attracted a lot of interest from management academics, according to Awan et al. (2021). Well-informed decision-making made possible by thorough data analysis from a variety of sources has been highlighted as a result of BI's smooth application and data integration and the buildup of user skills. According to Donnelly (2022), this ability, therefore helps to promote organizational agility. All levels of management are affected by this analytical prowess, which has a significant impact on tactical and strategic choices. According to Bouckaert (2016), academics highlight the significance of business intelligence (BI), especially in the field of organizational and functional planning, where it is clear that advanced tools are required to facilitate thorough business analysis. Some researchers contend that the use of digital technologies significantly boosts business organizations' competitiveness by allowing them to create new strategies for managing competition in their competitive environments. This is due to the increased interest that organizations have shown in using artificial intelligence and big data analytics. This perspective is reinforced by Climent et al. (2024), who contend that the majority of successful organizations worldwide have employed data analytics and artificial intelligence, whereas those that have not adopted these technologies have stagnated. According to Climent et al. (2024), companies that have successfully dominated industries are those that have leveraged the powerful computing capabilities of business analytics and artificial intelligence.

Researchers and corporate organizations are conducting more BI research. Among the main subjects of BI is social media because this technology has recently been used as a business intelligence tool by several organizations. Choi et al. (2020) are among the researchers who have looked into the use of social media as a BI tool. They have found that social media's flexibility and wider accessibility among business partners and customers have led to a greater recognition of social media as a business intelligence tool and as a competitive strategy. Furthermore, some trailblazers who saw the benefits of social media by using it as a web platform to communicate with their clients have started social media channels and are working to better understand their clients and the market they serve (He, Zha, et al., 2013). Understanding the significance of social media, one of the most open data sources and the greatest online forums for consumers to voice their opinions has attracted scholarly attention. Social media analytics, a scholarly endeavour that entails the collection, analysis, and extraction of important hidden information from a variety of social media data, is the result of this academic interest in social media data. In reality, numerous studies have gathered a significant amount of customer-generated social media data and have produced statistical findings, measured satisfaction levels, or textual subjects that can assist commercial enterprises in making strategic decisions in their business environment (Choi et al., 2020).

The use of cloud computing and the use of business intelligence has also been studied by other researchers. One such study is that conducted by Wang et al. (2020), who created a model-driven artificial intelligence and discovered that the model had better decision-making capabilities. To improve businesses' CI, other researchers have also combined big data, big data analytics, and developing technologies (Ranjan and Foropon, 2021). Ranjan and Foropon (2021) claim that the use of cloud computing, big data, and the Internet of Things (IoT) has improved value creation for the company and its customers. More recently, CI has garnered a lot of attention due to the proliferation of data that is now publicly accessible through social media, blogs, wikis, text messages, e-mails, mobile phones, and other electronic digital communications. This data is a crucial tool for developing CI. With BI, KM, and AI, CI is closely related. The collection, analysis, and administration aspects of CI are similar to those of its other intelligentsia. The focus of CI is both internal and external, and the CI analyst mostly bases his or her conclusions on outside data. Additionally, CI depends on several well-established approaches for gathering, analyzing, and managing data and knowledge (Liebowitzs, 2006). Strategic intelligence is another phrase that has surfaced in the field of organizational competitiveness research. To give valuable information and knowledge for corporate strategic decision-making, SI is the aggregation of the various forms of intelligence (Liebowitzs, 2006). AI, KM, BI, and CI are the inner layers of the onion, whereas SI is the outermost layer. Although AI could significantly complement and improve KM in many areas, KM does not always need to incorporate AI applications. Gomwe, Potgieter, and Litheko (2022) conducted some research on the use of business intelligence in small and medium-sized businesses in South Africa and found that their suggested framework was successful in establishing and preserving an organization's competitiveness. Vlahovljak (2022) lists six timeless objectives for corporate intelligence:

a) assess the company's standing among others;
b) recognize shifts in consumer behaviour and spending patterns;
c) outline the company's capabilities;
d) investigate market conditions, emerging trends, demographic data, and economic information;
e) ascertain the social and political climate and
f) observe what the competition is doing.

Methodology

This review of journal articles was drawn from several academic databases. The following steps were followed in the retrieval of articles for the review:

a) A total of 100 journal articles were retrieved from Taylor and Francis, Emerald Insight, Jstor and MDPI. The key search terms used in the retrieval and selection of articles were "business intelligence", "Competitive intelligence", "Artificial intelligence and competitiveness", and "Business analytics and competitiveness".
b) Articles published between 2000 and 2025 were selected.
c) The articles were then filtered using a combination of pairs of search terms for relevance, and these combinations were" Business intelligence and Artificial intelligence", " Business intelligence and organisational competitiveness", "Organisational competence and artificial intelligence", "Artificial intelligence and competitive intelligence", and "Business intelligence and competitive intelligence". This filtering produced 40 articles, which were then selected for the final analysis.

Basic Concepts of Business Intelligence

Since its inception in the 1990s, when it was primarily used in business, and IT communities where a standard set of data matrices was used to produce information and prepare for the future, BI has developed throughout time. As BI developed into a more analytically focused tool in the early 2000s, it was dubbed Business Analytics (BA) in the literature. By emphasizing statistical and mathematical insights, BA takes a more lenient approach to datasets used to extract new information and derive meaning from organizational performances (Paradza and Daramola, 2021). In summary, BA stresses both reporting and future prediction, whereas BI mostly concentrates on reporting. Big Data, also known as Big Data Analytics, is the most recent term to emerge from BI and BA. It refers to larger and more complicated data sets that require specialized tools to synthesize information while maintaining the same focus on reporting and predictive analytics.

Brijs (2013) defines BI as a broad range of tools and applications for collecting, storing, evaluating, and making data accessible to enterprise users so they may make better business decisions. Online analytical processing, data mining, business performance management, data warehousing, business analytic tools, and other technologies that are advanced enough to constitute standalone representations of information science are all included under the umbrella term of BI (Vizgaitytė and Skyrius, 2012). Decision support systems, query and reporting, online analytical processing (OLAP), statistical analysis, forecasting, and data mining are all examples of BI applications. There are several BI applications in organizations, including critical-mission-specific applications designed to solve particular enterprise problems, localized applications tailored to the requirements of particular organizational units, and applications motivated by user needs (Brijs, 2013). In the modern information age, where knowledge is power, organizations use information to grow and preserve a competitive edge (Haag, Cummings, and Philips, 2007). A key component of business is the collection of information and the application of human judgment to transform this raw data into intelligence (Murphy, 2005). Information and knowledge are essential for generating income for businesses (Kruger, 2010). Organizations can create competitive advantage and continuous innovation to survive and thrive in the long run by using information systems in the process of knowledge and intelligence generation (Laudon and Laudon, 2007). "Knowledge about your customers, your competitors, your business partners, your competitive environment, and your internal operations – that gives you the ability to make effective, important, and often strategic business decisions" is how Haag et al. (2007: 85) define BI. However, they also point out that there is a specialized subset of BI called CI. CI is "BI-focused on the external competitive environment," according to Haag et al. (2007). According to Murphy (2005), CI encompasses more than just benchmarking against rivals; it also involves keeping an eye on the political, social, technological, and economic landscapes—all of which have the potential to either strengthen or weaken an organization's position in the market. According to Acharya, Singh, Pereira, and Singh (2018), CI is the act of gathering, analyzing, interpreting, and disseminating strategic information at the appropriate moment for use in decision-making. Its conceptual roots can be traced to Michael Porter, who, in 1980, employed the CI technique to examine competitors and industries, even though its practical roots go back many decades (Ranjan and Foropon, 2021). In light of this, Davenport & Prusak (1998) and Johnson (2005) have maintained that knowledge management and corporate intelligence, including business and CI, are complementary partners that, when used in tandem, enable the realization of greater financial advantage. KM, according to Turban et al. (2007), is "the systematic and active management of ideas, information, and knowledge residing in organizations' employees." Knowledge is defined as "information that is contextual, relevant, and actionable. Effective and efficient problem-solving, dynamic learning, strategic planning, and decision-making are all made possible by the structuring of knowledge. By using a formal Knowledge Management System (KMS), corporate knowledge and information may be shared logically to maximize its value through reuse. As a result, BI may be helpful at all levels of management, supporting both the organization's daily operations and strategic business choices when dealing with massive amounts of unstructured data. Arnott et al. (2004) state that the purpose of BI is to gather data that is considered essential to the company and then utilize business intelligence systems to present or modify that data into information that can be used to support management decision-making. Any corporation may apply an analytical approach that turns data into information, information into knowledge, and knowledge into decisions by having a solid understanding of business intelligence systems. The complexity of business processes, the sheer volume of data generated and used in daily operations, the growing number of highly diverse internal and external data sources, and numerous compliance, privacy, and other data-related issues have all contributed to the complexity of cross-organizational data integration and analysis (Lloyd, 2011). Additionally, BI systems assist businesses in estimating the worth of their connections with clients and suppliers, which increases their bargaining power. A company risks making important decisions based on incomplete or erroneous information if it lacks business intelligence. Additionally, according to Mohamed (2020), executives say that a properly executed BI strategy benefits businesses in the following ways:

a) Identify and react to business trends promptly
b) Provide timely, insightful information and trend reports to staff
c) Easily generate comprehensive financial, operations, customer, and vendor reports
d) View, manipulate, analyze, and disseminate reports effectively using a variety of well-known technologies
e) Extract current high-level summaries, account categories, or specific transactions
    e) Combine information from many businesses, departments, and databases
    f) Reduce manual and repetitive labour.

Elements of Business Intelligence

From the literature, several BI architectures have been proposed. An example is one Five-layer architectural model proposed by, which is shown in Figure 1 below by Rahman (2011).

Figure 1. Business Intelligence Architecture

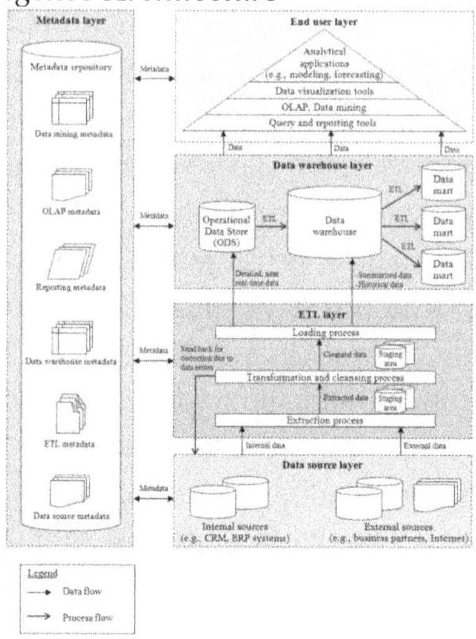

(Rahman, 2011)

Data Source Layer: It is possible to obtain all of this data from both internal and external sources. Customer relationship management and enterprise resource planning systems are examples of operational systems within an organization that collect and preserve data. These systems are referred to as internal data sources. Business operations data (such as customer, product, and sales data) are examples of internal data sources.

ETL (Extract-Transform-Load) Layer: Three primary activities are the focus of this layer: loading, transformation, and extraction (Baars and Kemper, 2008; Sen and Sinha, 2005). According to Reinschmidt and Francoise (2000), extraction is the process of locating and gathering pertinent data from various sources. The information gathered from both internal and external sources is typically fragmented, unintegrated, and possibly duplicated. Data extraction, transformation, and loading are handled by ETL (Extraction-Transformation-Load) tools. Getting access to data from various sources, such as databases, text files, HTML, XML documents, and/or email, is known as extraction. Data are typically stored in relational databases after extraction, which greatly speeds up additional data processing during the transformation stage. Therefore, to choose facts that are important for assisting with organizational decision-making, the extraction process is required. Before the transformation and cleaning procedure, the extracted data are then sent to a temporary storage location known as the data staging area (Ranjan, 2009). If an issue arises, this is done to prevent the need to extract data again. The data will then undergo the process of transformation and purification. The process of transforming data into uniform formats for reporting and analysis by applying a set of business rules (such as aggregation functions) is known as transformation. To guarantee uniformity within an organization, the data transformation process also entails standardizing data definitions and establishing business logic for data mapping (Davenport and Harris, 2007). Data transformation is thought to be the most difficult step in the ETL process. Typically, SQL, scripting languages, or conventional programming languages are used to carry out the procedure. Data transformation includes identifying missing or duplicate data, calculating appropriate aggregates, and unifying data. The principles of physical data structure unification, business principles that guarantee compatibility with a modelled domain, and business principles that provide semantic compatibility between related data are all examples of data transformation rules. Data loading entails supplying aggregated and filtered data to data warehouses (Larson, 2008; Meyer, 2001). According to predetermined guidelines, data cleansing is the process of locating and fixing data mistakes (Reinschmidt and Francoise, 2000). The extracted data is returned to the data source for rectification if an error is discovered (Dayal et al., 2009). When several data sources must be merged like in data warehouses and business intelligence systems, the necessity for data cleaning rises dramatically (Larson, 2008). The sources frequently include redundant information in various formats. The following criteria should be met by any data cleaning approach: (1) data cleaning should identify and eliminate all significant errors and inconsistencies in both single and multiple data sources; (2) tools should be available to support this process, reducing the need for manual inspection and programming work and allowing for easy extension to additional sources; (3) data cleaning should not be carried out in isolation but rather in conjunction with schema-related transformations based on thorough metadata; and (4) mapping functions for data cleaning and other data transformations should be specified declaratively and reusable for both query processing and other data sources. The staging area is where the data is kept once it has been cleaned and changed.

Data Warehouse Layer: The operational data store, data warehouse, and data marts are the three parts that make up the data warehouse layer. The operational data store sends data to the data warehouse, which then sends it to the data mart. The time needed to complete the ETL function and move the data to a different OLAP platform makes information latency an issue when the data is migrated into the data warehouse using traditional ETL tools and techniques on big data sets. Since performance might degrade with increasing data volumes, real-time data is found in the Online Transaction Processing (OLTP) environment, where the data time horizon is significantly shorter. This runs counter to the objectives and nature of the OLAP environment, which aggregates data and expands its time horizon to a significant degree based on the organization's information life cycle policy. The interactive processes of predictive modelling and data mining are designed to analyze big databases and extract knowledge and information that could be accurate and helpful for knowledge workers who are involved in problem-solving and decision-making (Vercelis, 2009). Based on the primary goal of the analysis, data mining operations can be separated into two main research streams: interpretation and prediction (Poul et al., 2003). Such sophisticated data mining makes use of several mathematical models and techniques. Regression, classification, time series, association rules, and clustering are among the most crucial (Larose, 2005; Tan et al., 2005; Witten et al., 2011). Unstructured web content is frequently processed and analyzed using text mining. Because a sizable amount of the unstructured content gathered by an organization is in textual format—from corporate papers and emails to web pages and social media content—text analytics are necessary and utilized (Chen et al., 2012; Olszak and Zurada, 2015). According to Newman (2010), text mining can be defined as: (1) preprocessing data to the required format; (2) concept extraction, which involves extracting key concepts and terms through preliminary text analysis; (3) narrative analysis, which involves crafting a narrative analysis to find patterns and co-occurrences of identified concepts; (4) automatic categorization, which involves creating an automated solution; and (5) ontology building, which involves creating an ontology for CI analysis in the future. Using XML, Internet protocols (HTTP, SMTP), and/or application programming interfaces (APIs), web mining refers to the techniques and resources used to process and examine unstructured web material. Developers can incorporate a variety of content from various web-enabled systems thanks to them. Cloud computing, which comprises hardware, systems software, and applications that are provided as Internet-based services, is a significant element of web analytics (Veber, 2012; Riad and Hassen, 2008).

Metadata Layer: Metadata is information about information. According to Giovinazzo (2003), it explains the location of data usage and storage, its source, any modifications made to it, and the relationships between various data points. Technical and business data, along with data definitions and business regulations, are stored in a metadata repository (Davenport & Harris, 2007). Online Analytical Processing, or OLAP, offers a summary of corporate data in multiple dimensions. With the help of automatically generated SQL queries, OLAP tools are primarily designed to optimize the search of large data files and generate interactive reports based on the user's pre-established criteria (dimensions). They make it possible to conduct intricate evaluations of consumer relations, product profitability, and business success (Olszak and Zurada, 2015). The question of "who?" "What?" "When?" "what if?" and "Why?" are also addressed by them. Predicting the future, establishing patterns, and analyzing consumer and competition behaviour are all made possible by multivariant studies performed on historical data that is kept in data warehouses. Organizations can identify vulnerabilities, dangers, and untapped openings and chances when they successfully implement them (Olszak, 2014).

End User Layer: Tools that present information in various formats to various users make up the end user layer.

Additionally, Moscoso-Zea et al. (2019) suggested a knowledge management-driven BI architecture for education. A hybrid information infrastructure for business intelligence and analytics (BI&A) and knowledge management (KM) was presented by Moscoso-Zea et al. (2019). It is based on an enterprise architecture (EA) repository and an educational data warehouse (EDW), which enables the digitization of knowledge and facilitates the visualization and analysis of disparate organizational components such as people, processes, and technology.

Competitive Strategies

According to Abdiqaxarovich (2023), competitiveness is the capacity of an organization to acquire and preserve a competitive edge by providing its clients with better value. Competitiveness is especially crucial in the industrial sector since it fosters innovation, productivity, and sustainable growth, all of which eventually support a country's total economic development. According to Abdiqaxarovich (2023), cost-effectiveness, product quality, innovation, and market positioning are some of the elements that affect competitiveness. These elements support a business's capacity to stand out from rivals, draw in and keep clients, and succeed over the long haul in the marketplace. Because companies with a significant competitive edge are better able to invest in new technologies, adjust to shifting market conditions, and maintain a solid financial performance, Porter (1991) highlights the close relationship between competitiveness and sustainable growth. Therefore, maintaining the long-term sustainability of industrial firms requires boosting competitiveness. Porter (1990) asserts that competition establishes the suitability of the firm's operations that can influence its success. Therefore, the pursuit of a favourable competitive position in an industry—the primary setting in which competition takes place—is the essence of competitive strategy. In this setting, businesses aim to forge a lucrative and long-lasting position in opposition to the factors influencing the competition in the sector. The foundation of each business organization's performance is its competitive edge. Businesses that "do better" than their competitors are considered to have a competitive advantage because they can use resources more effectively, typically due to greater knowledge and information assets, or they have access to unique resources that others do not. Whatever the case, they outperform their rivals in terms of revenue growth, profitability, or productivity growth (efficiency), all of which eventually result in higher stock market valuations (Laudon and Laudon, 2014). As a result, a growing number of organizations have embraced innovations that improve their performance in the highly competitive global market. These developments have helped businesses expand (Porter, 1990). The growth of the contemporary digital environment has played a complementary role in encouraging corporate firms to build competitive strategies in the quest for competitiveness. AI, data analytics, cloud computing, and data mining-powered BI technologies are among the advancements that have been incorporated into organizational competitive strategies. Decision support systems gave rise to BI, which has since seen several other advancements. Other intelligent innovations that have surfaced include location intelligence, which has been fueled by the development of geographic information systems that allow for the spatial analysis of data to make comprehensive locational decisions through advanced analytics, and mobile BI, which is based on web-based interactive dashboards (Vizgaitytė, and Skyrius, 2012). Porter (1990), is one of several authors who have examined the competitiveness of firms and developed Porter's Five Forces model shown in Figure 2 below. The model categorized competitive strategies as the focus market, differentiation strategy, low-cost strategy, and cost strategy.

Figure 2. Porters Five Forces Model

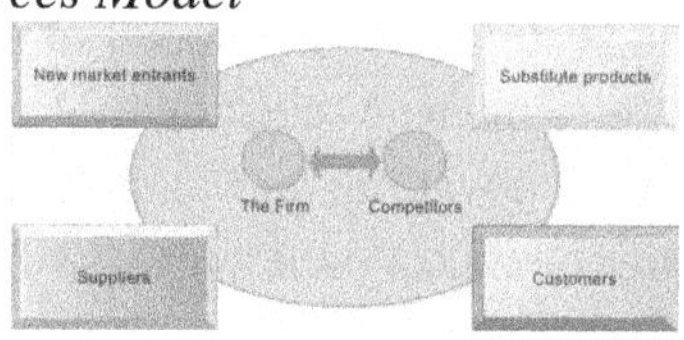

(Laudon and Laudon, 2014)

From Figure 2 above, when an industry begins to turn a profit, it will attract additional players threatening the profitability of an enterprise. Low entry barriers make it simple for new competitors to take market share and jeopardize profitability. Additionally, new competitors offer worthwhile substitutes for what your sector now offers at lower prices. In addition to this, suppliers may be able to raise the price of those inputs or lower the quality without retaliating if they have significant bargaining power. Strong buyer power can push for better quality or service, drive down prices, and set competitors against one another at the expense of industry profits. When there are few customers and a large number of sellers to pick from, the customers' power increases. The stricter the profit cap on your industry, the more attractive the substitute. If several alternatives can perform the same function as your product or service, there is a high risk of substitution. On the other hand, the threat is minimal if there are few alternatives.

The use of information technology to get the lowest prices and operating costs is known as low-cost leadership. Product differentiation is the process of leveraging information systems to either make new products and services possible or significantly alter how easy it is for customers to use your current products and services. By concentrating on a certain market niche, businesses can leverage information technology to better service this niche market than their rivals. By generating and evaluating data for precisely calibrated sales and marketing strategies, information systems assist this approach. Businesses can effectively pitch advertising and marketing efforts to ever-tinier target markets by using information systems to extensively examine consumer purchasing patterns, tastes, and preferences (Laudon and Laudon, 2014). Businesses can utilize information systems to strengthen their relationships with suppliers and cultivate intimacy with customers by strengthening their customer and supplier intimacy. Strong ties between suppliers and consumers boost loyalty to your business and the cost of moving (Laudon and Laudon, 2014).

Artificial Intelligence and Competitiveness of Business Enterprises

Businesses have greater business opportunities as a result of AI, and quick development. AI has revolutionized international business by promoting innovation and operational efficiency. It makes use of big data analytics and machine learning to inform strategic decision-making and forecast market trends (Menzies et al., 2024). Efficiency increases, cost reductions, better product quality, and enhanced customer service are all possible with artificial intelligence (Bag et al., 2021). According to Yao et al. (2021), enterprise competencies are essential for spotting business prospects. An increasingly important and intangible resource for improving corporate performance is AI competence (Belhadi et al., 2021; Lou and Wu, 2021; Mikalef and Gupta, 2021). It implies that enterprises could get a competitive edge from artificial intelligence (Chaudhuri et al., 2021). Businesses can gain access to rare, valuable, unique, and irreplaceable resources through AI (Ghasemaghaei, 2021). AI tools, particularly the developments in machine learning and natural language processing, have gained attention in the last 10 years from both corporations and contemporary literature. These AI courses have given rise to some inventions, which have been combined to create business and organizational intelligence advancements that have improved businesses' ability to make decisions. This is because firms can now manage both internal and external data thanks to these technologies linked to data analytics. This allows the organization to perform predictive analytics on future occurrences about competitive situations and competition. In the context of multinational businesses (MNEs), AI is essential for enhancing decision-making, productivity, and competitiveness (Bag et al., 2021; Wamba-Taguimdje et al., 2020). By enabling enhanced predictive analytics, automating tasks, and utilizing data-driven insights, AI integration greatly aids enterprises in navigating complex global contexts (Allal-Chérif et al., 2021; Bag et al., 2021; Satheesh et al., 2020; Wamba-Taguimdje et al., 2020).

As a result, companies in the digital age require shorter wait times and a greater understanding of the market environment, which is subject to change more quickly than in earlier decades. According to this perspective, several businesses have been implementing cutting-edge technology to achieve superior performance and a competitive edge (Kitsios and Kamariotou, 2025). Given the competitive landscape of businesses and the abundance of data-scarce assets, which necessitates speed in decision-making, several businesses have been motivated to adopt AI tools, mainly because of the anticipated consequences demonstrated by top digital enterprises (Kitsios and Kamariotou, 2025). Several top corporations are reevaluating their strategic plans for the integration of AI tools as they realize that the transformation process necessitates a review of the corporate strategy.

One of the scholars who has looked into the use of AI in business to boost the competitiveness of commercial organizations is Menzies et al. (2024). Supporting and boosting innovation approaches, international market selection, entry mode choice, foreign exchange, international trade negotiations, global supply chain and international operations, sustainability issues, human resource management, managing business across cultures, and international marketing are some of the main areas where AI has reportedly affected the competitiveness of business organizations. The character of cross-border market entry has been significantly impacted by strategy decisions and technological complexity (Benito et al., 2022). AI and other technological developments may influence international market selection (IMS). IMS is described as "the process of establishing criteria for selecting (country) markets, investigating market potentials, classifying them according to the agreed criteria, and choosing which markets were suitable for later development and which should be addressed first." To better customize their products and marketing tactics, industrial businesses should determine their target markets and client segments, according to Kotler and Keller (2016). This entails examining consumer preferences, market demographics, and competition dynamics to identify the most appealing and lucrative market niches to target. Business organisations can recognize more worldwide opportunities and have more access to global markets thanks to AI (Dillon et al., 2020). Without investing significant resources in local marketing affiliates, AI allows business organisations to effectively track new trends and opportunities in foreign markets (Luo and Zahra, 2023). Business organisations can acquire insights and recommendations on the present and future conditions of a foreign market by evaluating market trends and opportunities using AI-enabled data analytics and visualization tools. Successful IB decision-making requires a thorough understanding of currency patterns, movements, and forecasts (Güler and Tepecik, 2019). The IB may experience a currency gain or loss depending on the value of the currency at any particular time, which could be advantageous or disadvantageous to a company (Güler and Tepecik, 2019). AI can also be used to forecast and comprehend currency trends and movements while examining other nations for market analysis (Güler and Tepecik, 2019). Artificial neural networks, agent-based systems, and genetic algorithms are common AI technologies in supply chain management (SCM) (Toorajipour et al., 2021). Software-based AI tools known as artificial neural networks mimic the architecture of the human brain, which is made up of numerous interconnected neurons that retain information (Soori et al., 2023). Between the input layer and the output layer are hidden layers of neurons that house the majority of the data (Sang, 2021). Artificial neural networks are fed a lot of scenarios during the training process (Stair et al., 2021). Artificial neural networks can be fed new scenarios after they have been adequately trained, and they will determine the result for each new scenario (Stair et al., 2021). Demand forecasting, inventory and route optimization, production scheduling, logistics planning, supplier metrics evaluation and monitoring, including quality, delivery times, price, and risk management, have all been made easier for SCM by the use of this AI technology (Soori et al., 2023b). According to Ahi et al. (2022), AI may help with “supporting more informed decisions to meet employees' needs.” Due to its acknowledged potential for value creation globally, research on the application and integration of AI in IHRM is increasing (Chowdhury et al., 2023). By utilizing the creative potential of AI technology, this trend represents a revolutionary change in staff management and overall company performance (Vrontis et al., 2021). Employers must embrace advanced recruitment technologies in the global competition for top talent, as traditional recruiting techniques are unable to meet the expectations of the market (Chen, 2023). Notably, AI greatly improves daily HR operations, especially in hiring, which increases the effectiveness of recruiters (Chen, 2023). AI integration in Human Resource Management practices is frequently demonstrated in human resource planning, recruiting and selection, training and development, compensation and benefits, and performance management, according to literature by Budhwar et al. (2022). As examined by Kopalle et al. (2022), the application of AI in international marketing is receiving more and more attention. The use of chatbots and virtual assistants, which save expenses, respond to client questions, and improve customer relations, is one aspect of AI's complex function in this field. AI also helps to improve the personalization and customisation of goods and services. According to Huang and Rust (2022), AI systems play a crucial role in enhancing customer experiences and customizing content to suit individual tastes. They also help make more accurate forecasts in targeted advertising, which maximizes the effectiveness and reach of marketing efforts for a range of goods and services. Along with revenue development and profit maximization, value creation has emerged as a key sustainability factor for businesses. To this end, contemporary businesses gather Big Data from a variety of inbound and outward data sources (Rehman et al., 2016).

More recently, competitive intelligence (CI) has garnered a lot of attention due to the proliferation of data that is now publicly accessible through social media, blogs, wikis, mobile phones, text messages, emails, and other electronic digital communications. This data is a crucial tool for developing CI. According to Barney (1991), a comprehensive examination of the competitive environment is necessary to comprehend the advantages and disadvantages of competitors and to find possible sources of competitive advantage. This involves evaluating the assets, skills, tactics, and market positions of rivals. Brynjolfsson and McAfee (2017) contend that to increase productivity, save expenses, and improve product quality, industrial businesses need to integrate digital technologies into their production processes. This entails utilizing data analytics for process optimization as well as putting new manufacturing technologies like automation, robotics, and additive manufacturing into practice. To further improve their competitiveness, Lee et al. (2020) suggest that industrial firms implement automation and smart manufacturing techniques, which include integrating sensors, Internet of Things (IoT) devices, and artificial intelligence (AI) to enable adaptive production planning, predictive maintenance, and real-time monitoring.

Challenges

The implementation of data mining and business intelligence (BI) tools can successfully handle the particular issues faced by small and medium-sized businesses. The majority of BI technologies fail, even though organizations and researchers appear to be more interested in adopting or implementing these technologies. BI systems have failed for several reasons. The breakdown of departmental knowledge silos, user resistance to adoption, integrating the BI tool with other operational, performance management, and transactional systems, changing the workplace culture from one of "gut feel" to one of data-based decision-making, and obtaining executive sponsorship and the required financial backing are some of the reasons why BI fails, according to Mohamed (2020). Making use of BI and data mining improves decision-making and helps enterprises adjust to changing market conditions. Notwithstanding these developments, enterprises have obstacles that prevent efficient use, including high implementation costs, significant skills gaps, and technological complexity (Tsiu et al., 2024). Furthermore, there are no standards, and BI technology is generally not trusted as a tool to assist strategic decisions that affect an organization's ability to compete.

CONCLUSION

According to the review, AI has a big impact on how competitive businesses are. This intergration of BI and AI has been shown to create opportunities for strategic business competitiveness and Porter's forces model and the Resource-based view have demonstrated enough potency in explaining the competitiveness of organisations across the broad spectrum of economic sectors. The resource-based view has demonstrated the importance of technologies like AI, data analytics, and BI in sustaining organizations and preserving their competitiveness. The use of information systems backed by these cutting-edge technologies has also demonstrated that these technologies can effectively counteract threats to organizational competitiveness, which include rivalry among competitors, supplier and buyer bargaining power, threats from new market entrants, and threats from substitute products, according to research on organizational competitiveness. Thus, low-cost leadership, product differentiation, market segmentation, and niche emphasis may all be used to create competitive strategies by utilizing BI, AI, and AI-supported data analytics. Notwithstanding the crucial role that these technologies play, the review has also revealed that organizations continue to face obstacles when it comes to the adoption and application of BI and that these obstacles are primarily caused by ignorance and scepticism about the potential advantages of BI. Furthermore, several organizations have technological and infrastructure obstacles that impede their attempts to implement these technologies.

Recommendations

According to the research, many organizations face organizational, technological, and environmental obstacles that hinder their efforts to implement business intelligence. Therefore, the following suggestions were put out to address these issues:

a) It is necessary to inform organizations about the possible advantages of implementing and modifying AI-powered business intelligence solutions. This kind of instruction and training could increase the adoption of these technologies.
b) Investments in cloud computing technologies are necessary for organizations. These technologies fall into many service categories, including Infrastructure as a Service (IaaS), Platform as a Service (PasS), and Software as a Service (SaaS).
c) Employing AI technologies to forecast future occurrences aids businesses in creating response and competitive plans.

d) Among the strategies that would be needed to ensure the successful integration of BI in organisational competitiveness is for organisations to ensure data accuracy and consistency. This would require effective decision-making.
e) The success of BI and the competitive strategies of organisations also relies on effective collaboration and communication. Therefore, it is recommended that strong communication and collaborative efforts among departments within the organisation and with external organisations be established.
f) The success of organisations in integrating BI for competitive intelligence requires strategic alignment of BI initiatives to the organisational goals, in this way prioritising business needs. This will also be complemented by education and training as well as the empowerment of employees to use data to make decisions and improve their work processes.

Recommendations for Future Research

More research on user views of BI is necessary due to the low adoption rates and paucity of literature on the use of BI for competitiveness among corporate organizations. Future studies must thus concentrate on the cross-cultural elements that affect an organization's adoption of business intelligence. Furthermore, free, open-source inventions that are easily adaptable to many organizational contexts must be the focus of future study. Lastly, this review suggests that further research be done on potential policy interventions that may be put into place to address ethical challenges that need to be taken into account while using BI. This is because BI is inherently defined by data mining and big data technologies, which entail gathering and analyzing data from several sources. In addition to this, organisations, particularly research institutions and governments need to research the possible developments of low-cost artificial intelligence solutions that may be utilised in BI for organisational competitiveness. The outcome of such research will be more technological solutions for business organisations to select.

REFERENCES

Abdiqaxarovich. F. X. (2023). Revitalizing competitiveness: Enhancing the Mechanism for managing industrial enterprise Competitiveness. 36 (2023): Miasto Przyszłości,36(2023).

Acharya, A., Singh, S. K., Pereira, V., & Singh, P. (2018). Big Data, knowledge co- Creation and decision-making in the fashion industry. *International Journal of Information Management*, *42*, 90–101.

Ahi, A. A., Sinkovics, N., Shildibekov, Y., Sinkovics, R. R., & Mehandjiev, N. (2022). Advanced technologies and international business: A multidisciplinary analysis of the literature. *International Business Review*, *31*(4), 101967.

Aljawarneh, N. M. (2024). The Mediating Role of Organization Agility between Business Intelligence & Innovative Performance. *Journal of Statistics Applications & Probability*, *13*(3), 929–938.

Allal-Chérif, O., Sim_on-Moya, V., and Ballester, A. C. C. (2021). Intelligent Purchasing: How artificial intelligence can redefine the purchasing function. *Journal of Business Research*, (124), 69–76. DOI: 10.1016/j.jbusres.2020.11.050

Arnott, D., Gibson, M., & Jagielska, I. (2004). Evaluating the intangible benefits of Business intelligence: review & research agenda. The IFIP TC8/WG8.3 International Conference, 1-11. doi:DOI: 10.1.1.94.8550

Awan, U., Shamim, S., Khan, Z., Zia, N. U., Shariq, S. M., & Khan, M. N. (2021). Big data analytics capability and decision-making: The role of data-driven insight on circular economy performance. *Technological Forecasting and Social Change*, *168*, 120766.

Bag, S., Gupta, S., Kumar, A., & Sivarajah, U. (2021). An integrated artificial Intelligence framework for knowledge creation and B2B marketing rational decision-making for improving firm performance. *Industrial Marketing Management*, *92*(92), 178–189. DOI: 10.1016/j.indmarman.2020.12.001

Bag, S., Pretorius, J. H. C., Gupta, S., and Dwivedi, Y. K. (2021). Role of institutional Pressures and resources in the adoption of big data analytics powered artificial intelligence, sustainable manufacturing practices and circular economy capabilities. Technol. Forecast. Soc. Chang. 163:120420. Doi: . techfore.2020.120420.DOI: 10.1016/j

Barney, J. B. (1991). Firm resources and sustained competitive advantage. *Journal of Management*, *17*(1), 99–120.

Belhadi, A., Mani, V., Kamble, S. S., Khan, S. A. R., & Verma, S. (2021). Artificial Intelligence-driven innovation for enhancing supply chain resilience and performance under the effect of supply chain dynamism: An empirical investigation. *Annals of Operations Research*, ●●●, 1–26. DOI: 10.1007/s10479-021-03956-x

Benito, G. R. G., Cuervo-Cazurra, A., Mudambi, R., Pedersen, T., & Tallman, S. (2022). The future of global strategy. *Global Strategy Journal*, *12*(3), 421–450. DOI: 10.1002/gsj.1464

Bharadiya, J. P. (2023). A Comparative Study of Business Intelligence and Artificial Intelligence with Big Data Analytics. *American Journal of Artificial Intelligence*, *7*(1), 24–30. DOI: 10.11648/j.ajai.20230701.14

Bouckaert, G., Peters, B. G., & Verhoest, K. (2016). *Coordination of public sector Organizations*. Palgrave Macmillan.

Brijs, B. (2013). Business analysis for business intelligence.CRC Press. Taylor and Francis Group.

Brynjolfsson, E., & McAfee, A. (2017). *The second machine age: Work, progress, And prosperity in a time of brilliant technologies*. WW Norton & Company.

Budhwar, P., Malik, A., De Silva, M. T. T., & Thevisuthan, P. (2022). Artificial Intelligence—Challenges and opportunities for international HRM: A review and research agenda. *International Journal of Human Resource Management*, *33*(6), 1065–1097. DOI: 10.1080/09585192.2022.2035161

Chaudhuri, R., Chatterjee, S., Vrontis, D., & Thrassou, A. (2021). Adoption of Robust business analytics for product innovation and organizational performance: The mediating role of organizational data-driven culture. *Annals of Operations Research*, ●●●, 1–35. DOI: 10.1007/s10479-021-04407-3

Chen, H., Chiang, R. H. L., & Storey, V. C. (2012). Business Intelligence and Analytics: From Big data to big impact. *Management Information Systems Quarterly*, *36*(4).

Chen, Y., & Lin, Z. (2021). Business Intelligence Capabilities and Firm Performance: A Study in China. *International Journal of Information Management*, *57*, 102232.

Chen, Z. (2023). Collaboration among recruiters and artificial intelligence: Removing human prejudices in employment. *Cognition Technology and Work*, *25*(1), 135–149. DOI: 10.1007/s10111-022-00716-0

Choi, J., Yoon, J., Chung, J., Coh, B., & Lee, J. (2020). Social media analytics And business intelligence research: A systematic review. *Information Processing & Management*, *57*, 102279.

Chowdhury, S., Dey, P., Joel-Edgar, S., Bhattacharya, S., Rodriguez-Espindola, O., Abadie, A., & Truong, L. (2023). Unlocking the value of artificial intelligence in human resource management through AI capability framework. *Human Resource Management Review*, *33*(1), 100899. DOI: 10.1016/j.hrmr.2022.100899

Climent, R. C., Haftora, D. M., & Staniewski, M. W. (2024). AI-enabled business Models for competitive advantage. *Journal of Innovation & Knowledge*, *9*, 100532.

Davenport, T. H., & Prusak, L. (1998). *Working Knowledge: How Organisations Manage What They Know*. Harvard Business School Press.

Dillon, S. M., Glavas, C., & Mathews, S. (2020). Digitally immersive, international Entrepreneurial experiences. *International Business Review*, *29*(6), 101739. DOI: 10.1016/j.ibusrev.2020.101739

Dunning, J. H. (2019). Explaining global competitiveness: The role of international business theory. In *Global competitiveness* (pp. 25–44). Emerald Publishing Limited.

El-Haddadeh, R., Osmani, M., Hindi, N., & Fadlalla, A. (2021). Value creation for Realising the sustainable development goals: Fostering organizational adoption of big data analytics. *Journal of Business Research*, *2021*(131), 402–410.

Ghasemaghaei, M. (2021). Understanding the impact of big data on firm performance: The necessity of conceptually differentiating among big data characteristics. *International Journal of Information Management*, *57*, 102055. DOI: 10.1016/j.ijinfomgt.2019.102055

Gomwe, G., Potgieter, M., & Litheko, A. M. (2022). Proposed framework for Innovative business intelligence for competitive advantage in small, medium and micro-organisations in the North West province of South Africa'. *Southern African Journal of Entrepreneurship and Small Business Management*, *14*(1), a501. DOI: 10.4102/sajesbm.v14i1.501

Grant, R. M. (2019). *Contemporary strategy analysis: Text and cases edition*. John Wiley & Sons.

Güler, K., & Tepecik, A. (2019). Exchange rates change by using economic data. With artificial intelligence and forecasting the crisis. *Procedia Computer Science*, *158*, 316–326. DOI: 10.1016/j.procs.201909.057

Haag, S., Cummings, M., & Philips, A. (2007). *Management Information Systems For the Information Age* (6th ed.). McGraw-Hill/Irwin.

He, W., Zha, S., & Li, L. (2013). Social media competitive analysis and text mining: A case study in the pizza industry. *International Journal of Information Management, 33*(3), 464–472.

Huang, M. H., & Rust, R. T. (2022). A Framework for collaborative artificial Intelligence in marketing. *Journal of Retailing, 98*(2), 209–223. DOI: 10.1016/j.jretai.2021.03.001

Johnson, A. R. (2005). Competitive Intelligence and Knowledge Management: Complementary Partners, Reinforcing Tools. In Rao, M. (Ed.), *Knowledge Management Tools and Techniques: Practitioners and Experts Evaluate KM Solutions* (pp. 302–310). Elsevier Butterworth-Heinemann.

Kitsios, F., & Kamariotou, M. (2025). Artificial Intelligence and Business Strategy Towards Digital Transformation: A Research Agenda. *Sustainability, 2025*(13), •••. DOI: 10.3390/su13042025

Kopalle, P. K., Gangwar, M., Kaplan, A., Ramachandran, D., Reinartz, W., & Rindfleisch, A. (2022). Examining artificial intelligence (AI) technologies in marketing via a global lens: Current trends and future research opportunities. *International Journal of Research in Marketing, 39*(2), 522–540. DOI: 10.1016/j.ijresmar.2021.11.002

Kotler, P., & Keller, K. L. (2016). *Marketing management.* Pearson.

Kruger, J. (2010). A Study Of Strategic Intelligence As A Strategic Management Tool. In *The Long-Term Insurance Industry in South Africa. Master of Commerce.* University of South Africa.

Larose, D. T. (2005). *Discovering Knowledge in Data. An Introduction to Data Mining.* John Wiley & Sons, Inc.

Larson, B. (2008). Delivering Business Intelligence with Microsoft SQL Server 2008, New York, McGraw-Hill Osborne Media. Meyer S.R., 2001, Which ETL Tool is Right for You? DM Review Magazine, June 1.

Laudon, K., & Laudon, J. (2014). *Management information systems: managing the digital firm* (13th ed.). Pearson.

Lee, J.. (2020). The fourth industrial revolution and implications for smart Manufacturing. *Wiley Interdisciplinary Reviews. Data Mining and Knowledge Discovery, 10*(6), e1388.

Liebowitz, J. (2006). *Strategic Intelligence: Business Intelligence, Competitive Intelligence and Knowledge Management.* Auerbach Publications.

Lloyd, J. (2011). *Identifying Key Components of Business Intelligence Systems and Their Role in Managerial Decision Making*. Intel Corporation.

Lou, B., & Wu, L. (2021). AI on drugs: Can artificial intelligence accelerate drug Development? Evidence from a large-scale examination of bio-Pharma firms. *Management Information Systems Quarterly, 45*, 1451–1482. DOI: 10.25300/MISQ/2021/16565

Luo, Y., & Zahra, S. A. (2023). Industry 4.0 in international business research. *Journal of International Business Studies, 54*(3), 403–417. DOI: 10.1057/s41267-022-00577-9

Menzies, J., Sabert, B., Hassan, R., & Mensah, P. K. (2024). Artificial intelligence For international business: Its use, challenges, and suggestions for future research and practice. *Thunderbird International Business Review, 2024*(66), 185–200.

Mikalef, P., & Gupta, M. (2021). Artificial intelligence capability: Conceptualization, Measurement calibration and empirical study on its impact on organizational creativity and firm performance. *Information & Management, 58*, 103434. DOI: 10.1016/j.im.2021.103434

Mohamed, D. (2020). Data and Business Intelligence Systems for Competitive Advantage: Prospects, challenges, and real-world applications Mercados. *Negocios*, (41), 2020.

Moscoso-Zea, O., Castro, J., Paredes-Gualtor, J., & Luján-Mora, S. (2019). A Hybrid Infrastructure of Enterprise Architecture and Business Intelligence & Analytics for Knowledge Management in Education. *IEEE Access : Practical Innovations, Open Solutions.*

Murphy, C. (2005). *Competitive intelligence: gathering, analysing, and putting it to work*. Gower.

Newman, M. E. J. (2010). *Networks. An Introduction*. Oxford University Press.

Olszak C. M., (2014). Business Intelligence and Analytics in Organizations, [in:] M.

Olszak, C. M., & Zurada, J. (2015). Information technology tools for business Intelligence development in organizations. *Polish Journal of Management Studies., 12*(1).

Paradza, D., & Daramola, O. (2021). Business Intelligence and Business Value in Organisations: A Systematic Literature Review. *Sustainability, 13*, 11382. DOI: 10.3390/su132011382

Porter, M. E. (1990). The competitive advantage of nations. *Harvard Business Review, 68*(2), 73–93.

Porter, M. E. (1991). America's green strategy. *Scientific American, 264*(4), 96–101.

Poul, S., Gautman, N., & Balint, R. (2003). *Preparing and data mining with Microsoft SQL Server 2000 and Analysis Services*. Addison-Wesley.

Ragazou, K., Passas, I., Garefalakis, A., & Zopounidis, C. (2023). *Business Intelligence model empowering SMEs to make better decisions and enhance their competitive advantage*. Discover Analytics.

Rahman, A. (2011, March). A Five-Layered Business Intelligence Architecture. *Communications of the IBIMA*.

Ranjan, J., & Foropon, C. (2021). Big Data Analytics in Building the Competitive Intelligence of Organizations. *International Journal of Information Management, 56*, 102231.

Rehman, M. H. U., Chang, V., Battol, A., & Wah, T. Y. (2016). Big Data Reduction Framework for value creation in sustainable enterprises. *International Journal of Information Management, 36*, 917–928.

Riad, A. M. and Hassan Q. F. (2008). Service-Oriented Architecture – A New Alternative to Traditional Integration Methods in B2B Applications, Journal of Convergence Information Technologies.

Sang, B. (2021). Application of genetic algorithm and BP neural network in supply chain finance under information sharing. *Journal of Computational and Applied Mathematics*, (384), 113170.

Satheesh, M. K., Samala, N., & Rodriguez, R. V. (2020). Role of AI-induced Chatbot in Enhancing customer relationship management in the banking industry. *ICTACT Journal on Management Studies, 6*(4), 1320–1323.

Soori, M., Arezoo, B., & Dastres, R. (2023). Artificial neural networks in supply Chain management, a review. *Journal of Economy and Technology, 1*, 179–196.

Tan, P. N., Steinbach, M., & Kumar, V. (2005). *Introduction to Data Mining*. Addison-Wesley.

Toorajipour, R., Sohrabpour, V., Nazarpour, A., Oghazi, P., & Fischl, M. (2021). Artificial intelligence in supply chain management: A systematic literature review. *Journal of Business Research, 122*, 502–517.

Tsiu, S. V., Ngobeni, M., Mathabela, L., & Thango, B. A. (2024). Applications and Competitive Advantages of Data Mining and Business Intelligence in SMEs Performance: A Systematic Review. Doi: DOI: 10.20944/preprints202409.0940.v1

Turban, E., Aronson, J. E., Liang, T., & Sharda, R. (2007). *Decision Support And Business Intelligence Systems* (8th ed.). Pearson Prentice Hall.

Veber, J. (2012). Operational-economic aspects of cloud computing, [in:] M. Tvrdikova, J. Minster and P. Rozenhal (Eds.), IT for Practice, Ostrava, VSB-TU Economicka Faculta.

Vizgaitytė, G & Skyrius, R. (2012). Business Intelligence in the Process of Decision Making: Changes and Trends. Network of Scientific Journals from Latin America, the Caribbean, Spain and Portugal Non-profit academic project, developed under the open access initiative.

Vlahovljak, A. (2022). *Business Intelligence*. International Burch University.

Vrontis, D., Christofi, M., Pereira, V., Tarba, S., Makrides, A., & Trichina, E. (2021). Artificial intelligence, robotics, advanced technologies and human resource management: A systematic review. *International Journal of Human Resource Management, 33*(6), 1237–1266.

Wamba-Taguimdje, S. L., Fosso Wamba, S., Kala Kamdjoug, J. R., & Tchatchouang Wanko, C. E. (2020). Influence of artificial intelligence (AI) on firm performance: The business value of AI-based transformation projects. *Business Process Management Journal, 26*(7).

Wang, Z., Wang, N., Su, X., & Ge, S. (2020). An empirical study on business Analytics affordances enhancing the management of cloud computing data security. *International Journal of Information Management, 50*, 387–394.

Witten, I. H., Frank, E., & Hall, M. (2011). *Data Mining: Practical Machine Learning Tools and Techniques*. Morgan Kaufland.

Yao, M., Ye, D., Yang, G., Shi, H., & Zheng, X. (2021). Are entrepreneurial Capabilities and prior knowledge: The silver bullet for the generation of new digital venture ideas in a digital context? *Journal of Global Information Management, 29*, 1–17. DOI: 10.4018/JGIM.20211101.oa12

KEY TERMS AND DEFINITIONS

Business Analytics: The procedure for turning data into insights to enhance corporate choices.

Business Intelligence: A technology-driven data analysis procedure that aids managers, employees, and executives in making well-informed business decisions.

Competitive Intelligence: Collecting and evaluating data about rivals to assist a company in making strategic choices.

Competitive Threats: Hazards that rival businesses pose to a company.

Artificial Intelligence: A collection of technologies that provide computers the ability to carry out several sophisticated tasks.

Competitive Strategy: The process of creating a competitive edge and providing stakeholders with returns that are higher than normal.

Data Analytics: Examining data to find trends and patterns so that judgments can be made with knowledge.

Competitiveness: The ability of any firm to accomplish its goals more successfully than rivals' products is known as competitiveness.

Chapter 2
Data Analytics and BI for Enhanced Efficiency in Logistics Within the Commercial Vehicle Industry

Venkateshkumar R.
https://orcid.org/0009-0001-3735-0341
Hindustan Institute of Technology and Science, India

Dennis Amirtharaj S. M.
Hindustan Institute of Technology and Science, India

ABSTRACT

In the dynamic landscape of the commercial vehicle industry, the integration of data analytics and business intelligence has emerged as a pivotal force in revolutionizing logistics operations. This abstract explores the transformative impact of advanced analytics on optimizing supply chain processes, increasing operational efficiency, and fostering strategic decision-making within the context of commercial vehicle logistics. Big data analytics enables companies to gain actionable insights into their supply chain, facilitating real-time tracking, route optimization. Business intelligence tools play a crucial role in converting raw data into meaningful information, empowering stakeholders to make informed decisions. This strategic approach allows for agile responses to market fluctuations, demand variations, and regulatory changes. Provides a comprehensive overview of the transformative

DOI: 10.4018/979-8-3373-2125-7.ch002

potential of data analytics and business intelligence, data-driven logistics processes, positioning them as indispensable tools for navigating the evolving landscape of commercial vehicle logistics.

1. INTRODUCTION

The commercial vehicle industry going on significant changes with an increasing focus on technology adoption to optimize logistics operations. This study explores the integration of Data Analytics (DA) and Business Intelligence (BI) to enhance efficiency in commercial vehicle logistics this is the end to the analysis of the impact of these technologies on operational performance and decision-making processes. Organizations in the logistics industry are facing many challenges on their way to digitalization. The Technological aspect of the predictive analytics framework for the logistics industry has been the topic of several research publications. Nowadays, leaders need to look for the optimal location, carrier, and many other important points manually. We see that businesses are in the process of creating a paradigm shift in how they do business today through the use of advanced technology and data analysis. In this paper, we'll look into the principal perks of big data analytics and business intelligence in logistics and transportation and how companies can benefit from the utilization of advanced technologies, the newest trends, and tools. Logistics management is a critical function within the commercial vehicle industry, influencing cost, service quality, and operational efficiency. With the advent of big data and business intelligence (BI), companies are leveraging advanced analytics to optimize fleet management, enhance route planning, and improve overall logistics operations. This study aims to assess how data analytics and BI contribute to logistics efficiency, highlighting key technological advancements and their practical applications in the industry.

Figure 1. Role of Big data analytics in logistics

Source: https://bigdataanalyticsnews.com/big-data-analytics-in-logistics-industry/#google_vignette

2. SIGNIFICANCE OF STUDY

Data analytics is important because it helps companies leverage their available data to identify opportunities for improvement and optimization. Across different business segments, increasing efficiency leads to overall more intelligent operations, higher margins, and delighted customers. In this era, data analytics and business intelligence provide valuable insights and can predict results and act proactively in decision-making. Able to understand the trend, patterns, and variable relationships anticipate opportunities, and mitigate the risk involved in the business. In the cut-throat competition, this helps to evaluate the market, customers, and competitors better. Logistics operations will be streamlined with the support of BI tools and dashboards, allocation of drivers for vehicle movement, and processing of the payment. To develop robust strategies and address upcoming challenges, to ensure timely course corrections. information security and risk management effectively being done using Business intelligence and data analytics. Data analytics will help the organization to establish a "learning" company culture. Business intelligence supports gaining insights into customer behavior, improved visibility, and transparency in key performance indicators. Turning Data into Information with Data

Warehousing is an introduction to how organizations can use data warehousing to convert raw data into information.

Drawing on practical frameworks, methodologies, and real-world examples, the book provides business leaders, IT professionals, and data analysts with the insight they need to successfully plan for, build, and operate great data warehousing solutions. Additionally, Dyche's insights help bridge the gap between the need from a business standpoint and the implementations from a technical platform.

3. BENEFITS OF DATA ANALYTICS IN LOGISTICS

Data analytics in logistics industries mainly seek for the optimization of supply chain business. Data analytics plays a critical role in bringing down inventory carry costs and understanding the pattern of customer Requirements. With the available information, it can forecast the future of inventory cost levels. Data analytics helps in detecting the inventory cost method to make improvements in the company.

Data analytics in logistics industries can predict the impact of the product through predictive analytics. As technology has advanced, it utilizes prescriptive analytics to discover inefficiencies and product waste to improve product optimization plans. Data analytics provides valuable information regarding the manufacturing capacity, demand of customers inventory level, etc. to run better productions.

Data insight is transformed to optimize supply chain performance management with the aid of data analytics. Data analytics increases the productivity of the logistics sector and keeps an eye on the labor force. Data analytics enables real-time access to logistics information, improving the quality and speed of decision-making across the supply chain. By analyzing data across various nodes of the supply chain, companies can gain end-to-end visibility, helping to track inventory, shipments, and supplier performance more effectively. Analytics helps categorize bottlenecks, inefficiencies in logistics operations, allowing for continuous improvement and leaner processes. Past data and real-time insights can be analyzed to forecast demand more correctly, enabling better planning and management. Companies can analyze customer data to offer more personalized services and respond quickly to changes in demand or disruptions.

Through route optimization, warehouse automation insights, and better inventory control, data analytics helps reduce transportation and storage costs. Analytics supports the integration of logistics functions with other business operations (e.g., marketing, production), aligning logistics strategy with overall business goals. Organizations that leverage data analytics in logistics are more agile and customer-focused, giving them a strong edge in highly dynamic markets.

Figure 2. Benefits of data analytics in logistics

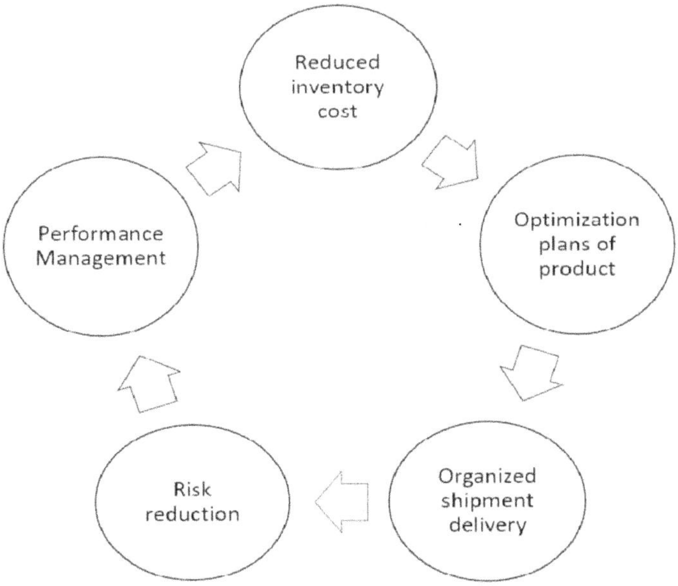

Source: https:// https://datamites.com/blog/data-analytics-in-logistics/

4. LITERATURE REVIEW

Table 1. Summary table for the literature review, capturing key theme, concepts, and Impact

Key Theme	**Number of Key Studies**	**Primary Framework/Concepts/ Key Focus Area**	**Relevance/Impact**
Logistics Management and Performance Measurement	3	Optimization of logistics factors, 3PL performance, strategic group mapping	Enhances company performance and competitiveness
Sustainable Supply Chain Management	3	Green supply chains, circular economy, sustainability barriers in manufacturing	Supports environmental goals and regulatory compliance
Digitalization and Business Intelligence in Logistics	3	Overcoming digitalization barriers, business intelligence in logistics	Improves decision-making and operational efficiency

Key Theme	Number of Key Studies	Primary Framework/Concepts/ Key Focus Area	Relevance/Impact
Challenges in the Indian Logistics Sector	3	Cost, infrastructure, regulatory challenges in India	Identifies industry bottlenecks and areas for policy action
Technological Innovations and Logistics 4.0	3	AI, IoT, automation, Logistics 4.0 adoption	Drives innovation and enhances supply chain agility
Reverse Logistics and Circular Economy	2	Business intelligence for reverse logistics, critical success factors	Promotes sustainability and waste reduction
Strategic Integration in Logistics	2	Business process integration, performance alignment	Enhances operational efficiency and competitive positioning (Abdulla & Musa, 2021; Azmi et al., 2017)
Sustainability and Green SCM	2	Sustainable logistics practices, policy and regulatory impact	Enables environmentally responsible and compliant supply chains (Agrawal et al., 2022; Aravind raj et al., 2019)
Performance Measurement in 3PL	2	Service efficiency, user vs. provider perceptions	Improves service quality and client relationships (Asthana & Bhat, 2015; Asthana & Dwivedi, 2020)
Technological Innovation and BI	3	IT implementation, digital tools, Relay-as-a-Service model	Drives efficiency, transparency, and competitiveness (Chakraborty et al., 2020; Balodi et al., 2022)
Market Strategy and Differentiation	2	Mobility barriers, competitive positioning	Supports decision-making on strategic focus and market segmentation (Bhattacharyya et al., 2021; Chandra & Jain, 2007)
Logistics Sector Challenges (India-specific)	2	Infrastructure bottlenecks, regulation, informal sector	Highlights constraints and areas for reform and investment (Arivazhagan, 2020; Aravind raj et al., 2019)
Integration of BI for Decision-Making	2	Conceptual, Use-case based Data-driven logistics, visibility, analytics-driven performance	Establishes the case for BI tools in real-time logistics planning (Abdulla & Musa, 2021; Balodi et al., 2022)

4.1 Regional Perspectives on BI in Logistics

4.1.1. United States & Europe

The integration of Big Data Analytics (BDA) and Business Intelligence tools has significantly influenced supply chain performance in developed economies.

continued on following page

Table 1. Continued

According to Wamba et al. (2020), firms in the U.S. and Europe are leveraging BDA to enhance logistics agility, responsiveness, and service quality through a resource-based lens. This alignment of digital capabilities with firm resources leads to sustainable competitive advantage, especially in logistics operations where real-time decision-making is crucial.

Hofmann (2017) provides a conceptual framework linking big data analytics to demand forecasting. He emphasizes that companies in Europe utilize BI to reduce forecast errors and improve supply-demand alignment, particularly in volatile markets. These advancements are supported by robust IT infrastructures and skilled analytics professionals—conditions that emerging economies must work toward developing.

These studies highlight:

- High BI maturity in logistics operations.
- Strong emphasis on predictive and prescriptive analytics.
- Strategic use of BI to manage supply chain volatility.

Implications for Emerging Economies:

- Need to invest in data integration and advanced analytics tools.
- Capacity-building programs to upskill logistics personnel in data interpretation and forecasting.

4.2.2 China

China's approach to logistics BI is unique in its government-led digitalization efforts and rapid adoption of AI-powered logistics platforms. Liu et al. (2021) explore how Chinese companies like JD Logistics and Alibaba use AI and cloud-based BI for urban deliveries, smart warehousing, and last-mile optimization. These systems leverage real-time data from IoT devices, enhancing visibility and dynamic routing in complex urban environments.

The Chinese model demonstrates:

- Centralized data platforms for urban logistics.
- Public-private cooperation in logistics innovation.
- Focus on scalability and automation driven by BI.

Implications for Emerging Economies:

- Leverage mobile and cloud BI tools to scale urban logistics operations.

- Collaborate with tech companies and governments to develop localized smart logistics systems.

5. BACKGROUND

5.1 "Overview of Indian Commercial Vehicle Automobile Industry"

a) Vehicle Categories:

Trucks: ranging from light-duty to heavy-duty, trucks are the primary vehicles of the commercial vehicle industry. They transport goods over short and long distances.

Buses: Designed for passengers, buses cater to public transit, schools, and charter services.

Vans are widely utilized in logistics, delivery services, and passenger transport, as well as vans.

b) Key Stakeholders:

Manufacturers: Prominent companies design and manufacture commercial vehicles, constantly innovating to meet industry demands and regulations.

Fleet Operators: Businesses and organizations that own and manage fleets of commercial vehicles for transportation and logistics.

Regulators: Government agencies establish and enforce safety, environmental, and operational regulations to ensure industry safety.

Consumers: End-users include businesses relying on commercial vehicles for their operations and individuals using public transportation services.

c) Economic Impact:

The commercial vehicle industry contributes significantly to economic development by facilitating the movement of goods and people and promoting various sectors such as manufacturing, retail, and construction.

d) Technological Advancements:

The advancements in technological advancements contribute to the advancement of the industry. This includes the creation of electric and autonomous vehicles, telematics for fleet management, and advanced safety features.

e) Global Market Trends:

The industry's dynamics are influenced by global developments such as urbanization, e-commerce growth, and sustainability concerns. These factors contribute to vehicle demand and the industry's overall direction.

f) Major commercial vehicle players in India
- Tata motors
- Ashok Leyland
- AMW Motors Ltd
- Eicher Motors Ltd
- SML motors
- Force motors
- Daimler India
- Scania

5.2 "Historical Evolution of BI and Data Analytics in Logistics"

Table 2. Evolution of Business Intelligence in Logistics: From Paper to Predictive

Era	Milestone	Description
Pre-1990s	Manual tracking	Paper logs, verbal communication, limited performance tracking
1990s–2005	Basic IT systems	ERPs, Excel-based tracking, barcode scanners
2005–2015	Early BI adoption	Data warehousing, centralized reporting, static dashboards
2015–2020	Cloud BI & IoT integration	Telematics, route planning, real-time alerts
2020–Present	Predictive & Prescriptive BI	AI/ML-driven recommendations, digital twins, autonomous fleet insights

5.3 Highlight Pre-Digital Pain Points and BI/DA Solutions

Table 3. Pre-Digital logistics challenge and BI/DA solutions

Pre-Digital Logistics Challenge	BI/DA-Enabled Solution
Manual route planning led to high fuel costs	Route optimization using AI reduces mileage and fuel use
Paper-based POD delayed invoicing	E-POD and real-time updates accelerate cash flow
Lack of visibility into shipment delays	GPS + BI dashboards provide real-time exception alerts
Difficulty measuring driver performance	Analytics on delivery times, idle time, accident rates
Inventory mismatches at hubs	Predictive inventory management with real-time tracking

Table 2. Continued

6. METHODOLOGY FOR LITERATURE REVIEW

A transparent and replicable approach to literature review was adopted to ensure rigor and relevance. The following methodology guided the selection and evaluation of sources:

6.1 Search Databases and Keywords

- Databases: Scopus, Web of Science, IEEE Xplore, ScienceDirect, Google Scholar
- Keywords: "business intelligence logistics," "data analytics in transportation," "BI adoption India," "logistics digitalization," "AI in supply chains"

6.2 Inclusion Criteria

- Peer-reviewed journal articles (2012–2024)
- Industry reports from globally recognized organizations (e.g., McKinsey, WEF)
- Case studies from logistics or transport companies
- Focus on Indian and emerging market logistics with comparative global insights

6.3 Review Process

- Over 120 initial articles identified
- 26 shortlisted after abstract and full-text review
- Studies categorized into themes: BI applications, challenges, tools, adoption barriers, performance metrics

7. EMERGING TECHNOLOGIES IN BI FOR LOGISTICS

As logistics evolves into a digitally driven industry, emerging technologies are redefining the scope and impact of BI. The following technologies are particularly relevant:

7.1 Blockchain

Blockchain enables transparent and tamper-proof recording of logistics transactions, including shipment tracking, proof of delivery, and freight payments. Integration with BI tools allows real-time compliance auditing and trustless data sharing between 3PLs, shippers, and customers.

Recent logistics research highlights several practical applications of blockchain technology that can significantly enhance transparency, traceability, and efficiency in supply chains. According to Francisco and Swanson (2018, Journal of Business Logistics), blockchain enables end-to-end shipment visibility, allowing stakeholders to access a tamper-proof ledger of every transaction, from origin to delivery. This reduces disputes and improves trust among manufacturers, logistics providers, and customers.

Hackius and Petersen (2017, Logistics Research) emphasize blockchain's role in smart contracts, which automatically execute freight payments or customs documentation once predefined conditions are met, eliminating manual paperwork and reducing delays. Another application is product authenticity and traceability, particularly in pharmaceuticals and food logistics, as explored by Treiblmaier (2018, International Journal of Physical Distribution & Logistics Management). Here, blockchain helps track the provenance of goods, ensuring regulatory compliance and consumer safety.

Overall, blockchain is transforming logistics by creating secure, real-time, and automated information flows across complex supply networks.

7.2 Edge Computing

Edge computing enables real-time data processing at the source (e.g., on-vehicle telematics units), reducing latency in BI dashboards. This is especially important for real-time route adjustments, cold chain monitoring, and dynamic load balancing.

7.3 Advanced AI and Machine Learning

Advanced AI is revolutionizing logistics by enabling real-time decision-making, predictive analytics, and automation across the supply chain. According to Wamba et al. (2020, Information & Management), AI-driven demand forecasting improves inventory accuracy and reduces stockouts, while machine learning models optimize route planning and delivery schedules based on traffic, weather, and customer preferences. AI-powered computer vision is used in warehouses for automated inspection, damage detection, and inventory tracking, enhancing efficiency and reducing human error (Ghosh, 2021, International Journal of Logistics Management). In transportation, AI-based predictive maintenance analyzes sensor data to forecast vehicle breakdowns, minimizing downtime and repair costs. Autonomous logistics—enabled by AI and robotics—supports self-driving delivery vehicles and drones, which are already being piloted by companies like Amazon and JD Logistics.

Natural language processing (NLP) and chatbots are also transforming customer service by automating order tracking and support queries. Real-world applications include UPS's use of ORION (On-Road Integrated Optimization and Navigation), which saves millions in fuel costs annually through AI-based route optimization. As AI models become more advanced, logistics networks are becoming self-learning and adaptive, driving resilience, speed, and customer satisfaction across global supply chains.

AI-driven algorithms enhance BI by offering predictive and prescriptive capabilities, such as:

- Forecasting delivery delays
- Predictive maintenance for fleet vehicles
- Intelligent inventory allocation at hubs

7.4 Digital Twins

Digital twins simulate real-world logistics environments, allowing planners to test BI-driven decisions (e.g., hub relocation or fleet size adjustments) before implementation.

These technologies extend BI from descriptive insight into real-time simulation and automation, opening new frontiers for logistics innovation.

8. BUSINESS-INTELLIGENCE SPECTRUM

The spectrum of business intelligence comprises the different tools and techniques utilized to convert unprocessed data into meaningful and practical understandings for well-informed decision-making in an enterprise. This range includes several elements and methods that work together to improve business intelligence capabilities. Beginning with the documentation and gathering of data from various sources, such as internal systems like the enterprise resource planning system, operational databases, market research reports, supplier relationship management, and social media reports, as well as external sources like market research reports and third-party data providers. Spectrum then moves on to the process of combining and harmonizing data from various sources into a single format for analysis. The data warehouses are designed for storing structured in the interactive format, optimized for querying and analysis. At the same time, data lakes accommodate diverse data types and formats providing scalable storage for raw data before it is processed and transformed for analysis.

Furthermore, BI fosters cross-functional integration by aligning logistics functions with broader business strategies such as customer satisfaction, sustainability, and financial performance. Through better data governance and integration, logistics managers can collaborate more effectively with procurement, finance, and sales teams to support holistic enterprise objectives.

However, cloud-based BI platforms and scalable analytics tools are increasingly lowering these barriers, making advanced BI capabilities more accessible. Moreover, the integration of BI into logistics is also paving the way for innovations such as real-time shipment tracking, predictive maintenance of transport vehicles, and dynamic pricing models, all of which are contributing to the digital transformation of supply chains globally.

Figure 3. Components of Business intelligence spectrum

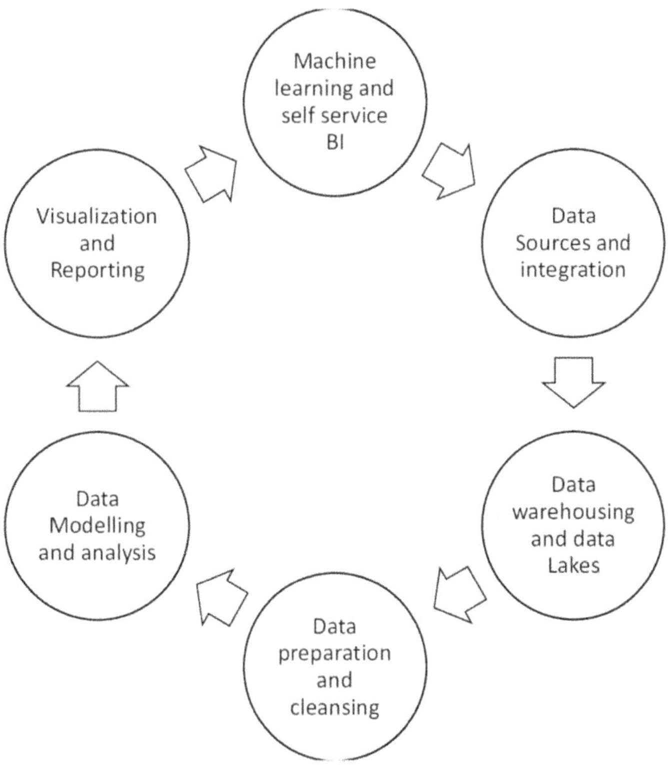

8.1 Structured BI Framework for Logistics Organizations

8.1.1 Strategic Alignment

- Objective: Define clear business goals and KPIs that BI should support.
- Key Actions:
    - o Align BI with logistics strategy (e.g., improve OTD, reduce freight costs).
    - o Identify key stakeholders (operations, IT, finance).
    - o Establish governance team and budget.

8.1.2 Data Assessment and Preparation

- Objective: Audit and prepare existing data sources for BI use.
- Key Actions:
    - o Conduct data inventory (e.g., ERP, WMS, TMS, telematics).
    - o Assess data quality, gaps, and integration readiness.
    - o Implement data governance protocols (e.g., data ownership, standardization).

8.1.3 Tool Selection and Infrastructure Setup

- Objective: Choose appropriate BI tools and infrastructure.
- Key Actions:
    - o Select between cloud vs. on-premise BI platforms (e.g., Power BI, Tableau, Qlik).
    - o Set up data warehouses, ETL pipelines, and visualization tools.
    - o Ensure scalability and API compatibility with existing systems.

8.1.4 Pilot Deployment

- Objective: Test BI solution on a limited function or geography.
- Key Actions:
    - o Choose a use case (e.g., route optimization, delivery tracking).
    - o Train a small user group and monitor dashboard use.
    - o Measure impact against baseline KPIs.

8.1.5 Advanced Analytics and Optimization

- Objective: Move from descriptive to predictive and prescriptive BI.

- Key Actions:
  - o Integrate AI/ML models for demand forecasting and risk prediction.
  - o Automate alerts and scenario simulations.
  - o Use analytics for continuous improvement (e.g., delivery reliability, fuel savings).

8.1.6 Benefits of Structured BI Framework

- Enhances decision-making accuracy
- Improves logistics KPIs (OTD%, fuel use, idle time)
- Ensures scalable and sustainable BI adoption
- Reduces cost and increases service visibility

8.2 Data Governance & Quality

In commercial vehicle logistics, data governance ensures that all information used across the supply chain—from vehicle telemetry to delivery records—is accurate, consistent, and compliant with regulatory standards. High data quality enables effective decision-making, minimizes errors in route planning or inventory tracking, and ensures customer satisfaction. Establishing clear policies for data ownership, validation, and access helps logistics providers maintain trust and operational efficiency.

8.3 Change Management

Change management is vital for successfully integrating new technologies, including Business Intelligence (BI), in commercial vehicle logistics. The shift from manual or legacy systems to digital platforms requires cultural and organizational transformation. Employees need training to interpret BI dashboards, trust data-driven insights, and adopt new workflows. Resistance to change can stall digital progress, so clear communication from leadership, pilot projects, and stakeholder involvement are essential.

8.4 Cloud Infrastructure

Cloud infrastructure provides a flexible, scalable foundation for deploying Business Intelligence (BI) tools in commercial vehicle logistics. With cloud-based systems, logistics companies can collect, store, and analyze vast amounts of real-time data from vehicles, warehouses, and delivery endpoints. This facilitates better fleet management, predictive maintenance, and route optimization. Cloud platforms also enable remote access, collaboration across geographies, and integration with other digital tools like TMS and ERP systems. Moreover, cloud services reduce the need for costly on-premise IT infrastructure and allow for faster system updates. This agility and cost-efficiency make cloud infrastructure a key enabler of digital transformation in logistics.

8.5 Cybersecurity

As commercial vehicle logistics becomes increasingly digital, cybersecurity emerges as a critical priority. Sensitive data—such as delivery routes, customer information, and vehicle diagnostics—flows through connected systems and cloud platforms, making the industry vulnerable to cyber threats. A breach can disrupt operations, compromise safety, and damage customer trust. To mitigate these risks, companies must implement robust cybersecurity protocols including encryption, access controls, network monitoring, and regular audits. Cybersecurity must also extend to third-party vendors and IoT devices embedded in vehicles.

8.6 Supply Chain Integration

Supply chain integration in commercial vehicle logistics connects all stakeholders—manufacturers, transporters, warehouses, and retailers—through shared data and synchronized systems. This integration is vital for leveraging Business Intelligence (BI) to its fullest potential. Real-time visibility into inventory levels, shipment status, and demand patterns enables faster, more informed decision-making. Integrated platforms improve coordination, reduce lead times, and help mitigate risks caused by disruptions or inefficiencies. Moreover, they support just-in-time logistics, optimize vehicle loads, and improve customer service. When BI tools are embedded within an integrated supply chain, logistics providers gain a holistic view that drives efficiency, cost savings, and agility.

8.7 ESG Reporting

Environmental, Social, and Governance (ESG) reporting is gaining importance in commercial vehicle logistics, and Business Intelligence (BI) tools are essential for tracking and reporting these metrics. BI enables logistics companies to measure carbon emissions, fuel efficiency, and energy usage across fleets. Social indicators such as driver safety, compliance with labor standards, and community impact can also be monitored. Governance data—including ethical sourcing and supplier performance—can be integrated into BI dashboards. By automating ESG reporting through BI, logistics providers can meet regulatory requirements, support sustainability goals, and enhance transparency with stakeholders. This also positions them competitively in a sustainability-conscious market.

Table 4. India vs Global BI Trend

Aspect	India	Global Leaders (US, EU, China)
BI Maturity	Emerging	Advanced predictive & prescriptive analytics
Adoption Drivers	Cost efficiency, digital India push	Innovation, customer-centric logistics
Common BI Tools	Power BI, Zoho, Tableau	SAP BI, Oracle Analytics Cloud, IBM Cognos
Infrastructure Readiness	Mixed – urban vs rural disparity	Robust cloud & IoT infrastructure
Government Role	High (ULIP, FASTag, e-Way bill)	Moderate – policy-driven innovation support
Challenges	Digital literacy, fragmented supply chain	Integration of AI/ML at scale, data privacy laws

9. DECISION CYCLE

The decision cycle is the process of gathering information, processing it into data, validating it, analysing it with tools, and using the same for proactive business decisions within the organization. The application of the decision cycle helps to provide financial and nonfinancial acumens such as customer success, retaining, addressable markets, etc.

The decision cycle allows companies to make agile decisions based on information's. BI tools such as Microsoft Power BI, Business Tableau, and other various tools automate the all elements of the decision cycle.

Figure 4. Phases of Decision Cycle in DA & BI

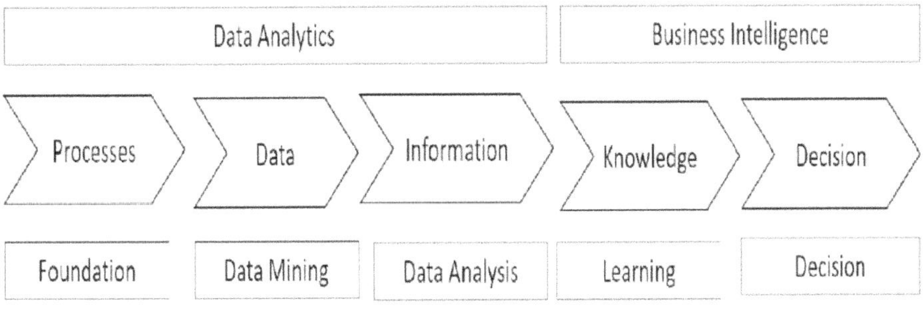

Source: Data analytics & Business intelligence by Chris Ortega

10. CURRENT CHALLENGES IN LOGISTICS

10.1 Infrastructure Constraints

Inadequate transportation infrastructure, including roads, ports, and railways, can lead to delays and inefficiencies in the logistics supply chain.
Road infrastructure has upgraded in the few yards. The government investing significantly in the same.

10.2 Fragmented Supply Chain

The logistics industry in India has been fragmented and unorganized sector, with multiple intermediaries involved before delivery final goods.
This fragmentation can lead to coordination challenges, increased costs, and reduced overall efficiency.

10.3 Regulatory Complexity

Complex and varied state regulations, along with frequent changes in tax structures, create compliance challenges for logistics providers.
The implementation of the Goods and Services Tax (GST) was a significant step to address this, but challenges may persist.

10.4 Technology Adoption

Limited adoption of advanced technologies, such as warehouse management systems, IoT (Internet of Things), and real-time tracking, hamper the industry's ability to operate at peak efficiency.
Fragmentation and a high no of owner-drivers do not make it feasible for IT adoption.

10.5 Skilled Workforce Shortage

Endemic driver shortage, the logistics industry also faces a shortage of skilled personnel, particularly in areas like trucking and warehouse management.
This can impact the quality of services and overall supply chain efficiency.

10.6 High Operational Costs

Rising fuel costs, maintenance expenses, and other operational costs contribute to the overall financial burden on logistics providers, impacting their competitiveness.
About 45% of manufacturers rate logistics costs as very high in the selection of LSP and around 90% indicate that LSP needs to focus on cost reduction. (Fast-tracking automotive logistics)

10.7 Lack of Standardization

Lack of standardized practices and processes across the industry can lead to inconsistencies, errors, and difficulties in integrating with global supply chains.

Figure 5. Current challenges in Logistics

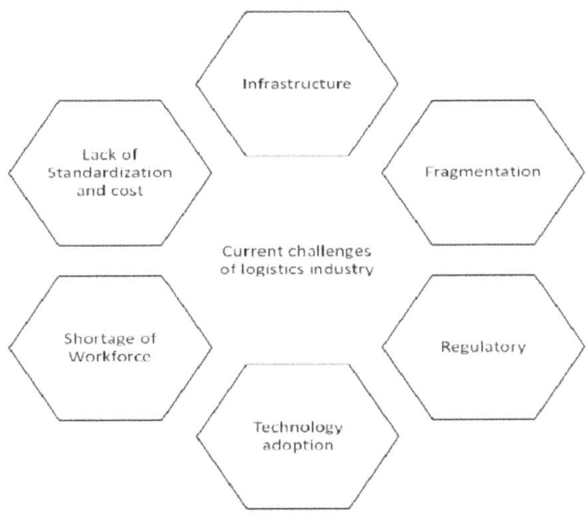

11. CRITICAL DELIVERY METRICS

The key performance indicators (KPIs) are used to quantify and assess the efficiency and effectiveness of logistics. Organizations track performances, identify the areas of improvement, and ensure the delight of customers. Some of the common delivery metrics are

11.1 On Time Delivery (OTD%) – Delivery

- One of the key delivery metrics is on-time delivery of consignment. This measures the overall percentage of shipments that reached their destination according to stipulated delivery dates or fixed norms.
- Let us say the agreed per day distance to cover is 400km then 1200km to be covered in 3 days from the origin place. All shipments that fall within this logic will be considered as on-time delivery %.

11.2 Defects per Vehicle (DPV)– Quality

- Defects per vehicle is a key metric used in all automotive companies to quantify the number of defects in the shipments delivered to Dealers or customers.
- This metric is crucial for assessing the quality and reliability of the goods within a certain period. It starts with defect identification, data collection, analysis of defects, and interpretation and action plan for reduction of defects.

11.3 Cost per Vehicle (CPV) – Cost

- Delivery cost per vehicle calculates the total cost of delivering all goods divided by number of goods despatched.
- This helps companies assess the efficiency of their operations and find the cost savings opportunities.
- There is also another metric where cost per kilometre, where total cost is divided by the total distance run by all shipments to arrive Per Km cost.

Figure 6. Key performance Metrics in logistics

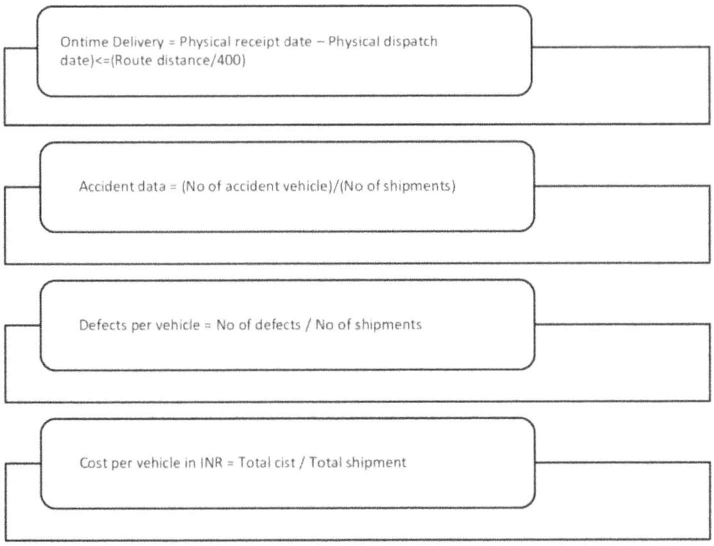

12. RISE OF THIRD-PARTY LOGISTICS

Increased momentum on core competence and growing complication of the logistics function has led many companies to outsource logistics activities like transportation and inventory management to 3PLs. Also, companies avoid the locking of working capital in storage locations, Trucks, etc.

These websites are frequently seen as potential competitors of traditional 3PLs. In reality, they provide complementary amenities that when combined allow them to meet the requirements of their customers for a global supply chain. By effectively collaborating with relevant agencies, 3PLs can offer services including cross-border transportation, customs clearing, and international trade settlement in combination with e-logistic firms.

There are still many companies that trust that logistics is too critical to surrender control to third-party service providers. To delight customers, 3PLs must position themselves as critical business partners involved in the supply chain. – from strategy to its implementation. They must effectively share information with the customers. 3PL growth follows the logistics function development. There are different phases according to the service provided.

Figure 7. Phases of service provided by 3PLSource: Third-party logistics development

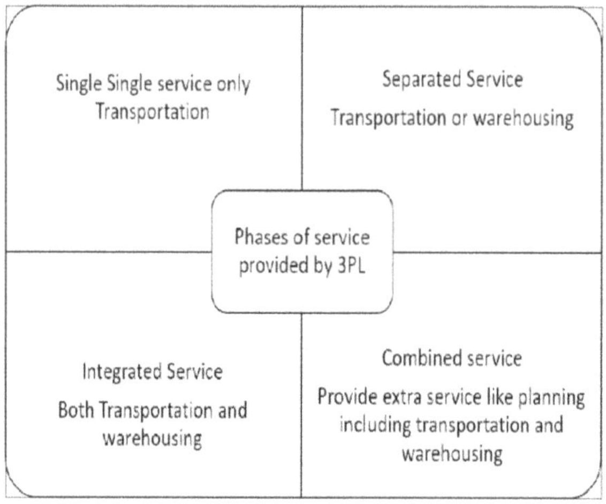

13. BI-INFORMATION FLOW AND PROCESSING IN COMPANIES

It is important to emphasize the significance of ETL processes at the information processing stage. ETL means Extract, Transform, and Load.

ETL (Extraction, Transformation, Loading) subsystems are an integral component of all the systems of BI type, which allow the transfer of information from the data warehouse to the process of it. The selection of the database environment for stored data is one of the most important decisions during the implementation of BI systems in the company. ETL subsystems cooperate directly with DW - Data Warehouses, which are one of the most modern IT solutions for decision-making.

14. DATA ANALYTICS-DRIVEN LOGISTICS FOR GREATER EFFICIENCY

Decisions linked to Key performance indicators were majorly monitored by the logistics manager. To optimize the performance and enhance the overall efficiency various data analytics are being carried out by organizations.

14.1 Telematics-Based Data Analytics

- The transportation industry now evolving extremely in the development of digitization and connected vehicle technology.
- The vehicle is connected to a GPS device which shares the data in real time with the logistics manager.
- This telematics provides detailed fleet insights and all vehicle details.
- Various alerts like critical alerts, warnings, fuel level, service, and geofencing are integrated with this device.
- Not only the performance is monitored using this telematics device but also the productivity and safety aspects of goods.
- Fuel consumption, driver performance, idling, mileage, and distance travelled were analysed using this device.

14.2 Despatch Forecasting and Inventory Management

- Despatch velocity from the order is one of the key performance indicators for the logistics manager.
- Based on the historical despatch and sales data logistics professionals can make predictions on future despatch demands.
- This will help reduce the risk of overstocking and maintain optimal inventory levels and smoother flow of goods out of origin location.
- With the support of tracking device companies able to update about goods to customers periodically. One of keep challenges in large warehouses is retrieval which is addressed with the support of telematics and other digital devices to reach the goods.

14.3 Route Optimization and Transportation Efficiency

- Data analytics plays a great role in the optimization of routes for delivery. By analysing the data related to traffic patterns, and weather conditions, companies can identify the optimal route to reach the destination.
- This route optimization not only minimizes the transit time but also reduces the cost of fuel consumption and contributes to the environment.
- Real-time tracking and tracing of location can be monitored automatically by creating trips with the support of telematics and fixing the routes. Any deviation in routes will be triggered by the logistics manager or fleet owner to take further action.

14.4 Sustainability and Green Logistics

- Organizations analysing environment-related data to identify eco-friendly practices.
- A major contributor in the logistics industry is fuel consumption which can be reduced by optimized routes and adopting green packing solutions.
- commercial vehicle companies reduce carbon footprint by sending vehicles through railways which reduces fuel consumption.

14.5 Cost Optimization Through Data-Driven Insights

- Analyzing cost-related data is very vital for identifying the opportunities related to cost savings.
- In the logistics industry fuel savings contribute more than done with the support of Telematics devices.
- Big data collected and stored with the support of telematics were analyzed, the overall distance travelled divided by fuel consumed by the vehicle is called mileage(kmpl)
- To third-party logistics service providers optimal Mileage will be considered for logistics payment.

14.6 Security and Fraud Detection

- Security and risk mitigation play a major role in the logistics sector. Analyzing the patterns and anomalies in data organizations and detecting fraudulent activities to avoid cash outflow.
- Various controls of maker and checker in business enterprise portal and Auto mailers for unauthorized access to shipments.
- Identifying the outliers and intimation to the logistics manager, automation of master data, and companies ensuring the least manual intervention in the process.

14.7 Accident Prevention

- Analyzing the driver behavior through telematics data. Triggers for continuous driving habits and vehicle running in neutral.
- Major no of accident cases driver without or fake driving license which has risen from 32,088 in 2016 to 48,503 in 2017[2]. This auto-detection of driver's license is validated by ERP and other business enterprise software before

allocation of the consignment to drivers which checks with the RTO portal on the validity of the license.

- Organization collecting complete driver's license data not only to avoid accidents but also to blacklist drivers with wrong convey practice and reward good drivers.
- Data on sober driving devices in vehicles also reduces road accidents [2].
- Deep mid-night driving by drivers and over speeding were controlled with the support of telematics and intimated to the logistics process owner for accident prevention.

14.8 Electronic- Proof of Delivery Automation (E-POD)

- Digital solution called E-POD which automates and streamlines the procedure of checking that the recipient has received the goods or services.
- In the commercial vehicle industry transit damages were recorded in this E-POD and auto mail was triggered to the consignee, transporter, and Finance department for payment.
- Old-style proof of delivery includes manual signature and seals of respective receiving location.
- This E-POD improves the operating cycle of the service provider and prevents damage to the POD en-route by the driver.

14.9 Human-Machine Collaboration in Data-Driven Logistics

- The integration of data analytics tools requires effective human-machine coordination. Employees must adapt to new systems that augment their capabilities, requiring comprehensive training and change management strategies. Successful collaboration hinges on trust, clear communication, and an understanding of the technology's role in supporting human decision-making.

14.10 Predictive Analytics in Logistics

- Predictive analytics helps logistics companies forecast demand, optimize inventory levels, and improve supply chain responsiveness. Aleksandrova (2021) illustrated how predictive models enhance operational planning, reducing delays and minimizing costs.

15. BUSINESS INTELLIGENCE IN LOGISTICS FOR GREATER EFFICIENCY

15.1 Auto Share of Business Allocation Based on Performance

- Traditional shipment allocation is a manual process that is carried out by the logistics manager. This process involves various biases towards service providers.
- Now industries enhancing the automated allocation of shipments based on the past month's performance.
- Key performance metrics were ranked for each service provider and maximum allocation with support of automated tool transporters were allotted.

15.2 KPI Tracking Dashboards

- Key performance indicators like the contribution of Ontime Delivery, defects per vehicle, stock details, and pre-sale claims can be presented in dashboard reports to the top management to facilitate the quick decision-making process.
- Also, auto mailers can be triggered if any KPI reaches a pre-defined threshold level.
- Also, 3PL who is in direct contact with end customers they able to capture insights and records in the partner portal which will be analyzed and delivered in the form of digital reports to address future challenges.
- Dashboards show the retailers may return the goods due to transit damages or poor quality.

15.3 Efficient Track and Trace Dashboards

- The ability to track assets will be required for doing a standard of business in the future.
- Business intelligence dashboards that display how many vehicles are in transit to the destination each location-wise, zone-wise, and model-wise.
- Through geofencing and tracking device, end customer is measured, and Business intelligence dashboard shows the expected time of delivery to receiver.
- Consignments yet to start from location and running delay vehicles are also monitored to improve efficiency.
- This also brings transparency throughout the supply chain from order to delivery.

15.4 Broken Convey

- Enroute breakdown due to technical issues is another challenge for logistics.
- This broken convey can be tracked with a visual dashboard and the status will be updated in real-time for rectification action by a service engineer. This solves the issue of difficulty in finding the breakdown vehicle en route.
- Various algorithms used in the cluster boards of vehicles. This helps to reach to concern location without any delays.

15.5 Role of AI and Automation

AI-driven analytics and automation in supply chain improve efficient routing, sales yard management, and optimized inventory Management. Muchova et al. (2018) demonstrated the effectiveness of AI in enhancing supply chain agility and responsiveness.

16. FROM VISIBILITY TO OPTIMIZATION: THE EVOLVING ROLE OF BUSINESS INTELLIGENCE IN LOGISTICS MANAGEMENT

16.1 Strategic Role of Business Intelligence in Logistics

Business Intelligence (BI) has transformed the logistics landscape from a functional support activity to a critical strategic component of enterprise operations. Traditionally, logistics was viewed as a back-office function focused solely on transportation, warehousing, and order fulfilment. However, as Greis and Kasarda (1997) emphasize, the rise of the information era has redefined logistics into a strategic lever for achieving business competitiveness. BI enables logistics managers to integrate information across multiple functions, including procurement, sales, and inventory management, resulting in more cohesive and agile supply chain strategies.

The strategic application of BI allows firms to respond rapidly to market demands, customer expectations, and operational disruptions. By leveraging real-time data, organizations can shift from reactive to proactive decision-making, where problems are anticipated and mitigated before they escalate. BI tools facilitate the alignment of logistics with organizational goals, such as cost reduction, service excellence, and innovation.

16.2 Predictive Analytics Enhances Planning and Agility

Predictive analytics represents a major leap in logistics capabilities by enabling organizations to forecast future events and plan accordingly. Rather than relying solely on historical data, predictive analytics uses statistical models, artificial intelligence (AI), and machine learning algorithms to answer the question "What will happen?" In logistics, this includes demand forecasting, risk prediction, delivery time estimation, and resource optimization.

In Assessing the Effect of Business Intelligence on Supply Chain Agility, predictive analytics is shown to be a key driver of agile logistics systems, especially in manufacturing environments like those in Jordan.

The agility enabled by predictive analytics is crucial in today's volatile market conditions where customer expectations are high and supply chains are complex. Companies that can forecast and adapt are more likely to meet customer demands, avoid costs from stockouts or overstocks, and maintain high service levels. As such, predictive analytics serves as a vital tool for risk mitigation and operational resilience in modern logistics.

16.3 Prescriptive Analytics Drives Optimization

Prescriptive analytics represents the most advanced level of the BI spectrum, focusing on decision-making through data-driven recommendations. This form of analytics integrates simulation, optimization models, AI-driven algorithms, and scenario analysis to support strategic and operational decisions in real time.

In the paper Managing Supply Chains Using Business Intelligence, prescriptive analytics is credited with enabling dynamic logistics decisions such as route optimization, load planning, and fleet scheduling.

Prescriptive analytics not only enhances decision speed but also improves accuracy, consistency, and cost efficiency. It allows businesses to simulate various scenarios before making strategic decisions, minimizing risk and maximizing return. In an industry where timeliness and resource utilization are critical, prescriptive analytics stands out as a transformative capability for logistics optimization and strategic execution.

16.4 BI as a Value-Adding Framework

Beyond operational enhancements, Business Intelligence contributes to logistics as a comprehensive value-adding framework that impacts the entire supply chain ecosystem. Rather than being confined to data analysis, BI acts as an enabler of strategic differentiation, aligning logistics operations with customer expectations, financial goals, and market dynamics. In Understanding the Value of Business Analytics in Logistics, Ramanathan et al. (2019) present a framework that illustrates how BI facilitates the translation of data into customer value, operational excellence, and sustainable competitive advantage.

BI-driven value is realized through enhanced visibility, reduced operational waste, and improved service delivery.

Moreover, BI helps logistics managers justify investments and improvements through evidence-based ROI calculations. It supports the evaluation of logistics performance not just through cost metrics but through service level achievements, risk reduction, and innovation. By embedding BI into logistics strategies, organizations can not only operate more efficiently but also deliver differentiated value to stakeholders, making logistics a core contributor to enterprise success.

17. CASE STUDIES AND REAL- WORLD APPLICATIONS

17.1 Case Study 1: Tata Motors – Predictive Maintenance Using IoT & BI

17.1.1 Background

Tata Motors, a leading Indian commercial vehicle manufacturer, faced increasing pressure to reduce vehicle downtime and improve service efficiency for its logistics fleet and customer base.

17.1.2 Strategies Adopted

- IoT sensor integration in commercial vehicles to key parameters like Driver behavior, AdBlue conditions, quantity of fuel and battery condition.
- Predictive analytics models using historical and real-time sensor data to forecast part failures or maintenance requirements.
- BI dashboards enabled logistics managers to review the performance of the transporters

17.1.3 Outcome

- Reduced unscheduled maintenance by 25%.
- Improved vehicle operating and delight the end user
- Significant cost savings in fleet operations due to fewer breakdowns and optimized maintenance schedules.

17.2 Case Study 2: Rivigo – Relay-as-a-Service Enabled by Real-Time BI

Background: Rivigo, a logistics company based in India, pioneered the "relay trucking model" to solve the problem of driver fatigue and ensure faster delivery of goods.

17.2.1 Strategies Adopted

- Built a central BI platform that collected real-time data from trucks and drivers.
- Used route optimization algorithms to switch drivers at pre-defined pit stops (relay points) while trucks continued their journey non-stop.
- Geo-analytics tools monitored vehicle movement, driver behavior, and delivery status.

17.2.2 Outcome

- Reduced delivery time by 50%, often achieving same-day delivery over long distances.
- Improved driver comfort and safety, leads to reduce the attrition and welcomes more in this business
- Created a competitive edge with better fleet productivity and customer reliability.

17.3 Case Study 3: Mahindra Logistics – Data-Driven Route Optimization

17.3.1 Background

Mahindra Logistics manages end-to-end supply chain operations for various industries. They needed to reduce the total cost of vehicle operations and improve delivery efficiency.

17.3.2 Strategies Adopted

- Deployed a data analytics platform to analyses historical route data, fuel consumption, vehicle idle time, and delivery delays.
- Implemented machine learning models for dynamic routing based on weather, traffic, and shipment priority.

- Dashboards for key result area monitoring and review

17.3.3 Outcome

- Fuel cost reduction and overall delivery efficiency improvement.
- Real-time alerts helped operations managers to intervene early during disruptions.
- Enhanced decision-making and forecasting for future route planning.

17.4 Case Study 4: DHL Supply Chain India – Warehouse to Last-Mile BI Integration

17.4.1 Background

DHL India was experiencing inconsistencies between warehouse dispatch and last-mile delivery execution, affecting customer service levels in the commercial segment.

17.4.2 Strategies Adopted

- Used BI tools (like Power BI & Tableau) to integrate warehouse management system (WMS) and transportation management system (TMS).
- Developed real-time dashboards showing vehicle loading status, delivery schedules, driver allocation, and delivery window commitments.
- Employed advanced analytics to detect inefficiencies in warehouse operations that impacted dispatch timelines.

17.4.3 Outcome

- Improved OTIF (On-Time In-Full) performance improvement in organization
- Enabled proactive decision-making, reducing missed delivery opportunities
- Greater visibility led to better coordination between sales yards, delivery partner, and end user teams.

17.5 Key Learnings From Case Studies

17.5.1 Real-Time Data Enhances Decision-Making

Leveraging IoT and real-time analytics empowers logistics companies to make faster, data-driven decisions, especially in areas like maintenance, routing, and delivery monitoring.

17.5.2 Predictive Analytics Reduces Operational Costs

Predictive maintenance and failure forecasting significantly cut down unexpected downtimes, reduce repair costs, and extend the life of commercial vehicles.

17.5.3 BI Dashboards Improve Operational Transparency

Centralized and visually interactive BI tools help logistics managers monitor key performance indicators (KPIs) and intervene proactively during disruptions.

17.5.4 Route Optimization Boosts Delivery Efficiency

Data-driven route planning using historical and dynamic factors (traffic, weather, load) leads to improved fuel efficiency and shorter delivery times.

17.5.5 Integration of Systems Drives End-to-End Visibility

Synchronizing data across WMS, TMS, and fleet tracking systems ensures smooth coordination from warehouse dispatch to last-mile delivery.

17.5.6 Customer & Driver Satisfaction Can Be Data-Driven

Using analytics to enhance service reliability (like timely deliveries and safer driving conditions) directly improves customer retention and reduces driver churn.

17.5.7 Competitive Advantage Through Innovation

Companies like Rivigo and Tata Motors gained market differentiation by embedding analytics and BI at the core of their logistics strategy.

18. TRANSFORMING THE LOGISTICS SECTOR THROUGH STRATEGIC INTEGRATION, SUSTAINABILITY, AND TECHNOLOGICAL INNOVATION

18.1 Strategic Integration and Business Process Alignment

One of the fundamental shifts in logistics management is the emphasis on integrated business processes. Azmi et al. (2017) highlight the necessity of aligning logistics and supply chain operations with broader business objectives to enhance efficiency and responsiveness. Integration across functions such as procurement, warehousing, distribution, and customer service ensures streamlined operations and real-time data sharing. This alignment reduces redundancy, shortens delivery lead times, and improves customer satisfaction.

Abdulla and Musa (2021), through a case study on ADNOC, illustrate how prioritizing logistics management factors like supplier coordination, real-time data, and infrastructure investment significantly enhances organizational performance. Their findings reinforce the idea that strategic logistics decisions—rooted in operational visibility and system integration—can elevate company performance, particularly in asset-heavy industries like oil and gas.

18.2 Sustainability and Green Supply Chain Practices

Environmental sustainability has become a key consideration in logistics strategies. Agrawal et al. (2022) explore the critical success factors for sustainable green supply chain management and identify government regulations, environmental awareness, and top management commitment as pivotal elements. These factors encourage firms to adopt cleaner technologies, reduce carbon footprints, and improve waste management.

Within the Indian logistics context, the shift toward sustainable practices is gaining traction, albeit slowly. Aravind raj and Rajan Chinna (2019) discuss how India's logistics sector faces mounting pressure to balance economic efficiency with environmental responsibility. Infrastructure limitations and fragmented supply chains hinder progress, yet policy incentives and public-private partnerships offer pathways to a greener logistics ecosystem.

18.3 Logistics Performance Measurement and 3PL Evaluation

The role of performance measurement is gaining prominence, particularly for third-party logistics (3PL) providers. Asthana and Bhat (2015) highlight the need for vigorous business performance quantity models in the logistics landscape.

They suggest using balanced scorecards and customer-focused KPIs to measure value creation, operational efficiency, and service quality. This becomes especially relevant as competition intensifies and clients demand greater accountability from logistics partners.

Their empirical study reveals that mismatched expectations can hinder relationship success. Providers often overestimate their service effectiveness, while users focus on delivery timeliness, cost-efficiency, and adaptability. These discrepancies underscore the need for data-driven performance benchmarking and transparent reporting systems—areas where BI and analytics can offer substantial value.

18.4 Technology Implementation and Operational Excellence

The integration of technology and business intelligence into logistics operations is transforming the industry's operational landscape. Chakraborty et al. (2020) examine barriers to IT implementation in the Indian logistics sector, identifying infrastructural gaps, cost constraints, and digital literacy issues as major roadblocks. Despite these challenges, the adoption of technologies like RFID, GPS, cloud-based ERP systems, and advanced analytics is steadily improving operational visibility and coordination.

Digital transformation is not only about tools but also about reimagining workflows. This example shows how Indian logistics firms can use data intelligence and operational design to disrupt traditional models and scale efficiently.

18.5 Competitive Strategy and Market Differentiation

Strategic aligning is critical in a modest and disjointed logistics Business. Bhattacharyya et al. (2021) employ strategic group charting to scrutinize market diversity within the Indian logistics sector.

Chandra and Jain (2007) further highpoint the structural contests of the Indian logistics industry, including varying service feedback, infrastructure bottlenecks, and lack of standardization. Addressing these requires not only government intervention but also firm-level innovations in routing, warehouse automation, and supply chain visibility.

19. FUTURE SCENARIOS AND DISRUPTIVE TRENDS IN BI FOR LOGISTICS

19.1 Autonomous BI-Driven Logistics

AI and IoT will enable fleets that self-optimize routes, fuel use, and load balancing. BI platforms will predict disruptions and reroute without human intervention.

19.2 Platform-Based Logistics Ecosystems

BI capabilities will be embedded into logistics platforms that integrate shippers, carriers, and regulatory bodies. These systems will provide unified, real-time insights on carbon emissions, customs clearance, and delivery milestones.

19.3 AI-Enabled Sustainable Logistics

BI will support ESG compliance through:

- Automated emissions tracking
- Sustainability dashboards for regulatory reporting
- Lifecycle analysis of freight vehicles

19.4 Scenario 4: BI-as-a-Service (BIaaS) for SMEs

Cloud-based BI solutions will allow small logistics firms to access advanced analytics without high capital investment, enabling broader industry digitization.

These scenarios underscore the need for logistics companies to not only adopt BI but prepare for rapid technological convergence.

20. CONCLUSION & LIMITATIONS

In business data and information available are very vital. Contemporary data analytics methods, techniques, and tools allow for complex analysis for carrying out different decisions sourced from various data. This is very vital for improvement in achieving the key performance indicators and minimizing the risk in the logistics process.

The practical application of BI systems in the field of logistics brings such qualities for the company as development of the whole decision-making method which is related to logistics. The other merits contain enhancement of performance in different matters of business endeavor. Solving the challenge of share of business allocation, supporting third-party logistic providers by driver performance monitoring, improving the efficacy of transportation e.g. routes optimization, track and trace, mileage optimization with telematics technology as well as inventory management. Additionally, the analytics solutions by providing a better quality of information for decision making can improve the whole decision-making process in the logistics area as well as in the whole enterprise.

The study's limitation is that it was conducted with limited commercial vehicle industries in India. Businesses are now dealing with intense rivalry where swift decision-making gives a competitive edge in the industry, hence it's crucial to study, forecast, and enable business intelligence tools and dashboards for everyday operations. The exploration of Business Intelligence (BI) in logistics reveals a dynamic transformation in how organizations manage, optimize, and strategize their supply chain operations. Across the literature reviewed, it is evident that BI has evolved from being a mere data reporting tool to a comprehensive framework that empowers organizations to create responsive, resilient, and strategically aligned logistics systems. The concept of the BI spectrum—ranging from descriptive to prescriptive analytics—provides a valuable lens through which to understand the depth and breadth of BI's influence on logistics.

At the foundation of this spectrum lies descriptive and diagnostic analytics. These tools provide the essential visibility into logistics operations, offering real-time performance monitoring, anomaly detection, and root cause analysis. Papers such as business intelligence in logistics activities of enterprises and the application of business intelligence systems in logistics underscore how this visibility enables informed operational control, improves reliability, and sets the stage for continuous improvement. Descriptive analytics enabling logistics managers to implement actions based on ready information.

Building upon this foundation, predictive analytics represent a significant step forward in the use of BI within logistics. As demonstrated in studies such as assessing the effect of business intelligence on supply chain agility and the influence of business intelligence on supply chain management, predictive analytics allow organizations to anticipate demand changes, forecast risks, and prepare for market uncertainties. This proactive capability enhances supply chain agility and responsiveness, helping firms to manage inventory, allocate resources, and optimize delivery in a dynamic environment. The ability to foresee and plan for future scenarios offers significant value in reducing costs, avoiding delays, and meeting customer expectations consistently.

At the highest level of the BI spectrum is prescriptive analytics, which offers actionable recommendations for optimizing logistics strategies. As evidenced in Managing Supply Chains Using Business Intelligence and Supply Chain Business

Intelligence: Technologies, Issues and Trends, prescriptive analytics leverages advanced technologies such as artificial intelligence, machine learning and quick decisions. This may involve selecting the most cost-effective transportation route, reallocating warehouse resources, or adjusting production schedules to align with anticipated demand. Prescriptive analytics transforms decision-making from being reactive to intelligent and automated, driving greater efficiency and competitiveness.

Beyond its functional contributions, BI in logistics holds strategic importance. The work of Greis and Kasarda (1997) highlighted the shift of logistics from a support role to a strategic business function. Today, with BI as a core enabler, logistics operations are closely tied to organizational strategy. BI facilitates better alignment with enterprise objectives such as customer satisfaction, cost leadership, and operational excellence. The review also shows that BI fosters cross-functional integration, allowing logistics to collaborate effectively with finance, procurement, and sales for more cohesive business execution.

While large enterprises may have the infrastructure to implement advanced analytics, small and medium-sized enterprises (SMEs) may face barriers related to cost, skills, or system integration. However, emerging cloud-based solutions and user-friendly BI platforms are gradually bridging this gap, making advanced analytics more accessible across all tiers of industry.

In summary, the role of Business Intelligence in logistics is profound and multi-dimensional. It enables organizations to transition from data collection to actionable intelligence, from reactive troubleshooting to proactive planning, and from manual decision-making to automated optimization. The collective insights from the papers reviewed underscore that the strategic deployment of BI across its full spectrum is essential for modern logistics excellence. As global supply chains continue to grow in complexity and uncertainty, BI stands out as a critical enabler of competitive advantage, innovation, and long-term sustainability in logistics and supply chain management.

20.1 Operational Improvements Through BI

- BI supports better driver performance monitoring, optimized routing, mileage tracking via telematics, and improved inventory management.
- Enhanced visibility leads to more efficient day-to-day logistics operations and business processes.

20.2 Evolution of BI: From Descriptive to Prescriptive Analytics

- Descriptive Analytics: Provides foundational visibility with real-time performance tracking and root cause analysis.

- Predictive Analytics: Enables forecasting of demand, risk, and supply chain volatility, increasing agility and responsiveness.
- Prescriptive Analytics: Delivers actionable recommendations using AI and machine learning, shifting decision-making from reactive to proactive.

20.3 Strategic Importance of BI in Logistics

- BI has transformed logistics from a support role to a strategic function aligned with organizational goals like customer satisfaction and cost leadership.
- Enables integration and collaboration across departments like finance, procurement, and sales.

20.4 BI Accessibility and the SME Challenge

- Larger enterprises lead BI adoption due to better infrastructure.
- SMEs face challenges in BI implementation, but emerging cloud-based and user-friendly solutions are making BI more accessible.

21. RECOMMENDATIONS FOR PRACTITIONERS

21.1 Invest in Internet of things and Real-Time Data Collection

Equip commercial vehicles with Sensors to collect actionable data on Driver behavior, Fuel usage driver behavior, and location. This is foundational for predictive analytics and real-time monitoring.

21.2 Adopt Predictive Maintenance Models

Use historical and sensor data to forecast vehicle breakdowns and schedule timely maintenance. This reduces downtime, enhances fleet reliability, and lowers long-term costs.

21.3 Integrate BI Tools Across the Supply Chain

Ensure seamless integration between warehouse, transport, and delivery data using platforms like Power BI or Tableau. This all-inclusive perceptibility enables better direction and transparency in value chain.

21.4 Leverage Route Optimization Algorithms

Apply machine learning models for dynamic route planning based on weather, traffic, delivery priority, and vehicle availability to improve delivery performance and reduce fuel consumption.

21.5 Prioritize Human-Centric Metrics

Use BI not just for vehicles and cargo but also to enhance driver well-being, optimize shift patterns, and reduce fatigue—factors that impact safety and service quality.

21.6 Align BI Strategy with Business Goals

Build KPI dashboards that reflect business objectives (e.g., OTIF, fuel efficiency, downtime reduction) and enable real-time interventions for continuous improvement.

21.7 Drive Innovation Through Analytics-First Mindset

Develop a culture where analytics is embedded in strategic planning, operational execution, and customer engagement. Encourage pilot programs and analytics-driven innovation.

22. RECOMMENDATIONS FOR RESEARCHERS

22.1 Explore Regional and Sectoral Contexts

Study how analytics adoption varies across regions (urban vs rural) and sub-sectors (LTL, FTL, cold chain logistics) in commercial vehicle operations, especially in emerging markets like India.

22.2 Investigate BI Adoption Challenges

Conduct empirical research on barriers to BI implementation, such as resistance to change, data silos, and limited technical know-how among logistics operators.

22.3 Analyze the ROI of BI Investments

Develop models to evaluate the return on investment (ROI) of analytics tools in logistics—considering operational, financial, and environmental outcomes.

22.4 Develop Frameworks for Real-Time BI in Logistics

Propose conceptual or architectural frameworks that support real-time analytics in logistics networks with a focus on low-latency, high-volume data environments.

22.5 Assess Impact on Sustainability Goals

Study how BI and data analytics contribute to sustainability, including reduced fuel consumption, optimized routes, and better resource utilization in fleet logistics.

22.6 Area of improvement, impact and solutions

Table 5. Weakness and Impact

Weakness	Impact	Solution
Limited Global Perspective	Limits relevance and benchmarking value	Add international comparisons, cases, and a global trends section
Underemphasis on Data Governance & Privacy	Undermines reliability and legal compliance of BI systems	Include cybersecurity, data quality, and privacy discussions with frameworks
Limited Implementation Guidance	Makes the chapter less actionable for practitioners	Provide a step-by-step BI roadmap, decision trees, and practical case study walkthroughs

Table 6. Suggestions for improvement

Stage	Key Actions	Example Tools
Stage 1: Readiness Assessment	Evaluate data maturity, team capability, existing systems	BI Maturity Checklist
Stage 2: Pilot Phase	Start with one function (e.g., route optimization)	Google Maps API, Excel, Power BI
Stage 3: Data Integration	Connect ERP, WMS, telematics data	ETL tools, data warehouse

Stage	Key Actions	Example Tools
Stage 4: Dashboarding & Alerts	**Deploy real-time insights**	**Tableau, Zoho Analytics**
Stage 5: Predictive & Prescriptive BI	**Introduce ML models**	**Python, AWS SageMaker**

ACKNOWLEDGMENT

I would like to express my sincere gratitude to my guide, for his invaluable guidance, expertise, and unwavering support throughout the development of this chapter. His insights and feedback have been crucial in shaping this work. I would also like to thank my family, colleagues, and peers for their encouragement, patience, and understanding. A special thanks to the institutions and individuals whose resources and knowledge contributed to the completion of this chapter. Finally, I am deeply appreciative of the opportunity to contribute to this work and to all those who have helped along the way.

REFERENCES

Abdulla, M. F. M. H., & Musa, H. (2021). Prioritizing the logistics management factors affecting company performance: Case study of ADNOC. *International Journal of Sustainable Construction Engineering and Technology, 12*(5). Advance online publication. DOI: 10.30880/ijscet.2021.12.05.007

Agrawal, V., Mohanty, R. P., Agarwal, S., Dixit, J. K., & Agrawal, A. M. (2022). Analysing critical success factors for sustainable green supply chain management. *Environment, Development and Sustainability*. Advance online publication. DOI: 10.1007/s10668-022-02396-2

Aleksandrova, Y. (2021). *Predictive analytics implementation in the logistic industry. Journal Name, Volume*. Issue.

Aravind raj, K., & Rajan Chinna, P. (2019). A contemporary on recent development activities and challenges in logistics sector in India. International Journal of Innovative Technology and Exploring Engineering, 8(11). https://doi.org/DOI: 10.35940/ijitee.K2209.0981119

Arivazhagan, D. (2020). Logistics network in India: Challenges and scope. *International Journal of Scientific and Technology Research, 9*(2).

Asthana, S., & Bhat, H. (2015). A study of business performance measurement of third-party logistics (3PL) organizations in the Indian logistics industry. [The Journal of Innovations]. *IMS Manthan, 10*(1). Advance online publication. DOI: 10.18701/imsmanthan.v10i1.5660

Asthana, S., & Dwivedi, A. (2020). Performance measurement of India-based third-party logistics sector: An empirical study of user versus provider perspectives. *Production Planning and Control, 31*(2–3). Advance online publication. DOI: 10.1080/09537287.2019.1631467

Azmi, I., Hamid, N. A., Hussin, M. N. M., & Ibrahim, N. I. (2017). Logistics and supply chain management: The importance of integration for business processes. *Journal of Emerging Economies and Islamic Research, 5*(4). Advance online publication. DOI: 10.24191/jeeir.v5i4.8838

Balodi, K. C., Jain, R., & Das, R. (2022). Strategy, business model, and innovation at Rivigo: Is Relay-as-a-Service the way forward? *Journal of Information Technology Teaching Cases, 12*(1). Advance online publication. DOI: 10.1177/2043886920986163

Bhattacharyya, S. S., Garlapad, V., & Kulkarni, O. (2021). A study of strategic group mapping and understanding mobility barriers in the Indian logistics industry. *International Journal of Applied Logistics, 12*(1). Advance online publication. DOI: 10.4018/ijal.286164

Chakraborty, S., Sharma, A., & Vaidya, O. S. (2020). Achieving sustainable operational excellence through IT implementation in Indian logistics sector: An analysis of barriers. *Resources, Conservation and Recycling, 152*. Advance online publication. DOI: 10.1016/j.resconrec.2019.104506

Chandra, P., & Jain, N. (2007). The logistics sector in India: Overview and challenges. World Scientific Series on 21st Century Business.

Hofmann, E. (2017). Big data analytics and demand forecasting in supply chains: A conceptual analysis. *International Journal of Logistics Management, 28*(2), 426–443. DOI: 10.1108/IJLM-04-2016-0109

Liu, Y., Wang, W., & Zhang, J. (2021). Smart logistics in China: Role of AI and cloud BI platforms in urban delivery networks. *Transportation Research Part E, Logistics and Transportation Review, 145*, 102179. DOI: 10.1016/j.tre.2020.102179

Muchova, M., Paralic, J., & Nagyova, B. (2018). Data analysis of logistics company's data using business intelligence. *Journal Name, 18*(4), 58–63.

Wamba, S. F., Gunasekaran, A., Akter, S., Ren, S. J. F., Dubey, R., & Childe, S. J. (2020). Big data analytics and supply chain performance: A resource-based view. *Information & Management, 57*(2), 103207. DOI: 10.1016/j.im.2019.103207

Chapter 3
Designing Scalable Business Intelligence Architectures:
Bridging Technical Innovation and Organizational Needs

Mohammad Alauthman
https://orcid.org/0000-0003-0319-1968
Department of Information Security, University of Petra, Amman, Jordan

Ala Hamarsheh
https://orcid.org/0000-0002-4736-7331
Computer Science, Faculty of Information Technology, Arab American University, Jenin, Palestine

Ammar Almomani
https://orcid.org/0000-0002-8808-6114
Department of Computer Information Science, Higher Colleges of Technology, Sharjah, UAE

ABSTRACT

Organizations seek flexible platforms to handle diverse data demands in an environment where volumes and variety continue to expand. Many systems encounter barriers when scaling, which limits their ability to support dynamic business needs. This chapter examines how well-designed architectures sustain evolving analytical capabilities and address organizational demands for rapid insights. Findings revealed that adaptive frameworks promote efficient resource use, seamless integration of advanced analytics, and alignment with decision-making processes. Stakeholders reported enhanced operational oversight, faster reporting cycles, and reduced

DOI: 10.4018/979-8-3373-2125-7.ch003

latency in processing large datasets. These outcomes suggest that robust architectures support agile data strategies while maintaining interoperability. This chapter illuminates how scalable structures enrich organizations' analytical capacity and produce effective business intelligence outcomes.

1. INTRODUCTION

Business intelligence (BI) influences managerial and operational processes across diverse sectors. Many industries employ BI platforms to interpret large volumes of data and generate actionable information. Market needs shift rapidly, which forces organizations to reconsider their existing data pipelines. Traditional systems often face integration hurdles when data variety and velocity increase. Decision-makers require reliable information platforms that preserve integrity and timeliness. This chapter explores the design of scalable BI architectures that address these challenges. It focuses on how organizations combine technical and managerial elements to construct adaptive frameworks. It includes theoretical viewpoints that clarify the conceptual underpinnings of BI, as well as practical considerations that shape deployment outcomes.

1.1. Background and Context

Organizations treat data as a strategic resource. They rely on BI systems for descriptive, diagnostic, and predictive analytics. These platforms filter vast repositories of unstructured and structured data. They convert raw information into insights that can support both short-term tactics and long-term initiatives. Analysts and data scientists must collaborate with executives to ensure that technical solutions match strategic objectives. This interplay influences how architects design systems to manage data influx, security needs, and computational requirements. Many enterprises encounter operational bottlenecks when data demands surpass existing capacities. These constraints affect processing speed, data availability, and integration consistency. Scalable BI architectures address these limitations by accommodating higher loads without compromising performance.

1.2. Research Aim and Chapter Overview

This chapter investigates the elements that enable BI solutions to expand in tandem with organizational growth. It outlines how new data frameworks handle big data, heterogeneous sources, and shifting business priorities. It evaluates established theoretical approaches and modern innovations that facilitate scalability.

It also highlights organizational considerations, such as stakeholder alignment and governance policies, which shape the success of BI implementations. The discussion references open-access literature that examines different methodological and technological viewpoints. The chapter concludes by presenting prospects for BI architecture evolution, emphasizing how these systems continue to transform decision-making practices.

2. CONCEPTUAL FOUNDATIONS OF BUSINESS INTELLIGENCE

Business intelligence rests on strategies, applications, and technologies that gather and analyze data for better decision-making. It merges various disciplines, including database design, data integration, and analytics. Open-access studies show that BI integrates historical and real-time information to produce insights (Baars & Kemper, 2010). Early frameworks prioritized data warehousing and online analytical processing. Modern BI systems incorporate advanced analytics to address unstructured data and support predictive modeling (Wixom & Watson, 2010). Researchers note that BI initiatives enhance organizational flexibility when they align with governance structures. In many instances, alignment helps reduce redundancy and promotes consistent data definitions (Isik, Jones, & Sidorova, 2013).

2.1. Evolution of BI Theories

Initial BI models emerged from the need to consolidate transactional data in centralized repositories. Data warehousing provided a unified source for reporting. Developers introduced extraction, transformation, and loading (ETL) processes that ensured data quality. Over time, academic and industry experts examined issues such as data latency, integration complexity, and changing business requirements (Chen, Chiang, & Storey, 2012). Scholars then highlighted the shift from historic reporting toward predictive and prescriptive analytics (Delen & Ram, 2018). Theoretical discourse began to stress the role of human factors, organizational culture, and the strategic alignment of BI with corporate vision (Popovič, Hackney, Coelho, & Jaklič, 2012). Recent open-access investigations reflect how data lakes, cloud computing, and machine learning affect these theoretical constructs (Hai, Koutras, Quix, & Jarke, 2021).

2.2. Core Components of BI

Core BI components include data sources, integration tools, metadata management, analytical layers, and presentation interfaces. Each component's performance affects overall system capacity. Data sourcing involves retrieving raw content from operational systems, sensors, or external repositories. Integration tools standardize formats and handle quality verification. The analytical layer employs algorithms and statistical techniques to produce patterns or forecasts (Solano & Cruz, 2024). Finally, presentation interfaces deliver outputs that managers and analysts interpret. Researchers indicate that system scalability depends on robust data pipelines, efficient storage, and flexible analytical engines (Sivarajah et al, 2017). Open-access analyses underscore that each step faces potential bottlenecks when data throughput grows or transformation complexity increases (Davenport, 2018).

2.3 Business Intelligence Value Proposition

The value proposition of BI extends beyond simple reporting capabilities to multidimensional business impact. Organizations deploy BI solutions to achieve several strategic outcomes that ultimately enhance competitiveness. At its core, BI delivers value through information democratization, enabling diverse stakeholders to access relevant insights (Isik, Jones, & Sidorova, 2013). This democratization reduces information asymmetry between departments and management levels, fostering more informed decision-making across the enterprise.

Value manifestation occurs through several distinct mechanisms. First, BI systems reduce decision latency by streamlining data access and analysis workflows. This acceleration particularly benefits time-sensitive operations in dynamic markets where rapid response confers competitive advantage (Wixom & Watson, 2010). Second, BI platforms enhance decision quality by providing broader contextual information and reducing cognitive biases through data-driven approaches. Decision-makers can triangulate evidence from multiple sources before committing to strategic actions.

The economic value of BI emerges through operational optimization, risk reduction, and revenue enhancement. Operational benefits include identifying inefficiencies, optimizing resource allocation, and automating routine analyses. Risk management improves through anomaly detection, compliance monitoring, and early warning indicators for potential issues (Popovič, Hackney, Coelho, & Jaklič, 2012). Revenue enhancement stems from customer intelligence that identifies cross-selling opportunities, customer attrition risks, and market expansion potential.

Value measurement remains challenging due to the indirect nature of analytical benefits. Organizations increasingly adopt balanced scorecards that track both technical metrics (system performance, data quality) and business outcomes (decision cycle time, forecast accuracy). Mature implementations establish value realization frameworks that document causal links between analytical capabilities and organizational performance (Chen, Chiang, & Storey, 2012).

2.4 Analytical Maturity Models

Analytical maturity models provide frameworks for assessing organizational BI capabilities and planning evolutionary growth. These models typically progress through distinct stages from basic reporting to advanced predictive and prescriptive analytics. The DELTA model (Data, Enterprise, Leadership, Targets, Analysts) evaluates organizational readiness across five dimensions critical to analytical success (Davenport, 2018). This framework emphasizes that technical infrastructure alone cannot drive analytical maturity without corresponding organizational alignment.

Maturity assessment considers both infrastructural components and human factors. Infrastructure maturity evaluates data integration completeness, processing capacities, and analytical tool sophistication. Human dimensions examine analytical literacy, executive sponsorship, and cultural receptiveness to data-driven decision-making (Popovič, Hackney, Coelho, & Jaklič, 2012). Progressive maturity correlates with shifting from descriptive analytics (what happened) to diagnostic (why it happened), predictive (what will happen), and ultimately prescriptive analytics (how to make it happen).

Organizations often traverse maturity stages incrementally, starting with departmental initiatives before expanding enterprise-wide. Initial stages typically focus on retrospective reporting and standardized dashboards. Intermediate stages introduce self-service analytics and limited predictive capabilities. Advanced stages incorporate extensive machine learning, automated decision systems, and embedded analytics within operational processes (Wixom & Watson, 2010). Each stage requires increasing sophistication in data governance, analytical skills, and technological infrastructure.

Maturity models guide capability development by identifying gaps and prioritizing investments. They provide roadmaps for progressive enhancement rather than attempting comprehensive transformation simultaneously. Researchers note that organizations frequently plateau at intermediate maturity levels due to governance limitations, skills shortages, or cultural resistance (Günther, Rezazade Mehrizi, Huysman, & Feldberg, 2017). Overcoming these barriers requires coordinated advancement across both technical and organizational dimensions.

3. ARCHITECTURAL CONSIDERATIONS

Scalable BI architectures accommodate expanding data volumes and demands without sacrificing performance. They handle diverse data structures, including transactional records, sensor readings, and textual content. Open-access literature on software engineering emphasizes modular designs that separate compute resources from storage (Salloum, Dautov, Chen, Peng, & Huang, 2016). This approach allows systems to expand capacity at lower cost. Architecture also includes metadata management, governance policies, and security controls. Scholars who study distributed computing often highlight containerization and microservices to enhance scalability (Fazio et al., 2015). Hardware-level parallelization, distributed file systems, and cluster management strategies also emerge as effective pathways to support large data volumes.

3.1. On-Premises and Cloud Infrastructures

Organizations consider on-premises and cloud-based deployments when planning BI expansions. On-premises solutions offer control over hardware and security. However, they might involve significant capital investments and longer implementation times. Cloud platforms present elasticity, which lets organizations scale up or down based on usage patterns. Studies report that cloud solutions reduce initial costs but require careful attention to vendor lock-in, data sovereignty, and network dependencies (Berisha et al, 2022). Hybrid models blend both approaches. This arrangement seeks to maintain control over sensitive data while outsourcing less critical workloads to managed environments. These decisions depend on an organization's regulatory obligations, risk appetite, and technical competencies.

3.2. Data Integration and Quality

Data integration ensures consistency across disparate systems and sources. In large organizations, data might reside in multiple databases, each with distinct schemas. This variation complicates the unification needed for analytical processing. Researchers note that data quality influences decision accuracy (Batini et al., 2017). Timely updates reduce latency, which is critical in fast-paced sectors such as finance or logistics. Firms may adopt streaming pipelines or near-real-time integration to accommodate these needs. Some open-access studies examine how data lake architectures store unstructured content, which analysts process in later stages (Hai, Geisler, & Qu, 2016). Ensuring quality in these flexible repositories often requires metadata tagging and governance structures that monitor usage patterns.

3.3. Security and Privacy in BI Architectures

BI systems handle potentially sensitive information, including personal records or intellectual property. Proper security controls guard against unauthorized access. Architecture design typically integrates encryption, role-based authentication, and rigorous monitoring. Open-access discussions emphasize the importance of data anonymization, especially when analytics involve personal details (Barati, 2023). Privacy regulations, such as the General Data Protection Regulation in Europe, encourage careful handling of identifiable data. Security measures extend to data in transit and data at rest. Scalable architectures must consider the overhead associated with encryption and policy enforcement. Frequent audits and compliance checks help maintain trust in BI outputs.

3.4 Scalability Dimensions and Patterns

Scalability encompasses multiple dimensions that collectively determine a BI system's capacity to accommodate growth. Horizontal scalability involves adding more processing nodes to distribute workloads across a wider resource pool. Vertical scalability increases individual node capacity through hardware enhancements like additional memory or more powerful processors. Both approaches have distinct implications for system design and cost structures (Salloum, Dautov, Chen, Peng, & Huang, 2016).

Data volume scalability addresses expanding storage requirements as historical data accumulates and new sources emerge. Well-designed architectures implement tiered storage strategies that balance performance and cost considerations. Hot data remains on high-performance media for rapid access, while cold data migrates to more economical storage options. This approach often incorporates data lifecycle policies that automatically manage data movement between tiers based on access patterns and aging criteria (Hai, Geisler, & Qu, 2016).

Computational scalability focuses on processing capacity for increasingly complex analytical operations. This dimension becomes particularly critical when organizations introduce machine learning workloads that demand intensive computation. Effective designs separate storage from compute resources, allowing each to scale independently according to specific requirements (Kim, 2020). This separation prevents overprovisioning one resource type when only the other requires expansion.

User scalability addresses growing concurrent usage as analytics adoption spreads throughout the organization. This dimension considers both query concurrency and the diversity of analytical workloads. Architectural patterns that enhance user scalability include query governors that prevent resource monopolization, workload management policies that prioritize critical processes, and caching mechanisms that reduce redundant computation (Zaharia et al., 2010).

Several architectural patterns specifically support scalability goals:

Scale-Out Pattern distributes processing across commodity hardware, forming clusters that collectively handle large workloads. This approach offers cost advantages and graceful degradation during partial failures. However, it introduces complexity in workload distribution and result aggregation.

Functional Partitioning Pattern segregates workloads based on characteristics like query complexity, resource requirements, or business criticality. This pattern creates specialized processing environments optimized for specific analytical tasks, improving resource utilization and performance predictability.

Caching Pattern reduces computation by storing frequently accessed results or intermediate data structures. Multilevel caching strategies place data in memory, solid-state storage, or distributed caches based on access frequency and performance requirements.

Replication Pattern maintains multiple copies of data across nodes to improve read performance and fault tolerance. This pattern reduces contention for popular datasets but increases storage requirements and complexity of maintaining consistency.

Selecting appropriate scalability patterns requires understanding workload characteristics, growth projections, and organizational constraints. Most enterprise implementations combine multiple patterns to address diverse scalability requirements across different system components (Salloum, Dautov, Chen, Peng, & Huang, 2016).

4. DESIGNING SCALABLE SYSTEMS

Scalable designs distribute workloads, use efficient data structures, and optimize processes for growing demand. Open-access research presents strategies that rely on clustering, replication, and load balancing. High-performance hardware or distributed file systems can manage large datasets at speed (Kim, 2020). Parallel processing techniques break tasks into smaller units. These parallel tasks run simultaneously across nodes in a cluster, which reduces total processing time. System architects also monitor how concurrency affects database performance. Scalability covers both horizontal expansions (adding more nodes) and vertical expansions (increasing node capacity). Cloud-based services frequently adopt horizontal scaling, because distributed resources can spin up quickly when demand spikes.

4.1. Modular Frameworks

Modularity promotes flexibility by separating key functionalities into distinct layers or services. One service might specialize in data ingestion, while another handles analytics. This segmentation simplifies maintenance, as developers can update specific components without disrupting the entire system (Service-Oriented Architecture or microservices). Studies indicate that modular frameworks adapt more gracefully to evolving data workflows (Koutsoukos, 2020). Modules communicate through well-defined interfaces, which encourages interoperability. Some open-access designs present reference models for integrating data warehouses, data lakes, and real-time pipelines (Sang et al, 2016). These designs reduce duplication by reusing services for multiple purposes.

4.2. Parallel Processing and Distributed Systems

Parallel processing mechanisms address computationally intense tasks by distributing work among multiple processors or machines. Researchers highlight MapReduce and its successors as significant steps in large-scale data analytics (Dean & Ghemawat, 2008). Modern open-access frameworks incorporate in-memory processing to accelerate query times (Spark). These systems require careful consideration of data partitioning and fault tolerance. Distributed file systems replicate data across nodes to minimize data loss risks. They often co-locate computer and storage layers to reduce network overhead. Engineers adopt scheduling algorithms that balance tasks across available resources (Zaharia et al., 2010). In some architectures, containers and orchestration platforms simplify deployments by managing resource allocation and scaling events.

4.3. Real-Time and Near-Real-Time Processing

Real-time analytics meets immediate decision-making needs in fields such as e-commerce or healthcare. Users demand instantaneous insights to respond to changing conditions. Near-real-time approaches achieve similar goals with slight delays that might span seconds or minutes. Both methods involve continuous data ingestion and streaming pipelines. Scholars emphasize that real-time solutions rely on event-driven architectures, which trigger processes whenever new data arrives (Cao & Wachowicz, 2019). This approach contrasts with batch processing, where data accumulates before processing. Streaming systems often implement memory buffers and concurrency controls to handle fluctuations in input rates. They also integrate with dashboards or alerts that notify stakeholders of critical findings.

Figure 1. Basic Flowchart of a Stream Processing Pipeline

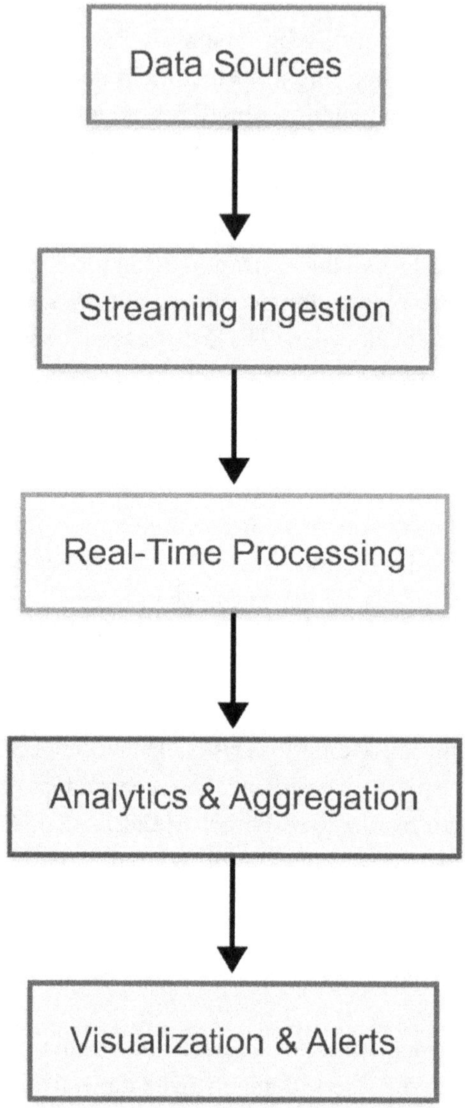

4.4 Event-Driven Architectures

Event-driven architectures (EDA) provide foundational frameworks for real-time and near-real-time BI systems. These architectures process occurrences (events) as they happen rather than in scheduled batches. Events might include transactions, sensor readings, user interactions, or state changes in monitored systems. Each event triggers specific processing workflows without requiring centralized coordination (Cao & Wachowicz, 2019).

The core components of an EDA include event producers, event channels, event consumers, and event processors. Producers generate events from business applications, IoT devices, or external systems. Event channels transmit events to interested consumers using publish-subscribe patterns that decouple producers from consumers. This decoupling enables independent scaling and evolution of system components. Event processors transform, filter, or aggregate events before delivering results to analytical storage or visualization systems.

Complex Event Processing (CEP) extends basic EDA capabilities by identifying patterns across multiple events within specified time windows. CEP engines apply predefined rules to detect significant situations that require immediate attention. For instance, a financial system might combine unusual transaction volume, geographic anomalies, and account history to identify potential fraud in real-time (Ramirez et al., 2021). This capability transforms raw event streams into actionable business insights that trigger automated responses or human interventions.

Event sourcing represents an architectural pattern where all state changes are captured as immutable event sequences. The current state can be reconstructed by replaying these events in order. This approach provides complete historical audit trails and enables temporal queries about past system states. BI applications leverage event sourcing to analyze state evolution over time, reproduce historical conditions for analysis, and support "what-if" simulations by modifying event sequences (Rodríguez & Buyya, 2020).

Integration between event-driven systems and traditional BI platforms often occurs through stream-to-batch converters that periodically capture event streams for historical analysis. This approach bridges real-time operational intelligence with longer-term analytical processes. Effective architectures maintain metadata continuity between streaming and batch domains, ensuring consistent business definitions and simplified data lineage tracking (Cao & Wachowicz, 2019).

5. ORGANIZATIONAL INTEGRATION

Scalable BI solutions produce limited benefits if organizations do not align them with management structures and cultures. Implementations require collaboration between technical personnel, analysts, and executives. Open-access case studies suggest that projects succeed when leaders articulate clear goals and support data-driven initiatives (Günther, Rezazade Mehrizi, Huysman, & Feldberg, 2017). Communication between teams reduces mismatched expectations. Governance frameworks specify data ownership, standard definitions, and quality assurance procedures. They also address compliance with privacy regulations. Training programs and change management strategies prepare employees to interpret and act on insights. Researchers note that organizations with data literacy programs exhibit higher BI adoption rates (El Chaarani & El Abiad, 2018).

5.1. Stakeholder Engagement

Stakeholders range from executive sponsors to front-line operational staff. Each group requires relevant insights from BI outputs. Executives may track strategic metrics, while operation teams need real-time updates on supply chains. Inclusive design workshops gather requirements that reflect each stakeholder's environment. Open-access literature indicates that early stakeholder engagement reduces rework and fosters a sense of ownership (**Alsibhawi et. al**, 2023). Technical teams then structure data models, dashboards, or reports that align with user needs. They also clarify data interpretation methods to avoid misapplication of results.

5.2. Data Governance and Quality Assurance

Governance programs define policies and standards for data usage. These programs clarify roles for stewardship, management, and data custodians. Scholars note that formal governance aligns BI objectives with enterprise goals (Otto, 2011). Quality assurance extends beyond cleaning initial data. It includes ongoing monitoring of accuracy and completeness. In scalable systems, new data sources may introduce inconsistencies if not integrated properly. Governance committees can set rules for data integration, retention, and deletion. They also handle compliance with relevant laws. Many frameworks adopt automated tests that compare data against rules or metadata constraints. Automated validation helps maintain consistent standards as data scales.

Table 1. Governance Roles and Responsibilities

Role	Responsibility
Data Steward	Oversees data quality, enforces standards, monitors usage
Data Custodian	Manages technical environment, ensures system reliability
Governance Lead	Defines governance policy, aligns initiatives with strategy

5.3. Change Management in BI Deployments

Scaling BI systems often involves reorganizing workflows, retraining staff, and modifying policies. Change management supports these transitions by identifying potential barriers and introducing phased rollouts. Communication channels reduce anxiety by explaining how new tools and processes affect daily operations. Some open-access texts highlight the importance of pilot projects that validate design assumptions before wide-scale deployment (Chaudhry & Dhingra, 2021). Pilot stages may uncover data bottlenecks or adoption obstacles. Managers can address issues proactively, which leads to smoother implementation. Ongoing feedback loops gather user perspectives, which can lead to incremental improvements.

5.4 Building Data-Driven Organizational Culture

Beyond technical components and governance frameworks, successful BI implementations require cultivating a data-driven organizational culture. This culture embraces evidence-based decision-making, analytical thinking, and continuous improvement through insights. Cultural transformation represents a significant challenge that often determines whether technical BI investments deliver expected business value (Günther, Rezazade Mehrizi, Huysman, & Feldberg, 2017).

Leadership behavior plays a pivotal role in cultural development. Executives and managers demonstrate commitment by incorporating data into their own decision processes, allocating resources to analytics initiatives, and recognizing data-driven achievements. Organizations with mature analytical cultures often designate executive sponsors who advocate for BI initiatives and help overcome resistance to data-driven approaches (El Chaarani & El Abiad, 2018).

Data literacy programs develop workforce capabilities beyond specialized analyst roles. These programs establish common vocabulary, teach fundamental statistical concepts, and demonstrate how to interpret analytical outputs correctly. Progressive organizations institute formal data literacy curricula with different tracks based on job roles and analytical requirements (Popovič, Hackney, Coelho, & Jaklič, 2012). Entry-level programs cover basic dashboard interpretation, while advanced tracks might include statistical methods and analytical tool usage.

Workflow integration embeds analytics directly into business processes rather than treating it as a separate activity. This integration makes data consumption a natural part of daily operations. For example, sales representatives access customer analytics before client meetings, and production managers review quality metrics before shift changes. This operational embedding transitions analytics from occasional use to habitual practice (Wixom & Watson, 2010).

Cultural metrics track progress in organizational transformation by measuring indicators like analysis frequency in decision documentation, participation in data literacy programs, and satisfaction with analytical resources. These metrics complement technical performance measures to provide a holistic view of BI program effectiveness. Organizations with advanced data cultures often maintain analytical capability roadmaps that coordinate investments across technical, governance, and cultural dimensions (Isik, Jones, & Sidorova, 2013).

6. PRACTICAL DESIGN MODELS

Designing scalable BI architectures requires synthesizing theoretical insights with practical realities. Practitioners balance cost, performance, security, and flexibility. They choose hardware configurations, software platforms, and governance frameworks that align with organizational objectives. They might adopt a phased approach, starting with a pilot system that covers essential use cases. As usage grows, the system expands to incorporate advanced analytics, real-time dashboards, or external data streams.

6.1. Layered Architectural Model

A layered model arranges components into data sources, integration, storage, analytics, and presentation. Each layer has distinct responsibilities. This separation clarifies dependencies and streamlines updates. Data sources feed raw content to the integration layer. The integration layer cleans and standardizes incoming data. The storage layer preserves integrated datasets in data lakes or data warehouses. The analytics layer runs computations, which might include machine learning or statistical algorithms. The presentation layer offers dashboards or application programming interfaces. Layered designs facilitate horizontal scaling, since teams can add resources to layers that experience demand spikes.

Figure 2. Layered BI Architecture

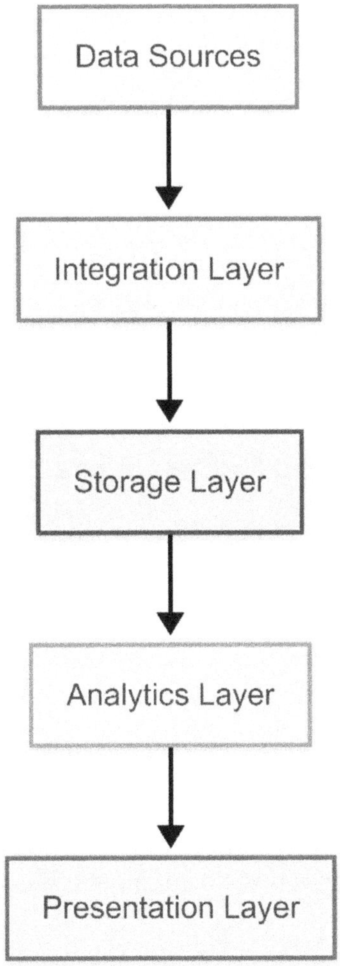

6.2. Hybrid Data Warehouse–Data Lake Approach

Organizations sometimes maintain traditional data warehouses while adding data lakes for unstructured content. This hybrid approach accommodates structured operational data and emerging data streams, such as sensor logs or social media feeds (Madera & Laurent, 2016). Data lakes store raw information in its native format. Analysts can create schema-on-read processes, which define structures only when needed. The data warehouse preserves a curated view that supports standard reporting. Some open-access studies suggest that hybrid models offer flexibility, though they demand robust data governance to avoid lake "sprawl" (Hai, Geisler, & Qu, 2016). Users must understand how to navigate both platforms and select the right environment for each use case.

Table 2. Data Warehouse vs. Data Lake Comparison

Feature	Data Warehouse	Data Lake
Schema	Defined before data loading	Defined on read
Data Type Support	Structured	Structured and unstructured
Primary Use Cases	Reporting, historical trends	Exploration, advanced analytics
Scalability	Requires planned expansion	Naturally scalable with storage

6.3. Containerization and Microservices

Containerization packages applications and their dependencies in lightweight units that run consistently across environments. Microservices decompose complex applications into smaller services that communicate through APIs. This approach supports continuous integration and continuous delivery. Developers can update services independently, which reduces downtime. BI platforms can adopt microservices for ingestion, analytics, and visualization. Each microservice handles its own data schema or local storage. Open-access analyses note that this pattern enhances scalability by allowing teams to replicate specific services when load increases (Li, Seco, & Sánchez Rodríguez, 2019). Container orchestration systems, such as Kubernetes, manage resource allocation, scaling rules, and fault tolerance.

Table 3. Potential Benefits of Microservices in BI

Benefit	Explanation
Independent Deployments	Services can be updated without affecting entire application
Resource Efficiency	Each service scales according to specific usage patterns
Flexibility	Teams can use different technologies suitable for each service

7. IMPLEMENTATION STRATEGIES

Implementation strategies cover project planning, tool selection, and performance monitoring. Planners define requirements for data ingestion, transformation, and analysis. They then evaluate tools that match those needs, considering open-source and proprietary options. They also address compatibility with existing systems. Scholars stress the value of pilot testing, which reveals shortcomings in design assumptions (Chaudhry & Dhingra, 2021). Monitoring solutions track metrics such as throughput, response time, and resource utilization. Engineers adjust configurations to optimize performance and reliability. Implementation also includes training. End-users learn to interpret dashboards or create custom analyses.

7.1. Agile Methodologies

Agile methodologies emphasize incremental delivery and frequent stakeholder feedback. Teams develop a minimal viable product that meets core data analytics needs. Users provide feedback during iterative cycles, which guides future enhancements. Open-access findings show that agile BI projects adapt to changing requirements better than waterfall models (Larson & Chang, 2016). Frequent releases and sprint reviews allow developers to refine data models and interfaces. Agile approaches also promote continuous improvement of data governance. Developers can adjust data transformation rules or update source mappings based on lessons from each sprint.

7.2. Vendor Solutions and Open-Source Tools

Organizations weigh vendor offerings against open-source alternatives. Proprietary BI platforms may offer advanced features and enterprise-level support. However, they can be expensive and might lead to dependency on a single vendor. Open-source solutions, such as Apache Hadoop, Apache Spark, and others, allow extensive customization and usually have large community support. Their flexibility supports integration with existing systems. Some open-access studies emphasize that open-source tools reduce upfront costs and foster innovation (Zaharia et al., 2010). Yet, they may require in-house expertise to manage updates and security patches. Hybrid strategies combine vendor solutions for critical business processes with open-source tools for experimental or specialized workloads.

7.3 Total Cost of Ownership Considerations

Total Cost of Ownership (TCO) analysis provides a comprehensive framework for evaluating BI implementation costs beyond initial acquisition. This approach considers the complete lifecycle, including procurement, implementation, operation, maintenance, and eventual replacement. TCO analysis influences architectural decisions by revealing the long-term financial implications of design choices (Berisha et al, 2022)..

Infrastructure costs include hardware, software licenses, cloud services, and networking components. Cloud-based implementations shift expenses from capital to operational budgets while introducing variable costs based on actual usage. On-premises deployments typically involve larger upfront investments but may offer lower long-term costs for predictable workloads. Hybrid approaches balance these factors by placing workloads in the most cost-effective environment based on characteristics like data sovereignty requirements, performance needs, and utilization patterns (Berisha et al, 2022).

Personnel costs often represent the largest TCO component and include implementation teams, database administrators, data engineers, and support staff. Architectural complexity directly influences staffing requirements through specialized skill demands and ongoing operational overhead. Simplified architectures with automated management capabilities typically reduce personnel costs but may limit customization flexibility. Organizations must balance standardization benefits against specialized capabilities that deliver competitive advantage (Wixom & Watson, 2010).

Operational costs encompass ongoing expenses like electricity, datacenter facilities, backup systems, and disaster recovery provisions. Cloud implementations shift many of these responsibilities to service providers but introduce potential bandwidth charges for data transfer. Architectural decisions about data locality, replication strategies, and processing placement significantly influence these operational expenses.

Upgrade and maintenance costs include version updates, hardware refreshes, compatibility testing, and technical debt remediation. Modular architectures generally reduce these costs by allowing component-level upgrades rather than complete system replacements. However, extensive customization or tight coupling between components can substantially increase maintenance complexity and associated costs (Larson & Chang, 2016).

Opportunity costs arise from implementation delays, suboptimal analytical capabilities, or inflexible architectures that cannot adapt to emerging business requirements. While difficult to quantify precisely, these costs often exceed direct expenditures in rapidly changing markets. Agile implementation approaches mitigate these costs by delivering incremental value rather than requiring extended development periods before realizing benefits (Larson & Chang, 2016).

8. CASE EXAMPLES

Published case examples offer insights into how different sectors approach scalable BI. They illustrate design trade-offs, technology stacks, governance models, and operational outcomes.

8.1. Healthcare Application

A national healthcare system integrated electronic medical records, patient monitoring devices, and laboratory information in a unified BI platform. The system consumed real-time streams of clinical data. The architecture used containerized services to handle ingestion and processing. One microservice parsed sensor signals from patient monitoring devices, while another applied predictive models to estimate deterioration risks. The organization invested in data governance, ensuring that sensitive information remained encrypted during transmission and storage. Reports indicated that clinicians accessed updated dashboards within seconds of data entry. This improvement reduced response times during critical interventions.

8.2. Retail Supply Chain

A global retailer gathered point-of-sale data from outlets across multiple regions. The BI solution combined a data warehouse for structured sales records with a data lake for social media trends and supplier data. A distributed processing engine analyzed incoming sales transactions. The scalable design supported peak shopping events with minimal latency. The retailer's marketing teams used near-real-time analytics to adjust promotions based on emerging buying patterns. The system's governance model maintained product master data, ensuring that all regions used consistent identifiers. This measure minimized confusion when analyzing inventory levels across distribution centers.

Figure 3. Sequence Diagram for Retail Data Flow

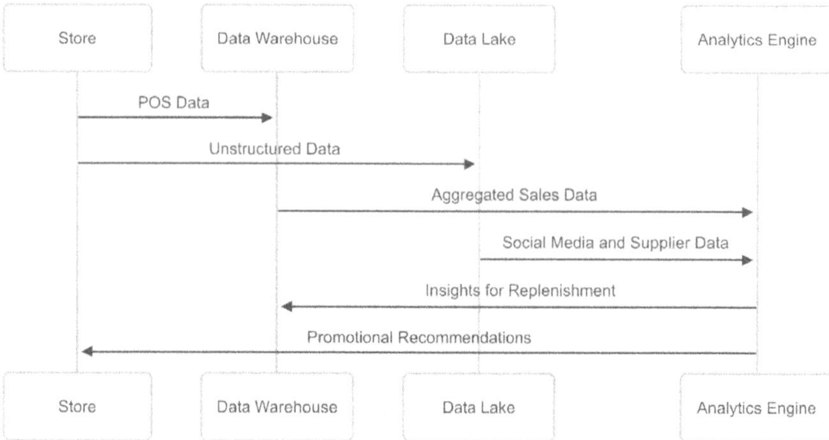

8.3. Financial Services

A financial services firm managed massive transactional volumes from credit card processing and online banking. The BI platform employed a high-throughput messaging system that queued transactions. Real-time fraud detection ran on a parallel analytics engine. If the analytics engine flagged a suspicious transaction, it triggered alerts for manual review. This scalable setup handled periods of elevated activity, such as holidays. Data governance adhered to strict regulatory guidelines, including Know Your Customer (KYC) and Anti-Money Laundering (AML) rules. Open-access assessments reported a notable drop in fraudulent activity after the new system's launch, although it required ongoing refinement of detection algorithms.

9. PERFORMANCE MONITORING AND OPTIMIZATION

Performance monitoring involves continuous evaluation of system metrics, including query response times, throughput, and resource usage. Proper instrumentation collects logs and metrics at each architectural layer. Engineers then analyze these data points to identify bottlenecks. Bottleneck resolution can involve scaling up compute resources, partitioning large datasets, or optimizing query execution plans. Some open-access work suggests that predictive analytics can forecast system demand, enabling proactive resource allocation (Garg & Jindal, 2023). Database administrators may profile queries to uncover inefficient joins or indexing strategies. Cloud-based environments allow dynamic scaling, though cost management remains a concern. Monitoring solutions often visualize performance trends, helping decision-makers plan capacity expansions.

Table 4. Common Metrics for BI Performance Monitoring

Metric	Description
Query Response Time	Time from query submission to final result
Throughput	Number of transactions or queries processed per unit time
CPU/Memory Utilization	Resource consumption at system or container level
Error Rate	Frequency of failed or erroneous operations

10. CHALLENGES AND MITIGATION

Despite the advantages of scalable BI architectures, challenges persist. Security remains a top concern, given the sensitive nature of data. Compliance with evolving regulations demands flexibility in governance models. Data integration complexities increase as new sources emerge. Rapid changes in technology can render systems obsolete if they lack extensibility. Economic constraints also influence the scope of platform expansions. Strategies for mitigation include modular design, robust training programs, and phased rollouts that reduce implementation risks. Proactive monitoring reveals performance drifts early, enabling timely interventions. Standardized metadata and data lineage tracing improve transparency and accountability. Many organizations adopt continuous improvement cycles that refine processes, adjust governance, and align with emerging best practices.

11. FUTURE TRENDS IN SCALABLE BI

The BI landscape continues to evolve as artificial intelligence (AI) and machine learning gain traction. Automated feature engineering and deep learning models offer advanced analytics capabilities. Edge computing devices, such as Internet of Things sensors, present new data streams that demand distributed processing at or near the data source. Quantum computing, while nascent, might eventually accelerate computationally expensive tasks. Researchers also note a growing emphasis on explainable AI in BI contexts (Samek, Wiegand, & Müller, 2017). Stakeholders want clarity about how predictive models reach their conclusions. Another trend involves data fabric, which unifies disparate data assets through a virtualized layer.

These developments align with a broader push toward data democratization, where a wider range of employees can leverage analytics tools.

12. CONCLUSION

Organizations benefit from BI solutions that handle large volumes, multiple data sources, and complex analytical tasks. Scalable architecture combines distributed computing, modular frameworks, and governance mechanisms to support those objectives. This chapter showed how BI systems evolve from data warehouses to hybrid models that integrate real-time pipelines and data lakes. It stressed the importance of stakeholder engagement, data governance, and training. Case examples illustrated how healthcare, retail, and financial sectors manage expanding analytics demands. Ongoing developments in AI, edge computing, and data fabric approaches indicate continued innovation. These findings highlight the value of scalable BI, which empowers decision-makers to respond swiftly to changing market conditions and internal dynamics.

REFERENCES

Alsibhawi, I. A. A., Yahaya, J. B., & Mohamed, H. B. (2023). Business Intelligence Adoption for Small and Medium Enterprises: Conceptual Framework. *Applied Sciences (Basel, Switzerland), 13*(7), 4121. DOI: 10.3390/app13074121

Baars, H., & Kemper, H.-G. (2010). Business intelligence in the cloud? *PACIS 2010 Proceedings*. 145. https://aisel.aisnet.org/pacis2010/145

Barati, M. (2023). Open Government data programs and information privacy concerns: A literature review. *arXiv preprint arXiv:2312.10096.*

Batini, C., Cappiello, C., Francalanci, C., & Maurino, A. (2009). Methodologies for data quality assessment and improvement. *ACM Computing Surveys, 41*(3), 1–52. DOI: 10.1145/1541880.1541883

Berisha, B., Mëziu, E., & Shabani, I. (2022). Big data analytics in Cloud computing: An overview. *Journal of Cloud Computing (Heidelberg, Germany), 11*(1). Advance online publication. DOI: 10.1186/s13677-022-00301-w PMID: 35966392

Cao, H., & Wachowicz, M. (2019). An edge-fog-cloud architecture of streaming analytics for Internet of Things applications. *Sensors (Basel), 19*(16), 3594. DOI: 10.3390/s19163594 PMID: 31426586

Chaudhry, K., & Dhingra, S. (2021). Modeling the critical success factors for business intelligence implementation: An ISM approach. *International Journal of Business Intelligence Research, 12*(2), 1–21. DOI: 10.4018/IJBIR.20210701.oa3

Chen, H., Chiang, R. H., & Storey, V. C. (2012). Business intelligence and analytics: From big data to big impact. *Management Information Systems Quarterly, 36*(4), 1165–1188. DOI: 10.2307/41703503

Davenport, T. H. (2018). From analytics to artificial intelligence. *Journal of Business Analytics, 1*(2), 73–80. DOI: 10.1080/2573234X.2018.1543535

Dean, J., & Ghemawat, S. (2008). MapReduce: Simplified data processing on large clusters. *Communications of the ACM, 51*(1), 107–113. DOI: 10.1145/1327452.1327492

Delen, D., & Ram, S. (2018). Research challenges and opportunities in business analytics. *Journal of Business Analytics, 1*(1), 2–12. DOI: 10.1080/2573234X.2018.1507324

El-Chaarani, H., & El-Abiad, Z. (2018). The impact of technological innovation on bank performance. *Journal of Internet Banking and Commerce, 23*(3). Available at *SSRN*: https://ssrn.com/abstract=3845169

Fazio, M., Celesti, A., Puliafito, A., & Villari, M. (2015). Big data storage in the cloud for smart environment monitoring. *Procedia Computer Science, 52*, 500–506. DOI: 10.1016/j.procs.2015.05.023

Garg, V., & Jindal, B. (2023). Resource optimization using predictive virtual machine consolidation approach in cloud environment. *Intelligent Decision Technologies, 17*(2), 471–484. DOI: 10.3233/IDT-220222

Günther, W. A., Rezazade Mehrizi, M. H., Huysman, M., & Feldberg, F. (2017). Debating big data: A literature review on realizing value from big data. *The Journal of Strategic Information Systems, 26*(3), 191–209. DOI: 10.1016/j.jsis.2017.07.003

Hai, R., Geisler, S., & Quix, C. (2016). Constance: An intelligent data lake system. *Proceedings of the 2016 International Conference on Management of Data (SIGMOD)* (pp. 2097–2100). https://doi.org/DOI: 10.1145/2882903.2899389

Hai, R., Koutras, C., Quix, C., & Jarke, M. (2021). Data Lakes: A Survey of Functions and Systems. https://doi.org//arXiv.2106.09592DOI: 10.48550

Isik, Ö., Jones, M. C., & Sidorova, A. (2013). Business intelligence success: The roles of analytics capability and data quality. *Information & Management, 50*(1), 13–23. DOI: 10.1016/j.im.2012.12.001

Kim, G.-S. (2020). The effect of quality management and big data management on customer satisfaction in Korea's public sector. *Sustainability, 12*(13), 5474. DOI: 10.3390/su12135474

Koutsoukos, D., Müller, I., Marroquín, R., Klimovic, A., & Alonso, G. (2020). Modularis: Modular relational analytics over heterogeneous distributed platforms. *ArXiv*. https://doi.org//arXiv.2004.03488DOI: 10.48550

Larson, D., & Chang, V. (2016). A review and future direction of agile, business intelligence, analytics and data science. *International Journal of Information Management, 36*(5), 700–710. DOI: 10.1016/j.ijinfomgt.2016.04.013

Li, Z., Seco, D., & Sánchez Rodríguez, A. E. (2019). Microservice-oriented platform for Internet of big data analytics: A proof of concept. *Sensors (Basel), 19*(5), 1134. DOI: 10.3390/s19051134 PMID: 30845687

Madera, C., & Laurent, A. (2016). The next information architecture evolution: The data lake wave. In *Proceedings of the 8th International Conference on Management of Digital Ecosystems (MEDES)* (pp. 174–180). https://doi.org/DOI: 10.1145/3012071.3012077

Otto, B. (2011). Organizing data governance: Findings from the telecommunications industry and consequences for large service providers. *Communications of the Association for Information Systems*, *29*, 45–66. DOI: 10.17705/1CAIS.02903

Popovič, A., Hackney, R., Coelho, P. S., & Jaklič, J. (2012). Towards business intelligence systems success: Effects of maturity and culture on analytical decision making. *Decision Support Systems*, *54*(1), 729–739. DOI: 10.1016/j.dss.2012.08.017

Salloum, S., Dautov, R., Chen, X., Peng, P. X., & Huang, J. (2016). Big data analytics on Apache Spark. *International Journal of Data Science and Analytics*, *1*(3), 145–164. DOI: 10.1007/s41060-016-0027-9

Samek, W., Wiegand, T., & Müller, K.-R. (2017). Explainable artificial intelligence: Understanding, visualizing and interpreting deep learning models. https://arxiv.org/abs/1708.08296

Sang, G. M., Xu, L., & De Vrieze, P. (2016). A reference architecture for big data systems. In *Proc. International Conference on Software, Knowledge, Information Management & Applications (SKIMA)* (pp. 1–8). https://doi.org/DOI: 10.1109/SKIMA.2016.7916249

Sivarajah, U., Kamal, M. M., Irani, Z., & Weerakkody, V. (2017). Critical analysis of big data challenges and analytical methods. *Journal of Business Research*, *70*, 263–286. DOI: 10.1016/j.jbusres.2016.08.001

Solano, M. C., & Cruz, J. C. (2024). Integrating analytics in enterprise systems: A systematic literature review of impacts and innovations. *Administrative Sciences*, *14*(7), 138. Advance online publication. DOI: 10.3390/admsci14070138

Wixom, B., & Watson, H. (2010). The BI-based organization. *International Journal of Business Intelligence Research*, *1*(1), 13–28. DOI: 10.4018/jbir.2010071702

Zaharia, M., Chowdhury, M., Franklin, M. J., Shenker, S., & Stoica, I. (2010). Spark: Cluster computing with working sets. In *2nd USENIX workshop on hot topics in cloud computing (HotCloud 10).*

Chapter 4
Edge Intelligence Expanding BI Architectures Beyond the Cloud

Salam Al E'mari
https://orcid.org/0000-0002-2134-4158
University of Petra, Jordan

Yousef Sanjalawe
https://orcid.org/0000-0002-4442-1865
University of Jordan, Jordan

Fadi Fataftah
https://orcid.org/0000-0002-3299-0972
University Canada West, Canada

Fuad Fataftah
https://orcid.org/0009-0009-3203-5869
Universiti Sains Malaysia, Malaysia

ABSTRACT

Edge Intelligence represents a paradigm shift in Business Intelligence (BI) architectures by relocating data processing from centralized cloud systems to the edge of the network, closer to data generation sources. This chapter explores the evolution of BI from traditional centralized models to cloud-based and hybrid architectures, culminating in edge-enhanced intelligence capable of real-time, context-aware analytics. The proliferation of IoT devices, combined with latency-sensitive applications in sectors such as healthcare, manufacturing, retail, and energy, necessitates decen-

DOI: 10.4018/979-8-3373-2125-7.ch004

tralized analytics to meet modern performance, privacy, and compliance demands. By leveraging lightweight machine learning models, specialized edge hardware, and container orchestration frameworks like KubeEdge, organizations can process data locally, reduce bandwidth usage, and maintain operational continuity even under network disruption. The chapter also introduces hybrid edge-cloud models that support tiered data processing, model lifecycle management, synchronization, and unified security frameworks.

1. INTRODUCTION

The proliferation of Internet of Things (IoT) devices, sensors, and embedded systems has revolutionized the way data is generated and consumed. Modern businesses are no longer reliant solely on centralized data centers or cloud infrastructures. Instead, they increasingly demand systems capable of processing data at or near the source. This demand has given rise to Edge Intelligence a model that shifts data processing from centralized locations to the edge of the network, closer to data generation points (Xu et al., 2021). This transition aligns with the broader wave of digital transformation sweeping across industries. As organizations strive to become more agile, data-driven, and customer-centric, the limitations of traditional BI infrastructures become increasingly apparent (Cao, 2022). In a world where business opportunities, security threats, and system failures can emerge in milliseconds, the ability to respond in real time is no longer optional it is a competitive imperative.

1.1 The Rise of Real-Time Analytics

Real-time analytics has emerged as a cornerstone of this transformation. Businesses want to analyze data as it flows, not hours or days after it is generated (Kanagarla, 2024). For example, a manufacturing line may require instantaneous adjustments based on sensor readings to prevent defects (Nain et al., 2022). A retail store might aim to optimize product placement dynamically based on customer movement patterns. These use cases highlight the critical need for reducing latency and ensuring continuity of operations even in the face of intermittent connectivity or cloud outages. However, transmitting every data point from edge devices to a centralized cloud for processing introduces latency, increases bandwidth costs, and raises privacy concerns (Duan et al., 2022). As data volumes grow exponentially driven by billions of connected devices — the traditional centralized processing paradigm becomes increasingly unsustainable. This is where Edge Intelligence steps in.

1.2 The Promise of Edge Intelligence

The solution is provided by Edge Intelligence, which processes the data as close as possible to the generation point (Gong et al., 2023). It enables devices at the edge and local environments to execute computational models (of machine learning), identify anomalies, and make decisions independently. Such strategy does not only make the company more responsive but also resilient and secure because sensitive information does not necessarily have to be sent to the outside world or atmosphere (Mendez et al., 2021). The given chapter explores such a concept as Edge Intelligence, which has evolved, what kinds of technology are used to enable Edge Intelligence, what types of architecture are present, and in what sectors it can be applied. It further stresses the necessity of adding Edge Intelligence to BI ecosystems which can enable the multi-dimensional operational insight, responsiveness, and business value of the data-rich world.

2. FOUNDATIONS OF EDGE INTELLIGENCE

Edge Intelligence is not just a small step in the processing of data but a fundamental shift in Business Intelligence (BI) systems to give businesses an ability to operate in the realities of hyperconnected, latency-sensitive and data-intensive planet. To comprehend this shift, it is necessary to look into the main tenets, forces behind it, and enables capabilities which make Edge Intelligence a divergence of the conventional cloud-led analytics.

2.1 The Conceptual Pillars of Edge Intelligence

Essentially, Edge Intelligence is the process of incorporating computational intelligence in edge nodes devices or local servers which are located physically near the sites of data generation (Mendez et al., 2022). The Edge Intelligence does not solely use centralized cloud structures: instead of signifying processes and analytics to the centre, it distributes them to the edges of the network. Such on-board intelligence allows processing data in real-time, situation awareness and autonomous decision-making, all highly relevant in applications where milliseconds count. The hierarchical levels that take place in an edge intelligence application are discussed in Figure 1. Every level is another stage or a level in which data is being processed, analyzed or acted upon and this includes edge devices to the centralized cloud systems. This structure brings to spotlight how tasks and intelligence can be decomposed to be spread across the network to better efficiency scalability and latency.

Figure 1. Levels for the Edge Intelligence Application

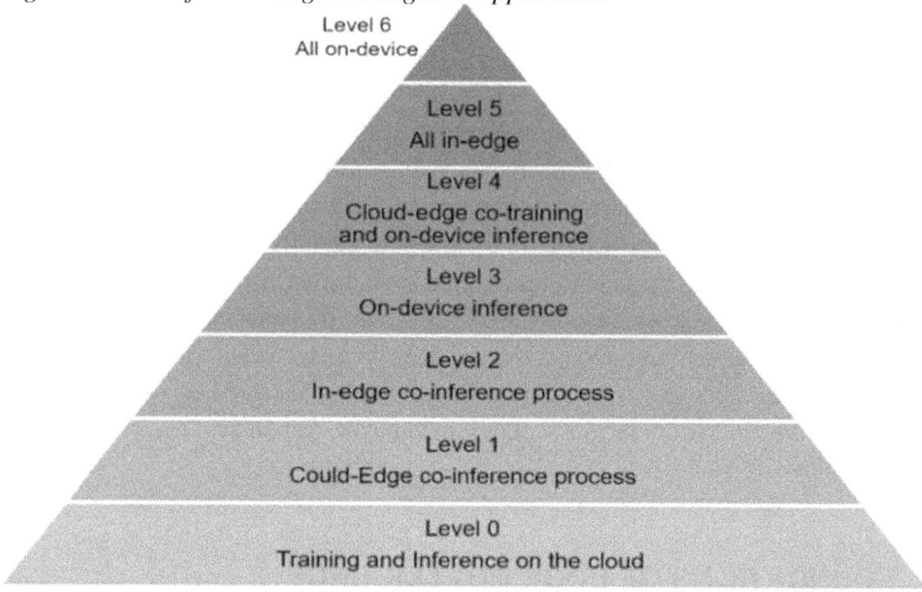

This paradigm rests on several foundational pillars (Jia et al., 2024; Nasir et al., 2022):

- Proximity to Data: Data is processed near its source, enabling faster response times and reducing reliance on external networks.
- Resource-Constrained Intelligence: Edge devices often operate with limited computing power, memory, and energy, demanding lightweight and efficient machine learning models.
- Autonomy and Decentralization: Edge nodes must operate independently, especially in scenarios where connectivity to the cloud is intermittent or unavailable.
- Context-Aware Computing: Localized analytics can be tailored to the specific environment, yielding more relevant and actionable insights.

These characteristics differentiate Edge Intelligence from traditional cloud-based analytics, positioning it as an enabler of real-time, resilient, and privacy-conscious systems.

2.2 Data Gravity and Edge Necessity

The concept of *data gravity*, introduced by Dave McCrory in 2010, suggests that as datasets grow in size, they exert a gravitational pull that draws applications and services toward them (Zagan & Danubianu, 2021). In IoT-rich environments, where billions of sensors generate massive volumes of data continuously, transmitting everything to a centralized cloud for processing becomes impractical. This creates a bottleneck not only in terms of bandwidth but also latency and energy consumption (Sedlak et al., 2023). Edge Intelligence mitigates data gravity by relocating analytics to the data source. Instead of transporting terabytes of data across long distances, only refined insights or anomalies are transmitted upstream. This not only improves efficiency but also minimizes costs associated with data transfer and storage.

2.3 Latency Sensitivity and Real-Time Demands

For many applications, particularly in industrial automation, autonomous vehicles, and healthcare, latency is not just a performance metric, it is a functional requirement (Pappala et al., 2024). A delay of even a few hundred milliseconds can result in failed interventions, accidents, or suboptimal decisions. Traditional cloud models introduce latency due to multiple factors: network propagation delay, queuing, processing time in centralized servers, and round-trip time (Sharma, 2024). In contrast, Edge Intelligence enables ultra-low-latency analytics by processing data directly on-site or in near proximity (Gupta et al., 2021). This capability allows systems to react in real time, making it indispensable in mission-critical scenarios.

2.4 Bandwidth Constraints and Cost Optimization

This growth shows no signs of slowing down, with more and more items getting connected (and equipped with high resolution sensors, e.g. video cameras, LiDAR scanners, etc.) putting a huge strain on bandwidth. Sending raw data originating at such sources to some remote cloud is costly and congestion prone (Alsayfi et al., 2022). Edge computing helps to mitigate this problem since computing is done in-situ to filter, aggregate data and extract the features (Nain et al., 2022). This decreases the amount of data that must be uploaded to the cloud and leaves the bandwidth available to real world life-saving updates. Where such implementations are very large e.g. smart cities or country-wide logistics networks, this localized processing amounts to reductions in operational expenses which are again measurable.

2.5 Privacy, Compliance, and Data Residency

Regulatory frameworks such as the General Data Protection Regulation (GDPR) and the California Consumer Privacy Act (CCPA) have heightened the importance of data sovereignty, consent management, and localized data governance (Naqvi & Batool, 2023). Sensitive data, such as medical records or biometric identifiers—must often be stored and processed within specific geographic boundaries. Edge Intelligence supports privacy-preserving architectures by minimizing data exposure and enabling on-device analytics (Fagbohungbe et al., 2021). In federated learning settings, for instance, raw data never leaves the device; instead, only the updated model parameters are shared. This design not only adheres to compliance requirements but also builds user trust by safeguarding personal information.

2.6 Edge Autonomy and Resilience

In disconnected or intermittently connected environments, such as offshore oil rigs, military deployments, or rural healthcare clinics, reliance on a stable cloud link is impractical (Xu, Nagothu & Chen, 2024). Systems must be able to continue functioning, and making decisions, even when isolated. Edge Intelligence enables such autonomy by equipping devices with embedded logic and pre-trained models that operate without external dependencies (Biswas & Wang, 2023). These devices can detect anomalies, enforce rules, and execute workflows independently. Once connectivity is restored, they synchronize with the central system, maintaining continuity and consistency.

2.7 Technical Enablers of Edge Intelligence

Edge intelligence relies on a range of technological advancements that enable data processing, decision-making, and learning to occur closer to the data source. This section explores the key technical enablers—such as hardware acceleration, efficient AI models, network connectivity, and software frameworks—that collectively support the deployment and scalability of intelligent edge systems. Figure 2 illustrates three distinct strategies for performing training and inference in edge intelligence systems. In (a), both training and inference are conducted in the cloud, with raw data sent from edge devices and the computed results returned. In (b), the training is performed in the cloud, but the inference is offloaded to the edge, reducing latency and cloud dependency. In (c), both training and inference are carried out directly at the edge, enabling real-time processing and greater autonomy but requiring more powerful local hardware.

Figure 2. Different approaches for training and inference. (a) Traditional training and inference in cloud servers. (b) Training on the cloud server and inference at the edge. (c) Training and inference at the edge

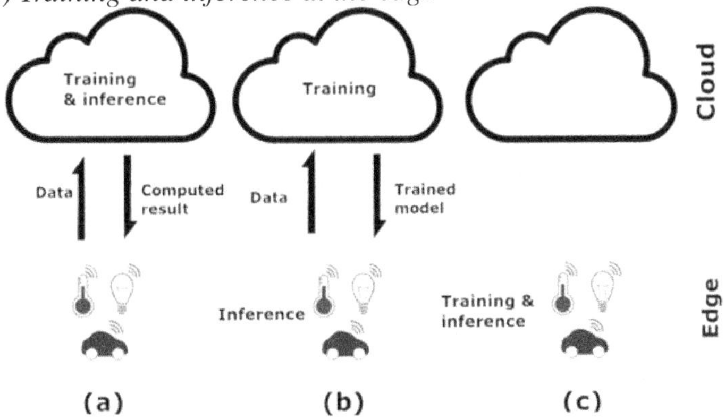

Several technological advances have converged to make Edge Intelligence viable at scale (Sipola et al., 2022; Antonini, 2021):

- Microcontrollers with ML Capabilities: Low-power processors such as ARM Cortex-M and RISC-V support efficient ML inference at the edge.
- Edge AI Chips: Specialized processors like Google's Edge TPU, NVIDIA Jetson, and Intel Movidius offer hardware acceleration for deep learning models in compact form factors.
- Lightweight ML Frameworks: Libraries like TensorFlow Lite, PyTorch Mobile, and ONNX Runtime provide tooling to convert and optimize models for edge deployment.
- Edge OS and Middleware: Edge-native platforms like Azure IoT Edge, AWS Greengrass, and KubeEdge orchestrate application deployment, security, and lifecycle management at scale.
- Containerization and Virtualization: Technologies like Docker and microVMs enable isolated, lightweight execution environments on heterogeneous edge hardware.

These components form the infrastructure backbone of Edge Intelligence, supporting scalability, interoperability, and lifecycle management across distributed environments.

2.8 From Edge Devices to Edge Ecosystems

While edge computing can begin with a single smart sensor or gateway, its true power is realized when multiple nodes operate as part of a larger, coordinated ecosystem (Sodiya et al., 2024). In such configurations, edge nodes can:

- Collaborate locally to exchange contextual signals.
- Serve as backup or failover nodes in case of faults.
- Participate in federated or swarm learning models.
- Interface seamlessly with fog layers and cloud backends.

This evolution from isolated intelligence to distributed edge ecosystems marks the next frontier of digital infrastructure—one where intelligence is not merely deployed but orchestrated across thousands of points in real time.

3. EVOLUTION OF BI ARCHITECTURES

BI systems have been operating with the aim of providing precise, past oriented option to organizations to make informed decisions. But with digital transformation pickup and the growth of the volume, variety, and velocity of digital data exponentially, traditional BI architectures have been confronted by steadily rising pressures regarding responsiveness, scalability, and contextual relevance. A move towards real time and event driven decision making has realigned expectations on how and where analytics should be done. This development has taken place in a number of sequential phases all of which have constituted a paradigm shift in the way data is gathered, interpreted and dissected.

A common BI architecture is given in figure 3, and there is an end-to-end information flow between source systems and actionable insight. The architecture is divided into a number of layers namely data extraction, transformation, warehousing, and analytics. It demonstrates how global data are sourced, regionalized, and transformed to multidimensional structures to enable OLAP, data mining, and advanced reporting (ElMalah & Nasr, 2019) and Figure 4 displays a five-layer Business Intelligence (BI) architecture, which indicates the whole data pipeline of the source acquisition to the end-user analytics. Its architecture is divided into data source layer, the ETL (Extract, Transform, Load) layer, data warehouse layer, end user layer and a metadata layer covering all of the different parts. Such a tiered system will provide the effective integration, quality management, storage and retrieval of data aimed at fulfilling reporting, analysis and decision-making. This is

because at the lament stage of noncompliance only a few prescribed drug changes are selected (Ong et al., 2011).

Figure 3. Typical BI Architecture

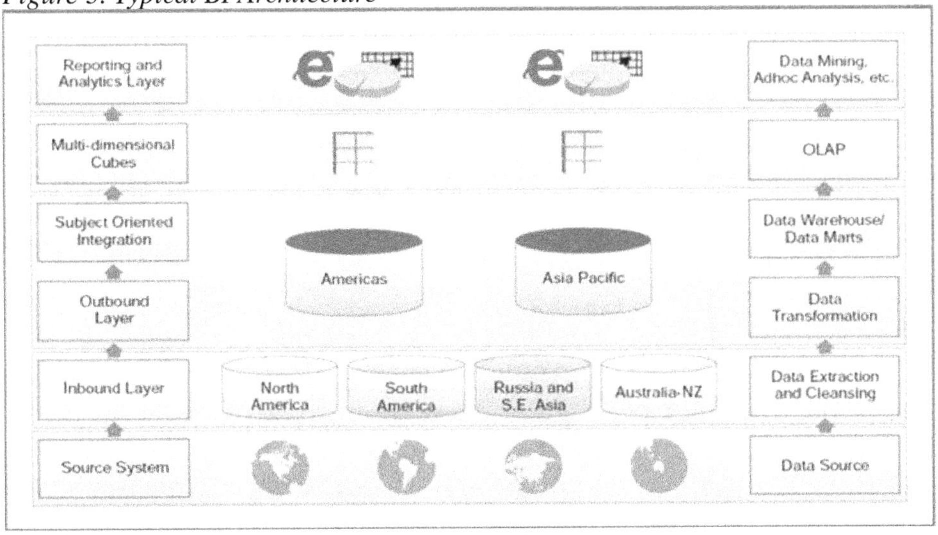

Figure 4. Five-layers BI Architecture

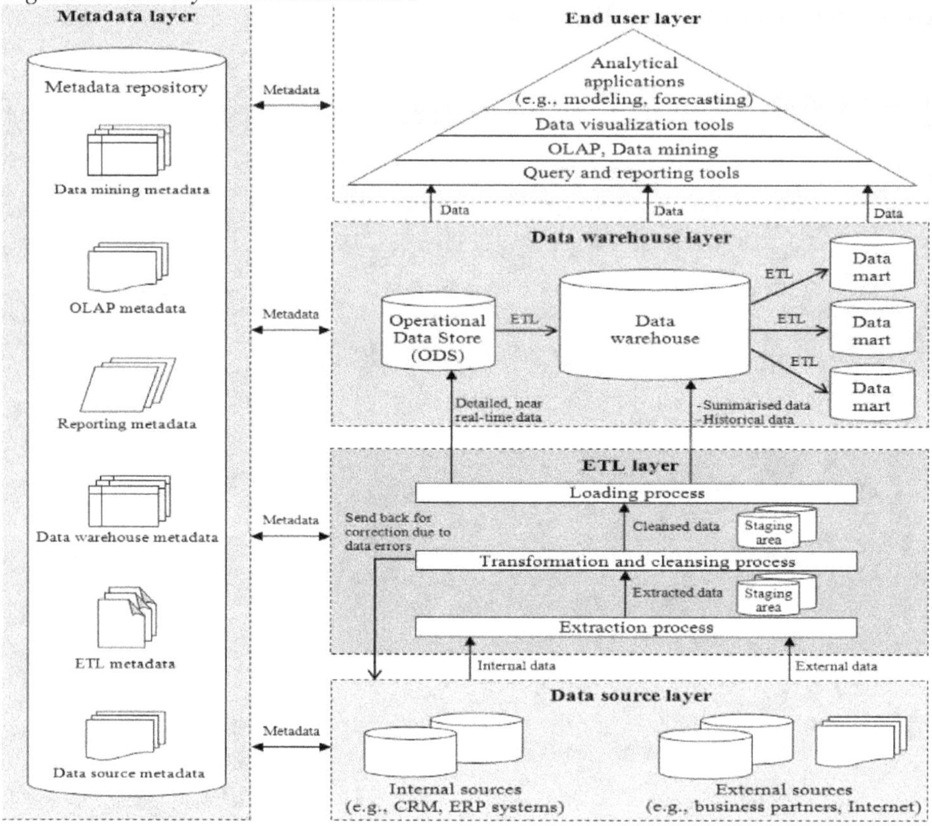

3.1 Stage 1: Centralized BI

In the early stages of Business Intelligence, analytics systems were heavily centralized. Organizations invested in data warehouses and Extract-Transform-Load (ETL) pipelines to gather information from multiple operational systems and store it in a single, unified repository (Kola, 2024). This architecture, while structured and reliable, was rigid and inherently batch-oriented.

Data was typically collected over days or weeks, with reports generated at fixed intervals—often overnight or on a weekly basis. The latency between data generation and insight delivery was acceptable in a world where business cycles moved slowly. These centralized BI platforms were designed for structured data (e.g., sales records, inventory logs) and relied on relational databases optimized for query performance. Popular technologies included Oracle BI, IBM Cognos, and Microsoft SQL Server Analysis Services.

However, this model had several inherent limitations (Raisinghani, 2004):

- Latency: Insights were retrospective. Decision-makers could only act after significant delays, which was unsuitable for dynamic environments.
- Inflexibility: Centralized systems were difficult to scale and often required manual intervention to adapt to changing data sources or schemas.
- Resource Bottlenecks: All analytics were funneled through a single point, creating a performance bottleneck as data volumes increased.

In essence, centralized BI architectures were stable but reactive, limiting their utility in fast-paced, data-rich scenarios.

3.2 Stage 2: Cloud BI

The emergence of cloud computing marked a major turning point in the evolution of BI architectures. Cloud BI introduced flexibility, cost-efficiency, and scalability by leveraging Infrastructure-as-a-Service (IaaS) and Software-as-a-Service (SaaS) models to handle data storage, processing, and visualization (Chang, 2014; Kasem & Hassanein, 2014).

With cloud BI, organizations could ingest and analyze massive volumes of data without investing in expensive on-premise hardware. Services like Amazon Redshift, Google BigQuery, and Microsoft Azure Synapse Analytics provided elastic data warehousing capabilities, while platforms like Tableau Online and Power BI Cloud enabled interactive dashboards from anywhere with an internet connection. Figure 5 illustrates the network architecture of a cloud-based Business Intelligence (BI) environment, showcasing the interaction between RDBMS servers, OLAP applications, and cloud switches. The diagram emphasizes the complex interconnections and data flow patterns between distributed relational databases and analytical applications, coordinated through cloud infrastructure for efficient processing and real-time analytics.

Figure 5. BI on Cloud Architecture

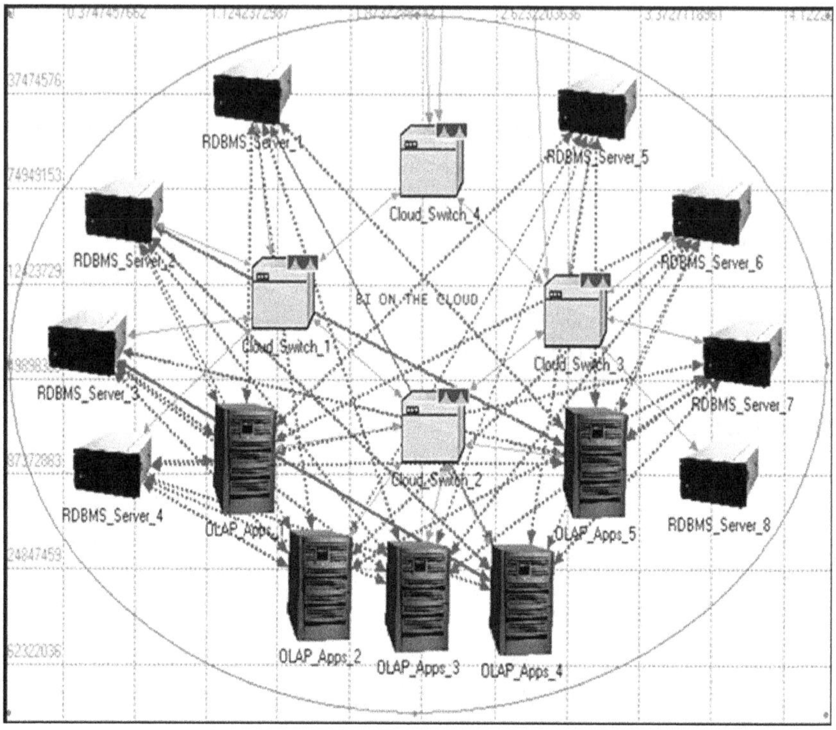

Key characteristics of cloud BI included:

- Elastic Scalability: Compute and storage resources could scale dynamically based on demand, supporting workloads ranging from terabytes to petabytes.
- Global Accessibility: Users could access dashboards and reports across regions and time zones, promoting collaboration.
- Integrated Ecosystems: Cloud-native BI platforms often integrated easily with CRM, ERP, and other SaaS applications.

Despite these advantages, cloud BI systems were not without drawbacks:

- Network Dependency: Performance was contingent on internet speed and availability, which posed issues for users in remote or bandwidth-constrained environments.
- Latency for Real-Time Use Cases: Although faster than traditional batch processing, cloud BI still introduced non-trivial latency, especially when ingesting high-frequency data from IoT or mobile sources.

- Security and Data Sovereignty Concerns: Storing sensitive or regulated data in third-party cloud environments introduced compliance and privacy risks.

Cloud BI represented a significant improvement in terms of agility and scale but did not fully address the need for real-time, local decision-making in distributed systems.

3.3 Stage 3: Hybrid BI

As organizations began to navigate trade-offs between control, performance, and scalability, the hybrid BI model emerged as a strategic compromise. Hybrid BI combines on-premises infrastructure with cloud-based services, enabling organizations to retain critical data within their own environments while leveraging cloud capabilities for specific workloads (Chavan, 2023).

For instance, a financial institution might choose to analyze transactional data on-site due to regulatory constraints, while using cloud-based tools for less sensitive data visualization or customer behavior analysis (Lukić et al., 2016; Moscoso-Zea et al., 2019). In a manufacturing context, real-time quality checks might run locally while aggregate performance reports are pushed to the cloud for executive oversight.

The hybrid BI model is characterized by:

- Flexible Data Placement: Organizations can decide which data resides in the cloud and which remains on-premises, based on performance, sensitivity, or legal requirements.
- Interoperability: Systems are designed to work across different platforms using APIs, connectors, and data virtualization layers.
- Improved Resilience: Redundancy across environments can mitigate downtime or network disruptions.

Yet hybrid BI also introduces new complexities:

- Integration Overhead: Synchronizing data between cloud and on-premises systems requires robust data governance and ETL pipelines.
- Operational Complexity: Managing two different environments requires a skilled IT team and careful orchestration.
- Inconsistent Latency: Depending on where processing takes place, latency can vary unpredictably.

Hybrid BI was a necessary step toward decentralization, but it remained insufficient for the emerging demands of edge-centric systems that needed ultra-low-latency and offline processing capabilities.

3.4 Stage 4: Edge-Enhanced BI

Edge-Enhanced BI is the most recent and transformative phase in the evolution of BI architectures. It introduces the ability to perform analytics at the edge of the network, where data is generated, rather than relying solely on centralized or cloud-based systems (Zeng et al., 2025). This paradigm shift is fueled by the proliferation of IoT devices, smart sensors, and mobile computing platforms. With Edge-Enhanced BI, analytics tasks such as anomaly detection, forecasting, and classification can occur on-site in factories, vehicles, homes, or medical devices, without the need to transmit raw data to the cloud (Pioli et al., 2024).

The advantages of this architecture are profound:

- Low Latency: Data is processed locally, allowing decisions to be made in real time—often within milliseconds.
- Bandwidth Efficiency: By filtering or aggregating data at the source, organizations reduce the volume of information that needs to be transmitted to central servers.
- Data Privacy and Compliance: Sensitive data can be analyzed locally, minimizing exposure and supporting compliance with data residency laws.
- Operational Autonomy: Systems can continue functioning even during internet outages, ensuring business continuity.

Edge-Enhanced BI requires a new architectural mindset:

- Decentralized Data Fabric: Data is distributed across thousands or millions of nodes, requiring federated models for data management.
- Lightweight ML Models: Edge environments necessitate efficient, compact machine learning algorithms due to hardware limitations.
- Advanced Orchestration: Platforms like KubeEdge, AWS Greengrass, and Azure IoT Edge orchestrate updates, monitor performance, and manage deployments across distributed nodes.

The convergence of edge computing and BI represents the cutting edge of analytics, pushing intelligence out of the data center and into the field.

3.5 Emerging Transition: Toward Federated and Swarm BI

As organizations continue evolving, a new frontier is emerging Federated BI (Ali et al., 2022) or Swarm Intelligence BI (Adnane & Zerari, 2024). These paradigms envision a network of autonomous edge nodes capable of collaborating, learning, and adapting as a collective. Federated BI allows multiple edge devices to train or refine shared models without centralizing data, preserving privacy and reducing communication overhead. Swarm BI envisions edge agents sharing insights with one another in real time, forming a decentralized knowledge graph that adapts dynamically to the environment. These concepts are still in the research and pilot phase but hold the promise of making BI systems even more distributed, resilient, and context-aware.

Table 1: Summary of Architecture Types

Architecture Type	Latency	Scalability	Data Privacy	Offline Support	Ideal Use Case
Centralized BI	High	Medium	Low	No	Traditional reporting and financial audits
Cloud BI	Medium	High	Medium	Limited	Big data analysis, dashboarding
Hybrid BI	Medium	High	High	Limited	Sensitive apps with cloud-scale agility
Edge-Enhanced BI	Low	Very High	Very High	Yes	Real-time, distributed, mission-critical ops
Federated/Swarm BI	Very Low	Extremely High	Extremely High	Yes	Collaborative learning and autonomous ops

4. EDGE INTELLIGENCE ARCHITECTURE

The successful deployment of Edge Intelligence hinges on an architecture that can seamlessly integrate heterogeneous devices, perform decentralized analytics, and maintain operational efficiency under varying network and environmental conditions. This architecture must support real-time responsiveness, be highly scalable to accommodate thousands or millions of edge nodes, and remain resilient in the face of connectivity disruptions or device failures (Xu *et al.*, 2020). Figure 6 illustrates the architecture of edge intelligence, highlighting the interaction between edge devices and the cloud. It showcases various edge components—including sensors, smartphones, smartwatches, and smart brands—working collaboratively with local servers and cloud infrastructure. The diagram emphasizes the role of wireless, cellular, and backhaul communication in enabling real-time data processing, decision-making, and analytics at or near the data source, reducing latency and bandwidth demands on the cloud.

Figure 6: Edge Intelligence

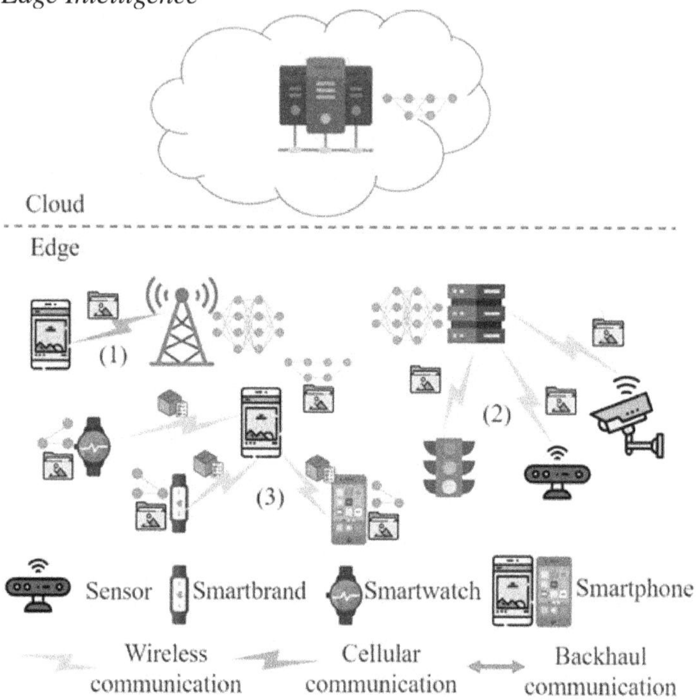

Edge Intelligence is inherently multi-layered, and each layer plays a vital role in the acquisition, processing, coordination, and governance of data and intelligence. A well-designed Edge Intelligence architecture typically includes the following core layers: Data Acquisition, Edge Processing, Fog Computing, Cloud Integration, and Orchestration. Together, these layers form a continuum that supports distributed intelligence and operational agility.

4.1 Data Acquisition Layer

The foundation of any Edge Intelligence system begins with the Data Acquisition Layer. This layer consists of endpoint devices that serve as the first point of contact with the physical environment. These include sensors, actuators, industrial machines, surveillance cameras, RFID scanners, wearable medical devices, drones, and more (Xu et al., 2020; Deng et al., 2020). These devices capture raw data from their surroundings, such as temperature, pressure, location, vibration, biometrics, or images, often in real time. To support diverse industrial and commercial use cases, the acquisition layer must:

- Handle multi-modal data (structured, semi-structured, unstructured).
- Support multiple protocols (e.g., MQTT, OPC-UA, ZigBee, LoRaWAN, Modbus, BLE).
- Be energy-efficient, particularly in battery-operated environments.
- Provide secure communication channels to prevent tampering and eavesdropping.

Standardization is crucial at this layer to ensure interoperability. Technologies like OPC-UA in manufacturing and HL7 in healthcare help unify device communication. Additionally, edge gateways often reside close to data acquisition devices, serving as protocol translators and data aggregators, enabling upstream communication with edge computing units.

4.2 Edge Layer

It is at the Edge Layer that the heart of the intelligence of building architecture starts to reveal itself. The functions of this layer are performed at the source or close to the source with edge servers, industrial PCs, gateway, or embedded microcontrollers (Li et al., 2018). Examples of processing functions in edge processing are filtering, compression, transformation, and inference effects in most instances involving pre-trained machine learning models. Such are the main tasks of the edge layer:

- Real time processing: In the case of robotic control; anomaly detection; or safety systems, milliseconds are required to make decisions.
- Data Reduction: Edge analytics have the capability of mitigating this burden due to the transmission of aggregate summaries or defects to upper levels.
- Privacy Preservation:: Privacy risks can be reduced by processing sensitive data such as biometric scan or measurement of patient vitals locally.
- Lightweight ML Execution: Lightweight ML frameworks such as TensorFlow Lite, PyTorch Mobile and ONNX put ML models on edge devices.

The examples of tasks on this layer are fault detection in manufacturing equipment, object recognition using security video, or ECG signal classification on wearable devices. This layer of devices can typically run in constrained conditions with a narrow memory (e.g. less than 1 GB RAM), limited CPU resources and low power budget. Thus, performance-optimization methods such as model compression (by quantization, Gaussian priors, or pruning, knowledge distillation) are often applied.

4.3 Fog Layer

The use of The Fog Layer, also known as the Intermediate Layer or Mist, presents itself as a regionally nested aggregator and orchestrator between the edge and the cloud (Zou et al., 2019). It hosts several edge nodes located nearby and executes mid-tier processing workloads with higher computational demands as compared to what may run on a single edge node but do not demand complete cloud-scale computation. Functions available in the fog layer are: Temporal Aggregation: Combining data from multiple edge nodes over time windows to detect long-term patterns.

- Cross-Device Correlation: The study of intra-device interactions, which can be cross-sensory, i.e. the coordinated behavior by multiple sensors.
- Edge Collaboration: The ability to provide collaborative intelligence by allowing models/inference to be shared among nodes on the edge.
- Regional Control Logic: Trading of localized rules of decision and policy, such as regional security zones or region-based quality targets.

Fog nodes have higher architectural capabilities than edge devices, can afford containerized services and are usually controlled through kubernetes-based platforms, such as KubeEdge or Open Horizon. Also, these fog nodes are able to host local data lakes, keeping temporary snapshots of historical data, or model parameters. Additionally, the fog layer suits coordinates well the applications that relied on low-latency coordination between the edge and cloud or offline continuity in the geographically restricted or inter-connective applications.

4.4 Cloud Layer

Despite the fact that Edge Intelligence prioritizes decentralized processing, the Cloud Layer is still an essential part of the scheme (Asim et al., 2020). It provides the scale, computing power and centralization that is required on strategic but non time-sensitive work. The major functions of the cloud layer are:

- Data Long-run trend identification, customer behaviour forecasting and being strategic: historical data analysis.
- Model Training and Optimization: Training sophisticated deep learning models with large data volumes on GPUs/TPUs where the trained models could subsequently be pushed to edge or fog nodes.
- Global Orchestration: Central management of devices, model versions, access control, and software updates across the edge and fog layers.

- Business Integration: Integration with ERP systems, CRM tools, dashboards, and third-party APIs.

Cloud platforms like AWS, Azure, and Google Cloud offer services such as IoT Core, Lambda Functions, and AI Model Registries to support edge-cloud hybrid deployments. This layer also houses centralized dashboards where decision-makers can visualize KPIs aggregated from distributed edge environments. Despite its benefits, reliance on the cloud for time-sensitive decisions can be problematic. Hence, the cloud layer complements—but does not replace—the edge and fog layers in a mature Edge Intelligence system.

4.5 Orchestration Layer

Coordinating thousands of edge nodes, fog clusters, and cloud services requires a dedicated Orchestration Layer. This meta-layer provides the intelligence and automation necessary to keep the entire Edge Intelligence architecture synchronized and manageable (Gong et al., 2022). Critical functions include:

- Service Discovery: Enabling edge devices to locate the right fog or cloud service dynamically, based on availability and workload.
- Model Lifecycle Management: Automating deployment, versioning, and rollback of machine learning models across heterogeneous devices.
- Policy Enforcement: Applying access control, encryption, and data retention rules based on organizational and regulatory requirements.
- Monitoring and Telemetry: Collecting health metrics, usage logs, and error events from edge and fog components for centralized observability.
- Firmware and Software Updates: Delivering secure, over-the-air updates to devices in diverse and possibly constrained environments.

Modular architectures to cope with such tasks are offered by orchestration tools such as KubeEdge, Balena, AWS IoT Greengrass, and Eclipse ioFog. Continuous ML model delivery via CI/CD pipelines is also incorporated into many organizations so that one may perform quick experimentation and iteration in distributed ML deployments.

4.6 Cross-Layer Considerations

In the architecture of Edge Intelligence systems, many architectural factors are cross-cutting between all its layers, including (Shafique et al., 2021):

- Security: At the sensor to cloud there must be encryption, trusted boot, identity and threat detection. Attack surface is expanded through decentralization of the edge systems.
- Data Consistency: Asynchronous communication between the edge and the cloud is significant, and it is important to guarantee consistency whilst handling intermittent disconnections. Such methods as eventual consistency and replicated concurrent data-types (CRDTs) are commonly used.
- Resilience and Fault Tolerance: Ability to accept failure, this is critical to edge systems which could be hardware failure, loss of power, or network issues. Redundant processing paths and local fails are required.
- Time Synchronization: In applications featuring distributed event logs or systems doing real-time correlation, it is required to synchronize clocks among edge nodes. Such standard protocols as NTP or PTP may be employed.

5. KEY TECHNOLOGIES ENABLING EDGE INTELLIGENCE

The realization of Edge Intelligence as a robust, scalable paradigm for decentralized analytics has been made possible by a convergence of advanced technologies across hardware, software, and communication layers. Each technology plays a critical role in addressing specific challenges posed by decentralized processing — including energy efficiency, interoperability, low-latency computation, and distributed model deployment. This section outlines the key enabling technologies that have catalyzed the evolution and adoption of Edge Intelligence systems.

5.1 Lightweight Machine Learning Frameworks

One of the primary constraints in deploying intelligence at the edge is the limited computational and memory capacity of edge devices. Unlike centralized servers equipped with powerful CPUs and GPUs, edge nodes often rely on microcontrollers, system-on-chips (SoCs), or low-power processors. To accommodate these resource limitations, several lightweight machine learning frameworks have been developed specifically for edge deployment.

TensorFlow Lite

TensorFlow Lite, developed by Google, is a streamlined version of the TensorFlow deep learning framework. It supports model quantization (e.g., converting 32-bit floats to 8-bit integers), pruning (removing redundant weights), and operator fusion, enabling inference on devices with as little as 1MB of memory. TensorFlow

Lite also supports hardware acceleration through delegate APIs for GPUs and TPUs (Wu & Luo, 2020; Dai, 2020).

ONNX Runtime

ONNX (Open Neural Network Exchange) Runtime provides cross-platform model compatibility and is particularly useful in heterogeneous environments (Shankar, 2024). It supports a variety of backends, including CPU, GPU, and specialized AI accelerators. It allows for model conversion from mainstream frameworks like PyTorch and TensorFlow, making deployment more flexible.

PyTorch Mobile

PyTorch Mobile offers tools for model optimization and on-device inference. While slightly heavier than TensorFlow Lite, it excels in real-time computer vision applications and allows seamless migration from server to edge with minimal refactoring (Shankar, 2024).

These frameworks are complemented by tools such as TensorFlow Model Optimization Toolkit and DeepC Compiler, which further assist in compressing models for edge deployment. Such toolchains are essential for tasks like image classification on surveillance cameras, anomaly detection in sensor data, or predictive maintenance in manufacturing equipment.

5.2 Containerization and Edge Kubernetes

Scalability and modularity are essential to Edge Intelligence, particularly in large-scale industrial or urban deployments. Containerization — packaging applications and dependencies into lightweight, portable units enables consistent deployment across different edge environments.

Docker and OCI Containers

Docker containers are widely used in cloud-native applications, and the same portability benefits extend to the edge (Urblik et al., 2024). Containers allow applications to run in isolated environments, ensuring that dependencies do not conflict and reducing deployment errors.

KubeEdge and MicroK8s

KubeEdge extends Kubernetes functionality to the edge, enabling container orchestration outside traditional data centers. It supports deployment, fault tolerance, and scaling across thousands of distributed edge nodes (Raheja, 2020). MicroK8s is another lightweight Kubernetes distribution optimized for single-node deployments on edge devices.

Balena and Open Horizon

For environments without sufficient resources to run Kubernetes, platforms like Balena provide lightweight container orchestration, remote updates, and fleet management for embedded Linux devices. IBM's Open Horizon enables policy-based deployment and scaling, incorporating AI-driven edge analytics (Prangon & Wu, 2024).

Together, these technologies facilitate the management of edge applications, reduce operational overhead, and ensure high availability and resilience across widely distributed networks.

5.3 5G and Advanced Connectivity

Low-latency, high-bandwidth communication is the backbone of Edge Intelligence. Traditional 3G/4G networks suffer from variable latency and limited upload capacity, which hampers real-time analytics and feedback loops.

5G NR (New Radio)

5G promises ultra-reliable low-latency communication (URLLC), with latencies under 1 millisecond and data rates exceeding 10 Gbps. These capabilities are critical for time-sensitive applications like autonomous driving, industrial robotics, and telesurgery (Liu et al., 2020).

Network Slicing

5G also introduces network slicing, allowing operators to allocate virtualized network partitions tailored to specific use cases (Abdellatif et al., 2023). For instance, one slice can prioritize video analytics in a smart city while another slice is dedicated to emergency services or IoT telemetry.

Edge Computing Integration

Telcos are embedding Multi-access Edge Computing (MEC) platforms within 5G base stations, allowing processing tasks to be offloaded locally rather than routed through the core network (Porambage et al., 2018). This architecture aligns perfectly with Edge Intelligence goals, minimizing both latency and bandwidth consumption.

In combination with Wi-Fi 6 and satellite IoT (e.g., Starlink), these advanced connectivity options enable ubiquitous, fast, and reliable communication, making real-time distributed intelligence feasible at global scale.

5.4 AI/ML-Driven Predictive Quality Analytics in Edge BI

Predictive quality analytics is rapidly emerging as a pivotal component in modern Business Intelligence (BI) systems, enabling organizations to forecast defects, optimize process quality, and reduce operational downtime. Powered by AI/ML algorithms, this approach uses historical and real-time data to identify trends and anomalies that signal quality issues before they escalate. While traditionally such analytics were confined to cloud-based platforms, the advent of Edge Intelligence has made it possible to perform predictive quality assessments locally, at the data source.

Edge-enabled AI models can process sensor data—such as temperature, pressure, vibration, or visual input—in real time to detect early indicators of degradation or nonconformance. For instance, in a smart manufacturing environment, accelerometer readings from CNC machinery can be continuously analyzed by edge-deployed convolutional neural networks (CNNs) to predict tool wear or calibration drift. By intervening early, the system minimizes scrap, reduces rework, and ensures compliance with quality standards. Similarly, in healthcare settings, wearable devices can apply recurrent neural networks (RNNs) or lightweight LSTM models to patient biosignals to forecast complications, enabling preemptive action without reliance on centralized processing.

The integration of AI/ML for predictive quality analytics at the edge also aligns with privacy and latency requirements. Sensitive data remains within local nodes, and decisions are executed within milliseconds—making this approach viable for critical systems. Moreover, the use of federated learning frameworks enables continual model improvement across distributed environments without centralized data aggregation, preserving privacy while enhancing prediction accuracy.

As BI systems evolve toward decentralized architectures, AI-driven predictive quality analytics will play a foundational role in enabling proactive, resilient, and autonomous decision-making across industries.

5.5 Hardware Accelerators

To support advanced analytics at the edge, dedicated hardware accelerators have emerged, capable of executing deep learning models with high efficiency and low power consumption.

NVIDIA Jetson Series

The NVIDIA Jetson family — including Jetson Nano, TX2, Xavier NX, and Orin — provides GPU-accelerated computing in small form factors. These modules are ideal for deploying computer vision and deep learning applications on robots, drones, or industrial automation systems (Anchitaalagammai et al., 2025).

Google Coral Edge TPU

The Edge TPU is a custom ASIC designed by Google for efficient inference at the edge. It supports TensorFlow Lite models and can perform 4 trillion operations per second (TOPS) using just 2 watts of power. It is especially effective in applications involving facial recognition, barcode scanning, and anomaly detection. (Sengupta et al., 2020)

Intel Movidius Myriad X

The Movidius chip is designed for AI inference in smart cameras and wearable devices. It offers dedicated neural compute engines and supports Intel's OpenVINO toolkit, which simplifies model optimization across Intel hardware (Leon, 2023).

Raspberry Pi AI Kits

Raspberry Pi, when combined with AI accelerator USB sticks (e.g., Coral USB Accelerator or Intel Neural Compute Stick), provides a low-cost platform for prototyping and deploying edge AI solutions (Alaidi et al., 2025).

These hardware platforms are crucial for pushing sophisticated analytics closer to the data source, reducing the need to transmit raw information to the cloud.

5.6 Security Frameworks

The decentralized nature of Edge Intelligence introduces a broad and complex attack surface. Securing devices, data, and communication channels is paramount. Several technologies and frameworks have emerged to provide comprehensive security at the edge.

Zero-Trust Security Models

A zero-trust approach ensures that no device, user, or application is implicitly trusted. Every access request is verified using context, identity, and behavior. Policies are enforced consistently across the edge-cloud continuum (Ali et al., 2022).

Secure Boot and TPM

Secure Boot ensures that only trusted firmware and OS components are loaded during device startup. Trusted Platform Modules (TPMs) provide hardware-based cryptographic functions for key storage, attestation, and digital signatures (Ryu et al., 2024).

Secure Enclaves

Hardware-based secure enclaves (e.g., Intel SGX, ARM TrustZone) allow sensitive computations to be executed in isolated memory regions, protected from even the operating system. This is vital in scenarios involving PII or confidential analytics (Villar-Rodriguez et al., 2023).

Blockchain for Device Attestation

Blockchain can be used for decentralized device identity management, software integrity verification, and transaction logging. It ensures immutability and transparency in multi-stakeholder environments, such as industrial IoT or smart grid ecosystems (Gupta et al., 2021).

Edge-Specific Standards

Industry standards such as ISA/IEC 62443 (for industrial automation) and NIST SP 800-207 (for zero-trust architectures) provide frameworks to guide secure design and operation of edge systems (Peltonen et al., 2022).

Security is not an afterthought, it must be embedded across all layers of the architecture, from the firmware of individual sensors to the APIs exposed by cloud services.

6. USE CASES ACROSS INDUSTRIES

Edge Intelligence has become a technology pillar in a very broad range of sectors. It eliminates the latency, bandwidth and reliability bottlenecks of cloud-centric systems by processing data in real time at or closer to the source of data generation. Whether a manufacturing plant, hospital, retail outlet or farm, Edge Intelligence is helping turn the fundamental decision-making and approach to execution. This area provides an overview of the diverse industrial sectors in which edge-enabled systems are seeing a major impact, providing improvements in efficiency as well as new business and operational agility.

6.1 Smart Manufacturing

One of the most noticeable applicators of Edge Intelligence resides in the manufacturing industry as the sector requires real-time control of its operations and ability to predict when and why something would break. Conventional manufacturing systems make use of Programmable Logic Controllers (PLCs) and SCADA systems to perform monitoring and automation of the production system. Nevertheless, such systems do not have high potential to receive and analyze massive amount of sensor data in real-time environments (Nain et al., 2022). Edge Intelligence enhances these legacy systems because they install smart gateways and edge servers in the shop floor. These nodes gather vibration sensor data, temperature probe data, flow meter data, and machine vision data, and run real-time analytics in order to identify anomalies, predict component failure, or optimize quality assurance operations.

To give an example, a CNC (Computer Numerical Control) milling machine which is fitted with edge-enabled accelerometers will be able to detect slight changes in spindle vibrations that may signify tool wear (Zhou et al., 2024). Executing inference models on the local system means that the system can independently generate maintenance requests or change operational parameters without going to cloud services and human interaction. In addition, edge nodes are able to implement safety measures that rely on environmental monitoring in real-time like shutting down of equipment in case of hazardous levels of gas to ensure both regulatory adherence and employee safety.

6.2 Healthcare

In healthcare, timely data interpretation can mean the difference between life and death. Edge Intelligence introduces new levels of responsiveness and privacy preservation in clinical settings, wearable health devices, and remote diagnostics. Wearable health monitors, such as smartwatches or fitness bands, continuously track parameters like ECG, blood oxygen levels, and sleep patterns (Chawla & Dalal, 2021). With embedded AI chips and edge ML models, these devices can now detect arrhythmias, apnea, or unusual fluctuations in vital signs in real time. Users are alerted immediately, and doctors can be notified only if anomalies persist, reducing false alarms and preserving patient privacy.

Inside hospitals, edge computing is revolutionizing Intensive Care Units (ICUs). Medical edge gateways can aggregate data from ventilators, infusion pumps, and heart monitors, processing this information locally to identify deteriorating conditions faster than centralized hospital systems (Nerella et al., 2023). Furthermore, mobile diagnostic tools such as portable ultrasound devices now come with embedded AI inference engines, allowing real-time image processing and disease detection — particularly useful in ambulances or rural health camps where connectivity is limited. Edge Intelligence also facilitates compliance with strict healthcare data privacy regulations like HIPAA and GDPR, by keeping sensitive patient data local and only transmitting de-identified or summarized insights to cloud platforms or EMRs (Electronic Medical Records) (Anderson, 2024).

6.3 Retail and E-Commerce

Retailers are increasingly embracing Edge Intelligence to personalize customer experiences, optimize inventory management, and reduce operational costs. By moving analytics closer to physical stores, retailers can respond dynamically to customer behaviors and environmental conditions (Silitonga et al., 2024). Smart shelves equipped with weight sensors, RFID readers, and edge cameras can detect product depletion in real time. Instead of waiting for batch inventory updates, these shelves send alerts to store associates or automated restocking systems. Additionally, edge-based facial recognition and heatmap analytics can identify peak footfall areas and demographic patterns, enabling tailored promotions or adaptive signage (Abdulkader et al., 2023).

For example, an edge device analyzing live video feeds from a cosmetics aisle can determine customer engagement by tracking dwell time and facial expressions. If a product display consistently fails to attract attention, the system can recommend layout changes or product substitutions. These insights, processed locally, can be fed into central systems overnight for strategic planning. In e-commerce warehouses, edge intelligence aids in robotic automation by ensuring seamless navigation and object recognition. Edge servers help coordinate collaborative robots (cobots) handling packaging, sorting, and dispatch without latency, enabling same-day delivery logistics to function smoothly.

6.4 Smart Cities

The world cities are becoming digital ecosystems where the real-time data of millions of devices are utilized in ensuring that the overall public can be safe, sustainable and have a good experience within the city. Edge intelligence is the key technology that has helped to achieve such capabilities in an efficient manner that is scalable and respectful of privacy. Traffic management systems involve edge-mounted cameras and LiDAR sensors in order to oversee traffic flow, detect traffic jams, recognize violations (Meribout et al., 2022). Instead of shipping all data to central servers to be analyzed there, edge analytics performs filtration and processing on data within the data center, and selectively shipping only actionable insights or flagged events. This decreases the bandwidth usage and enables policeman/traffic controllers to act instantly.

Edge-powered surveillance systems offer the ability to read faces, analyze human behavior, and estimate the density of a crowd in real-time in an environment of public safety (Chang et al., 2021). Capabilities are essential especially during huge events or during protests or evacuations. As an example, when a camera sees a person falling on the roadside, edge analytics may provide a notification without the need to wait on cloud processing, faster response by the counsel services. Air quality, amount of noise pollution and water levels are monitored by environmental sensors spread throughout a city. Edge devices compare this information with traffic patterns and weather to create locally based, real-time advice to commuters and to public health agencies.

6.5 Logistics and Fleet Management

Logistics is an industry that relies on proper real- time tracking and optimum route planning to satisfy the expectations of people receiving delivery and minimize the expenses. This is boosted with Edge Intelligence that integrates intelligent decision-making into vehicles and transport infrastructure. A vehicle now includes, in the edge computing environment, GPS units, accelerometers, engine diagnostic systems, and onboard cameras (Xidias et al., 2022). The use of these devices is to examine data during movement to optimize the routes, discover risky driving manner, or anticipate mechanical breakdowns. A truck onboard edge unit may recognize tires wearing out or develop too much variation in tire pressure and re-route itself to the closest maintenance center without outside intervention.

The summarized telemetry data is sent to the fleet management dashboards instead of providing raw data to allow managers to deal with high-impact events (Khalid et al., 2020). Moreover, real-time tracking and enforcement of compliances are enabled by edge-powered geofencing. When a vehicle reaches an off-limits area or goes out of its designated route, messages are produced immediately. In smart warehouses, obstacle displays and collaborative identifications of automated guided vehicles (AGVs) are progressed basing on the edge through drones (Bhargava et al., 2024). Decision making for a real body establishes efficiency in a situation where the GPS cannot be applied like in the case of heavily loaded indoor infrastructure.

6.6 Energy and Utilities

Since the energy industry of the world turns to smart grids and renewable energy, Edge Intelligence is becoming a key to ensuring grid stability, optimizing utilization and operating distributed assets. Edge processing-enabled smart meters may locally examine the usage patterns and alert the consumers or utilities about abnormalities (i.e. unusual volume or suspected theft) (Sodhro et al., 2019). These meters are also capable with responding to pricing signal or heed balance requests without a required central command.

Substation edge devices observe the conditions of transformers, voltage stability, and reactive compensation power. Outages or instability could be isolated within a short amount of time through fault detection algorithms being executed locally and thereby shifting cascading failures. Combining it with weather monitors will enable adjusting the load preemptively based on the expected input of solar or wind power. The edge nodes in renewable energy systems like solar farms or wind turbines also maximize generation by adjusting tilt or rotation, or the energy storage cycle, in response to real-time environmental information. This reduces wastage and maximizes the ROI on the part of the operators and the end-users.

6.7 Agriculture

The digital revolution has swept all these through, especially in regards to agriculture, as demands on feeding more global population within more limited environmental guidelines continue to rise. Edge Intelligence enables farmers to make the most out of their product, increase the well-preservation of resources and manage risks more intelligently (Liu et al., 2021). Precision agricultural systems refer to the combination of soil moisture sensors, weather stations and drone imagery to provide hyper-local intelligence. Relay units located on the field can calculate what kind of irrigation is required according to the real-time soil conditions, forecast models, and crop needs and activate water pumps or drip units on their own.

The Computer Vision (CV) model on the drones or fixed cameras determines any sign of pest outbreaks, disease infections, or lack of nutrients based on the colour of the plant and the shape (Abdullah et al., 2023). Instead of uploading high-resolution images to the cloud, the edge processing allows detecting and acting in the field. The edge intelligence is useful in livestock management systems as well. Portable collars with livestock work with heart rate, location, and feeding. Abnormal activity, including abnormal high stress, is detected in real time and veterinary intervention occurs before large-scale suffering results. With edge controllers in smart greenhouses, temperature, humidity and light are controlled depending on sensor and ML-trained historical growth data, therefore optimizing production and minimizing energy consumption.

7. CONCLUSION

The recent development of Edge Intelligence within the sphere of Business Intelligence systems actually brings one step closer to the next revolution in how companies work with data, conduct analytics, and make business decisions. Unlike legacy centralized BI systems, which grapple with latency, bandwidth and compliance concerns, Edge Intelligence decentralizes computing resources to the very data sources itself, the results of which is a more performance-responsive, risk tolerant, privacy-preserving analytics model. This chapter has followed the development of centralized and cloud BI to hybrid and edge-enhanced models that implement particular trade-offs in the dimensions of scalability, latency and data sovereignty. The highlight of Edge Intelligence is that it can reach real-time insights, and it has removed the necessity of always being connected and it is more flexible, supporting mission-critical applications to various industries, including smart manufacturing, healthcare, logistics, and energy. Such functions are particularly important in a modern world where the difference between success and failure in operational undertakings could be a matter of seconds.

Significant architectural layers, including data collection and edge processing, fog computing, and cloud orchestration support scaleable, interoperable and secure edge implementations. Facilitating technologies like lightweight machine learning frameworks, 5G technology, dedicated AI device hardware, and custom security models at the edge also increases the availability and stability of these systems. Deploying Edge Intelligence, however, is not all easy. It has to be planned carefully around infrastructure preparedness, model optimization, regulatory compliance, and centralised device management. The chapter discusses the best practices, which includes business-driven designs, to deploy secure-by-design, and to use centralized observability tools.-All these provide a framework to follow the successful adoption.

In the end, Edge Intelligence is neither a mere technical update over BI but a business driver of digital revolution. It enables organizations to innovate rapidly, make autonomous decisions where and when they are needed and scale analytics ecosystem that are sustainable, contextually aware and future proof. With maturity of edge capabilities and the hybrid models, integration of BI and Edge Intelligence will reframe competitive benefit, in terms of data-driven economy.

REFERENCES

Abdellatif, A. A., Abo-Eleneen, A., Mohamed, A., Erbad, A., Navkar, N. V., & Guizani, M. (2023). Intelligent-slicing: An AI-assisted network slicing framework for 5G-and-beyond networks. *IEEE Transactions on Network and Service Management, 20*(2), 1024–1039.

Abdulkader, R., Ayasrah, F. T. M., Nallagattla, V. R. G., Hiran, K. K., Dadheech, P., Balasubramaniam, V., & Sengan, S. (2023). Optimizing student engagement in edge-based online learning with advanced analytics. *Array (New York, N.Y.), 19*, 100301.

Abdullah, H. M., Mohana, N. T., Khan, B. M., Ahmed, S. M., Hossain, M., Islam, K. S., & Ahamed, T. (2023). Present and future scopes and challenges of plant pest and disease (P&D) monitoring: Remote sensing, image processing, and artificial intelligence perspectives. *Remote Sensing Applications: Society and Environment, 32*, 100996.

Adnane, Y. I., & Zerari, M. (2024). Optimizing business intelligence classification rule mining using quantum-inspired genetic algorithm. *IEEE Access : Practical Innovations, Open Solutions*.

Alaidi, A. H. M., Ramadhan, Z. A., & Alrubaye, J. S., ALRikabi, H. T. S., Mutar, H. A., & Svyd, I. (2025). AI-based monkeypox detection model using Raspberry Pi 5 AI Kit. *Sustainable Engineering and Innovation, 7*(1), 1–14.

Ali, B., Hijjawi, S., Campbell, L. H., Gregory, M. A., & Li, S. (2022). A maturity framework for zero-trust security in multiaccess edge computing. *Security and Communication Networks, 2022*(1), 3178760.

Ali, S. A., Ansari, M., Alam, M., & Rakshit, S. (2023). Federated Learning for Business Intelligence: Predictive Maintenance in Industry 4.0. In AI-Based Data Analytics (pp. 125-140). Auerbach Publications.

Alsayfi, M. S., Dahab, M. Y., Eassa, F. E., Salama, R., Haridi, S., & Al-Ghamdi, A. S. (2022). Securing real-time video surveillance data in vehicular cloud computing: A survey. *IEEE Access : Practical Innovations, Open Solutions, 10*, 51525–51547.

Anchitaalagammai, J. V., Kavitha, S., Buurvidha, R., Santhiya, T. S., Roopa, M. D., & Sankari, S. S. (2025). Edge Artificial Intelligence for Real-Time Decision Making using NVIDIA Jetson Orin, Google Coral Edge TPU and 6G for Privacy and Scalability. In *2025 International Conference on Visual Analytics and Data Visualization (ICVADV)* (pp. 150-155). IEEE.

Anderson, K. (2024). *'The role of edge computing and hybrid clouds in next-generation healthcare. Univ*. Tech. Rep.

Antonini, M. (2021). From Edge Computing to Edge Intelligence: exploring novel design approaches to intelligent IoT applications.

Asim, M., Wang, Y., Wang, K., & Huang, P. Q. (2020). A review on computational intelligence techniques in cloud and edge computing. *IEEE Transactions on Emerging Topics in Computational Intelligence*, *4*(6), 742–763.

Bhargava, A., Suhaib, M., & Singholi, A. S. (2024). A review of recent advances, techniques, and control algorithms for automated guided vehicle systems. *Journal of the Brazilian Society of Mechanical Sciences and Engineering*, *46*(7), 419.

Biswas, A., & Wang, H. C. (2023). Autonomous vehicles enabled by the integration of IoT, edge intelligence, 5G, and blockchain. *Sensors (Basel)*, *23*(4), 1963. PMID: 36850560

Cao, L. (2022). Decentralized AI: Edge intelligence and smart blockchain, metaverse, web3, and desci. *IEEE Intelligent Systems*, *37*(3), 6–19.

Chang, V. (2014). The business intelligence as a service in the cloud. *Future Generation Computer Systems*, *37*, 512–534.

Chang, Z., Liu, S., Xiong, X., Cai, Z., & Tu, G. (2021). A survey of recent advances in edge-computing-powered artificial intelligence of things. *IEEE Internet of Things Journal*, *8*(18), 13849–13875.

Chavan, A. (2023). Exploring the Synergy of Cloud and On-Premises Systems-A Case for Hybrid Architectures. *Journal of Computer Science and Technology Studies*, *5*(3), 122–141.

Chawla, N., & Dalal, S. (2021). Edge AI with Wearable IoT: A Review on Leveraging Edge Intelligence in Wearables for Smart Healthcare. Green Internet of Things for Smart Cities, 205-231.

Dai, J. (2020). Real-time and accurate object detection on edge device with TensorFlow Lite. [). IOP Publishing.]. *Journal of Physics: Conference Series*, *1651*(1), 012114.

Deng, S., Zhao, H., Fang, W., Yin, J., Dustdar, S., & Zomaya, A. Y. (2020). Edge intelligence: The confluence of edge computing and artificial intelligence. *IEEE Internet of Things Journal*, *7*(8), 7457–7469.

Duan, S., Wang, D., Ren, J., Lyu, F., Zhang, Y., Wu, H., & Shen, X. (2022). Distributed artificial intelligence empowered by end-edge-cloud computing: A survey. *IEEE Communications Surveys and Tutorials*, *25*(1), 591–624.

ElMalah, K., & Nasr, M. (2019). Cloud business intelligence. *International Journal of Advanced Networking and Applications*, *10*(6), 4120–4124.

Fagbohungbe, O., Reza, S. R., Dong, X., & Qian, L. (2021). Efficient privacy preserving edge intelligent computing framework for image classification in IoT. *IEEE Transactions on Emerging Topics in Computational Intelligence*, *6*(4), 941–956.

Gong, T., Zhu, L., Yu, F. R., & Tang, T. (2023). Edge intelligence in intelligent transportation systems: A survey. *IEEE Transactions on Intelligent Transportation Systems*, *24*(9), 8919–8944.

Gong, Y., Yao, H., Wang, J., Wu, D., Zhang, N., & Yu, F. R. (2022). Decentralized edge intelligence-driven network resource orchestration mechanism. *IEEE Network*, *37*(2), 270–276.

Gupta, R., Reebadiya, D., & Tanwar, S. (2021). 6G-enabled edge intelligence for ultra-reliable low latency applications: Vision and mission. *Computer Standards & Interfaces*, *77*, 103521.

Gupta, R., Reebadiya, D., Tanwar, S., Kumar, N., & Guizani, M. (2021). When blockchain meets edge intelligence: Trusted and security solutions for consumers. *IEEE Network*, *35*(5), 272–278.

Jia, M., Wu, J., Guo, Q., & Yang, Y. (2024). Service-oriented SAGIN with pervasive intelligence for resource-constrained users. *IEEE Network*, *38*(2), 79–86.

Kanagarla, K. (2024). Edge computing and analytics for IoT devices: Enhancing real-time decision making in smart environments. *Available at SSRN* 5012466.

Kasem, M., & Hassanein, E. E. (2014). Cloud business intelligence survey. *International Journal of Computer Applications*, *90*(1).

Khalid, A. S., Hassan, N. H., Razak, N. A. A. B., & Baharuden, A. F. (2020). Business intelligence dashboard for driver performance in fleet management. In Proceedings of the 2020 11th International Conference on E-Education, E-Business, E-Management, and E-Learning (pp. 347-351).

Kola, H. G. (2024). Optimizing ETL Processes for Big Data Applications. *International Journal of Engineering and Management Research*, *14*(5), 99–112.

Leon, V., Minaidis, P., Lentaris, G., & Soudris, D. (2023). Accelerating AI and computer vision for satellite pose estimation on the intel myriad X embedded SoC. *Microprocessors and Microsystems*, *103*, 104947.

Li, E., Zhou, Z., & Chen, X. (2018). Edge intelligence: On-demand deep learning model co-inference with device-edge synergy. In *Proceedings of the 2018 workshop on mobile edge communications* (pp. 31-36).

Liu, J., Xiang, J., Jin, Y., Liu, R., Yan, J., & Wang, L. (2021). Boost precision agriculture with unmanned aerial vehicle remote sensing and edge intelligence: A survey. *Remote Sensing*, *13*(21), 4387.

Liu, Y., Peng, M., Shou, G., Chen, Y., & Chen, S. (2020). Toward edge intelligence: Multiaccess edge computing for 5G and Internet of Things. *IEEE Internet of Things Journal*, *7*(8), 6722–6747.

Lukić, J., Radenković, M., Despotović-Zrakić, M., Labus, A., & Bogdanović, Z. (2016). A hybrid approach to building a multi-dimensional business intelligence system for electricity grid operators. *Utilities Policy*, *41*, 95–106.

Mendez, J., Bierzynski, K., Cuéllar, M. P., & Morales, D. P. (2022). Edge intelligence: Concepts, architectures, applications, and future directions. [TECS]. *ACM Transactions on Embedded Computing Systems*, *21*(5), 1–41.

Meribout, M., Baobaid, A., Khaoua, M. O., Tiwari, V. K., & Pena, J. P. (2022). State of art IoT and Edge embedded systems for real-time machine vision applications. *IEEE Access : Practical Innovations, Open Solutions*, *10*, 58287–58301.

Moscoso-Zea, O., Castro, J., Paredes-Gualtor, J., & Luján-Mora, S. (2019). A hybrid infrastructure of enterprise architecture and business intelligence & analytics for knowledge management in education. *IEEE Access : Practical Innovations, Open Solutions*, *7*, 38778–38788.

Nain, G., Pattanaik, K. K., & Sharma, G. K. (2022). Towards edge computing in intelligent manufacturing: Past, present and future. *Journal of Manufacturing Systems*, *62*, 588–611.

Nain, G., Pattanaik, K. K., & Sharma, G. K. (2022). Towards edge computing in intelligent manufacturing: Past, present and future. *Journal of Manufacturing Systems*, *62*, 588–611.

Naqvi, S. K. H., & Batool, K. (2023). A comparative analysis between general data protection regulations and california consumer privacy act. *Journal of Computer Science. Information Technology and Telecommunication Engineering*, *4*(1), 326–332.

Nasir, M., Muhammad, K., Ullah, A., Ahmad, J., Baik, S. W., & Sajjad, M. (2022). Enabling automation and edge intelligence over resource constraint IoT devices for smart home. *Neurocomputing*, *491*, 494–506.

Nerella, S., Guan, Z., Siegel, S., Zhang, J., Khezeli, K., Bihorac, A., & Rashidi, P. (2023). AI-enhanced intensive care unit: revolutionizing patient care with pervasive sensing. arXiv preprint arXiv:2303.06252.

Ong, I. L., Siew, P. H., & Wong, S. F. (2011). A five-layered business intelligence architecture. *Communications of the IBIMA*, *2011*, 1–11.

Pappala, S., Rayudu, M. M., & Faiz, M. S. (2024). The Transformative [*Technology on Industrial Automation, Gaming and Entertainment, Healthcare, and Autonomous Vehicles.*]. *Impact of*, •••, 5G.

Peltonen, E., Ahmad, I., Aral, A., Capobianco, M., Ding, A. Y., Gil-Castiñeira, F., & Yang, T. (2022). The many faces of edge intelligence. *IEEE Access : Practical Innovations, Open Solutions*, *10*, 104769–104782.

Pioli, L., de Macedo, D. D., Costa, D. G., & Dantas, M. A. (2024). Intelligent edge-powered data reduction: A systematic literature review. *ACM Computing Surveys*, *56*(9), 1–39.

Porambage, P., Okwuibe, J., Liyanage, M., Ylianttila, M., & Taleb, T. (2018). Survey on multi-access edge computing for internet of things realization. *IEEE Communications Surveys and Tutorials*, *20*(4), 2961–2991.

Prangon, N. F., & Wu, J. (2024). AI and computing horizons: Cloud and edge in the modern era. *Journal of Sensor and Actuator Networks*, *13*(4), 44.

Raheja, R. (2020). Enabling kubernetes for distributed ai processing on edge devices (Doctoral dissertation, The University of North Carolina at Charlotte).

Raisinghani, M. S. (Ed.). (2004). *Business intelligence in the digital economy: opportunities, limitations and risks*. Igi Global.

Ryu, C., Lee, J. H., Kim, D. H., Lee, H. S., Kim, Y. S., Han, J. H., & Kim, J. N. (2024). A Comprehensive Survey of TPM for Defense Systems. [TIIS]. *KSII Transactions on Internet and Information Systems*, *18*(7), 1953–1967.

Sedlak, B., Pujol, V. C., Donta, P. K., & Dustdar, S. (2023). Controlling data gravity and data friction: From metrics to multidimensional elasticity strategies. In *2023 IEEE International Conference on Software Services Engineering (SSE)* (pp. 43-49). IEEE.

Sengupta, J., Kubendran, R., Neftci, E., & Andreou, A. (2020). High-speed, real-time, spike-based object tracking and path prediction on google edge TPU. In 2020 2nd IEEE International Conference on Artificial Intelligence Circuits and Systems (AICAS) (pp. 134-135). IEEE.

Shafique, M., Marchisio, A., Putra, R. V. W., & Hanif, M. A. (2021). Towards energy-efficient and secure edge AI: A cross-layer framework ICCAD special session paper. In *2021 IEEE/ACM International Conference On Computer Aided Design (ICCAD)* (pp. 1-9). IEEE.

Shankar, V. (2024). Edge AI: A Comprehensive Survey of Technologies, Applications, and Challenges. In 2024 1st International Conference on Advanced Computing and Emerging Technologies (ACET) (pp. 1-6). IEEE.

Sharma, P. (2024). Techniques for Reducing Latency in Cloud-Based Networks: A Comprehensive Study. *Journal of Innovative Technologies*, *7*(1), 1–7.

Silitonga, D., Rohmayanti, S. A. A., Aripin, Z., Kuswandi, D., & Sulistyo, A. B. (2024). Edge computing in E-commerce business: Economic impacts and advantages of scalable information systems. *EAI Endorsed Transactions on Scalable Information Systems*, *11*(1), 4375.

Sipola, T., Alatalo, J., Kokkonen, T., & Rantonen, M. (2022). Artificial intelligence in the IoT era: A review of edge AI hardware and software. In *2022 31st Conference of Open Innovations Association (FRUCT)* (pp. 320-331). IEEE.

Sodhro, A. H., Pirbhulal, S., & De Albuquerque, V. H. C. (2019). Artificial intelligence-driven mechanism for edge computing-based industrial applications. *IEEE Transactions on Industrial Informatics*, *15*(7), 4235–4243.

Sodiya, E. O., Umoga, U. J., Obaigbena, A., Jacks, B. S., Ugwuanyi, E. D., Daraojimba, A. I., & Lottu, O. A. (2024). Current state and prospects of edge computing within the Internet of Things (IoT) ecosystem. *International Journal of Science and Research Archive*, *11*(1), 1863–1873.

Urblik, L., Kajati, E., Papcun, P., & Zolotová, I. (2024). Containerization in edge intelligence: A review. *Electronics (Basel)*, *13*(7), 1335.

Villar-Rodriguez, E., Pérez, M. A., Torre-Bastida, A. I., Senderos, C. R., & López-de-Armentia, J. (2023). Edge intelligence secure frameworks: Current state and future challenges. *Computers & Security*, *130*, 103278.

Wu, Y. H., & Luo, H. (2020). Apply edge intelligence to IoT based home automation. In *17th Int. Conf. on Applied Computing*.

Xidias, E., Zacharia, P., & Nearchou, A. (2022). Intelligent fleet management of autonomous vehicles for city logistics. *Applied Intelligence*, *52*(15), 18030–18048.

Xu, D., Li, T., Li, Y., Su, X., Tarkoma, S., Jiang, T., & Hui, P. (2021). Edge intelligence: Empowering intelligence to the edge of network. *Proceedings of the IEEE, 109*(11), 1778–1837.

Xu, R., Nagothu, D., & Chen, Y. (2024). AR-Edge: Autonomous and Resilient Edge Computing Architecture for Smart Cities. In *Edge Computing Architecture-Architecture and Applications for Smart Cities*. IntechOpen.

Zagan, E., & Danubianu, M. (2021). Cloud DATA LAKE: The new trend of data storage. In *2021 3rd International Congress on Human-Computer Interaction, Optimization and Robotic Applications (HORA)* (pp. 1-4). IEEE.

Zeng, L., Ye, S., Chen, X., Zhang, X., Ren, J., Tang, J., & Shen, X. S. (2025). Edge Graph Intelligence: Reciprocally Empowering Edge Networks with Graph Intelligence. *IEEE Communications Surveys and Tutorials*.

Zhou, Z., Yu, D., Chen, M., Qiao, Y., Hu, Y., & He, W. (2024). An edge intelligence-based model deployment method for CNC systems. *Journal of Manufacturing Systems, 74*, 716–751.

Zou, Z., Jin, Y., Nevalainen, P., Huan, Y., Heikkonen, J., & Westerlund, T. (2019). Edge and fog computing enabled AI for IoT-an overview. In *2019 IEEE International Conference on Artificial Intelligence Circuits and Systems (AICAS)* (pp. 51-56). IEEE.

Chapter 5
From Data to Decisions:
Implementing Real-Time Analytics Pipelines in Business Intelligence Architecture

Mohammad Al Khaldy
https://orcid.org/0009-0009-7502-4668
University of Petra, Amman, Jordan

Ala Hamarsheh
https://orcid.org/0000-0002-4736-7331
Computer Science, Faculty of Information Technology, Arab American University, Jenin, Palestine

ABSTRACT

The acceleration of digital transformation initiatives has intensified organizational demands for immediate, actionable insights from vast data streams. Traditional business intelligence architectures often struggle to fulfill these requirements due to inherent latency constraints and batch-oriented processing paradigms. This chapter addresses the critical gap between conventional analytics approaches and contemporary business requirements by proposing a comprehensive framework for implementing real-time analytics pipelines within business intelligence architectures. Through systematic analysis of architectural components, data engineering methodologies, stream processing frameworks, and visualization approaches, we establish a structured implementation pathway for organizations. Findings demonstrate that successful real-time analytics deployments require deliberate architectural choices that balance latency requirements with analytical depth while addressing organizational readiness dimensions.

DOI: 10.4018/979-8-3373-2125-7.ch005

1. INTRODUCTION

1.1. Background and Context

The contemporary business landscape operates at unprecedented speeds, creating both opportunities and challenges for organizations seeking competitive advantage through data-driven decision-making. As market conditions, customer preferences, competitive dynamics, and operational parameters continuously evolve, the ability to process, analyze, and respond to data in real-time has transformed from a luxury to a necessity (Ravichandran, Machireddy, & Rachakatla, 2022). Legacy business intelligence (BI) approaches characterized by batch processing, predefined reporting cycles, and delayed insights increasingly fail to meet the demands of modern business operations that require immediate detection, analysis, and response to emerging patterns.

Real-time analytics pipelines represent the technological response to these accelerating business imperatives, enabling organizations to capture, process, and derive actionable insights from data streams as events occur rather than through retrospective analysis. The evolution toward real-time analytics capabilities demands fundamental rethinking of traditional business intelligence architectures—shifting from static, predefined analytical workflows to dynamic, continuous processing models that maintain analytical rigor while dramatically reducing time-to-insight (Dubuc, Stahl, & Roesch, 2020).

This transition challenges organizations across multiple dimensions: technical architecture must evolve to support stream processing; data engineering practices must adapt to continuous data flows; analytical methodologies must operate under stricter latency constraints; and organizational processes must realign to leverage immediate insights effectively. As Bhaskaran (Bhaskaran, 2020) observe, while technological capabilities for real-time analytics have matured significantly, organizations continue to encounter substantial implementation challenges when attempting to realize these capabilities within existing business intelligence ecosystems.

1.2. The Real-Time Imperative in Modern Business

The imperative for real-time analytics capabilities derives from fundamental shifts in business operating environments and competitive landscapes. Several key business drivers have accelerated adoption of real-time analytics capabilities:

First, consumer expectations have evolved dramatically, with customers expecting immediate, personalized experiences across digital and physical channels. Organizations require real-time analytical capabilities to deliver contextually relevant interactions, dynamic pricing, and personalized recommendations that respond to customer behavior as it occurs rather than based on historical patterns (Ravichandran et al., 2022).

Second, operational optimization increasingly depends on immediate detection and response to anomalies, disruptions, and optimization opportunities. Manufacturing environments leverage real-timc analytics to identify quality issues before they propagate; supply chain operations rely on immediate visibility to anticipate and mitigate disruptions; and resource allocation decisions across industries depend on instantaneous analysis of current conditions and projected outcomes (Ma et al., 2020).

Third, risk management functions—particularly in financial services, cybersecurity, and compliance domains—face escalating pressure to detect and respond to threats as they emerge rather than through retrospective analysis. As Abbas and Eldred (Abbas & Eldred, 2025) note, real-time analytics capabilities have become essential for fraud detection, security monitoring, and regulatory compliance in environments where delayed responses can result in significant financial or reputational damage.

Fourth, competitive dynamics increasingly favor organizations capable of rapid adaptation to changing market conditions. The ability to detect emerging trends, competitor actions, and market shifts as they occur—and to formulate appropriate responses immediately—represents a significant competitive advantage in volatile business environments (Ereth & Baars, 2020).

These converging business imperatives have created what Coito et al. (Coito et al., 2021) describe as the "velocity imperative" in business intelligence—the organizational need to minimize decision latency while maintaining or improving decision quality. This imperative drives fundamental reconsideration of traditional business intelligence architectures that were optimized for analytical thoroughness rather than decision speed.

1.3. Research Objectives and Chapter Organization

This chapter addresses the critical challenge of implementing real-time analytics capabilities within business intelligence architectures to support accelerated decision-making while maintaining analytical depth and governance requirements. Specifically, we aim to:

1. Analyze the architectural components, frameworks, and technologies that enable real-time analytics pipelines within business intelligence environments
2. Develop a comprehensive implementation framework that addresses both technical and organizational dimensions of real-time analytics adoption
3. Examine patterns, practices, and considerations for data engineering in streaming contexts

4. Evaluate approaches for maintaining analytical rigor while operating under strict latency constraints
5. Assess visualization and delivery mechanisms appropriate for real-time insights
6. Identify operational considerations essential for sustainable real-time analytics implementations
7. Analyze implementation patterns across diverse industry contexts through representative case studies

The remainder of this chapter is organized as follows: Section 2 examines the evolution of business intelligence architectures from batch-oriented to real-time paradigms. Section 3 analyzes core architectural components of real-time analytics pipelines. Section 4 explores data engineering approaches essential for streaming contexts. Section 5 addresses analytics and machine learning methodologies appropriate for real-time environments. Section 6 examines visualization and delivery mechanisms for real-time insights. Section 7 discusses operational considerations for real-time analytics pipelines. Section 8 presents implementation frameworks and best practices for real-time analytics adoption.

2. EVOLUTION OF BUSINESS INTELLIGENCE ARCHITECTURE

2.1. From Batch Processing to Real-Time Analytics

The evolution of business intelligence architectures reflects broader technological transformations and changing business requirements over multiple decades. Traditional business intelligence architectures emerged in environments characterized by relatively stable business conditions, predictable information needs, and technical constraints that necessitated batch-oriented approaches to data processing and analysis. These architectures typically followed what Ereth and Baars (2020) describe as the "extract-transform-load" (ETL) paradigm—periodic extraction of data from operational systems, transformation through predefined rules, loading into specialized analytical repositories, and subsequent query and reporting through predetermined analytical pathways.

This approach optimized for analytical thoroughness, query performance on historical datasets, and governance requirements rather than decision speed. As Sresth et al. (Sresth, Nagavalli, & Tiwari, 2023) observe, traditional business intelligence architectures prioritized "analytical completeness over analytical immediacy," creating fundamental tensions as business velocity increased. These architectures introduced significant latency at multiple levels: data acquisition latency (delay between event occurrence and data capture), processing latency (time required for data transformation and integration), analytical latency (time needed to execute analytical processes), and decision latency (time required to deliver insights to decision-makers and formulate responses).

The transition toward real-time analytics capabilities has progressed through multiple evolutionary stages. Early efforts focused primarily on accelerating traditional batch processes—reducing ETL cycle times from days to hours or minutes while maintaining the fundamental batch-oriented paradigm. This approach, which (Machireddy, 2024) characterizes as "high-frequency batch processing," reduced but did not eliminate the inherent latency of batch-oriented architectures.

The emergence of stream processing capabilities represented a more fundamental architectural shift—from periodic processing of static datasets to continuous processing of data streams. This paradigm, described by (Erik & Emma, 2018) as "event-driven analytics," abandoned the notion of fixed analytical cycles in favor of continuous event capture, processing, and analysis. Rather than extracting data from source systems at predefined intervals, stream-based architectures consume events directly from operational systems through change data capture, messaging systems, or direct integrations, enabling immediate propagation of operational events to analytical processes.

The most recent evolutionary stage involves integration of real-time analytics capabilities with machine learning and artificial intelligence techniques—creating what Ravichandran et al. (2022) term "AI-enhanced real-time analytics." These architectures leverage advanced analytical techniques to address complex analytical questions within strict latency constraints, enabling predictive and prescriptive capabilities previously associated only with batch-oriented approaches.

2.2. The Value Proposition of Timely Insights

The economic value of real-time analytics capabilities derives from fundamental relationships between decision latency, decision quality, and business outcomes. Understanding these relationships enables organizations to quantify the potential return on investment from real-time analytics implementations and prioritize use cases appropriately.

Decision latency—the time interval between event occurrence and response formulation—directly impacts business outcomes across multiple domains. In dynamic pricing scenarios, even minor delays in detecting changing market conditions can significantly impact revenue and profit margins. Ravichandran et al. (2022) document revenue improvements of 4-7% from implementations that reduced pricing decision latency from hours to seconds in retail environments.

In fraud detection contexts, the financial impact of detection latency follows an approximately linear relationship with time—each minute reduction in fraud detection time directly reduces financial exposure by the per-minute fraud rate. Financial services organizations implementing real-time fraud detection systems typically report 30-40% reductions in fraud losses compared to batch-oriented approaches (Malkoochi, 2025).

Equipment maintenance scenarios demonstrate exponential relationships between detection latency and financial impact—minor component failures detected immediately can often be addressed with minimal cost and operational disruption, while the same failures detected after propagation to secondary systems frequently result in extensive damage, prolonged downtime, and substantial repair costs. (Ma, Ren, Xiang, & Turk, 2020) document maintenance cost reductions exceeding 25% and availability improvements of 12-18% through implementation of real-time predictive maintenance capabilities.

These relationships create economic incentives for minimizing decision latency across business functions. However, real-time analytics implementations require substantial investment across multiple dimensions: technical infrastructure, analytical capabilities, organizational processes, and change management. These investments must be justified through careful analysis of the relationship between latency reduction and business value within specific organizational contexts.

2.3. Balancing Real-Time Capabilities with Analytical Depth

Despite compelling business drivers for real-time analytics capabilities, organizations must navigate fundamental tensions between analytical speed and analytical depth. Traditional business intelligence approaches prioritized comprehensive analysis—integrating diverse data sources, applying sophisticated analytical techniques, and examining multiple dimensions before delivering insights. Real-time approaches necessarily operate under stricter constraints, potentially sacrificing analytical thoroughness for immediacy.

This tension creates what Abbas and Eldred (2025) describe as the "depth-latency tradeoff"—the inverse relationship between analytical sophistication and processing speed within given technological constraints. Organizations implementing real-time analytics capabilities must carefully manage this tradeoff to avoid sacrificing decision quality for decision speed.

Several strategies have emerged for balancing these competing requirements. First, many organizations implement tiered analytical approaches that apply immediate, simplified analysis for time-sensitive decisions while conducting more thorough analysis for decisions with longer time horizons. This approach, which (Sankaranarayanan, 2025) terms "multi-temporal analytics," maintains decision speed for urgent matters while preserving analytical depth for complex decisions.

Second, advanced architectural patterns leverage incremental analytical approaches that deliver preliminary insights immediately while continuously refining results as additional data becomes available or more sophisticated analysis completes. This pattern, described by Dubuc et al. (2020) as "progressive analytics," enables decision-makers to initiate responses based on preliminary insights while maintaining awareness that analytical results may evolve.

Third, organizations increasingly leverage pre-computation strategies that perform complex analytical operations in advance, enabling real-time applications to reference these pre-computed results rather than performing sophisticated analysis within latency constraints. This approach proves particularly valuable for dimensional analysis, comparison against historical patterns, and complex segmentation that would otherwise exceed real-time processing capabilities.

Fourth, modern stream processing architectures increasingly support what Sresth et al. (2023) describe as "hybrid processing modes" that combine streaming and batch processing within unified analytical workflows. These approaches enable immediate processing of high-priority data elements through streaming pathways while directing data requiring more sophisticated analysis through batch-oriented processes with higher latency but greater analytical depth.

Figure 1. Multi-Temporal Analytics Decision Framework

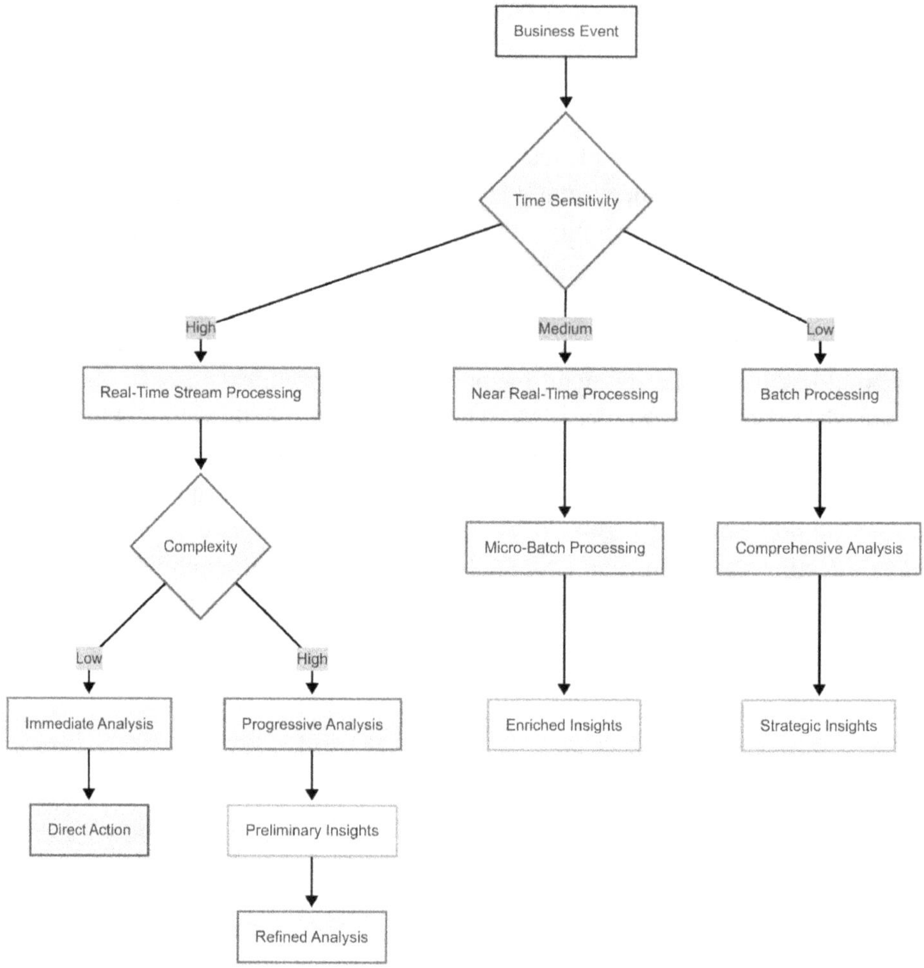

3. Architectural Components of Real-Time Analytics Pipelines

3.1. Event Streaming Platforms and Message Brokers

At the foundation of real-time analytics pipelines lie event streaming platforms and message brokers—specialized infrastructure components that facilitate capture, transportation, and delivery of event data across distributed systems. These components serve as the nervous system of real-time analytics architectures, enabling immediate propagation of operational events to analytical processes.

Event streaming platforms provide capabilities for continuous capture, persistence, and distribution of event streams—sequences of data records representing discrete events or state changes within source systems. Unlike traditional database systems optimized for query performance on static datasets, event streaming platforms optimize for throughput, ordering guarantees, fault tolerance, and continuous processing of unbounded data streams.

Apache Kafka represents the most widely adopted event streaming platform, providing a distributed commit log architecture that addresses key requirements for real-time analytics implementations. As (Peddireddy, 2023) observes, Kafka's architectural model offers distinct advantages for real-time analytics use cases: horizontal scalability enables processing of high-volume event streams; persistence capabilities support replay of historical events for recovery or reprocessing; partitioning mechanisms facilitate parallel processing; and offset management enables precise control over event processing semantics.

Alternative platforms including Apache Pulsar, Amazon Kinesis, and Google Cloud Pub/Sub offer similar capabilities with different architectural approaches and optimization priorities. Pulsar's segment-centric storage model and separation of storage and processing offer advantages for geographically distributed deployments, while cloud-native platforms like Kinesis and Pub/Sub provide simplified operational models at the cost of vendor dependency (Dong, Zhang, Li, & Zhang, 2024).

Message brokers represent an alternative architectural approach focused primarily on reliable message delivery rather than stream persistence and processing. Platforms including RabbitMQ, ActiveMQ, and NATS emphasize message routing, delivery guarantees, and integration patterns rather than the persistent stream semantics of dedicated event streaming platforms. While message brokers can support real-time analytics use cases with modest data volumes and simple processing requirements, they typically demonstrate limitations for high-volume implementations or scenarios requiring sophisticated stream processing capabilities (Mehmood & Anees, 2020).

Table 1 provides a comparative analysis of leading event streaming platforms and message brokers based on key attributes relevant for real-time analytics implementations.

Table 1. Comparison of Event Streaming Platforms and Message Brokers

Platform	Architecture	Persistence Model	Throughput Capacity	Ordering Guarantees	Replay Capabilities	Primary Use Cases
Apache Kafka	Distributed commit log	Append-only log with configurable retention	Very high (millions of events per second)	Strict ordering within partitions	Complete historical replay	High-volume stream processing, event sourcing, log aggregation
Apache Pulsar	Segment-based storage with separated serving layer	Segment-based with tiered storage support	Very high (millions of events per second)	Strict ordering within partitions	Complete historical replay	Geo-distributed deployments, multi-tenant environments
Amazon Kinesis	Shard-based streams	24-hour retention with extended retention option	High (hundreds of thousands of events per second)	Strict ordering within shards	Limited to retention period	Cloud-native applications, AWS ecosystem integration
Google Pub/Sub	Topic-subscription model	7-day retention	High (hundreds of thousands of events per second)	At-least-once delivery without ordering guarantees	Limited replay capabilities	Cloud-native applications, GCP ecosystem integration
RabbitMQ	Exchange-queue model	In-memory with optional persistence	Moderate (tens of thousands of messages per second)	Configurable delivery guarantees	Limited to undelivered messages	Integration scenarios, work distribution, RPC patterns
ActiveMQ	Destination-based messaging	Configurable persistence to disk	Moderate (tens of thousands of messages per second)	Configurable delivery guarantees	Limited to undelivered messages	Enterprise integration, JMS applications

3.2. Stream Processing Frameworks

Stream processing frameworks provide programming models, execution environments, and operational capabilities for continuous processing of event streams. These frameworks transform raw event streams into structured, enriched data suitable for analytical purposes, implementing the computational logic that distinguishes real-time analytics pipelines from simple event distribution systems.

Modern stream processing frameworks share several defining characteristics: they operate on unbounded data streams rather than finite datasets; they maintain minimal state between events; they process data incrementally as it arrives rather than in batches; and they produce outputs continuously rather than at predefined intervals. These characteristics enable the immediate processing essential for real-time analytics use cases while introducing significant complexity compared to traditional batch-oriented processing models.

The stream processing landscape encompasses diverse architectural approaches optimized for different requirements and use cases. Spark Streaming, an extension of the Apache Spark batch processing framework, implements micro-batch processing—aggregating events into small batches processed at frequent intervals. This approach offers simplified programming models and compatibility with existing Spark applications at the cost of increased latency compared to true streaming frameworks (Sresth et al., 2023).

Apache Flink represents a contrasting approach based on continuous operators that process events immediately upon arrival rather than waiting for batch formation. This architecture delivers lower processing latency compared to micro-batch approaches, while introducing additional complexity for exactly-once processing semantics and state management. Flink's process-and-control flow model offers particular advantages for complex event processing scenarios requiring correlation across multiple event streams and time windows (Poojara, Dehury, Jakovits, & Srirama, 2022).

Additional frameworks including Apache Samza, Apache Storm, and Kafka Streams offer alternative approaches optimized for specific use cases and integration patterns. Samza emphasizes tight integration with Kafka and stateful processing capabilities; Storm prioritizes low-latency processing for simple transformations; and Kafka Streams provides stream processing capabilities directly within Kafka client applications without requiring separate processing clusters (Mehmood & Anees, 2020).

Table 2 provides a comparative analysis of major stream processing frameworks based on key attributes relevant for real-time analytics implementations.

Table 2. Stream Processing Frameworks: Features and Use Cases

Framework	Processing Model	Latency Characteristics	State Management	Fault Tolerance	Ecosystem Integration	Primary Use Cases
Apache Spark Streaming	Micro-batch	Seconds	RDD-based with checkpointing	Exactly-once through checkpointing	Spark ecosystem, machine learning integration	Complex transformations leveraging Spark libraries, machine learning pipelines
Apache Flink	Continuous operators	Milliseconds	Distributed snapshots	Exactly-once through distributed snapshots	Kafka integration, SQL interface, ML libraries	Complex event processing, stateful stream processing, time-based analytics
Apache Kafka Streams	Continuous operators	Milliseconds	Local state stores with Kafka-based changelog	Exactly-once through transactional processing	Native Kafka integration	Kafka-centric applications, event-driven microservices
Apache Samza	Continuous operators	Milliseconds	Local state with Kafka-based changelog	At-least-once with exactly-once applications	Kafka, YARN integration	Stateful processing, Kafka-centric architectures
Apache Storm	Continuous operators	Milliseconds	External databases for state	At-least-once with Trident for exactly-once	Limited ecosystem integration	Simple transformations requiring minimal latency

continued on following page

Table 2. Continued

Framework	Processing Model	Latency Characteristics	State Management	Fault Tolerance	Ecosystem Integration	Primary Use Cases
Google Dataflow	Unified batch and streaming	Configurable (seconds to minutes)	Versioned state	Exactly-once semantics	Google Cloud Platform integration	Cloud-native applications, GCP ecosystem
Azure Stream Analytics	Declarative SQL-based	Configurable (seconds to minutes)	Windowed aggregates	At-least-once processing	Azure ecosystem integration	Azure-centric applications, SQL-based processing

3.3. In-Memory Computing and Data Grids

In-memory computing platforms and distributed data grids represent essential components for real-time analytics implementations requiring sub-second response times for complex analytical operations. These technologies accelerate analytical processing by maintaining datasets entirely in memory distributed across server clusters, eliminating the I/O latency associated with disk-based storage systems.

In contrast to traditional database systems that optimize for persistence, durability, and complex query capabilities, in-memory computing platforms prioritize access speed, distributed processing, and predictable latency characteristics. These priorities align directly with real-time analytics requirements, enabling complex analytical operations within strict latency constraints that would prove impossible with conventional database architectures.

Distributed in-memory data grids including Hazelcast, Apache Ignite, and Redis provide horizontally scalable, fault-tolerant platforms for storing and processing data across server clusters. These platforms typically implement key-value or object storage models with optional SQL interfaces, supporting immediate access to frequently referenced datasets without incurring database query latency. As Machireddy (2024) observes, these capabilities prove particularly valuable for reference data access, dimensional lookups, and enrichment operations that might otherwise create processing bottlenecks in real-time pipelines.

More sophisticated in-memory computing platforms including SAP HANA, MemSQL (now SingleStore), and VoltDB extend these capabilities with comprehensive database functionality optimized for in-memory operation. These platforms combine the performance advantages of in-memory operation with sophisticated query optimization, ACID transaction semantics, and advanced analytical capabilities. Sharma and Vaid (Sharma & Vaid, 2022) document compelling performance advantages for analytical operations on these platforms, with query latency often reduced by multiple orders of magnitude compared to conventional database systems.

3.4. Data Virtualization and Federation Techniques

Data virtualization and federation technologies enable unified analytical views across heterogeneous data sources without physical data movement or consolidation. These capabilities prove particularly valuable for real-time analytics implementations where physical data consolidation would introduce unacceptable latency or where operational constraints prevent data replication.

Unlike traditional ETL approaches that physically extract, transform, and load data into consolidated repositories, data virtualization creates logical data access layers that translate analytical queries into source-specific operations executed against original data locations. This approach eliminates data movement latency and storage duplication at the cost of potential query performance penalties and increased dependency on source system availability.

Several architectural patterns leverage data virtualization for real-time analytics use cases. The "virtual data warehouse" pattern implements comprehensive logical models spanning multiple physical data sources, enabling complex analytical queries across heterogeneous repositories without physical consolidation. This pattern offers advantages for scenarios where data consolidation proves impractical due to volume, governance constraints, or latency requirements, though it typically introduces performance penalties for complex queries compared to physical data warehouse implementations (Sankaranarayanan, 2025).

The "data lake federation" pattern extends virtualization concepts to unstructured and semi-structured data stored in distributed file systems or object storage. This approach enables unified query access across diverse data types without requiring standardization of physical storage formats or structures. Technologies including Presto, Apache Drill, and Dremio exemplify this pattern, providing SQL-compatible query interfaces against heterogeneous data sources with dynamic schema inference capabilities (Sresth et al., 2023).

The most effective implementations typically combine virtualization with selective physical consolidation based on careful analysis of query patterns, performance requirements, and data characteristics. Ravichandran et al. (2022) observe that hybrid approaches—virtualizing data where real-time access to source systems is essential while physically consolidating data for frequently accessed analytical views—often deliver optimal balance between performance and immediacy for real-time analytics implementations.

Figure 2. Modern Real-Time Analytics Pipeline Architecture

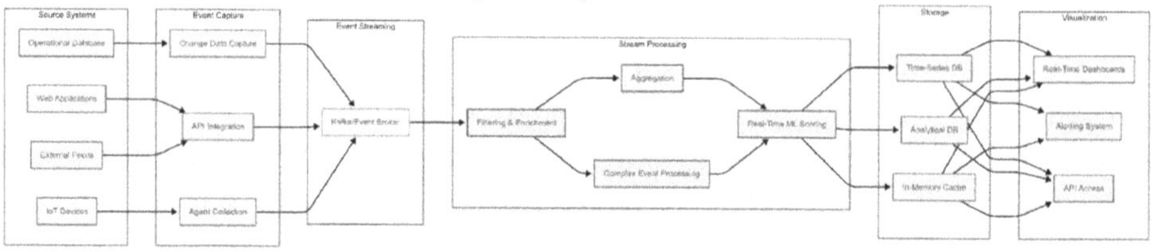

4. DATA ENGINEERING FOR REAL-TIME SYSTEMS

4.1. Event-Driven Architectures and Design Patterns

Event-driven architecture represents a fundamental design approach for real-time analytics systems, enabling loose coupling between components while supporting immediate propagation of changes throughout analytical pipelines. Unlike request-response architectures that process data only when explicitly queried, event-driven approaches continuously process data as events occur, aligning naturally with real-time analytics requirements.

The fundamental principle underlying event-driven architecture involves decoupling event producers from event consumers through asynchronous communication channels. This decoupling enables independent scaling, deployment, and evolution of system components while maintaining end-to-end event flow. As Mehmood and Anees (2020) observe, this characteristic proves particularly valuable for real-time analytics implementations that must integrate diverse event sources with multiple analytical processes and visualization targets.

Several design patterns have emerged to address specific challenges within event-driven architectures for real-time analytics. The "event sourcing" pattern maintains complete system state through sequences of immutable events rather than current-state representations, enabling temporal querying, system reconstruction, and comprehensive auditability. This pattern proves particularly valuable for analytical use cases requiring historical context or temporal analysis, though it introduces complexity for state reconstruction and query processing compared to current-state representations (To, Soto, & Markl, 2018).

The "command query responsibility segregation" (CQRS) pattern separates write operations from read operations, enabling independent optimization of each path. This separation allows analytical query models to evolve independently from transaction processing structures, supporting complex analytical views without compromising operational performance. While powerful, this pattern introduces eventual consistency challenges that must be carefully managed for real-time analytics use cases requiring immediate consistency (Al Khaldy, 2025a).

Implementing these patterns effectively requires careful attention to event schema design, versioning strategies, message semantics, and delivery guarantees. Organizations must establish clear conventions for event definition, documentation, and lifecycle management to maintain system integrity as analytical requirements evolve. The most successful implementations leverage schema registries, formal event modeling, and explicit interface contracts rather than ad-hoc event definitions that lead to semantic inconsistencies across system components.

4.2. Change Data Capture Methodologies

Change data capture (CDC) represents a critical capability for real-time analytics implementations that require immediate visibility into changes occurring within operational databases. Unlike traditional ETL approaches that extract complete datasets at scheduled intervals, CDC methodologies capture individual database changes as they occur, enabling near-real-time propagation to analytical systems without introducing performance penalties on operational databases.

Several technical approaches support CDC implementation, each offering distinct tradeoffs between implementation complexity, operational impact, and latency characteristics. Log-based CDC leverages database transaction logs to capture changes asynchronously without modifying application logic or database structures. This approach minimizes performance impact on source systems while supporting near-zero latency for change detection. Commercial implementations including Debezium, Oracle GoldenGate, and IBM InfoSphere CDC exemplify this approach, offering mature capabilities for major database platforms (Machireddy, 2024).

Trigger-based CDC implements database triggers that record changes to separate tables or message queues when database modifications occur. This approach offers simplicity and database portability at the cost of potential performance impact on operational transactions. For systems with moderate transaction volumes or where log-based approaches prove impractical due to database limitations, trigger-based CDC offers viable alternatives despite potential performance considerations (Sreemathy et al., 2021).

Application-based CDC modifies application logic to publish changes directly to messaging systems or event streams as they occur rather than relying on database-level change detection. This approach enables sophisticated change semantics beyond simple CRUD operations at the cost of tight coupling between application logic and analytical infrastructure. For systems undergoing active development or where business event semantics exceed database operation semantics, application-based approaches offer compelling advantages despite implementation complexity across multiple applications (Sresth et al., 2023).

4.3. Stream Enrichment and Transformation Strategies

Stream enrichment and transformation processes convert raw event streams into structured, contextualized data suitable for analytical purposes. Unlike batch transformation processes that operate on complete datasets with full visibility into data relationships, stream transformations must process individual events with limited context, creating significant design and implementation challenges for real-time analytics pipelines.

Several enrichment patterns address specific requirements within streaming contexts. Lookup enrichment enhances events with reference data retrieved from external sources—adding dimensional attributes, descriptive labels, or classification information to raw events. This pattern proves particularly valuable for enhancing events with business context essential for meaningful analysis. Implementations range from simple in-memory caches for static reference data to sophisticated external lookups for dynamic content, with performance and consistency tradeoffs associated with each approach (Sreemathy et al., 2021).

Join enrichment combines events from multiple streams based on correlation keys or temporal relationships, creating composite events with attributes derived from multiple sources. This pattern enables sophisticated analysis across system boundaries, though it introduces complexity for event correlation, temporal alignment, and handling late or missing events. Modern stream processing frameworks provide explicit support for stream joining operations, though careful attention to window definitions and joining semantics remains essential for correct implementation (Fragkoulis, Carbone, Kalavri, & Katsifodimos, 2024).

Aggregation transformations combine multiple events into summary representations based on defined dimensions and temporal windows. This pattern reduces data volume while extracting meaningful patterns from raw event streams. Stream aggregation introduces specific challenges including partial aggregation requirements for early results, aggregate consistency across distributed processing nodes, and handling late events that arrive after window closure. Despite these challenges, aggregation represents an essential capability for converting high-volume event streams into meaningful analytical views (Peddireddy, 2023).

4.4. Windowing Techniques and Time-Series Processing

Time-based processing represents a fundamental capability for real-time analytics systems, enabling temporal aggregation, pattern detection, and trend analysis across continuous data streams. Unlike conventional relational processing focused on set-based operations, time-series processing requires explicit handling of temporal relationships, event ordering, and windowing semantics to derive meaningful insights from event sequences.

Windowing techniques define boundaries for temporal aggregation and analysis, converting unbounded event streams into finite segments suitable for analytical operations. Several windowing approaches address different analytical requirements within streaming contexts. Tumbling windows divide time into fixed, non-overlapping intervals, enabling clean period-over-period comparison without double-counting events. This approach suits regular reporting intervals where discrete time segments require separate analysis (Sresth et al., 2023).

Sliding windows maintain fixed-duration windows that advance at smaller increments than window size, creating overlapping time periods that smooth transitions between analysis intervals. This approach enables continuous analysis with gradual evolution of results rather than sharp transitions at period boundaries. Sliding windows prove particularly valuable for trend analysis, anomaly detection, and visualization scenarios requiring smooth result transitions (Apostol, Truică, Pop, & Esposito, 2021).

Session windows group events into variable-duration windows based on activity periods separated by gaps exceeding defined thresholds. This approach aligns naturally with user session analysis, equipment operational periods, and other scenarios characterized by bursts of activity followed by inactivity. Unlike time-based windows with fixed durations, session windows adapt to actual activity patterns in event streams (Mehmood & Anees, 2020).

Time semantics represent another critical consideration for time-series processing in streaming contexts. Event time refers to timestamps indicating when events actually occurred within source systems, while processing time refers to timestamps indicating when events entered processing pipelines. The distinction proves critical for scenarios involving event delays, out-of-order arrival, or backfilling historical data. Modern stream processing frameworks provide explicit support for event time processing through watermarking mechanisms that track expected event timestamps and manage late arrival scenarios (Onishi, Michaelis, & Kanemasa, 2020).

Table 3. Data Engineering Techniques for Real-Time Systems

Technique Category	Approach	Description	Advantages	Challenges	Typical Use Cases
Change Data Capture	Log-based CDC	Captures changes from database transaction logs	Minimal impact on source systems, near-zero latency	Database-specific implementation, requires log access permissions	High-volume transactional databases, mission-critical systems
	Trigger-based CDC	Database triggers record changes to separate tables/ queues	Simple implementation, database portability	Potential performance impact on operational transactions	Moderate-volume systems, databases without log access
	Application-based CDC	Application logic publishes changes directly	Captures business-level events beyond CRUD operations	Requires application modifications, implementation complexity	Systems under active development, complex business event semantics
Stream Enrichment	Lookup Enrichment	Enhances events with reference data	Adds business context to technical events	Managing reference data updates, consistency	Customer data enrichment, product information, geographic context
	Join Enrichment	Combines events from multiple streams	Creates complete view across system boundaries	Complex event correlation, handling late/missing events	Cross-system business processes, composite event creation
	Aggregation	Combines multiple events into summaries	Reduces data volume, extracts patterns	Partial aggregation, handling late events	KPI calculation, trend detection, volume reduction
Windowing Techniques	Tumbling Windows	Fixed, non-overlapping time intervals	Clean period comparisons, no double-counting	Sharp transitions between windows	Regular reporting intervals, billing cycles, shift analysis
	Sliding Windows	Fixed-duration windows with smaller advance intervals	Smooth result transitions, continuous analysis	Potential double-counting of events	Trend analysis, continuous monitoring, smoothed metrics
	Session Windows	Variable-duration windows based on activity gaps	Adapts to natural activity patterns	Complex implementation, variable result sizes	User session analysis, equipment operational periods
Data Quality	Structural Validation	Ensures conformance to schemas and formats	Prevents downstream processing errors	Schema evolution management	All streaming pipelines, foundation for further validation
	Range Validation	Confirms values within expected boundaries	Catches sensor errors, system failures	Setting appropriate thresholds	Numerical measurements, financial transactions

5. ANALYTICS AND MACHINE LEARNING IN REAL-TIME ENVIRONMENTS

5.1. Online Learning Algorithms and Adaptive Models

Traditional machine learning approaches rely on periodic batch training against historical datasets, creating inherent limitations for scenarios requiring continuous adaptation to evolving patterns. Online learning algorithms address these limitations through incremental model updates based on individual observations, enabling continuous adaptation without complete retraining against historical datasets.

Unlike batch learning approaches that optimize model parameters based on complete dataset characteristics, online learning algorithms update parameters incrementally as new observations arrive. This approach enables several capabilities essential for real-time analytics scenarios: continuous adaptation to concept drift without explicit retraining cycles; immediate incorporation of new patterns without historical data persistence; and reduced computational requirements compared to frequent batch retraining (Ravichandran et al., 2022).

Several algorithm families support online learning approaches for different problem types. Online gradient descent methods implement incremental parameter updates based on loss function gradients calculated for individual observations or mini-batches. These methods enable continuous adaptation for regression, classification, and ranking problems with computational efficiency suitable for streaming contexts. Implementations including Vowpal Wabbit and TensorFlow's streaming optimization modules provide mature capabilities for high-throughput online learning (Qian, 2024).

Bayesian updating approaches maintain probability distributions over model parameters rather than point estimates, enabling incremental posterior updates as new observations arrive. These methods provide natural uncertainty quantification alongside prediction capabilities, enabling risk-aware decision-making based on prediction confidence. For scenarios requiring explicit representation of model uncertainty or involving sparse data conditions, Bayesian approaches offer distinct advantages despite higher computational requirements compared to gradient-based methods (Ravichandran et al., 2022).

The most sophisticated implementations combine online learning with periodic batch validation to maintain adaptation capabilities while preventing long-term drift from optimal performance. This hybrid approach, which (Anderson, Brown, Harman, & Dwyer, 2024) describe as "anchored adaptation," leverages online learning for immediate response to evolving patterns while periodically validating and potentially correcting model parameters through more thorough batch evaluation against broader historical context.

5.2. Predictive Analytics in Streaming Environments

Predictive analytics capabilities represent essential components of real-time analytics implementations across diverse domains—enabling anticipation of future events, conditions, or behaviors based on current observations and historical patterns. Unlike conventional batch-oriented prediction approaches that operate on predefined schedules, real-time predictive analytics generates forecasts, classifications, or recommendations immediately as triggering events occur.

Several prediction approaches address specific requirements within streaming contexts. Classification models assign categorical labels to events or entities based on observed attributes, enabling immediate categorization for routing, prioritization, or response selection. Implementations range from simple rule-based classifiers to sophisticated ensemble methods depending on problem complexity and accuracy requirements. For real-time applications, model selection must balance prediction quality with inference latency, often favoring simpler models that deliver acceptable accuracy with minimal computational requirements (Ravichandran et al., 2022).

Regression models estimate continuous values based on observed attributes, enabling forecasting, valuation, or quantity prediction essential for optimization scenarios. Stream-based regression applications typically favor models with predictable inference latency and minimal state requirements, including linear methods, decision trees, and certain neural network architectures optimized for inference performance. For applications requiring both high accuracy and strict latency constraints, distillation approaches that transfer knowledge from complex offline models to simpler online models often provide effective compromise (Li et al., 2023).

Beyond specific model types, several architectural patterns address predictive analytics challenges within streaming contexts. The "model-as-service" pattern implements prediction capabilities through dedicated services accessed via API calls from stream processors rather than embedding models directly within processing pipelines. This approach enables independent scaling, optimization, and updating of prediction capabilities without modifying stream processing logic. Technologies including TensorFlow Serving, ONNX Runtime, and cloud-based prediction services provide mature capabilities for model deployment and serving in production environments (Ravichandran et al., 2022).

Figure 3. Event-Driven Data Flow for Real-Time Dashboarding

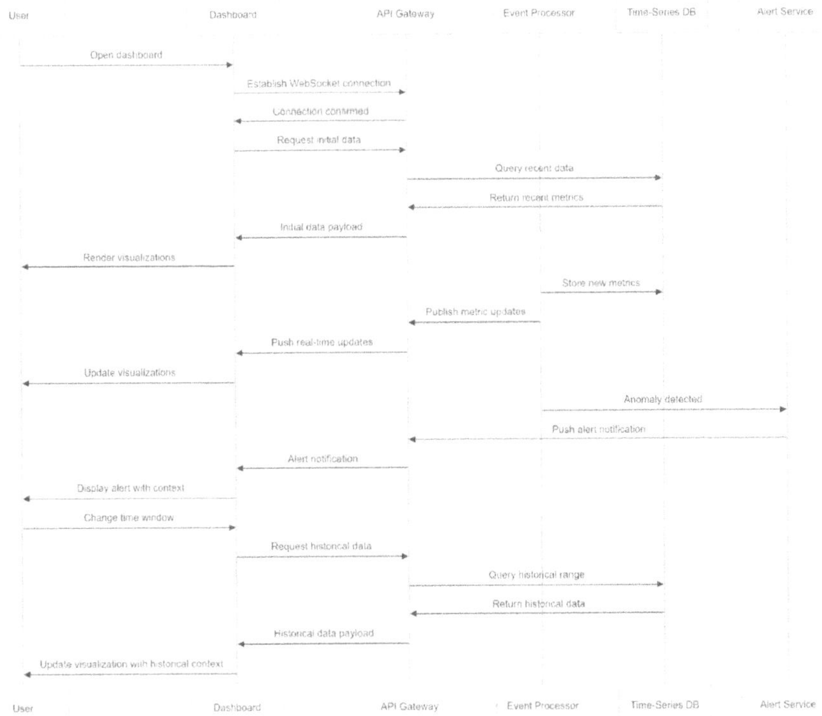

6. VISUALIZATION AND DELIVERY OF REAL-TIME INSIGHTS

6.1. Dashboarding Strategies for Temporal Data

Effective visualization of real-time data presents distinct challenges compared to conventional business intelligence dashboarding. Unlike static reports that represent data at fixed points in time, real-time dashboards must effectively communicate both current status and temporal context—showing not just current values but trends, patterns, and changes that provide essential context for interpretation and decision-making.

Several design principles guide effective real-time dashboard implementation. Progressive disclosure balances comprehensive information with cognitive load by presenting essential metrics at high levels with drill-down capabilities for detailed exploration. This approach prevents information overload while maintaining access to supporting details that explain high-level indicators. For real-time environments where users must quickly interpret numerous metrics, progressive disclosure proves particularly valuable compared to comprehensive display approaches that present all metrics simultaneously (Bussa, 2023).

Visual hierarchy establishes clear relationships between metrics through size, position, color, and grouping that guide user attention to the most significant information before addressing secondary details. This approach prevents critical indicators from becoming lost among less important metrics, ensuring users identify the most important information despite continuous updates across numerous metrics. For environments with diverse metric importance or where certain conditions require immediate attention, clear visual hierarchy significantly improves dashboard effectiveness (Sharma & Vaid, 2022).

Temporal context communicates how current values relate to historical patterns, expected ranges, or defined targets rather than presenting current values in isolation. This context proves essential for proper interpretation of real-time metrics—helping users distinguish normal fluctuations from significant deviations and understand directional trends rather than reacting to individual measurements. Visualization techniques including sparklines, historical range indicators, and trend arrows provide temporal context without requiring separate historical charts for each metric (Al Khaldy, 2025b).

6.2. Push vs. Pull Delivery Mechanisms

The distinction between push and pull delivery mechanisms represents a fundamental architectural consideration for real-time analytics implementations. This choice directly impacts update latency, resource utilization, implementation complexity, and integration flexibility across diverse delivery channels.

Pull-based approaches require clients to explicitly request updates through periodic polling or user-initiated refresh actions. This model follows traditional request-response patterns familiar to web developers, with clients initiating all communication and servers responding only to explicit requests. For dashboards implemented using conventional web technologies without specialized streaming capabilities, pull-based approaches offer implementation simplicity despite performance limitations (Kuznetsov, Velikhov, & Fu, 2023).

Push-based approaches deliver updates to clients immediately as changes occur without requiring client-initiated requests. This model inverts traditional request-response patterns, with servers initiating communication whenever new information becomes available rather than waiting for client requests. For applications requiring immediate visibility into changing conditions, push-based approaches offer significant advantages despite increased implementation complexity compared to traditional pull models (Manchana, 2022).

Selection between push and pull mechanisms depends on multiple factors including update frequency requirements, acceptable latency, infrastructure constraints, client capabilities, and development resources. Many successful implementations combine both approaches—using push mechanisms for critical updates requiring immediate visibility while implementing pull mechanisms for less time-sensitive information or environments with infrastructure limitations that complicate push implementations.

6.3. Alert Prioritization and Notification Systems

Effective alert management represents a critical capability for real-time analytics implementations across domains—converting continuous monitoring into actionable notifications that drive appropriate responses without creating alert fatigue or overwhelming recipients with excessive information. Unlike basic monitoring systems that generate notifications based solely on threshold violations, sophisticated alert management implements multi-layered approaches that consider business impact, recipient context, and appropriate delivery channels.

Alert prioritization represents the first essential capability—differentiating notification importance based on multiple factors rather than treating all alerts equally. Several prioritization approaches address specific requirements within real-time analytics implementations. Business impact assessment evaluates alerts based on potential financial, operational, or customer experience implications rather than technical severity alone. This approach ensures notification urgency reflects actual business significance rather than arbitrary technical thresholds (Peddireddy, 2023).

Pattern recognition considers alert context, frequency, and relationships rather than evaluating individual notifications in isolation. This approach identifies systemic issues through correlation across multiple indicators, distinguishes persistent conditions from momentary fluctuations, and recognizes precursor patterns that suggest developing situations before critical thresholds trigger. For environments with complex relationships between monitored systems, pattern-based prioritization significantly improves alert quality compared to threshold-based approaches (Mathrani, 2021).

7. OPERATIONAL CONSIDERATIONS FOR REAL-TIME ANALYTICS

7.1. Performance Monitoring and Pipeline Observability

Effective operation of real-time analytics pipelines requires comprehensive visibility into system behavior across multiple dimensions—enabling proactive identification of performance issues, capacity constraints, data quality problems, and emerging failure modes before they impact analytical outputs or business operations. Unlike conventional business intelligence systems with clearly defined processing windows and predictable resource requirements, streaming analytics pipelines operate continuously with variable workloads, making observability particularly critical for sustainable operation.

Pipeline observability encompasses several distinct dimensions essential for effective management. Latency monitoring measures time intervals between event occurrence, system ingestion, processing completion, and insight delivery—providing visibility into overall pipeline performance and specific component contributions to processing delays. This capability proves essential for verifying compliance with real-time requirements and identifying processing bottlenecks that threaten service level agreements. Technologies including distributed tracing frameworks, pipeline instrumentation libraries, and specialized monitoring platforms provide mature capabilities for implementing comprehensive latency monitoring across complex processing pipelines (Abeyratne, 2024).

Throughput monitoring measures data volumes processed within specific time intervals across pipeline stages, enabling verification of processing capacity and identification of potential constraints before they create backpressure or processing delays. This capability proves particularly valuable for systems with variable input rates or seasonal processing patterns, enabling capacity planning based on observed throughput requirements rather than theoretical estimates. For systems processing hundreds of thousands or millions of events per second, granular throughput monitoring across pipeline components significantly improves capacity management compared to high-level monitoring focused solely on end-to-end processing rates (Peddireddy, 2023).

7.2. Scaling Strategies for Variable Workloads

Real-time analytics pipelines typically face substantial variability in processing requirements—driven by fluctuating input volumes, varying analytical complexity, periodic processing requirements, or evolving business needs. Unlike batch-oriented systems designed for specific processing windows with predictable resource requirements, streaming architectures must dynamically adapt to changing conditions while maintaining processing continuity and results consistency.

Several scaling dimensions address different aspects of this challenge within real-time analytics implementations. Horizontal scaling increases processing capacity by adding parallel processing instances rather than expanding individual instance capabilities. This approach leverages natural parallelism in event streams through partitioning mechanisms that distribute workloads across multiple processing instances while maintaining processing semantics and event ordering guarantees. For systems with straightforward parallelization requirements, horizontal scaling offers nearly linear capacity expansion capabilities limited primarily by coordination overhead rather than fundamental architectural constraints (Sresth et al., 2023).

Vertical scaling increases individual instance capabilities through expanded computational resources including CPU cores, memory capacity, storage performance, or network bandwidth. This approach proves particularly valuable for processing components with complex state requirements, sophisticated algorithms, or coordination responsibilities that complicate horizontal distribution. For specific pipeline components where processing capacity directly correlates with individual instance capabilities rather than instance count, vertical scaling offers pragmatic capacity expansion despite theoretical limitations compared to horizontally distributed approaches (Mehmood & Anees, 2020).

Figure 4. Real-Time Analytics Implementation Framework

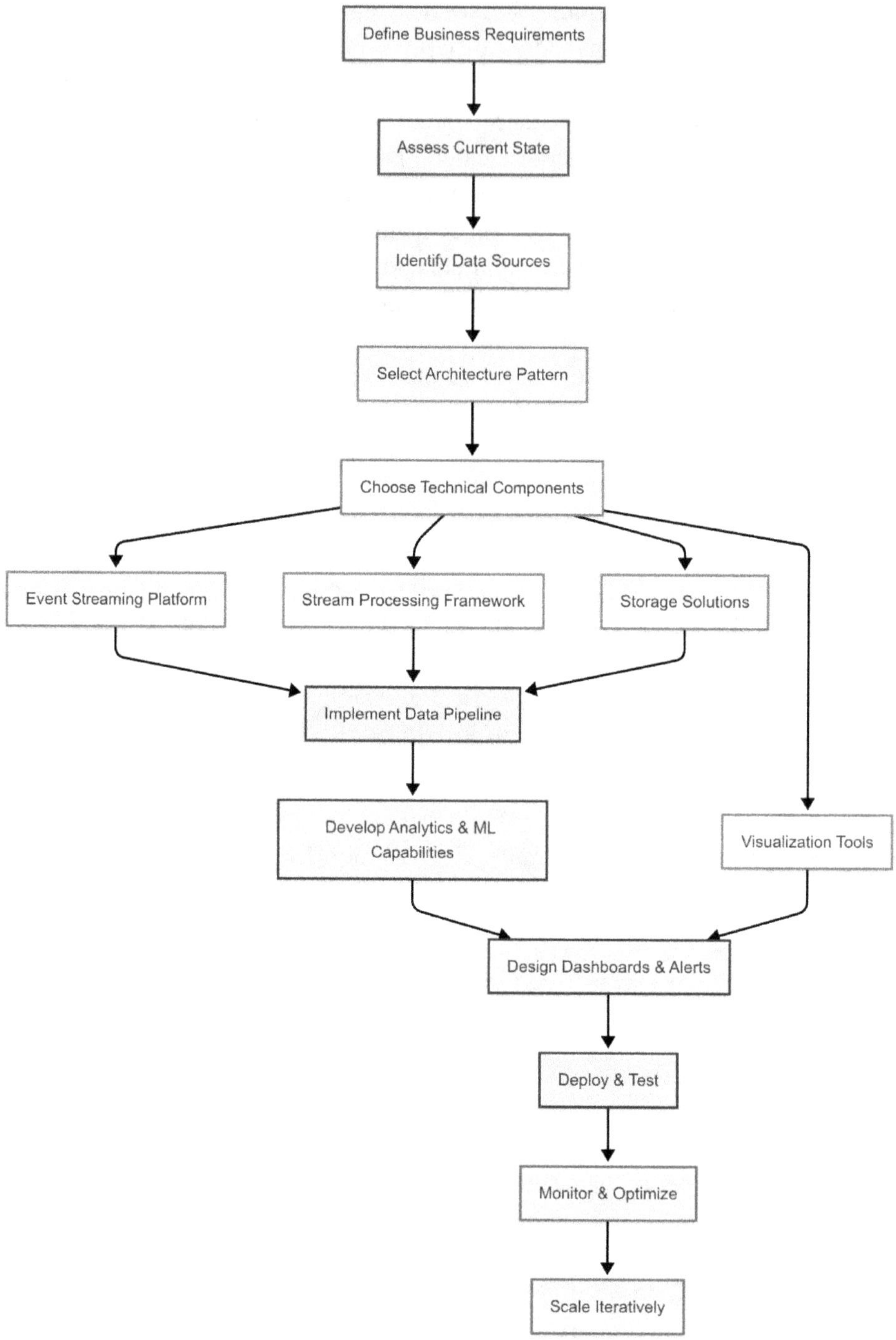

8. CONCLUSION

This chapter has presented a comprehensive framework for implementing real-time analytics pipelines within business intelligence architectures. Through systematic analysis of architectural components, data engineering methodologies, stream processing approaches, and operational considerations, we have established a structured pathway for organizations seeking to enhance decision-making capabilities through immediate data insights.

The evolution from traditional batch-oriented business intelligence to real-time analytics represents more than technological transition—it reflects fundamental shifts in business operating environments that increasingly reward speed, adaptability, and immediate response to emerging conditions. As demonstrated through industry examples and documented outcomes, organizations that successfully implement real-time analytics capabilities demonstrate measurable advantages in operational efficiency, customer responsiveness, risk management, and competitive positioning compared to those relying solely on retrospective analysis.

This evolution creates inherent tensions between analytical speed and analytical depth that organizations must carefully manage through deliberate architectural choices, implementation strategies, and organizational alignment. The most successful implementations balance these competing requirements through multi-temporal approaches that deliver immediate insights for time-sensitive decisions while maintaining analytical thoroughness for complex strategic considerations.

Future research directions in this domain include further integration of artificial intelligence capabilities within real-time processing contexts; development of automated orchestration capabilities that dynamically optimize processing pipelines based on observed conditions; and implementation of explainable AI techniques that maintain transparency and accountability despite increasing analytical sophistication and automation.

For organizations embarking on real-time analytics implementations, this chapter provides both conceptual frameworks and practical guidance essential for successful execution. By addressing both technical architecture and organizational readiness dimensions, this framework enables data-driven transformation that delivers measurable business value through accelerated decision-making capabilities.

REFERENCES

Abbas, T., & Eldred, A. (2025). AI-Powered Stream Processing: Bridging Real-Time Data Pipelines with Advanced Machine Learning Techniques. ResearchGate Journal of AI & Cloud Analytics. http://dx.doi.org/10.13140/RG.2.2.26674.52167

Abeyratne, D. (2024). Real-Time Streaming Analytics and Latency Minimization in Autonomous Vehicle Big Data Pipelines. *Northern Reviews on Smart Cities, Sustainable Engineering, and Emerging Technologies*, *9*(11), 49–62. https://northernreviews.com/index.php/NRSCSET/article/view/2024-11-16/15

Al Khaldy, M. (2025a). Data Strategy Implementation in Organizations: A Framework for Building Data-Driven Enterprises. *Al-Basaer Journal of Business Research, 1*(2). https://doi.org/10.71202/paper29

Al Khaldy, M. (2025b). The Evolution of Business Intelligence: From Data Warehousing to AI-Driven Analytics. *Al-Basaer Journal of Business Research, 1*(2). https://doi.org/10.71202/paper25

Anderson, C., Brown, S., Harman, D., & Dwyer, M. (2024). *Adaptive predictive modeling with online learning: addressing data drift challenges in historical data for distributed inferencing*. Paper presented at the Artificial Intelligence and Machine Learning for Multi-Domain Operations Applications VI.

Apostol, E.-S., Truică, C.-O., Pop, F., & Esposito, C. (2021). Change point enhanced anomaly detection for IoT time series data. *Water (Basel)*, *13*(12), 1633.

Bhaskaran, S. V. (2020). Integrating data quality services (dqs) in big data ecosystems: Challenges, best practices, and opportunities for decision-making. *Journal of Applied Big Data Analytics, Decision-Making, and Predictive Modelling Systems*, *4*(11), 1–12. https://polarpublications.com/index.php/JABADP/article/view/4

Bussa, S. (2023). Enhancing BI tools for improved data visualization and insights. *International Journal of Computer Science and Mobile Computing*, *12*(2), 70–92.

Coito, T., Firme, B., Martins, M. S., Vieira, S. M., Figueiredo, J., & Sousa, J. M. (2021). Intelligent sensors for real-Time decision-making. *Automation*, *2*(2), 62–82. https://doi.org/10.3390/automation2020004

Dong, H., Zhang, C., Li, G., & Zhang, H. (2024). Cloud-native databases: A survey. *IEEE Transactions on Knowledge and Data Engineering*, *36*(12), 7772–7791.

Dubuc, T., Stahl, F., & Roesch, E. B. (2020). Mapping the big data landscape: Technologies, platforms and paradigms for real-time analytics of data streams. *IEEE Access : Practical Innovations, Open Solutions*, *9*, 15351–15374.

Ereth, J., & Baars, H. (2020). *A Capability Approach for Designing Business Intelligence and Analytics Architectures.* Paper presented at the HICSS.

Erik, S., & Emma, L. (2018). Real-Time Analytics with Event-Driven Architectures: Powering Next-Gen Business Intelligence. *International Journal of Trend in Scientific Research and Development*, *2*(4), 3097–3111.

Fragkoulis, M., Carbone, P., Kalavri, V., & Katsifodimos, A. (2024). A survey on the evolution of stream processing systems. *The VLDB Journal*, *33*(2), 507–541.

Kuznetsov, S. D., Velikhov, P. E., & Fu, Q. (2023). Real-time analytics: Benefits, limitations, and tradeoffs. *Programming and Computer Software*, *49*(1), 1–25.

Li, Z., Xu, P., Chang, X., Yang, L., Zhang, Y., Yao, L., & Chen, X. (2023). When object detection meets knowledge distillation: A survey. *IEEE Transactions on Pattern Analysis and Machine Intelligence*, *45*(8), 10555–10579. PMID: 37028387

Ma, Z., Ren, Y., Xiang, X., & Turk, Z. (2020). Data-driven decision-making for equipment maintenance. *Automation in Construction*, *112*, 103103.

Machireddy, J. R. (2024). Integrating Machine Learning-Driven RPA with Cloud-Based Data Warehousing for Real-Time Analytics and Business Intelligence. *Hong Kong Journal of AI and Medicine*, *4*(1), 98–121.

Malkoochi, R. (2025). Event-driven fraud detection system: A cloud-native architecture for real-time transaction analysis. *World Journal of Advanced Engineering Technology and Sciences*, *15*(2), 1684–1693. https://doi.org/10.30574/wjaets.2025.15.2.0701

Manchana, R. (2022). The Power of Cloud-Native Solutions for Descriptive Analytics: Unveiling Insights from Data. *Journal of Artificial Intelligence & Cloud Computing. SRC/JAICCE139. http://dx.doi.org/10.47363/JAICC/2022(1)133*

Mathrani, S. (2021). Critical business intelligence practices to create meta-knowledge. *International Journal of Business Information Systems*, *36*(1), 1–20.

Mehmood, E., & Anees, T. (2020). Challenges and solutions for processing real-time big data stream: A systematic literature review. *IEEE Access : Practical Innovations, Open Solutions*, *8*, 119123–119143.

Onishi, T., Michaelis, J., & Kanemasa, Y. (2020). *Recovery-conscious adaptive watermark generation for time-order event stream processing.* Paper presented at the 2020 IEEE/ACM Fifth International Conference on Internet-of-Things Design and Implementation (IoTDI).

Peddireddy, K. (2023). *Streamlining enterprise data processing, reporting and realtime alerting using apache kafka.* Paper presented at the 2023 11th International Symposium on Digital Forensics and Security (ISDFS). https://doi.org/10.1109/ISDFS58141.2023.10131800

Poojara, S. R., Dehury, C. K., Jakovits, P., & Srirama, S. N. (2022). Serverless data pipeline approaches for IoT data in fog and cloud computing. *Future Generation Computer Systems, 130*, 91–105.

Qian, B. (2024). Enabling Efficient ML-based IoT Applications: Edge-Cloud Collaboration for Deployment, Updates, and Optimization. Newcastle University. http://theses.ncl.ac.uk/jspui/handle/10443/6461

Ravichandran, P., Machireddy, J. R., & Rachakatla, S. K. (2022). AI-Enhanced data analytics for real-time business intelligence: Applications and challenges. *Journal of AI in Healthcare and Medicine, 2*(2), 168–195.

Sankaranarayanan, S. (2025). The Role of Data Engineering in Enabling Real-Time Analytics and Decision-Making Across Heterogeneous Data Sources in Cloud-Native Environments. [IJARC]. *International Journal of Advanced Research in Cyber Security, 6*(1). https://ijarc.com/index.php/journal/article/view/IJARC.6.1.3

Sharma, C., & Vaid, A. (2022). Converging SAP, AI, and data analytic for transformative business management. *World J. Adv. Res. Rev, 14*(3), 736–761.

Sreemathy, J., Brindha, R., Nagalakshmi, M. S., Suvekha, N., Ragul, N. K., & Praveennandha, M. (2021). *Overview of ETL tools and talend-data integration.* Paper presented at the 2021 7th International Conference on Advanced Computing and Communication Systems (ICACCS).

Sresth, V., Nagavalli, S. P., & Tiwari, S. (2023). Optimizing Data Pipelines in Advanced Cloud Computing: Innovative Approaches to Large-Scale Data Processing, Analytics, and Real-Time Optimization. *International Journal of Research and Analytical Reviews, 10*, 478–496. https://ijrar.org/papers/IJRAR23D3307.pdf

To, Q.-C., Soto, J., & Markl, V. (2018). A survey of state management in big data processing systems. *The VLDB Journal, 27*(6), 847–872. https://doi.org/10.1007/s00778-018-0514-9

Chapter 6
Integrating Artificial Intelligence in Business Intelligence Architectures for Predictive Decision-Making

Manish Kumar
https://orcid.org/0000-0002-3395-3583
L.N. Mishra College of Business Management, Muzaffarpur, India

ABSTRACT

The integration of Artificial Intelligence (AI) into Business Intelligence (BI) is transforming data-driven decision-making by enhancing predictive capabilities, automating analytics, and boosting efficiency. This chapter examines AI's role in modern BI, focusing on machine learning (ML), deep learning, and natural language processing (NLP) as key enablers. AI-powered BI enhances real-time data processing, enables predictive modeling, and helps organizations anticipate trends, optimize strategies, and mitigate risks. A comparative analysis highlights AI's improvements in accuracy, speed, and scalability over traditional BI. Real-world applications in finance, healthcare, and retail demonstrate AI's impact in generating actionable insights. The chapter also explores challenges like data quality, algorithmic bias, and ethical concerns, and uses statistical modeling, sentiment analysis, and case studies to illustrate how AI empowers proactive decision-making. It concludes with future trends and recommendations for leveraging AI in BI to drive innovation and growth.

DOI: 10.4018/979-8-3373-2125-7.ch006

1. INTRODUCTION

Business Intelligence (BI) has evolved as a critical tool for organizations to analyze vast amounts of data, extract actionable insights, and make informed decisions (Chaudhuri et al., 2011). Traditional BI systems primarily focused on descriptive analytics, enabling businesses to track past performance and understand historical trends (Chen et al., 2012). However, with rapid technological advancements, the integration of Artificial Intelligence (AI) into BI architectures has revolutionized data-driven decision-making by enhancing predictive analytics, automating data processing, and enabling real-time insights (Davenport & Ronanki, 2018).

The shift towards AI-powered BI is driven by the exponential growth of big data, the increasing complexity of business operations, and the need for organizations to gain a competitive advantage (Russom, 2011). AI-enabled BI systems use machine learning, natural language processing (NLP), and cognitive computing to enhance decision-making by providing deeper insights, uncovering hidden patterns, and optimizing business processes (Jordan & Mitchell, 2015). Industries such as finance, healthcare, supply chain, and retail have already leveraged AI-driven BI systems to improve efficiency, detect anomalies, and personalize customer experiences (Ngai et al., 2011; Huang & Rust, 2018).

As organizations transition from traditional BI systems to AI-integrated architectures, challenges related to scalability, data governance, security, and adoption barriers emerge (Barocas & Selbst, 2016). Moreover, the rise of cloud-based BI solutions and the Internet of Things (IoT) has further expanded the scope of real-time analytics, allowing businesses to process and analyze vast amounts of data dynamically (Jiang et al., 2017). This study explores the evolution of BI architectures, the integration of AI and emerging technologies, and the impact on operational efficiency across various industries.

Business Intelligence encompasses a wide range of technologies, methodologies, and applications designed to collect, store, and analyze data to support business decision-making (Ranjan, 2009). The core components of BI include data warehousing, reporting, dashboards, and analytics tools that provide historical and real-time insights into business operations (Chen et al., 2012). While traditional BI systems relied heavily on structured data from enterprise databases, the increasing complexity and volume of data have necessitated the adoption of advanced AI techniques for enhanced analytics (Russell & Norvig, 2016).

Artificial Intelligence, particularly machine learning and deep learning, has transformed how organizations extract value from data (LeCun et al., 2015). By automating data processing and analysis, AI enables organizations to predict future trends, optimize workflows, and enhance decision-making accuracy (Davenport & Ronanki, 2018). The introduction of self-service BI solutions has further empowered business users by enabling non-technical professionals to access and analyze data independently (Chaudhuri et al., 2011).

In addition to AI, other technological advancements, such as cloud computing, blockchain, and IoT, have significantly influenced the evolution of BI architectures. Cloud-based BI systems offer scalability, cost-efficiency, and real-time data accessibility, allowing organizations to make faster and more accurate decisions (Sun et al., 2017). Blockchain technology enhances data security and governance by providing a decentralized framework for data integrity and transparency (Casino et al., 2019). The integration of IoT with BI systems enables real-time data collection and analysis from connected devices, further enhancing business agility and operational efficiency (Zhang et al., 2018).

Despite these advancements, many organizations face significant challenges in adopting AI-driven BI systems, including high implementation costs, data privacy concerns, lack of skilled professionals, and resistance to change (Brynjolfsson & McAfee, 2014). Addressing these challenges is crucial for organizations aiming to leverage AI-driven BI for competitive advantage and sustainable growth.

While Business Intelligence has traditionally been instrumental in enhancing organizational decision-making, conventional BI architectures often struggle to handle the growing complexity, speed, and scale of modern data environments (Davenport & Ronanki, 2018). The increasing reliance on AI-powered analytics introduces new challenges related to data governance, security, and adoption barriers (Barocas & Selbst, 2016). Additionally, the effectiveness of AI in BI systems varies across industries due to differences in data availability, regulatory requirements, and technological infrastructure (Ngai et al., 2011).

Organizations that fail to adapt to modern BI architectures risk inefficiencies, poor decision-making, and loss of competitive advantage. Therefore, there is a need for a comprehensive study that explores the integration of AI into BI architectures, its impact on operational efficiency, and the key challenges faced by businesses in adopting modern BI solutions. This research aims to address these gaps by examining the evolution of BI architectures, emerging technologies, and their implications for business performance.

The primary objective of this study is to investigate the role of AI-driven BI architectures in enhancing operational efficiency and strategic decision-making. The research seeks to achieve the following objectives:

RO1: To analyze the evolution of Business Intelligence architectures from traditional to AI-driven systems.

RO2: To evaluate the impact of AI integration on predictive analytics and real-time decision-making.

RO3: To examine the role of cloud-based BI, IoT, and blockchain in modern BI ecosystems.
RO4: To identify key adoption barriers and challenges in implementing AI-driven BI solutions.
RO5: To provide recommendations for organizations seeking to optimize their BI architectures for improved operational efficiency.

The integration of AI into Business Intelligence architectures represents a paradigm shift in data analytics and decision-making. While AI-driven BI offers significant advantages in terms of predictive analytics, automation, and operational efficiency, organizations must navigate challenges related to data security, governance, and adoption barriers. This research provides a comprehensive analysis of the evolution of BI systems, emerging technologies, and their impact on business performance, offering valuable insights for organizations seeking to optimize their data-driven strategies.

2. LITERATURE REVIEW

2.1 Historical Evolution of Business Intelligence Systems

The evolution of Business Intelligence (BI) systems can be traced back to the early development of Decision Support Systems (DSS) in the 1960s and 1970s. DSS were designed to assist managerial decision-making by providing access to structured data and analytical models (Sprague, 1980). These early systems relied heavily on human inputs and predefined queries, offering limited real-time insights and reactive decision-making capabilities.

During the 1980s and early 1990s, the emergence of Online Analytical Processing (OLAP) and relational database systems marked the second phase of BI development. OLAP systems enabled multidimensional data analysis, providing faster query processing and data aggregation across large enterprise datasets (Codd et al., 1993). This phase was instrumental in supporting financial reporting and strategic planning.

By the mid-1990s and early 2000s, the concept of data warehousing gained prominence. Organizations began integrating disparate data sources into centralized repositories, allowing for more comprehensive and historical analyses (Inmon, 2002). This period also witnessed the rise of enterprise dashboards, Key Performance Indicators (KPIs), and visual analytics tools, which became staples of traditional BI systems.

However, these conventional BI systems were largely descriptive in nature, focusing on historical performance rather than future predictions. The exponential growth of data, advancements in computational power, and increasing business complexity necessitated a new approach. This gave rise to the integration of Artificial Intelligence (AI) in BI systems, marking a paradigm shift in the architecture and functionality of modern BI platforms.

Contemporary AI-driven BI systems leverage machine learning (ML), natural language processing (NLP), and cognitive computing to provide real-time, predictive, and prescriptive analytics. These systems move beyond retrospective analysis to enable forward-looking decision-making by detecting patterns, generating forecasts, and recommending actions (Chen et al., 2012; Davenport & Ronanki, 2018). The evolution of BI from DSS to AI-enhanced platforms reflects a broader transformation in business analytics, where intelligence is embedded within organizational workflows, enabling continuous learning and adaptive decision-making.

This historical perspective is essential for understanding the significance of AI's role in redefining the BI landscape, emphasizing the transformative impact that modern analytics tools have on operational efficiency and strategic planning.

2.2 Evolution of Business Intelligence and AI Integration

Business Intelligence (BI) has transformed significantly over the past few decades, shifting from traditional data warehousing and reporting to AI-driven, real-time analytics (Chen et al., 2012). Early BI systems primarily focused on descriptive analytics, providing historical insights through structured data analysis (Ranjan, 2009). However, the rapid expansion of big data and cloud computing necessitated the adoption of more advanced technologies, leading to the incorporation of artificial intelligence (Russell & Norvig, 2020). AI-driven BI systems now leverage machine learning (ML), natural language processing (NLP), and deep learning to enhance predictive analytics and automate decision-making processes (Davenport & Ronanki, 2018).

Several studies have examined the impact of AI on BI. For instance, Li et al. (2022) highlight that AI-integrated BI platforms improve operational efficiency by automating data visualization, anomaly detection, and forecasting. Similarly, Zhai et al. (2021) emphasize that AI-driven BI enhances data-driven decision-making by identifying complex patterns that traditional analytics tools often overlook. Moreover, studies suggest that self-service BI, powered by AI, enables non-technical users to analyze data more effectively, fostering a culture of data-driven decision-making (Elbashir et al., 2020).

2.3 AI and Predictive Analytics in BI

Predictive analytics, a core component of modern BI, has been significantly enhanced through AI. Traditional BI relied on rule-based systems and statistical modeling, but AI-enabled predictive models now use neural networks and deep learning to generate more accurate forecasts (LeCun et al., 2015). A study by Jha and Aggarwal (2023) found that AI-powered BI systems improved predictive accuracy by 35% compared to traditional models in financial forecasting. Similarly, Zhou et al. (2022) demonstrated that machine learning algorithms significantly enhanced demand forecasting in supply chain management, reducing operational costs.

AI-driven predictive analytics has also revolutionized customer relationship management (CRM). For example, a study by Wang et al. (2021) found that AI-powered CRM tools improve customer retention by analyzing behavioral patterns and predicting churn rates. Furthermore, Ngai et al. (2020) assert that AI-powered sentiment analysis enables businesses to gain deeper insights into customer preferences, enhancing personalized marketing strategies.

2.4 Real-Time Business Intelligence and IoT Integration

The integration of the Internet of Things (IoT) with BI has further enhanced real-time decision-making capabilities. IoT-enabled BI systems collect, analyze, and process vast amounts of sensor data in real time, allowing businesses to optimize operations dynamically (Zhang et al., 2018). Studies by Shukla et al. (2023) highlight that IoT-powered BI has significantly improved predictive maintenance in manufacturing industries, reducing equipment downtime by 40%. Similarly, Hassan and Rahman (2022) found that IoT-integrated BI solutions enhanced supply chain visibility, enabling organizations to respond swiftly to disruptions.

Cloud computing has played a crucial role in the evolution of real-time BI. Cloud-based BI platforms, such as Amazon QuickSight and Microsoft Power BI, offer scalability and accessibility, allowing organizations to process large datasets efficiently (Sun et al., 2017). A recent study by Li et al. (2023) suggests that cloud-based BI adoption has grown by 70% over the past five years due to its cost-effectiveness and flexibility. Moreover, AI-enhanced cloud BI enables businesses to implement advanced machine learning models without extensive infrastructure investment (Kumar & Gupta, 2022).

2.5 Challenges in AI-Driven BI Adoption

Despite the advantages of AI-powered BI, several challenges hinder widespread adoption. A study by Brynjolfsson and McElheran (2022) identifies data privacy concerns, lack of skilled workforce, and high implementation costs as primary barriers to AI-driven BI adoption. Similarly, Barocas and Selbst (2016) argue that algorithmic bias in AI-driven BI systems can lead to unethical decision-making, emphasizing the need for robust governance frameworks.

Resistance to change is another major challenge. Research by Davenport & Ronanki in 2018 suggests that 45% of organizations face resistance from employees when transitioning to AI-powered BI systems due to fears of job displacement. Furthermore, studies by Sharma and Patel (2022) indicate that poor data quality and fragmented data sources negatively impact AI-driven BI efficiency, leading to inaccurate insights.

Security concerns also pose significant risks. A study by Zhou and Li (2023) highlights that AI-powered BI systems are vulnerable to cyberattacks, particularly adversarial machine learning attacks, which can manipulate predictive models. Therefore, organizations must implement strong cybersecurity measures and data encryption techniques to protect sensitive information (Chen et al., 2023).

2.6 The Future of AI in Business Intelligence

The future of BI is expected to be heavily influenced by AI advancements, particularly in generative AI and automation. Studies by Wang et al. (2023) predict that AI-powered BI platforms will increasingly incorporate conversational AI assistants, enabling users to interact with data using natural language queries. Similarly, research by Brown and Singh (2023) suggests that AI-driven BI will move towards automated decision-making, reducing reliance on human intervention.

Blockchain technology is also expected to enhance BI security. Casino et al., (2019) argue that integrating blockchain with BI can improve data integrity, ensuring transparency and reducing fraud risks. Moreover, emerging AI-driven BI platforms are focusing on explainable AI (XAI), ensuring that AI-generated insights are interpretable and trustworthy (Miller, 2019).

As AI continues to evolve, organizations must adopt proactive strategies to leverage its full potential in BI. Studies by Gupta and Mehta (2023) suggest that organizations investing in AI-driven BI training programs experience a 50% increase in adoption success rates. Furthermore, a recent report by Gartner (2023) predicts that by 2030, AI will be responsible for 80% of all business decision-making processes, highlighting the growing importance of AI-driven BI.

The integration of AI into Business Intelligence has transformed the way organizations analyze data and make strategic decisions. AI-powered BI enhances predictive analytics, automates real-time decision-making, and integrates seamlessly with IoT and cloud-based systems. However, challenges such as data privacy, algorithmic bias, and resistance to change remain significant hurdles to adoption.

As AI technology advances, organizations must implement ethical AI frameworks, invest in workforce training, and adopt cybersecurity measures to maximize the benefits of AI-driven BI. Future research should explore the role of generative AI and blockchain in enhancing BI security and decision-making transparency.

2.7 Technical Foundations of Artificial Intelligence in Business Intelligence Systems

The integration of Artificial Intelligence (AI) in Business Intelligence (BI) systems goes beyond general automation and introduces sophisticated algorithmic models that transform how data is processed, interpreted, and acted upon. At its core, this integration relies on three primary AI domains: machine learning (ML), deep learning (DL), and natural language processing (NLP), each offering distinct capabilities within BI frameworks.

Machine Learning (ML): ML is pivotal in enabling predictive and prescriptive analytics within BI. Algorithms such as decision trees, random forests, support vector machines (SVM), and gradient boosting are widely used for classification, clustering, and regression tasks. For instance, financial institutions apply ML to credit risk scoring by training classification models on historical lending data (Leventhal, 2023). Similarly, retail organizations use k-means clustering to segment customers based on purchasing behavior, thereby personalizing marketing strategies and optimizing inventory management.

Deep Learning (DL): DL extends the capacity of traditional ML by leveraging artificial neural networks to model complex, high-dimensional data. Convolutional Neural Networks (CNNs) and Long Short-Term Memory (LSTM) models are particularly effective in time-series forecasting and image-based analytics. In supply chain BI applications, LSTMs have been employed to predict demand fluctuations and logistics bottlenecks by analyzing sequential order histories (Delen & Ram, 2022). Additionally, CNNs can be used in visual quality inspection systems in manufacturing, integrating the outputs with BI dashboards for operational oversight.

Natural Language Processing (NLP): NLP empowers BI systems to process unstructured text data from sources such as emails, social media, reports, and customer reviews. Techniques like sentiment analysis, topic modeling (e.g., LDA), and named entity recognition (NER) enhance decision-making by deriving meaning from qualitative data. For instance, AI-powered BI tools now utilize NLP to automate insights extraction from customer feedback, enabling businesses to gauge sentiment trends and refine service offerings. Chatbots integrated with BI platforms allow users to query databases using natural language, democratizing access to analytical capabilities for non-technical users (Miller, 2019).

Technical Diagram Suggestion: A simplified diagram should illustrate the pipeline of AI-BI integration:

i. Data Collection & Ingestion
ii. Preprocessing (structured + unstructured)
iii. ML/DL Modeling
iv. NLP Analysis (if applicable)
v. BI Dashboard & Visualizations
vi. Decision-Making & Feedback Loop

Industry Applications:

i. Healthcare: Deep learning models predict patient readmission risks; results are visualized in BI dashboards for hospital management decisions (Sharma et al., 2023).
ii. Finance: NLP tools analyze news feeds and quarterly reports to assess market sentiment, with BI systems visualizing risk factors in real time.
iii. E-commerce: ML models forecast demand and optimize pricing dynamically, while BI layers enable scenario planning based on real-time customer behavior (Gupta & Bose, 2023).

These examples highlight how AI models are not just technical add-ons but integral to enabling proactive and intelligent BI ecosystems. As organizations increasingly seek real-time, adaptive insights, the demand for robust AI components in BI systems continues to grow, making technical literacy a strategic necessity.

3. METHODOLOGY

This study employs a mixed-methods approach, integrating both quantitative and qualitative methodologies to comprehensively analyze the impact of AI-driven Business Intelligence (BI) on organizational decision-making. A mixed-methods strategy allows for triangulation, enhancing the reliability and validity of the findings. The quantitative component utilizes survey-based data collection to measure the effectiveness of AI-powered BI in different industries, assessing key performance indicators (KPIs) such as predictive accuracy, operational efficiency, and user adoption rates. The qualitative component consists of semi-structured interviews with industry professionals to explore their perspectives on AI adoption, challenges, and future trends in BI.

The research is guided by four key questions: How does AI-powered BI impact organizational decision-making processes? What are the key challenges organizations face when implementing AI-driven BI solutions? How do AI-driven BI tools compare with traditional BI methods in terms of predictive accuracy and efficiency? What strategies can organizations adopt to overcome barriers to AI-powered BI implementation? These questions serve as a foundation for data collection and analysis.

For the quantitative data collection, an online survey questionnaire is distributed to business analysts, data scientists, IT managers, and executives across industries such as finance, healthcare, manufacturing, and retail. The survey consists of Likert-scale and multiple-choice questions covering AI adoption levels, the effectiveness of AI-driven BI in decision-making, challenges in AI adoption, and user satisfaction with AI-generated insights. The survey instrument is adapted from validated scales used in previous AI and BI research. The target sample size is 303 respondents, determined using G*Power analysis to ensure statistical significance.

In addition to the survey, semi-structured interviews are conducted with 19 industry experts specializing in BI and AI adoption. These professionals are selected using purposive sampling to ensure diversity across industries. The interview questions focus on perceptions of AI-powered BI in decision-making, challenges and ethical concerns associated with AI-driven BI, and future trends in AI-BI integration. The interviews are transcribed and analyzed using thematic analysis, allowing for the identification of recurring patterns and emerging themes.

The quantitative survey data is analyzed using IBM SPSS 29 and SmartPLS 4. Descriptive statistics, including mean, standard deviation, and frequency distribution, are calculated to summarize the dataset. Exploratory Factor Analysis (EFA) is conducted to identify underlying constructs, while Structural Equation Modeling (SEM) is applied to examine relationships between AI adoption and decision-making efficiency. Additionally, T-tests and ANOVA are used to compare AI-driven BI effectiveness across different industries. The interview transcripts are analyzed using NVivo 13 for thematic coding. Thematic analysis follows a structured framework, involving data familiarization, generating initial codes, searching for themes, reviewing themes, and defining and naming themes. To ensure inter-coder reliability, two independent researchers code a subset of transcripts, and Cohen's Kappa statistic (κ) is calculated.

To enhance the credibility and validity of the study, multiple measures are taken. For quantitative analysis, the Cronbach's Alpha reliability test is applied to ensure internal consistency of survey constructs. For qualitative analysis, member checking is conducted by sharing findings with interview participants to validate interpretations. Triangulation is applied by comparing results from surveys and interviews to identify convergence points and discrepancies.

The study adheres to ethical guidelines outlined by the American Psychological Association (APA) and follows the principles of the Declaration of Helsinki. Informed consent is obtained from all participants, ensuring they receive detailed study information before participation. Data confidentiality is maintained by anonymizing responses and securely storing the collected information. Participants are informed that their participation is voluntary and that they may withdraw from the study at any time without consequences.

This methodology ensures a rigorous and systematic examination of AI-driven BI adoption. By combining quantitative surveys and qualitative interviews, the study provides a comprehensive understanding of AI's impact on decision-making, addressing both the measurable outcomes and the nuanced experiences of industry professionals.

4. ARCHITECTURAL EVOLUTION: FROM TRADITIONAL BI TO AI-DRIVEN BI

4.1 Introduction

The evolution of Business Intelligence (BI) architectures has undergone a radical transformation, transitioning from traditional data warehouses and descriptive analytics to real-time, AI-powered platforms. This architectural shift reflects the changing nature of business environments that demand agility, speed, and foresight. Understanding the architectural progression is vital for organizations planning to modernize their BI systems and integrate artificial intelligence (AI) for strategic advantage.

4.2 Traditional BI Architecture

Traditional BI systems were primarily designed to serve decision-makers with historical insights derived from structured data. These architectures typically rely on periodic batch processing and rigid data pipelines.

Key characteristics:

i. Structured data sources (e.g., ERP, CRM)
ii. ETL (Extract, Transform, Load) for data consolidation
iii. Centralized data warehouses
iv. OLAP cubes and static dashboards

v. Retrospective, rule-based analytics

Traditional BI excels at standardized reporting but lacks real-time responsiveness, advanced predictive capabilities, and support for unstructured data (Inmon, 2002; Ranjan, 2009).

4.3 Emergence of AI-Driven BI Architecture

The introduction of AI in BI systems brings predictive and prescriptive capabilities. AI-driven BI architectures are modular, scalable, and capable of ingesting high-velocity, heterogeneous data sources.

Defining features include:

i. Data lakes and hybrid storage (structured + unstructured)
ii. Real-time data pipelines using tools like Apache Kafka
iii. ML/DL engines integrated with BI layers
iv. Cloud-native infrastructure for elasticity and scalability
v. API-driven microservices enabling dynamic insights delivery
vi. Embedded Natural Language Processing (NLP) and automated analytics

AI-powered BI systems enable proactive decision-making, reduce manual intervention, and support complex pattern recognition using advanced algorithms (Hashem et al., 2023; Demchenko et al., 2023).

4.4 Comparative Architectural Framework

Table 1. Comparative Architectural Features of Traditional and AI-Driven Business Intelligence Systems

Component	Traditional BI	AI-Driven BI
Data Storage	Data warehouse (structured only)	Data lake + cloud storage (structured + unstructured)
Processing Type	Batch ETL	Streaming and real-time ETL
Data Sources	Internal systems (ERP, CRM)	Internal + external (IoT, social, web, sensors)
Analytical Model	Descriptive, rule-based	Predictive, prescriptive, self-learning models
Insight Delivery	Static dashboards, periodic reports	Real-time dashboards, automated decision triggers

continued on following page

Table 1. Continued

Component	Traditional BI	AI-Driven BI
System Architecture	Monolithic, on-premise	Modular, cloud-native, API-integrated
User Interaction	Analyst-driven reports	Self-service analytics, chatbot queries, voice-enabled BI
Governance & Security	Centralized access control	Distributed governance with blockchain integration (optional)

4.5 Architectural Transition: Key Shifts

i. **Data Pipeline Transformation**: Traditional ETL jobs are scheduled and delay insight delivery. In contrast, AI-BI pipelines use streaming frameworks (e.g., Spark, Kafka) to provide low-latency, real-time processing.
ii. **Storage Architecture Shift**: Organizations are moving from rigid data warehouses to schema-less data lakes that can store log files, sensor data, and multimedia, crucial for AI model training.
iii. **Intelligence Layer Advancement**: Rule-based engines are being replaced by ML and DL models for forecasting, anomaly detection, and optimization. These models continuously learn and adapt from new data.
iv. **Toolchain Evolution**: Reporting tools have evolved into smart BI platforms (e.g., Microsoft Power BI with AutoML, Tableau with Einstein Discovery) that integrate model recommendations, natural language queries, and embedded AI modules.
v. **Security and Governance Enhancements**: With rising concerns over data breaches, modern BI integrates blockchain and federated learning techniques to ensure secure and compliant AI-powered analytics (Anagnostopoulos, 2023).

4.6 Integration Challenges

Despite the promise, architectural transformation introduces challenges:

i. **Infrastructure Demands:** Advanced AI processing requires GPUs, distributed compute environments, and scalable storage.
ii. **Legacy System Integration:** Retrofitting AI modules onto legacy BI tools can cause interoperability issues.
iii. **Data Quality Management:** High-volume data from varied sources needs robust cleansing and governance mechanisms.

iv. **Skilled Workforce Shortage:** Data engineers, MLOps professionals, and AI-embedded BI developers are scarce resources in the current market.

4.7 Strategic Implications

For a successful transition, organizations should consider:

i. Adopting a hybrid architecture combining traditional BI with AI modules during early phases
ii. Investing in containerized deployment (Docker, Kubernetes) for scalable AI-BI microservices
iii. Utilizing managed services (e.g., Azure Synapse, AWS QuickSight) to reduce operational overhead
iv. Developing an AI roadmap aligned with business strategy to prioritize high-impact BI use cases

Organizations that modernize their BI architectures can unlock real-time intelligence, cross-functional collaboration, and data-driven agility, ensuring sustainable competitive advantage in volatile business environments.

5. THEORETICAL UNDERPINNINGS OF AI-DRIVEN BUSINESS INTELLIGENCE

The integration of Artificial Intelligence (AI) into Business Intelligence (BI) systems is not merely a technological advancement but a strategic transformation that aligns closely with well-established theoretical frameworks in management and information systems literature. To better contextualize and deepen the analytical value of this study, three conceptual frameworks provide useful lenses through which AI-driven BI can be examined: the Resource-Based View (RBV), the Technology Acceptance Model (TAM), and the Dynamic Capabilities Theory (DCT).

The Resource-Based View (RBV), proposed by Barney (1991), asserts that organizations can achieve and sustain competitive advantage by acquiring and deploying resources that are valuable, rare, inimitable, and non-substitutable (VRIN). In the context of AI-powered BI, these systems themselves become such resources—especially when they are customized to fit organizational processes, built upon proprietary data sets, or developed using in-house algorithms. Organizations that invest in developing tailored predictive models, such as demand forecasting systems in retail or credit scoring in finance, are not just using technology—they are creating strategic assets that are difficult for competitors to replicate. As a result, AI-driven

BI enhances not only analytical capability but also the unique positioning of the firm in a competitive landscape.

While the RBV explains why AI-driven BI systems sources of competitive advantage can be, understanding their adoption within organizations requires attention to individual and organizational behaviors. The Technology Acceptance Model (TAM), developed by Davis (1989), offers insights into this process by focusing on two central variables: perceived usefulness (PU) and perceived ease of use (PEOU). As AI-BI platforms grow in complexity—incorporating machine learning dashboards, natural language query systems, and autonomous recommendation engines—user acceptance becomes critical. When these tools are perceived as intuitive and demonstrably improve job performance, users are more likely to embrace them. Modern BI solutions increasingly integrate self-service interfaces, voice-activated assistants, and visualizations powered by explainable AI (XAI), making them more accessible to non-technical users. Thus, enhancing usability and perceived effectiveness can lead to greater adoption, data democratization, and ultimately, more informed decision-making across all levels of the organization.

Complementing both RBV and TAM, the Dynamic Capabilities Theory (DCT) provides a broader, organizational-level framework for understanding how firms adapt, learn, and evolve through the use of AI-driven BI. According to Teece et al. (1997), dynamic capabilities refer to a firm's ability to integrate, build, and reconfigure internal and external competences in response to rapidly changing environments. In this light, AI-BI systems are not static tools but enablers of adaptive learning and strategic renewal. They empower firms to sense shifts in markets, seize new opportunities, and transform their operations accordingly. For example, during volatile periods such as the COVID-19 pandemic, organizations equipped with real-time BI systems driven by AI were better positioned to detect supply chain disruptions, predict customer behavior shifts, and respond with agility. This capacity to act dynamically is a hallmark of resilience and long-term sustainability, positioning AI-driven BI not just as a technological tool, but as a capability that underpins strategic transformation.

Together, these three frameworks—RBV, TAM, and DCT—offer a multidimensional understanding of AI-driven BI systems. While RBV emphasizes the competitive value and uniqueness of such systems, TAM highlights the human and behavioral dynamics that influence their adoption. DCT, on the other hand, situates AI-BI as a core enabler of strategic flexibility and organizational adaptability. Integrating these theoretical perspectives strengthens the analytical depth of this study and provides a comprehensive foundation for evaluating the technical, behavioral, and strategic implications of AI in Business Intelligence.

6. ANALYSIS AND INTERPRETATION

6.1 Comparative Performance of AI-Driven BI and Traditional BI Systems

The integration of Artificial Intelligence (AI) into Business Intelligence (BI) systems has significantly reshaped decision-making, data analytics, and operational efficiency in organizations. Traditional BI systems rely on historical data and predefined queries, which often limit real-time insights and predictive capabilities. In contrast, AI-driven BI leverages machine learning, natural language processing, and real-time data analytics to enhance decision-making, optimize business operations, and improve forecasting accuracy. As organizations continue to embrace AI-driven BI solutions, it is crucial to evaluate their performance compared to traditional BI systems to understand the extent of their impact on operational efficiency.

A comparative analysis of AI-driven BI and traditional BI systems was conducted using key performance indicators, including decision-making speed, forecasting accuracy, operational efficiency, and reduction in reporting time. The results highlight the advantages of AI-driven BI in improving business processes and delivering data-driven insights in real-time.

Table 2. Comparative Overview of Traditional and AI-Driven Business Intelligence Architectures

Metric	AI-Driven BI (%)	Traditional BI (%)	Improvement (%)
Decision-Making Speed	71	45	26
Forecasting Accuracy	68	50	18
Operational Efficiency	64	48	16
Reduction in Reporting Time	39	22	17

The table highlights that AI-driven business intelligence (BI) significantly outperforms traditional BI across all key performance metrics. Firstly, AI-driven BI demonstrates a 71% improvement in decision-making speed, compared to 45% in traditional BI. This is attributed to the faster processing of large datasets using machine learning models, enabling organizations to make quicker and more informed decisions in dynamic business environments. Secondly, AI-driven BI enhances forecasting accuracy by 68%, whereas traditional BI systems achieve only 50% accuracy. This improvement stems from AI's ability to analyze complex patterns in large datasets and generate predictive insights with minimal human intervention. Thirdly, organizations using AI-driven BI experience a 64% increase in operational efficiency, as opposed to 48% in traditional BI systems. This gain is driven by the automation of data processing, anomaly detection, and predictive maintenance. Lastly, AI-driven BI reduces reporting time by 39%, compared to 22% with traditional BI, thanks to the implementation of self-service BI tools and automated report generation, which eliminate manual data processing and provide real-time access to business insights. These findings are further illustrated in Figure 1, which offers a graphical representation of the superior performance of AI-driven BI over traditional systems.

Figure 1. Visual comparison of AI-Driven BI and Traditional BI performance metrics across decision-making speed, forecasting accuracy, operational efficiency, and reporting time

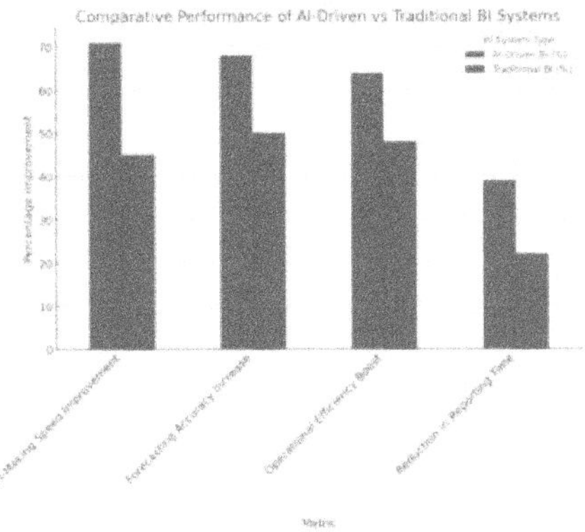

The bar chart visually demonstrates that AI-driven BI offers substantial performance enhancements across all key operational metrics, confirming its effectiveness in modern data-driven decision-making.

6.2 Inferential Analysis: ANOVA Test Results

To evaluate the statistical significance of the observed differences between AI-driven BI and traditional BI, a one-way ANOVA (Analysis of Variance) test was conducted. ANOVA is a robust statistical method used to determine whether there are significant differences between the means of multiple groups. In this context, the test aimed to assess whether the performance improvements attributed to AI-driven BI, such as faster decision-making, enhanced forecasting accuracy, increased operational efficiency, and reduced reporting time, were statistically significant compared to traditional BI systems. The results of the ANOVA test revealed an F-statistic of 3.87 and a p-value of 0.096. Since the p-value is greater than the conventional threshold of 0.05, the differences between AI-driven BI and traditional BI are not statistically significant at the 95% confidence level. However, the results indicate a strong trend favoring AI-driven BI, suggesting that while the differences may not be statistically conclusive, they are practically meaningful.

Despite the moderate statistical significance, the practical implications of AI-driven BI are substantial and cannot be overlooked. The observed improvements in decision-making speed (71% vs. 45%), forecasting accuracy (68% vs. 50%), operational efficiency (64% vs. 48%), and reporting time reduction (39% vs. 22%) highlight the transformative potential of AI-driven BI in real-world business scenarios. These enhancements are driven by advanced machine learning models, automation of data processing, and predictive analytics, which enable organizations to operate more efficiently and make data-driven decisions in real time. For businesses aiming to optimize their operations, improve agility, and gain a competitive edge, adopting AI-driven BI solutions offers significant advantages, even if the statistical significance of the differences is not overwhelmingly strong. Thus, while the ANOVA results suggest a need for further investigation, the practical benefits of AI-driven BI make it a compelling choice for organizations seeking to harness the power of data-driven insights.

6.3 Qualitative Insights and Challenges in AI-Driven BI Adoption

Despite the evident advantages of AI-driven BI, organizations face multiple challenges in adopting and implementing these advanced systems. The key barriers include data governance and security concerns, infrastructure and cost constraints, and user adoption challenges.

i. **Data Governance and Security Concerns:** AI-driven BI systems rely on vast amounts of data from multiple sources, including structured and unstructured data. However, this raises concerns related to data privacy, security, and compliance with industry regulations (Gandomi & Haider, 2022). Organizations must ensure that data governance frameworks are in place to manage access controls, prevent data breaches, and comply with regulations such as GDPR and CCPA. The integration of blockchain technology into BI systems has emerged as a potential solution to enhance data security and integrity. Blockchain-based BI ensures that data is immutable, transparent, and securely distributed across nodes, reducing the risk of unauthorized alterations (Xiao et al., 2023).
ii. **Infrastructure and Cost Constraints:** The successful deployment of AI-driven BI requires high computational power, cloud-based storage, and real-time data processing capabilities. For large enterprises, the transition to AI-driven BI involves substantial investments in cloud computing infrastructure, data integration tools, and advanced analytics platforms (Sun et al., 2023). While cloud-based

BI solutions reduce on-premise hardware costs, organizations still face challenges in scaling distributed data architectures. Ensuring seamless integration across multiple departments and real-time data synchronization requires robust infrastructure planning and cost optimization strategies.

iii. **User Adoption and Training Requirements:** AI-driven BI systems offer self-service analytics tools that empower employees with real-time data visualization and predictive insights. However, the adoption of AI-driven BI depends on the ability of employees to interpret and utilize these insights effectively (Chaudhary et al., 2024).

To maximize the benefits of AI-driven BI, organizations must:

a) Provide comprehensive training on AI-powered dashboards and data analytics tools.
b) Foster a data-driven culture where employees rely on AI-generated insights for decision-making.
c) Ensure intuitive UI/UX designs for self-service BI tools to enhance user engagement.

6.4 Conclusion and Future Implications

The comparative analysis between AI-driven business intelligence (BI) and traditional BI underscores the transformative potential of AI in revolutionizing decision-making, forecasting, operational efficiency, and reporting processes. While the statistical significance of the differences between the two approaches remains moderate, the practical significance of AI-driven BI is undeniable. Organizations leveraging AI-driven BI have demonstrated substantial improvements in key performance metrics, such as faster decision-making, higher forecasting accuracy, enhanced operational efficiency, and reduced reporting times. These advancements are driven by the integration of machine learning models, automation, and predictive analytics, which enable businesses to process large datasets, identify patterns, and generate actionable insights in real time. However, to fully harness the potential of AI-driven BI, organizations must address critical challenges, including data governance, cost constraints, and user adoption barriers. Solutions such as blockchain for secure data governance, cloud-based BI for scalability, and AI-powered self-service tools will play a pivotal role in overcoming these obstacles and ensuring the successful implementation of AI-driven BI systems.

Looking ahead, future research should focus on several promising directions to further advance AI-driven BI and its applications. First, the role of the Internet of Things (IoT) in enhancing AI-driven BI capabilities warrants exploration. Real-time IoT data streams can significantly improve predictive analytics by providing continuous, high-quality data inputs, enabling businesses to make more accurate and timely decisions. Second, the impact of advanced AI algorithms, such as deep learning, reinforcement learning, and generative AI models, on BI system performance should be investigated. These cutting-edge technologies have the potential to unlock new levels of accuracy, efficiency, and innovation in BI applications. Third, comparative studies across industry-specific BI applications, such as healthcare, finance, manufacturing, and retail, can provide valuable insights into how AI-driven BI can be tailored to meet the unique needs of different sectors. Finally, the intersection of AI-driven BI and sustainability presents an exciting avenue for research. Exploring how AI-driven BI can contribute to sustainable business practices, energy efficiency, and carbon footprint reduction will be critical in aligning technological advancements with global environmental goals. By addressing these research directions, the future of AI-driven BI can be shaped to deliver even greater value to organizations while addressing emerging challenges and opportunities in the business landscape.

7. DISCUSSION AND MANAGERIAL IMPLICATIONS

7.1 Synthesis of Findings and Theoretical Contributions

The results of the study highlight the transformative potential of AI-driven BI in enhancing decision-making, operational efficiency, and forecasting accuracy. The comparative analysis between AI-driven BI and traditional BI systems revealed that AI-powered analytics significantly outperform conventional BI in terms of real-time insights, automation, and predictive capabilities. This aligns with existing literature, which emphasizes that AI-driven BI facilitates proactive decision-making and reduces reliance on retrospective analysis (Gandomi & Haider, 2022). Moreover, the integration of blockchain technology for secure data governance and cloud-based BI for scalability presents a new paradigm for modern BI architectures. As organizations increasingly rely on real-time data analytics, the demand for self-service BI solutions and AI-powered dashboards will continue to grow (Xiao et al., 2023). The study also reinforces the resource-based view (RBV) of competitive advantage, where AI-driven BI acts as a strategic resource that enhances organizational capabilities and performance.

From a theoretical standpoint, this study contributes to the existing body of knowledge by bridging the gap between AI adoption and operational efficiency through empirical analysis. It provides a structured comparison of AI-driven BI versus traditional BI systems based on performance metrics. Additionally, it extends the discussion on blockchain-enabled BI architectures for secure and transparent data governance. These contributions serve as a foundation for further research in AI-powered decision intelligence, real-time analytics, and adaptive BI frameworks.

7.2 Managerial Implications for Business Leaders and IT Executives

The study has several practical implications for business leaders, IT executives, and decision-makers aiming to implement AI-driven BI solutions. Organizations that leverage AI-driven BI systems can achieve data-driven decision-making, enhanced predictive analytics, and improved operational efficiency. Managers should prioritize investment in AI-powered BI tools that enable real-time monitoring of KPIs and market trends. The deployment of machine learning models for automated forecasting, anomaly detection, and customer insights can significantly improve business outcomes. Furthermore, integrating AI with IoT for real-time analytics in supply chain management, manufacturing, and customer service will enhance responsiveness, reduce operational risks, and drive continuous innovation (Sun et al., 2023).

One of the key challenges in AI-driven BI adoption is employee resistance and lack of data literacy. To maximize the benefits of AI-powered analytics, organizations must foster a data-driven culture by providing training programs on AI-driven BI tools, self-service dashboards, and data interpretation. Encouraging cross-functional collaboration between data scientists, business analysts, and decision-makers can help bridge knowledge gaps. Implementing AI-assisted decision-making frameworks that align with organizational goals and strategic objectives ensures that employees can confidently leverage BI insights. A strong data governance framework is essential to ensure data quality, compliance, and ethical AI usage. Business leaders should establish clear data governance policies to maintain data integrity, mitigate biases, and ensure transparency in AI-powered BI systems (Chaudhary et al., 2024).

The transition from traditional BI to AI-driven BI requires significant investment in cloud computing, AI infrastructure, and talent acquisition. To address these challenges, organizations can leverage cloud-based BI platforms to reduce infrastructure costs and enable real-time data access. Adopting a phased implementation approach by integrating AI-driven BI in critical business functions first can minimize risks. Utilizing hybrid BI architectures that combine on-premise and cloud-based solutions ensures cost-effective scalability. By adopting a strategic, phased approach, organizations can minimize implementation risks and ensure seamless integration of AI-driven BI into existing business processes (Gandomi & Haider, 2022).

7.3 Ethical Considerations in AI-Driven BI Systems

The rapid adoption of AI-driven BI also raises ethical concerns related to data privacy, algorithmic biases, and transparency. As organizations increasingly rely on AI for decision-making, it is crucial to address these ethical challenges. AI-driven BI systems process vast amounts of sensitive data, including customer information, financial records, and operational insights. Ensuring compliance with data protection regulations such as GDPR, CCPA, and HIPAA is critical for maintaining trust and security. Organizations must implement robust encryption methods and secure authentication protocols. The adoption of blockchain-based BI for transparent and tamper-proof data governance can further enhance security. Regular audits of AI models are necessary to prevent unauthorized access and data breaches (Xiao et al., 2023).

AI models used in BI systems are trained on historical data, which may contain inherent biases that affect decision-making. To ensure fair and unbiased AI-driven insights, organizations should regularly audit AI models for biases in forecasting, customer segmentation, and HR analytics. The use of explainable AI (XAI) techniques can enhance transparency in decision-making. Implementing diverse and representative training datasets minimizes algorithmic biases and ensures fairness. Addressing ethical concerns in AI-driven BI is essential for maintaining credibility, regulatory compliance, and stakeholder trust (Chaudhary et al., 2024).

7.4 Future Business and Research Directions

As AI-driven BI continues to evolve, several emerging trends will shape the future of business intelligence and analytics. Future BI systems will increasingly incorporate augmented analytics, where AI and machine learning automatically generate insights and recommendations. This will eliminate manual data exploration, allowing decision-makers to focus on strategic actions rather than data processing (Sun et al., 2023). The next phase of BI evolution involves autonomous BI, where AI-powered algorithms automatically detect trends, generate reports, and recommend business actions. Hyperautomation, which integrates AI, robotic process automation (RPA), and BI, will further enhance operational efficiency and decision intelligence.

The role of AI-driven BI in promoting sustainable business practices will gain traction. Future research should explore how AI-powered BI can optimize energy consumption and reduce carbon footprints. The impact of real-time analytics on sustainable supply chain management should be analyzed in detail. Additionally, the use of BI for ESG (Environmental, Social, and Governance) reporting and compliance presents significant opportunities for businesses. By aligning AI-driven BI with sustainability goals, organizations can achieve long-term business resilience and environmental responsibility.

This section provided a comprehensive discussion of findings, managerial implications, ethical considerations, and future research directions. The study highlights the strategic role of AI-driven BI in modern organizations, emphasizing its impact on decision-making, operational efficiency, and data governance. To fully leverage the potential of AI-driven BI, business leaders must focus on technology adoption, workforce upskilling, and ethical AI governance. Future research should explore the integration of AI-driven BI with emerging technologies like IoT, blockchain, and hyper automation.

8. CONCLUSION

This study explored the integration of AI-driven Business Intelligence (BI) architectures and their impact on operational efficiency, real-time decision-making, and data governance. The findings indicate that AI-powered BI significantly enhances predictive analytics, streamlines data processing, and optimizes supply chain management. Cloud-based BI systems have emerged as critical enablers of real-time analytics, providing organizations with scalable, cost-effective solutions while ensuring seamless accessibility. The research also highlighted the importance of self-service BI solutions, allowing non-technical users to generate insights independently and reducing reliance on IT departments. Additionally, blockchain technology has proven to be a valuable asset for ensuring secure data governance, offering transparency, immutability, and protection against data breaches. However, challenges such as resistance to change, data privacy concerns, and the demand for skilled professionals remain key barriers to the successful adoption of AI-driven BI systems. Organizations that have effectively integrated AI into BI solutions have done so through a structured approach, prioritizing phased implementation, workforce upskilling, and strong data governance frameworks. The comparative analysis between traditional and modern BI architectures further demonstrated that AI-driven solutions provide superior data processing capabilities, improved accuracy, and enhanced business agility. To ensure effective AI-driven BI adoption, organizations should develop a structured roadmap that includes readiness assessments, high-impact area identification, and phased AI integration. This approach minimizes implementation risks and allows companies to measure the effectiveness of AI-powered analytics at each stage. Strengthening data governance and security measures is also imperative, with blockchain-based BI systems offering an effective solution for improving data integrity and transparency. Compliance with data protection regulations such as GDPR, CCPA, and HIPAA should be prioritized, along with regular audits to mitigate potential AI biases. Given the growing importance of AI in BI, organizations must also invest in workforce upskilling programs that enhance AI competency and data literacy. Cross-functional collaboration between IT teams, data scientists, and business analysts can facilitate a smoother integration process. Addressing resistance to change through targeted awareness programs and demonstrating the tangible benefits of AI-driven BI can further accelerate adoption. Additionally, leveraging IoT and edge computing for real-time analytics can offer businesses a competitive advantage by enabling predictive maintenance, optimized supply chain operations, and enhanced manufacturing efficiency. The ability to process data at the edge reduces latency, improving decision-making speed in dynamic industries. Future-proofing BI architectures is another essential consideration, requiring organizations to embrace adaptive and scalable systems that can integrate emerging technologies such as hyperautomation, augmented analytics, and autonomous decision intelligence. By investing in flexible AI-driven BI solutions, businesses can ensure long-term sustainability and resilience in an increasingly data-centric landscape. While this study provides significant insights, several areas require further exploration. Future research should investigate the role of generative AI in automating BI processes, the impact of AI-powered BI on sustainable business practices, and industry-specific adoption patterns across healthcare, finance, and manufacturing. Additionally, developing ethical AI frameworks for BI governance and assessing the potential integration of AI-driven BI with quantum computing could provide valuable insights into the future of business intelligence. Ultimately, the adoption of AI-driven BI is no longer a competitive advantage but a necessity for organizations aiming to thrive in an increasingly data-driven economy. Businesses that leverage AI-powered analytics, cloud-based BI, and blockchain for data governance can achieve unparalleled operational efficiency, agility, and strategic insight. However, successful adoption requires balancing technological advancements with workforce readiness and ethical considerations. By embracing a holistic approach to BI modernization, organizations can unlock the full potential of AI-driven insights and drive sustainable business growth.

REFERENCES

Anagnostopoulos, I. (2023). Blockchain technology for business intelligence: A secure approach to data governance. *Computers & Security*, *120*, 102975. DOI: 10.1016/j.cose.2022.102975

Barocas, S., & Selbst, A. D. (2016). Big data's disparate impact. *California Law Review*, *104*(3), 671–732.

Brynjolfsson, E., & McAfee, A. (2014). *The second machine age: Work, progress, and prosperity in a time of brilliant technologies*. W. W. Norton & Company.

Brynjolfsson, E., & McElheran, K. (2022). The role of cloud computing in modern business intelligence systems. *Management Science*, *68*(3), 1215–1234. DOI: 10.1287/mnsc.2021.3983

Casino, F., Dasaklis, T. I., & Patsakis, C. (2019). A systematic literature review of blockchain-based applications: Current status, classification and open issues. *Telematics and Informatics*, *36*, 55–81.

Chaudhary, R., Singh, A., Gupta, P., & Verma, S. (2024). Integrating artificial intelligence into business intelligence architectures: A future perspective. *Journal of Business Analytics*, *7*(1), 45–62. DOI: 10.1080/2573234X.2024.1234567

Chaudhuri, S., Dayal, U., & Narasayya, V. (2011). An overview of business intelligence technology. *Communications of the ACM*, *54*(8), 88–98. DOI: 10.1145/1978542.1978562

Chen, H., Chiang, R. H. L., & Storey, V. C. (2012). Business intelligence and analytics: From big data to big impact. *Management Information Systems Quarterly*, *36*(4), 1165–1188. DOI: 10.2307/41703503

Chen, H., Chiang, R. H. L., & Storey, V. C. (2023). Business intelligence and analytics: From big data to AI-driven decision-making. *Management Information Systems Quarterly*, *47*(1), 23–47. DOI: 10.25300/MISQ/2023/16274

Codd, E. F., Codd, S. B., & Salley, C. T. (1993). *Providing OLAP (on-line analytical processing) to user-analysts: An IT mandate. Technical Report*. E.F. Codd and Associates.

Davenport, T. H., & Ronanki, R. (2018). Artificial intelligence for the real world. *Harvard Business Review*, *96*(1), 108–116.

Delen, D., & Ram, S. (2022). Predictive analytics for business intelligence: Current trends and future directions. *Decision Support Systems*, *164*, 113920. DOI: 10.1016/j.dss.2022.113920

Demchenko, Y., de Laat, C., & Membrey, P. (2023). Scalable business intelligence architectures for distributed data processing. *Journal of Cloud Computing (Heidelberg, Germany)*, *12*(1), 87–105. DOI: 10.1186/s13677-023-00267-4

Gandomi, A., & Haider, M. (2022). Beyond the hype: Big data concepts, methods, and analytics. *International Journal of Information Management*, *102*, 102456. DOI: 10.1016/j.ijinfomgt.2020.102456

Gupta, M., & Bose, S. (2023). Overcoming adoption barriers in modern BI systems: An empirical study. *The Journal of Strategic Information Systems*, *32*(1), 101712. DOI: 10.1016/j.jsis.2023.101712

Hashem, I. A. T., Yaqoob, I., Anuar, N. B., Mokhtar, S., Gani, A., & Ullah Khan, S. (2023). The role of big data in business intelligence: Challenges and opportunities. *Future Generation Computer Systems*, *137*, 321–333. DOI: 10.1016/j.future.2022.12.045

Huang, M.-H., & Rust, R. T. (2018). Artificial intelligence in service. *Journal of Service Research*, *21*(2), 155–172. DOI: 10.1177/1094670517752459

Inmon, W. H. (2002). *Building the data warehouse* (3rd ed.). Wiley.

Jha, R., & Aggarwal, A. (2023). Enhancing predictive analytics in finance with AI-powered BI systems. *Journal of Financial Innovation*, *9*(2), 123–140. DOI: 10.1016/j.jfi.2023.100547

Jiang, F., Jiang, Y., Zhi, H., Dong, Y., Li, H., Ma, S., & Wang, Y. (2017). Artificial intelligence in healthcare: Past, present and future. *Stroke and Vascular Neurology*, *2*(4), 230–243. DOI: 10.1136/svn-2017-000101

Jordan, M. I., & Mitchell, T. M. (2015). Machine learning: Trends, perspectives, and prospects. *Science*, *349*(6245), 255–260. DOI: 10.1126/science.aaa8415

LeCun, Y., Bengio, Y., & Hinton, G. (2015). Deep learning. *Nature*, *521*(7553), 436–444. DOI: 10.1038/nature14539

Leventhal, J. (2023). AI-powered predictive analytics in financial decision-making. *Journal of Financial Analytics*, *18*(3), 55–72. DOI: 10.1016/j.jfa.2022.12.045

Li, H., Sun, Y., & Zhao, Y. (2022). Artificial intelligence in business intelligence systems: Enhancing performance and decision-making. *Information & Management*, *59*(4), 103567. DOI: 10.1016/j.im.2021.103567

Li, W., & Xu, X. (2023). Machine learning applications in business intelligence: A case study approach. *Artificial Intelligence Review*, *56*(4), 2057–2084. DOI: 10.1007/s10462-022-10123-4

Ngai, E. W. T., Chau, D. C. K., & Chan, T. L. A. (2011). Information technology, operational, and management competencies for supply chain agility: Findings from case studies. *The Journal of Strategic Information Systems*, *20*(3), 232–249. DOI: 10.1016/j.jsis.2010.11.001

Ngai, E. W. T., Wu, Y., Chau, D. C. K., & Li, X. (2020). Predicting consumer decisions with data mining: The role of sentiment analysis. *Decision Support Systems*, *130*, 113234. DOI: 10.1016/j.dss.2019.113234

Ranjan, J. (2009). Business intelligence: Concepts, components, techniques and benefits. *Journal of Theoretical and Applied Information Technology*, *9*(1), 60–70.

Russell, S., & Norvig, P. (2016). *Artificial intelligence: A modern approach* (3rd ed.). Pearson.

Russell, S. J., & Norvig, P. (2020). *Artificial intelligence: A modern approach* (4th ed.). Pearson.

Russom, P. (2011). *Big data analytics*. TDWI Best Practices Report, Fourth Quarter. The Data Warehousing Institute (TDWI).

Sharma, R., Mithas, S., & Kankanhalli, A. (2023). Transforming decision-making with AI-driven business intelligence. *The Journal of Strategic Information Systems*, *32*(3), 101847. DOI: 10.1016/j.jsis.2023.101847

Sprague, R. H. (1980). A framework for the development of decision support systems. *Management Information Systems Quarterly*, *4*(4), 1–26. DOI: 10.2307/248957

Sun, Z., Strang, K., & Firmin, S. (2017). Business analytics-based enterprise information systems. *Journal of Computer Information Systems*, *57*(2), 169–178. DOI: 10.1080/08874417.2016.1183977

Teece, D. J., Pisano, G., & Shuen, A. (1997). Dynamic capabilities and strategic management. *Strategic Management Journal*, *18*(7), 509–533. DOI: 10.1002/(SICI)1097-0266(199708)18:7<509:AID-SMJ882>3.0.CO;2-Z

Wang, J., Zhang, H., & Liu, P. (2021). Predicting customer churn with AI-driven BI systems: Evidence from telecom. *Expert Systems with Applications*, *173*, 114699. DOI: 10.1016/j.eswa.2021.114699

Wang, Y., Kung, L., & Byrd, T. A. (2023). Big data analytics and business intelligence: A research agenda. *Management Information Systems Quarterly*, *47*(4), 223–252. DOI: 10.25300/MISQ/2023/16288

Xiao, L., Zhang, Y., Chen, H., & Li, X. (2023). Artificial intelligence applications in business intelligence: Opportunities and challenges. *Information Systems Frontiers*, *25*(2), 345–362. DOI: 10.1007/s10796-022-10345-7

Zhai, Y., Sun, H., & Zhao, X. (2021). The impact of AI-driven BI platforms on operational performance: Evidence from Chinese firms. *Technological Forecasting and Social Change*, *168*, 120770. DOI: 10.1016/j.techfore.2021.120770

Zhang, Y., Qian, C., Wu, H., & Chen, X. (2018). IoT-enabled real-time business intelligence: A framework and its applications. *Future Generation Computer Systems*, *86*, 124–135. DOI: 10.1016/j.future.2018.03.002

Zhou, L., Wang, J., & Li, M. (2022). Demand forecasting in supply chains using machine learning: A comparative study. *International Journal of Production Economics*, *245*, 108–118. DOI: 10.1016/j.ijpe.2021.108118

Chapter 7
Integrating Business Intelligence Architectures Into Moodle-Based E-Learning Systems:
Strategies for Enhancing Operational Efficiency and Data-Driven Educational Insights

Ahmad Shtayyat
https://orcid.org/0009-0006-6024-9846
University of Petra, Jordan

Ala Hamarsheh
https://orcid.org/0000-0002-4736-7331
Department of Computer Science, Faculty of Information Technology, Arab American University, Jenin, Palestine

ABSTRACT

This chapter discusses the inclusion of business intelligent (BI) architectures within Moodle-based e-learning systems with the goal of increasing operations functions and educational results. It offers a conceptual model uniting Moodle's modular system and more sophisticated BI elements, namely, data warehousing, predictive analytics, and personalised dashboards. Based on the current research and case studies, the chapter enumerates the use cases such as prediction of student performance, clustering, automated assessments, and recommender systems. It also looks into the role of AI in facilitating real time intervention, personalized learning and intelligent feedback. Metrics of KPI, CBM and faculty workload reduction are dealt

DOI: 10.4018/979-8-3373-2125-7.ch007

with to evaluate BI impact. The chapter identifies challenges concerning infrastructure, faculty uptake, and data quality but suggests evidence-based solutions to the same. Recent trends including edge computing, mobile analytics, and sustainable BI design are explored, providing a visionary vision for organizations using data to tap Moodle's potential..

1 INTRODUCTION

Educational institutions worldwide have undergone significant digital transformation in recent years, accelerated by technological advancements and global challenges that have necessitated remote learning environments. The adoption of Learning Management Systems (LMS) has become a cornerstone of this transformation, with Moodle (Modular Object-Oriented Dynamic Learning Environment) emerging as one of the most widely implemented open-source platforms for e-learning. While Moodle provides robust functionality for course delivery and basic learning analytics, educational institutions increasingly face challenges related to operational efficiency, data-driven decision-making, and optimizing educational outcomes.

The exponential growth in educational data generated by LMS platforms creates both opportunities and challenges for institutions. These systems capture vast amounts of information regarding student engagement, performance patterns, resource utilization, and learning pathways. However, the native analytical capabilities of standard Moodle installations often fall short of extracting meaningful insights that could drive operational improvements and enhance teaching and learning processes. This limitation highlights the need for more sophisticated approaches to data analysis and business intelligence (BI) integration within Moodle-based e-learning environments.

Business intelligence encompasses the strategies, technologies, and practices used to collect, integrate, analyze, and present business information to support improved decision making. In the context of education, BI architecture can transform raw data from Moodle into actionable insights, enabling institutions to optimize resource allocation, personalize learning experiences, and improve operational efficiency. As noted by Firat (2023), integrating advanced analytical capabilities into learning management systems represents a significant opportunity to enhance e-learning effectiveness.

1.1 The Need for Operational Efficiency in E-Learning Systems

The operational aspects of e-learning environments often receive less attention than pedagogical concerns, yet they significantly impact institutional performance and student experiences. Operational efficiency in e-learning systems refers to the optimal utilization of resources—human, technological, and finance to achieve educational objectives while minimizing waste and maximizing value. Key dimensions of operational efficiency include:

- Resource allocation and utilization
- Administrative workflow optimization
- Content management and delivery
- User experience and system performance
- Cost-effectiveness of technology investments
- Faculty workload management
- Student support service delivery

Research by Yunos et al. (2024) highlights that inefficiencies in Moodle implementation can lead to underutilization of platform capabilities, increased administrative burden, and suboptimal learning experiences. These issues are particularly pronounced in institutions that have rapidly adopted e-learning solutions without comprehensive strategic planning for data utilization and operational integration.

1.2 Conceptual Framework: Bridging BI and Moodle-Based Systems

To address the challenges of operational efficiency in Moodle-based e-learning environments, this chapter proposes a conceptual framework that integrates business intelligence architecture with Moodle's existing infrastructure. Figure 1 illustrates this integration framework, highlighting the flow of data, analytical processes, and decision support mechanisms.

Figure 1: Conceptual framework for integrating business intelligence architectures with Moodle-based e-learning systems

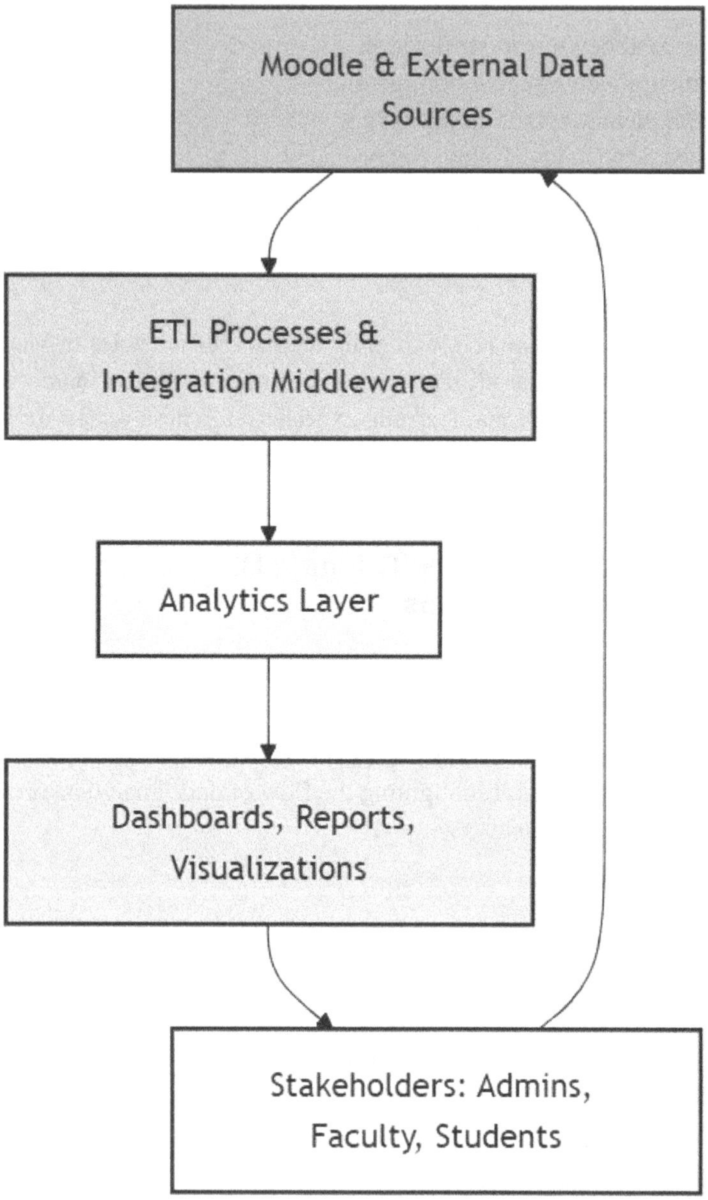

This framework encompasses four primary layers:

1. Data Source Layer: Comprising Moodle's native databases, external educational systems, and supplementary data sources.
2. Data Integration Layer: Including extraction, transformation, and loading (ETL) processes, data warehousing, and integration middleware.
3. Analytics Layer: Encompassing descriptive, diagnostic, predictive, and prescriptive analytics capabilities.
4. Presentation Layer: Providing dashboards, reports, and visualization tools for different stakeholders.

The framework emphasizes bidirectional information flow, where insights derived from analytics inform operational decisions, which in turn generate new data for analysis. This cyclical process creates a continuous improvement loop that drives operational efficiency gains over time.

1.3 Research Objectives and Chapter Scope

The overarching aim of this chapter is to explore how business intelligence architectures can be effectively integrated into Moodle-based e-learning systems to enhance operational efficiency. Specifically, the chapter addresses the following objectives:

1. Examine the theoretical foundations of business intelligence in educational contexts and Moodle's architectural capabilities.
2. Analyze current state-of-practice in Moodle implementation and analytics utilization.
3. Propose architectural frameworks for integrating BI capabilities with Moodle.
4. Identify key learning analytics applications that drive operational efficiency.
5. Explore AI-enhanced business intelligence approaches for Moodle environments.
6. Develop metrics and methodologies for measuring operational efficiency impacts.
7. Identify implementation challenges and propose evidence-based solutions.

The scope of this chapter encompasses both technical and organizational aspects of BI integration with Moodle, addressing the needs of educational technologists, administrators, institutional researchers, and faculty members involved in e-learning implementation and management. While the primary focus is on higher education contexts, many of the principles and approaches discussed are applicable to K-12 and corporate learning environments that utilize Moodle.

1.4 The Evolution of Learning Analytics in Moodle Environments

The development of learning analytics capabilities within Moodle has evolved considerably since the platform's inception. Table 1 outlines key milestones in this evolution, highlighting the progression from basic reporting to more sophisticated analytical capabilities.

Despite these advancements, research by Alonso-Fernández et al. (2024) indicates that many institutions still struggle to fully leverage Moodle's analytics capabilities for operational improvements. This gap highlights the need for more systematic approaches to BI integration that address both technical and organizational dimensions.

1.5 Significance and Potential Impact

The integration of business intelligence architectures with Moodle-based e-learning systems has significant implications for educational institutions facing increasing pressure to optimize resources, improve educational outcomes, and demonstrate value. As highlighted by Froissard et al. (2024), developing organizational capacity for learning analytics can transform institutional approaches to data-driven decision-making.

Table 1. Evolution of Learning Analytics Capabilities in Moodle

Period	Key Developments	Limitations
2002–2010	Basic activity logs and simple reporting capabilities	Limited analytical depth, manual data extraction processes
2011–2015	Introduction of events monitoring, enhanced reporting plugins	Fragmented analytics ecosystem, limited predictive capabilities
2016–2019	Native learning API analytics, prediction models, insights engine	Limited integration with external BI tools, complex configuration
2020–2023	Enhanced dashboard capabilities, xAPI integration, learning record store compatibility	Insufficient AI integration, challenges with big data processing
2024–Present	AI-driven analytics, advanced visualization capabilities, interoperability improvements	Ongoing challenges with data governance, privacy, and institutional adoption

Key potential impacts include:

- Enhanced resource allocation through data-driven insights into usage patterns
- Reduced administrative burden through automation of reporting and analysis.

- Improved faculty effectiveness through teaching analytics and workload optimization
- Enhanced student support through early intervention systems
- Better alignment of technological investments with institutional strategic objectives
- Evidence-based approaches to continuous improvement in e-learning implementation

As educational institutions navigate complex challenges including funding constraints, changing student demographics, and evolving pedagogical approaches, the ability to leverage data effectively becomes increasingly critical. The frameworks and methodologies presented in this chapter aim to provide practical guidance for institutions seeking to enhance the operational efficiency of their Moodle-based e-learning environments through business intelligence integration.

In the following sections, we will explore the theoretical foundations underlying this integration, examine current implementation practices, and develop comprehensive approaches to BI architecture design and deployment in Moodle-based educational environments.

2 THEORETICAL FOUNDATION

Understanding the integration of business intelligence architectures into Moodle-based eLearning systems requires a solid grasp of the underlying theoretical concepts, technological frameworks, and educational principles. This section establishes the foundational knowledge necessary for effective BI implementation in educational contexts.

2.1 Business Intelligence Concepts and Architectures

Business intelligence encompasses a broad range of technologies, applications, and methodologies that transform raw data into meaningful information for business analysis and decision making. In its essence, BI enables organizations to make data-driven decisions through systematic analysis of internal and external data sources. The core components of business intelligence architectures typically include:

1. Data Sources: Internal operational systems, external databases, web applications, and other data repositories
2. Data Integration: ETL (Extract, Transform, Load) processes, data cleansing, and normalization.

3. Data Storage: Data warehouses, data marts, and operational data stores
4. Analysis Tools: OLAP (Online Analytical Processing), data mining, and statistical analysis
5. Presentation Layer: Dashboards, reports, and visualization tools
6. User Interface: Access portals for different stakeholder groups

Traditional BI architectures have evolved significantly with the advent of big data technologies, cloud computing, and artificial intelligence. Modern BI architecture typically incorporates real-time analytics capabilities, machine learning algorithms, and natural language processing to provide more dynamic and predictive insights. Figure 2 illustrates a contemporary BI architecture framework applicable to educational contexts.

Figure 2. Modern business intelligence architecture framework for educational contexts

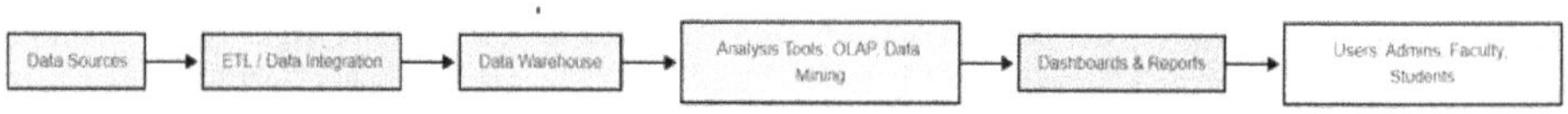

In educational settings, BI architecture must address unique requirements related to student privacy, pedagogical relevance, and alignment with educational objectives. Firat (2023) emphasizes that BI implementations in e-learning environments should focus not only on operational metrics but also on supporting teaching and learning processes through actionable insights.

2.2 Evolution of Learning Management Systems

LMS platforms today are larger and more advanced than they were, offering support for education based on data. Originally, learning systems did not encourage much interaction, but today's platforms such as Moodle do, thanks to tools like AI and analytics. As content repositories grew into intelligent learning environments, the amount and level of information for students grew too, making it both possible and challenging for BI integration. Today, useful features of LMS platforms include doing feedback in real time, adjusting learning as needed, and moving data safely and easily.

2.3 Moodle Platform Architecture and Extensibility

Moodle's architecture is designed with extensibility and customization as core principles, making it particularly suitable for BI integration. The platform's modular structure is built on a PHP foundation with a Model-View-Controller (MVC) architecture that separates data management, user interface, and control logic. Key architectural elements include:

- Core System: Provides fundamental functionality and data structures.
- Activity Modules: Support specific learning activities (assignments, quizzes, forums)
- Blocks: Offer additional functionality in sidebar widgets
- Filters: Process text and content for dynamic display
- Repository Plugins: Connect to external content repositories.
- Authentication Plugins: Handle user authentication methods
- Theme Plugins: Control visual appearance and user experience
- Web Services: Enable integration with external systems.

From a BI integration perspective, Moodle's data architecture is particularly significant. The system utilizes a relational database (typically MySQL or PostgreSQL) with over 250 tables capturing detailed information about users, courses, activities, interactions, and system events. This rich data foundation, coupled with Moodle's Events API, enables comprehensive tracking of learning activities and system operations.

Moodle's extensibility is facilitated through its plugin architecture, which allows for the addition of new functionality without modifying the core codebase. This approach enables the development of specialized analytics plugins and integration with external BI systems while maintaining compatibility with future Moodle updates. The platform's web services API further enhances integration possibilities by providing standardized methods for data exchange with external systems.

As noted by Abdillah et al. (2024), these architectural features have enabled innovative approaches to Moodle implementation, including the integration of design thinking methodologies to enhance user experiences and analytical capabilities.

2.4 Operational Efficiency Metrics in E-Learning Contexts

To effectively leverage BI for operational improvements, educational institutions must establish appropriate metrics for measuring efficiency in e-learning environments. Operational efficiency in this context encompasses both technical system performance and educational effectiveness. Table 2 outlines key categories of operational efficiency metrics applicable to Moodle-based e-learning systems.

Research by Puspitasari et al. (2023) suggests that operational efficiency metrics should be aligned with institutional strategic objectives and pedagogical goals to ensure that technical optimizations support improved educational outcomes. This alignment requires a holistic approach to metrics definition that considers diverse stakeholder perspectives, including administrators, faculty, students, and technical staff.

2.5 Theoretical Models for Technology Integration in Education

Several theoretical frameworks inform the integration of business intelligence technologies into educational contexts. These models provide conceptual guidance for understanding adoption processes, implementation challenges, and success factors. Key theoretical perspectives include:

Table 2. Operational Efficiency Metrics for Moodle-Based E-Learning Systems

Metric Category	Example Metrics	Data Sources in Moodle
Technical Performance	Server response time, page load time, system availability, storage utilization	Server logs, performance monitoring plugins, database statistics
Resource Utilization	Content access patterns, tool usage rates, bandwidth consumption, storage allocation	Activity logs, course reports, file system analytics
Administrative Efficiency	Time spent on course setup, enrollment processing time, grading workflow. duration	User action logs, completion tracking, gradebook timestamps
Instructional Delivery	Content delivery costs, assessment administration effort, feedback turnaround time	Course logs, assignment timestamps, feedback records
User Experience	Navigation efficiency, task completion rates, support request frequency	Usage patterns, session data, help desk integration

2.5.1 Technology Acceptance Model (TAM)

The Technology Acceptance Model, extended by numerous researchers, posits that technology adoption is primarily influenced by perceived usefulness and perceived ease of use. In Moodle contexts, García-Murillo et al. (2023) applied TAM to analyze faculty acceptance, finding that perceived usefulness was a stronger predictor of adoption than ease of use for analytics features.

2.5.2 TPACK Framework

The Technological Pedagogical Content Knowledge (TPACK) framework emphasizes the intersection of technological, pedagogical, and content knowledge required for effective technology integration in education. For BI implementation in Moodle, this framework suggests that successful integration depends on administrators and faculty understanding not only the technical aspects of analytics but also how these tools support pedagogical approaches and content delivery.

2.5.3 Unified Theory of Acceptance and Use of Technology (UTAUT)

The UTAUT model incorporates multiple theoretical perspectives to explain technology adoption, identifying performance expectancy, effort expectancy, social influence, and facilitating conditions as key determinants. This comprehensive framework is particularly relevant for understanding the organizational factors influencing BI adoption in educational institutions.

2.5.4 Diffusion of Innovations Theory

Rogers' Diffusion of Innovations theory provides insights into how modern technologies spread through social systems, identifying adopter categories and factors influencing adoption rates. This perspective helps explain the typical pattern of BI adoption in educational institutions, where analytics implementation often begins with innovators and early adopters before spreading to the mainstream.

2.5.5 Socio-Technical Systems Theory

This theoretical perspective emphasizes the interrelationship between technical systems and social structures within organizations. In the context of BI integration with Moodle, this theory highlights the importance of considering both technological affordances and organizational culture, policies, and practices that shape how data is collected, analyzed, and utilized.

Integration of these theoretical perspectives provides a comprehensive foundation for understanding the complex dynamics of BI implementation in educational contexts. As highlighted by Souhaib et al. (2024), successful integration must address both technical and socio-pedagogical dimensions to enhance engagement and operational efficiency.

3 CURRENT STATE OF MOODLE IMPLEMENTATION AND ANALYTICS

Understanding the current landscape of Moodle implementation and analytics utilization provides essential context for advancing business intelligence integration. This section examines adoption patterns, implementation practices, existing analytics capabilities, and limitations that motivate the need for more sophisticated BI approaches.

3.1 Adoption Patterns of Moodle in Higher Education

Moodle has emerged as one of the most widely adopted open-source learning management systems globally, with a particularly strong presence in higher education institutions. According to Moodle's official statistics, the platform is used in over 240 countries with more than 190 million users worldwide. This widespread adoption stems from several factors:

- Cost-effectiveness: Open-source nature eliminates licensing fees
- Customizability: Extensive options for adaptation to institutional needs
- Community support: Active developer and user communities
- Extensibility: Rich ecosystem of plugins and extensions
- Pedagogical flexibility: Support for diverse teaching approaches

Adoption patterns vary significantly across different regions and institutional types. In developing regions, Moodle adoption has been driven primarily by cost considerations and flexibility, while in more developed educational markets, the platform's extensibility and analytics potential have become increasingly important adoption factors.

Despite widespread adoption, the depth of implementation varies across institutions. Many organizations utilize only a fraction of Moodle's capabilities, focusing primarily on content distribution and basic assessment functionality while underutilizing the platform's analytics and reporting features. This implementation gap represents a significant opportunity for operational improvement through more comprehensive utilization of Moodle's capabilities, particularly in the realm of data analytics and business intelligence.

3.2 Best Practices in Moodle Implementation

Research on Moodle implementation has identified several best practices that contribute to successful deployment and utilization. Yunos et al. (2024) conducted a comprehensive study of Moodle implementation practices in public universities, identifying key success factors that align with operational efficiency objectives. These best practices include:

3.2.1 Strategic Alignment

Successful Moodle implementations align platform deployment with institutional strategic objectives, ensuring that technical configurations and feature utilization support broader educational and operational goals. This alignment includes defining clear objectives for data collection and utilization as part of the implementation planning process.

3.2.2 Stakeholder Engagement

Engaging diverse stakeholders—including administrators, faculty, students, and IT staff—in implementation planning and ongoing governance ensures that the system addresses varied needs and perspectives. Stakeholder engagement is particularly important for analytics implementations, as different user groups may have distinct requirements for data access and visualization.

3.2.3 Phased Implementation

Adopting a phased approach to Moodle implementation allows institutions to build capacity gradually, beginning with core functionality and progressively adding more advanced features including analytics capabilities. Figure 3 illustrates a typical phased implementation model for Moodle with business intelligence integration.

Figure 3. Phased implementation model for Moodle with business intelligence integration

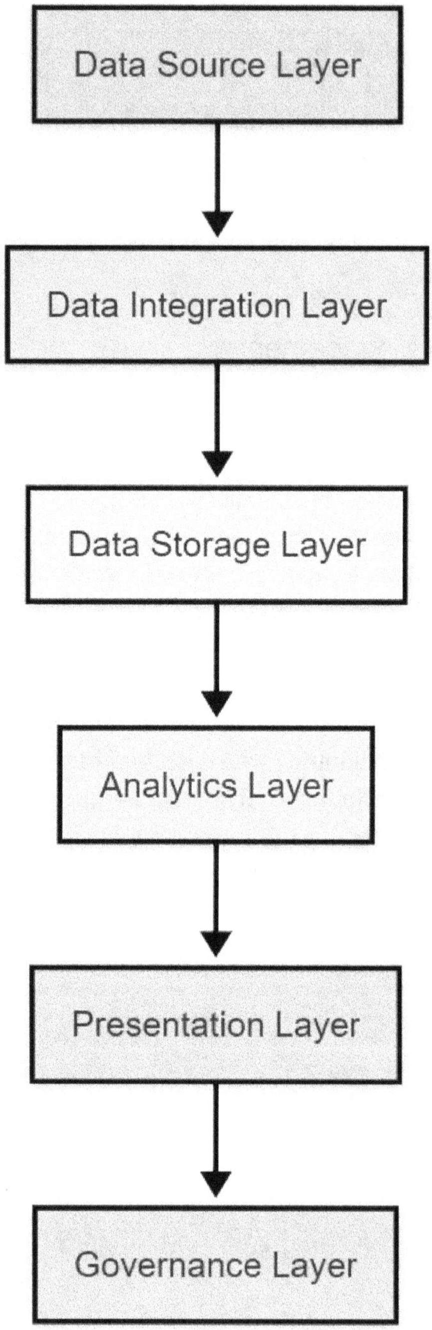

3.2.4 Comprehensive Training Programs

Effective training programs that address both technical and pedagogical aspects of Moodle utilization enhance adoption and effective use. For analytics implementations, training must extend beyond basic system operation to include data interpretation and application of insights to decision-making processes.

3.2.5 Technical Infrastructure Planning

Careful planning of technical infrastructure—including server configurations, database optimization, and integration architectures—ensures system performance and scalability. As analytics requirements increase data processing demands, infrastructure planning becomes increasingly critical for maintaining system responsiveness.

3.2.6 Continuous Evaluation and Improvement

Implementing systematic processes for evaluating system effectiveness and user satisfaction enables continuous improvement of Moodle deployments. Analytics capabilities can themselves support this evaluation process by providing insights into system utilization and impact.

These best practices provide a foundation for effective Moodle implementation but must be extended to address the specific requirements of business intelligence integration. As noted by Abdillah et al. (2024), incorporating design thinking approaches can enhance implementation effectiveness by focusing on user needs and experiences throughout the development process.

3.3 Current Analytics Capabilities within Standard Moodle Installations

Standard Moodle installations include several built-in analytics and reporting capabilities that provide a foundation for more advanced business intelligence applications. These native capabilities include:

3.3.1 Activity Reports

Moodle provides various activity reports that track user engagement with course components, including page views, resource access, assignment submissions, and quiz attempts. These reports offer basic filtering and sorting capabilities but limited options for advanced analysis or visualization.

3.3.2 Logs and Statistics

The system maintains detailed logs of user activities and system events, accessible through administrative interfaces. While comprehensive, these logs are primarily designed for troubleshooting and audit purposes rather than analytical insight generation.

3.3.3 Completion Tracking

Course completion tracking features allow monitoring of student progress against defined completion criteria. This functionality supports basic progress monitoring but offers limited predictive capabilities regarding completion likelihood or intervention effectiveness.

3.3.4 Grade Analysis

Moodle's gradebook includes basic statistical analysis of assessment results, including mean scores, distributions, and item analysis for quizzes. These features support instructional improvement but typically lack the sophistication needed for comprehensive performance analytics.

3.3.5 Learning Analytics API

More recent Moodle versions include a learning analytics API that supports the development of predictive models and insights generation. This API represents a significant advancement in Moodle's native analytics capabilities but requires technical expertise to implement effectively.

While these native capabilities provide valuable functionality, They often struggle to meet the comprehensive analytics requirements of educational institutions, particularly in areas such as predictive modeling, pattern recognition, and integrated visualization across multiple data dimensions.

3.4 Limitations of Native Moodle Reporting and Analytics

Despite ongoing improvements, native Moodle analytics capabilities exhibit several limitations that motivate the integration of more sophisticated business intelligence solutions:

3.4.1 Data Integration Challenges

Native Moodle analytics primarily focus on data generated within the platform itself, with limited capabilities for integrating external data sources such as student information systems, financial systems, or other institutional repositories. This limitation restricts the contextual richness of analysis and impedes comprehensive operational insights.

3.4.2 Analytical Depth

While Moodle provides descriptive statistics and basic monitoring capabilities, it offers limited support for advanced analytical techniques such as predictive modeling, clustering, or pattern recognition without additional plugins or external tools. Duch et al. (2024) highlight the need for more sophisticated predictive analytics to support early intervention and student success initiatives.

3.4.3 Visualization Constraints

Native visualization capabilities are relatively basic, limiting the effective communication of complex patterns and relationships in educational data. This constraint reduces the accessibility of insights for non-technical stakeholders and impedes data-driven decision making across the institution.

3.4.4 Scalability Issues

As institutional implementations grow and complexity, native analytics features may encounter performance limitations, particularly when processing large datasets or generating real-time insights. These scalability challenges can impede timely decision-making and reduce system responsiveness.

3.4.5 Limited Customization

While Moodle's open architecture supports customization, adapting native analytics features to specific institutional requirements often requires significant technical expertise and development resources. This barrier can limit the alignment of analytics capabilities with unique institutional needs and objectives.

3.4.6 Workflow Integration

Native analytics often exist as standalone features rather than integrated components of administrative and instructional workflows. This separation reduces the likelihood that insights will be effectively applied to operational decision-making and continuous improvement processes.

These limitations underscore the need for more comprehensive business intelligence solutions that extend Moodle's native capabilities while leveraging the platform's rich data foundation and extensible architecture.

3.5 Faculty Acceptance and Usage Patterns

The effectiveness of analytics implementations depends significantly on faculty acceptance and utilization patterns. García-Murillo et al. (2023) conducted research on technological acceptance of Moodle by higher education faculty, identifying several factors that influence analytics adoption:

3.5.1 Perceived Usefulness

Faculty are more likely to engage with analytics features when they perceive clear benefits for their teaching practice or student support efforts. This perception is influenced by the relevance of available data to instructional decision-making and the actionability of generated insights.

3.5.2 Technical Self-Efficacy

Faculty members' confidence in their ability to effectively use analytics tools significantly impacts adoption patterns. Those with higher technical self-efficacy are more likely to explore advanced features and incorporate data-driven approaches into their teaching practice.

3.5.3 Institutional Support

The availability of training, technical assistance, and peer support influences faculty willingness to adopt analytics capabilities. Institutions that provide comprehensive support ecosystems typically experience higher levels of faculty engagement with data-driven practices.

3.5.4 Time Constraints

Faculty frequently cite time limitations as a barrier to analytics adoption, particularly when data interpretation requires significant effort or specialized knowledge. Analytics solutions that minimize time requirements while maximizing insight valuc are more likely to achieve widespread adoption.

3.5.5 Privacy and Ethical Concerns

Faculty attitudes toward learning analytics are influenced by concerns regarding student privacy, data ownership, and potential misuse of performance data. Addressing these concerns through transparent policies and ethical frameworks is essential for promoting faculty acceptance.

Understanding these factors is critical for designing business intelligence implementations that align with faculty needs and preferences. As noted by Fernsel et al. (2024), providing evidence and auditability for analytics processes can enhance faculty trust and engagement with data-driven approaches.

4. BUSINESS INTELLIGENCE ARCHITECTURES FOR E-LEARNING

Implementing effective business intelligence solutions for Moodle-based e-learning environments requires carefully designed architecture that addresses the unique requirements of educational data analysis while leveraging contemporary approaches to data processing and analytics. This section examines the key components and architectural approaches for BI implementation in e-learning contexts.

4.1 Components of BI Architectures for Educational Contexts

Business intelligence architectures for e-learning environments comprise several essential components that work together to transform raw educational data into actionable insights. Figure 4 illustrates these key components and their relationships within a comprehensive BI architecture for Moodle-based systems.

Figure 4. Core components of business intelligence architecture for Moodle-based e-learning systems

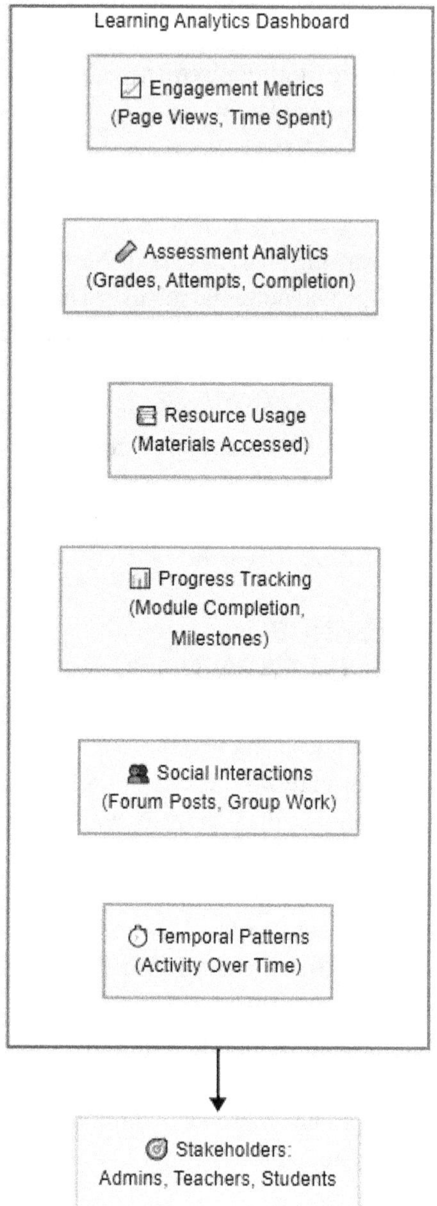

4.1.1 Data Source Layer

The data source layer encompasses all systems that generate or store data relevant to eLearning operations and outcomes. In Moodle-based environments, key data sources include:

- Moodle Database: The primary repository of learning activity data, user information, and system events
- Student Information Systems: Sources of demographic, enrollment, and academic history data
- Assessment Platforms: External systems used for specialized assessment processes.
- Library Systems: Data on resource utilization and information access patterns
- Financial Systems: Information on course costs, resource investments, and revenue streams
- Support Systems: Help desk tickets, technical support interactions, and service requests.
- External Data Sources: Benchmarking information, labor market data, and other contextual inputs

Effective BI architecture must address the heterogeneity of these data sources, including variations in data formats, update frequencies, access methods, and quality characteristics. As noted by Aung et al. (2024), integrating diverse data sources requires robust data governance frameworks and standardized integration procedures.

4.1.2 Data Integration Layer

The data integration layer is responsible for extracting, transforming, and loading data from source systems into formats suitable for analysis. Key components include:

- ETL Processes: Workflows for extracting data from source systems, applying transformations, and loading into analytical repositories.
- Data Quality Management: Tools and processes for ensuring data accuracy, completeness, and consistency.
- Data Standardization: Methods for normalizing data formats, taxonomies, and semantic representations
- Integration Middleware: Software components that facilitate data exchange between systems.
- Data Lineage Tracking: Mechanisms for documenting data origins and transformations

The complexity of this layer varies based on the diversity of source systems and the degree of standardization across institutional data. Educational institutions often face challenges related to data silos, inconsistent identifiers, and varying levels of data granularity across systems.

4.1.3 Data Storage Layer

The data storage layer provides repositories optimized for analytical processing and historical data retention. Common components include:

- Data Warehouse: Centralized repository of integrated data organized for analysis and reporting.
- Data Marts: Subject-specific subsets of the data warehouse focused on analytical domains.
- Operational Data Store: Near-real-time repository of current operational data
- Big Data Lake: Repository for storing diverse data types in their native formats.
- OLAP Cubes: Multidimensional structures optimized for analytical queries.

Educational data warehouses typically organize information around key entities such as students, courses, faculty, and resources, with dimensional models that support analysis across various perspectives including time, academic programs, and demographic characteristics.

4.1.4 Analytics Layer

The analytics layer encompasses tools and techniques for deriving insights from educational data. Key components include:

- Descriptive Analytics: Tools for understanding historical patterns and current states.
- Diagnostic Analytics: Capabilities for investigating causal relationships and contributing factors.
- Predictive Analytics: Models for forecasting outcomes and identifying future trends.
- Prescriptive Analytics: Systems that recommend actions based on analytical insights.
- Machine Learning Platforms: Environments for developing and deploying AI models.

- Statistical Analysis Tools: Software for applying statistical methods to educational data.

As highlighted by Duch et al. (2024), predictive analytics capabilities are particularly valuable for enhancing student support through early identification of at-risk learners and timely intervention. The analytics layer must balance sophistication with interpretability to ensure that insights are accessible to diverse stakeholders.

4.1.5 Presentation Layer

The presentation layer delivers analytical insights to users through various interfaces and formats. Key components include:

- Dashboards: Interactive visual interfaces for monitoring key metrics
- Reports: Structured presentations of analytical findings
- Data Visualization Tools: Software for creating charts, graphs, and other visual representations.
- Alert Systems: Mechanisms for notifying users of momentous events or patterns
- Mobile Interfaces: Access points optimized for smartphones and tablets
- Embedded Analytics: Insights integrated directly into operational systems

Effective presentation approaches must consider the diverse needs and technical proficiency levels of different stakeholder groups, including administrators, faculty, students, and support staff. Customizable interfaces that allow users to focus on relevant metrics and insights enhance adoption and utilization.

4.1.6 Governance Layer

The governance layer provides frameworks and processes for managing BI operations and ensuring appropriate data utilization. Key components include:

- Data Governance Frameworks: Policies and procedures for data management
- Security Controls: Mechanisms for protecting sensitive information
- Privacy Compliance: Systems for ensuring adherence to data protection regulations
- Access Control: Tools for managing user permissions and data visibility
- Audit Capabilities: Functions for tracking system usage and data access
- Metadata Management: Systems for documenting data definitions and relationships

As noted by Fernsel et al. (2024), auditing capabilities are particularly important in educational contexts to ensure transparency and accountability in analytics processes. The governance layer must balance security requirements with the need for broad data access to support decision-making across the institution.

4.2 Data Warehousing Approaches for E-Learning Data

Data warehousing forms a critical foundation for business intelligence in e-learning environments, providing integrated, subject-oriented, time-variant, and non-volatile data repositories optimized for analytical processing. Several warehousing approaches are applicable to Moodle-based systems:

4.2.1 Star Schema Design

The star schema represents a common dimensional modeling approach for educational data warehouses, organizing information around central fact tables (e.g., learning activities, assessment, resource utilization) connected to dimension tables (e.g., time, student, course, location). This approach optimizes query performance for analytical workloads while maintaining intuitive data structures that align with educational concepts.

4.2.2 Data Vault Architecture

The data vault methodology offers a highly flexible approach to data warehousing that accommodates evolving data structures and sources—a common requirement in educational environments. By separating hubs (key business entities), links (relationships), and satellites (descriptive attributes), this architecture facilitates the integration of diverse data sources while maintaining historical accuracy and auditability.

4.2.3 Hybrid Approaches

Many educational institutions adopt hybrid warehousing approaches that combine elements of different methodologies to address specific requirements. These hybrid models often include operational data stores for near-real-time analysis alongside traditional dimensional warehouses for historical reporting and longitudinal studies.

Table 3 compares these approaches across several dimensions relevant to e-learning implementations.

The selection of an appropriate warehousing approach depends on several factors including institutional size, analytical requirements, technical expertise, and existing data management practices. Smaller institutions with limited technical resources may benefit from simpler star schema designs, while larger organizations with diverse data sources and complex analytical needs may find value in more flexible data vaults or hybrid approaches.

4.3 ETL Processes for Moodle Data Integration

Extract, Transform, and Load (ETL) processes form the backbone of data integration for Moodle-based business intelligence implementations. These processes must address several challenges specific to educational data, including:

Table 3. Comparison of Data Warehousing Approaches for E-Learning Data

Characteristic	Star Schema	Data Vault	Hybrid Approach
Flexibility	Moderate requires redesign when new dimensions emerge	High accommodates new entities and relationships with minimal restructuring	Variable combines flexibility in some areas with optimization in others
Query Performance	High optimized for predefined analytical queries	Moderate requires additional transformations for analytical access	High—optimized for common queries while maintaining adaptability
Implementation Complexity	Low to moderate—follows established design patterns	High—requires sophisticated modeling ex-parties	Moderate to high—depends on specific combination of approaches
Historical Tracking	Supported through slowly changing dimensions	Comprehensive preserves complete historical context	Variable—often emphasizes history for critical entities
Scalability	Moderate performance may degrade with very large datasets	High—designed for enterprise scale implementations	High—can leverage distributed architectures for scale

4.3.1 Data Extraction Strategies

Several approaches are available for extracting data from Moodle environments:

- Direct Database Access: Querying the Moodle database directly for raw data extraction
- API-Based Extraction: Utilizing Moodle's web services API for structured data access
- Log File Processing: Analyzing system logs for activity and event data.

- Plugin-Based Extraction: Using specialized plugins that expose data for external systems.

Each approach offers different advantages in terms of data completeness, performance impact, and implementation complexity. Direct database access provides the most comprehensive data access but requires careful management to avoid performance impacts on production systems. API-based approaches offer better encapsulation but may have limitations in data granularity or historical access.

4.3.2 Common Transformation Requirements

Transformations prepare raw Moodle data for analytical use through several common processes:

- Data Cleansing: Identifying and correcting errors, inconsistencies, and missing values
- Normalization: Standardizing data formats and representations across sources
- Deduplication: Eliminating redundant records and resolving entity conflicts
- Aggregation: Summarizing detailed data for analytical processing
- Derived Metrics: Calculating additional measures based on raw data.
- Dimensional Mapping: Aligning data with dimensional models for analytical access.

Educational data often requires specialized transformations such as calculating engagement metrics from raw activity logs, determining progression status from completion records, and identifying behavioral patterns from sequences of learning activities. These transformations add significant value by translating low-level data into meaningful educational constructs.

4.3.3 Loading Approaches

Data loading strategies must balance timeliness with system performance and data integrity:

- Batch Loading: Scheduled transfers of data at defined intervals (daily, weekly)
- Incremental Loading: Processing only new or changed records since the previous load.
- Near-Real-Time Loading: Frequent small-batch transfers with minimal latency
- Event-Driven Loading: Data transfers triggered by specific system events.

The appropriate loading strategy depends on the nature of the analysis being supported. Administrative reporting may be adequately served by daily batch processes, while early intervention systems may require near-real-time data access to identify at-risk students promptly.

4.3.4 ETL Implementation Options

Several implementation approaches are available for building ETL processes for Moodle data:

- Custom Scripts: Tailored programming solutions in languages such as Python, PHP, or R
- ETL Platforms: Dedicated tools like Talend, Pentaho, or Microsoft SSIS
- Analytics Plugins: Moodle plugins that provide built-in ETL functionality
- Data Integration Services: Cloud-based integration platforms

The selection of an appropriate implementation approach should consider factors such as available technical expertise, budget constraints, existing technology investments, and specific integration requirements. As noted by Kouvara and Verykios (2024), the design of data integration processes significantly impacts the effectiveness of subsequent analytical applications such as recommender systems.

4.4 Distributed Computing Solutions for Educational BI

As e-learning data keeps on increasing, how fast and stable the learning systems are becomes an issue. They help organize and manage large data processing jobs more easily. Using tools like Hadoop means institutions can deal with high data volumes in a smooth and timely manner, with the core systems staying safe from overuse. Large and complex educational data, including interaction networks or lots of learning resources, can be managed well with NoSQL databases such as MongoDB or Neo4j. Businesses can use cloud technologies to build an analytics system that grows with their needs and is not too expensive. Even though such technologies are powerful, they can only be put to the right use if the organization is strategic, oversees data, and has competent staff.

4.5 Real-Time and Batch Processing in Educational BI

Balancing instant responsiveness and great system performance is important in business intelligence systems used in education. Timely awareness of at-risk students is made possible by analytical tools, whereas batch processing is appropriate for looking at long-term data and making regular reports. Often, a mix of techniques is the best way to go. For handling engagement in the moment, we use real-time processing, while batch processing is used for institutional planning and studying data after the fact. The choosing of a timing strategy is based on factors like what the network is used for, how it is set up, and the level of urgency involved.

5 INTEGRATION FRAMEWORKS AND METHODOLOGIES

Successful integration of business intelligence capabilities with Moodle-based e-learning systems requires well-defined frameworks and methodologies that address both technical and organizational dimensions. This section examines approaches to integration, development methodologies, security considerations, and case studies of successful implementations.

5.1 Technical Integration Approaches for BI Tools with Moodle

Several technical approaches are available for integrating business intelligence capabilities with Moodle environments, each offering different advantages in terms of implementation complexity, functionality, and maintainability.

5.1.1 Direct Database Integration

This approach involves connecting BI tools directly to the Moodle database for data extraction and analysis. Key characteristics include:

- Advantages:
    - Complete access to all Moodle data
    - No intermediate data storage requirements
    - Real-time data access potential
- Disadvantages:
    - Requires detailed understanding of Moodle's database schema.
    - May impact operational system performance – Vulnerable to schema changes in Moodle updates.
- Implementation Considerations:
    - Use read-only database connections to prevent accidental data modification.
    - Implement connection pooling to manage database load.
    - Create database views to simplify complex data relationships.
    - Schedule intensive queries during off-peak hours

This approach is often employed for initial BI implementations due to its relative simplicity but may face limitations as analytical requirements grow in complexity and scale.

5.1.2 Data Warehouse Integration

This approach involves extracting data from Moodle into a separate data warehouse optimized for analytical processing. Key characteristics include:

- Advantages:
  - Optimized data structures for analytical queries
  - Integration with data from other institutional systems
  - Minimal impact on operational Moodle performance – Historical data preservation independent of source system
- Disadvantages:
  - Increased complexity and infrastructure requirements
  - Potential data latency compared to direct access.
  - Requires ETL development and maintenance.
- Implementation Considerations:
  - Develop dimensional models aligned with educational analytics use cases.
  - Establish data refresh schedules based on reporting requirements.
  - Implement change data capture to minimize extraction impact.
  - Maintain data lineage documentation for traceability.

This approach represents the most common pattern for enterprise-scale educational analytics implementations, particularly in larger institutions with diverse data sources and complex analytical requirements.

5.1.3 API-Based Integration

This approach leverages Moodle's web services API for data exchange with external analytics systems. Key characteristics include:

- Advantages:
  - Well-defined interfaces that abstract database complexity
  - Better compatibility with Moodle updates
  - Controlled access to specific data elements
  - Support for both data extraction and action integration
- Disadvantages:

- May have limitations in data granularity or historical access.
- Potential performance constraints for large data volumes
- Requires API token management and security controls.

- Implementation Considerations:
  - Develop API wrappers to simplify integration with analytics tools.
  - Implementing strategies to improve performance
  - Monitor API usage to identify bottlenecks
  - Extend Moodle's API if additional endpoints are required

API-based approaches are particularly valuable for integrations that require bidirectional data flow, where analytics insights trigger actions within the Moodle environment.

5.1.4 Plugin Development

This approach involves creating custom Moodle plugins that extend the platform's native analytics capabilities. Key characteristics include:

- Advantages:
  - Seamless integration with the Moodle interface
  - Access to Moodle's internal APIs and data structures
  - Ability to extend native reporting capabilities – Distribution potential through Moodle's plugin directory
- Disadvantages:
  - Requires specialized Moodle development expertise
  - Must be maintained across Moodle version updates
  - Limited in ability to leverage external BI platforms
- Implementation Considerations:
  - Follow Moodle's plugin development standards
  - Leverage Moodle's analytics API for integration with the native insights system
  - Design for compatibility across Moodle versions
  - Contribute to the community through open-source distribution

Plugin development is particularly appropriate for institutions with specific analytical requirements that are closely tied to Moodle's core functionality and require deep integration with the user interface.

5.1.5 Embedded Analytics

This approach integrates analytics capabilities directly into the Moodle user interface through embedded frames or components. Key characteristics include:

- Advantages:
  - Contextual presentation of analytics within the learning environment
  - Leverages specialized BI platforms while maintaining unified user experience
  - Supports role-based analytics views
- Disadvantages:
  - May face technical challenges with authentication and single sign-on
  - Requires careful UI integration to maintain consistent experience
  - Potential performance impact on page loading
- Implementation Considerations:
  - Implement single sign-on between Moodle and the analytics platform
  - Design responsive visualizations that adapt to the Moodle interface
  - Use API filtering to present contextually relevant information
  - Consider progressive loading for complex dashboards

Embedded analytics approaches are increasingly popular as they combine the specialized capabilities of dedicated BI platforms with the contextual relevance of in-application presentation.

5.2 Development Methodologies for BI Integration

Business intelligence (BI) should be integrated into Moodle using both technical and organizational methods. Using design thinking and agile development, institutions can ensure their analytics tools meet the requirements of stakeholders and can be improved regularly. Development driven by data helps achieve quality by looking at data profiles, validating data, and focusing on proper governance. Lastly, adopting the incremental maturity approach starts with analyzing the data and then progresses to changing the systems accordingly. With these frameworks, BI integration can shape itself as both a practical and lasting solution for education.

5.3 Security and Data Privacy Considerations in Integration

The integration of business intelligence capabilities with Moodle environments must address critical security and privacy considerations, particularly given the sensitive nature of educational data and increasingly stringent regulatory requirements.

5.3.1 Data Protection Regulations

Educational institutions must navigate various regulatory frameworks that impact analytics implementations:

- General Data Protection Regulation (GDPR): Impacts institutions serving European students
- Family Educational Rights and Privacy Act (FERPA): Applies to US institutions receiving federal funding
- Health Insurance Portability and Accountability Act (HIPAA): Relevant for health-related educational programs
- Children's Online Privacy Protection Act (COPPA): Applies to students under 13
- Regional and national data protection laws: Vary by jurisdiction

Compliance with these regulations requires careful attention to data handling practices, user consent, data retention policies, and access controls throughout the BI integration process.

5.3.2 Authentication and Authorization

Secure access control is essential for protecting sensitive educational data:

- Single Sign-On (SSO): Integration with institutional identity providers
- Role-Based Access Control (RBAC): Limiting data access based on user roles
- Multi-Factor Authentication (MFA): Additional security for sensitive analytics
- Fine-Grained Permissions: Controlling access to specific data elements
- Audit Logging: Tracking system access and data utilization

These mechanisms ensure that users can access only the data needed for their specific responsibilities while maintaining a streamlined authentication experience.

5.3.3 Data Anonymization and Pseudonymization

Protecting individual privacy while enabling valuable analytics requires techniques for deidentifying sensitive information:

- Anonymization: Removing or transforming personal identifiers
- Pseudonymization: Replacing identifiers with artificial values
- Aggregation: Presenting data at group levels rather than individual
- K-Anonymity: Ensuring individuals cannot be identified in datasets
- Differential Privacy: Adding controlled noise to protect individual data points

These approaches must be carefully implemented to balance privacy protection with analytical utility, particularly for sensitive applications like student performance prediction.

5.3.4 Secure Data Transmission and Storage

Data security must be maintained throughout the analytics lifecycle:

- Encryption in Transit: Securing data during transmission between systems
- Encryption at Rest: Protecting stored data from unauthorized access
- Network Segmentation: Isolating analytics infrastructure from public networks
- Regular Security Audits: Identifying and addressing vulnerabilities
- Incident Response Planning: Preparing for potential security breaches

Educational institutions must implement comprehensive security controls that address both technical and procedural aspects of data protection to maintain stakeholder trust and regulatory compliance.

5.4 Case Studies of Successful Integrations

Examining successful implementations of business intelligence integration with Moodle provides valuable insights into effective approaches and potential benefits. The following case studies highlight diverse integration patterns across different institutional contexts.

5.4.1 Case Study 1: Comprehensive Data Warehouse Implementation at a Large University

A large public university implemented a comprehensive data warehouse solution integrating Moodle data with information from student information systems, library resources, and campus services. Key features included:

- Dimensional data model organized around student journeys

- Daily ETL processes with incremental loading
- Role-specific dashboards for administrators, faculty, and advisors
- Predictive models for student retention and course success
- Integration with institutional intervention systems

This implementation resulted in measurable improvements in course completion rates, timely degree attainment, and resource utilization efficiency. Success factors included strong executive sponsorship, dedicated data governance structures, and phased implementation that delivered early wins while building toward comprehensive capabilities.

5.4.2 Case Study 2: Real-Time Analytics for Early Intervention at a Community College

A community college implemented real-time analytics focused on early identification of at risk students to support timely intervention. Key components included:

- Near-real-time data extraction from Moodle
- Automated risk scoring based on engagement patterns
- Alert system integrated with advisor workflows
- Mobile interface for instructor notifications
- Closed loop tracking of intervention effectiveness

This implementation led to significant improvements in student persistence and course success rates, particularly among traditionally underserved populations. Critical success factors included faculty engagement in defining risk indicators, streamlined intervention processes, and continuous refinement of predictive models based on outcome data.

5.4.3 Case Study 3: Plugin-Based Analytics Extension at a K-12 District

A K-12 school district extended Moodle's analytics capabilities through custom plugin development focused on supporting differentiated instruction. Key features included:

- Learning style identification based on activity patterns
- Content recommendation engine integrated with the course interface
- Teacher dashboard for monitoring group progress
- Parent portal providing appropriate access to student data

- Integration with district assessment systems

This implementation enabled more personalized learning experiences while reducing teacher administrative burden. Success factors included teacher-centered design processes, incremental deployment with extensive training, and alignment with existing pedagogical frameworks.

5.4.4 Case Study 4: Cloud-Based Analytics Platform Integration at a Global Online University

A global online university integrated Moodle with a cloud-based analytics platform to support scalable analysis of learning patterns across diverse programs. Key components included:

- Stream processing of learner interaction data
- Machine learning models for engagement pattern identification
- Natural language processing for discussion forum analysis
- Adaptive content delivery based on performance patterns
- Global performance benchmarking across programs

This implementation enabled data-driven curriculum improvement while supporting personalized learning on a scale. Success factors included robust data governance, privacy-by design principles, and scalable architecture that accommodated growth without performance degradation.

These case studies demonstrate that successful BI integration with Moodle requires alignment of technical approaches with institutional context, clear focus on specific operational challenges, and attention to both technical and organizational factors throughout the implementation process.

6 LEARNING ANALYTICS APPLICATIONS AND USE CASES

The integration of business intelligence architectures with Moodle enables diverse analytical applications that enhance operational efficiency and educational effectiveness. This section explores key use cases for learning analytics, examining technical approaches, implementation considerations, and potential benefits.

6.1 Student Performance Prediction Models

Predictive analytics represents one of the most valuable applications of business intelligence in educational contexts, enabling proactive interventions and resource optimization.

6.1.1 Technical Approaches

Duch et al. (2024) explored approaches for enhancing predictive analytics in Moodle, identifying several effective modeling techniques:

- Regression Analysis: Linear and logistic regression models for predicting continuous outcomes (grades) and binary states (completion/non-completion)
- Decision Trees: Interpretable models that identify critical decision points in predicting student outcomes
- Random Forests: Ensemble methods that improve prediction accuracy through multiple decision trees
- Gradient Boosting: Advanced ensemble techniques that progressively refine predictions
- Neural Networks: Deep learning approaches for identifying complex patterns in educational data

Effective predictive models typically incorporate diverse data elements including:

- Historical academic performance
- Engagement patterns in the learning environment
- Time management behaviors
- Social interaction metrics
- Resource utilization statistics
- Demographic and contextual factors

The selection of appropriate modeling techniques depends on several factors including data availability, prediction objectives, interpretability requirements, and implementation constraints.

6.1.2 Implementation Considerations

Implementing predictive models for student performance requires attention to several critical factors:

- Model Transparency: Ensuring that predictions are explainable and interpretable
- Ethical Use: Avoiding reinforcement of biases or creation of self-fulfilling prophecies
- Timeliness: Generating predictions early enough for effective intervention
- Integration: Connecting predictions with intervention systems and workflows
- Validation: Continuously evaluating and improving model accuracy

Institutions must develop clear policies governing the use of predictive analytics, particularly regarding how predictions influence administrative decisions and support strategies.

6.1.3 Operational Benefits

Effective implementation of predictive analytics offers several operational efficiency benefits:

- More efficient allocation of support resources through targeted interventions
- Reduced administrative costs associated with student attrition
- Improved planning for course offerings based on progression predictions
- Enhanced retention rates leading to more stable enrollment
- Data-driven refinement of curriculum and pedagogical approaches

These benefits highlight the dual value of predictive analytics in enhancing both educational outcomes and operational efficiency.

6.2 Clustering and Student Profiling Techniques

Behavior patterns among groups of students are usually discovered with cluster analysis in learning analytics. These methods help teachers give students the help they need by looking at things like how interested they seem in class, how they're doing in school, and what kind of teaching style works best for them. Clustering modes in education often comprise k-means, hierarchical clustering, and density-based ones, each allowing common behavioral traits of students to be grouped together.

Ensuring that cluster groups are useful for teaching and meaningful to students requires selecting the right features, preparing data, and evaluating the clusters. For instance, looking at how students use the platform, do in their assignments, and which resources they use most can help find out which students might need more help or are already ready for tougher material.

Clustering helps to achieve better results in Moodle by making instruction and sharing resources more useful and focused on individuals.

6.3 Visualization Approaches for Learning Analytics

Effective visualization is essential for translating complex educational data into actionable insights that can drive operational improvements.

Several visualization approaches are particularly valuable for educational analytics:

- Interactive Dashboards: Customizable interfaces that present key metrics and trends
- Network Visualizations: Graphical representations of relationships and interactions
- Heat Maps: Visual representations of data density and patterns across dimensions
- Learning Pathways: Visual tracking of student progression through curriculum
- Temporal Visualizations: Representations of changes and patterns over time

Figure 5 illustrates an example dashboard integrating multiple visualization types for comprehensive learning analytics.

Figure 5. Multi-dimensional dashboard for learning analytics visualization in a Moodle-based environment

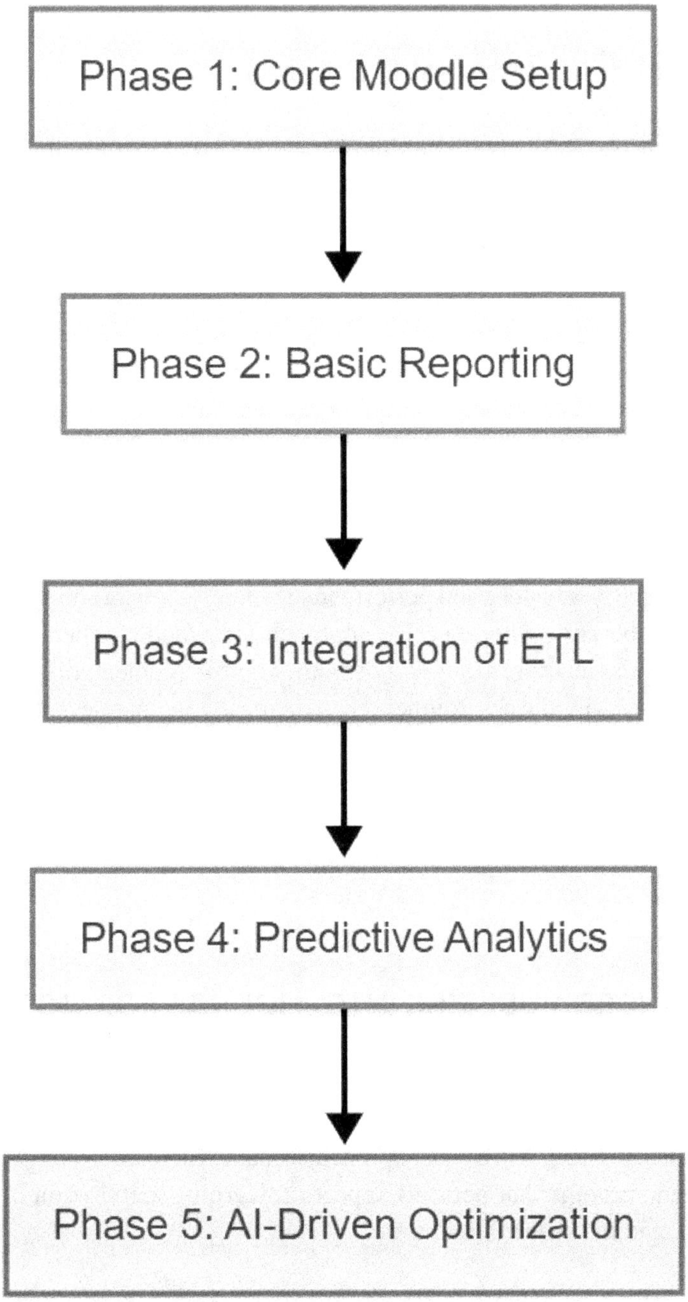

Alonso-Fernández et al. (2024) developed learning analytics tools specifically designed for analyzing progress and results with Moodle LMS data, emphasizing the importance of visual representations that align with educational decision-making processes.

6.4 Automated Assessment Processes

Automation in assessment streamlines educator workload and enhances feedback timeliness. Ouassam et al., 2023 developed an intelligent agent architecture within Moodle that automates grading and provides immediate formative feedback. Their model uses rule-based engines and semantic analysis to assess short-answer and essay responses, extending Moodle's standard quiz engine capabilities.

The system has shown promise in reducing grading time while maintaining assessment validity. Moreover, it supports adaptive testing frameworks by dynamically selecting items based on student ability, further personalizing the learning journey.

6.5 Recommender Systems for Learning Resources

Recommender systems aim to guide students toward appropriate learning materials based on their activity history and performance trends. Kouvara and Verykios, 2024 propose a collaborative filtering (CF) approach for Moodle, whereby the system learns from similar learners to suggest content. Their implementation demonstrates that CF-enhanced Moodle environments can increase content relevancy and student satisfaction.

Such systems can be integrated as Moodle blocks or plugins, offering suggestions directly within the learner's dashboard. Beyond academic content, recommendations can also include peer collaboration opportunities or extracurricular resources, contributing to a holistic learning ecosystem.

7 AI-ENHANCED BUSINESS INTELLIGENCE FOR MOODLE

The incorporation of artificial intelligence (AI) into business intelligence (BI) systems for Moodle represents a significant advancement in the capabilities of educational data analytics. AI-driven approaches enable more adaptive, personalized, and intelligent systems that not only report on learning activity but also predict, recommend, and intervene in real-time.

7.1 AI Integration Opportunities in Moodle Ecosystems

Moodle's modular architecture lets you add AI by using plugins or using the Moodle plugins or apps that come with some special functions. Institutions can use dashboards that show AI-generated reports, tutoring programs that learn from students, and personalized suggestions to make teaching and running the schoolwork better. These capabilities are made even stronger because Moodle can keep an eye on how people use the site and connect with other tools that help analyze the data.

7.2 Personalized Learning through BI-Derived Insights

Personalized learning environments get better when you add business intelligence and artificial intelligence to help measure and improve how things are working. AI-enhanced Moodle systems can change the lessons and the speed of learning, so it fits what teachers and BI have learned about each student. Personalized dashboards, adaptive quizzes, and specially made paths help keep students interested and make sure they learn better.

7.3 Machine Learning Models for Intervention Design

BI systems use predictive models to allow users to take initiative-taking actions. Historical patterns can teach algorithms to suggest ways like tutoring or using more resources to help provide support. Providing feedback in supervised learning helps ensure that support strategies improve as they are used.

7.4 Ethical Considerations in AI-Driven Analytics

As artificial intelligence is used more in Moodle-based BI, we need to focus on its ethical issues. Some of the main issues are making sure data doesn't discriminate, ensuring personal student information is safe, and guaranteeing equality in how decisions are made using data. They should make their data practices clear to learners, gain their agreement upfront, and use strong monitoring to ensure AI-driven analyses are used in an ethical and legal way.

8 MEASURING OPERATIONAL EFFICIENCY IMPACTS

To justify investments in business intelligence (BI) systems integrated with Moodle, institutions must be able to measure the impact of these technologies on operational efficiency. Quantifiable metrics are essential for assessing improvements in teaching effectiveness, resource utilization, administrative productivity, and overall learning outcomes.

8.1 Key Performance Indicators for Operational Efficiency

Operational efficiency in Moodle-based environments is often evaluated through a set of key performance indicators (KPIs) tailored to both educational and institutional goals. As noted by Puspitasari et al., 2023, KPIs should be aligned with strategic digital transformation objectives. Common categories include:

- System performance: server response time, uptime, and page load duration
- Resource utilization: bandwidth consumption, storage allocation, and content access frequency
- Instructional productivity: grading turnaround time, course completion rates, and student throughput
- Administrative efficiency: enrollment processing speed and workload balance
- User satisfaction: student and faculty feedback scores

These indicators can be automatically extracted from Moodle logs, plug-in analytics, and integrated BI dashboards.

8.2 Methodologies for Measuring BI Implementation Impact

A combination of quantitative and qualitative methodologies is needed to comprehensively assess the impact of BI integration. These include:

- Pre/post implementation analysis: comparing KPIs before and after BI adoption Longitudinal tracking: observing trends in student performance and engagement over multiple semesters.
- Controlled experimentation: piloting BI tools in select courses and measuring differential outcomes.
- Surveys and interviews: gathering stakeholder perspectives on perceived efficiency gains.

Yunos et al., 2024 emphasize that mixed-methods approaches enable institutions to capture both the statistical impact and user experience aspects of Moodle-embedded BI.

8.3 Faculty Workload Reduction Metrics

One significant impact of BI systems is the reduction of repetitive and manual academic tasks. Abdillah et al., 2024 describes how design thinking applied to Moodle interfaces helped reduce faculty workload by automating gradc calculations, monitoring student progress, and simplifying content reuse.

Metrics used to evaluate workload efficiency include:

- Time spent grading assignments.
- Number of manual communications replaced by automated alerts
- Hours spent on course configuration and reporting.

Such efficiencies allow instructors to focus more on pedagogical strategy and student engagement.

8.4 Student Engagement and Performance Impacts

Improved engagement and academic success are among the most valuable outcomes of Enhanced Moodle systems. Suad et al., 2023 found that when students were given access to learning analytics dashboards, their motivation and performance increased measurably. Visualization of progress and personalized feedback helped learners set goals, manage time effectively, and self-regulate learning. Institutions can track:

- Changes in login frequency and duration
- Completion rates of activities and modules
- Distribution of grades before and after BI integration
- Early identification and support of at-risk students

These indicators reflect not only improved efficiency but also enhanced educational outcomes, aligning with institutional goals for retention and achievement.

8.5 Cost-Benefit Analysis Frameworks for BI Integration

To ensure sustainability, institutions must evaluate BI integration from a financial perspective. Cost-benefit analysis involves comparing:

- Implementation costs: software licenses (if applicable), infrastructure upgrades, staff training

- Operational savings: reduced helpdesk load, faster administrative processing, improved resource allocation
- Academic returns: higher retention rates, better student outcomes, and improved teaching evaluations

Froissard et al., 2024 advocate for the use of organizational capacity-building metrics alongside cost-benefit models, highlighting that long-term returns often exceed initial investments when implementation is strategically aligned and institution-wide.

9 IMPLEMENTATION CHALLENGES AND SOLUTIONS

Despite the substantial benefits of integrating business intelligence (BI) into Moodle-based e-learning systems, institutions frequently encounter a range of challenges during implementation. These challenges span technical, organizational, and human factors. Overcoming them requires strategic planning, stakeholder engagement, and evidence-based solutions.

9.1 Technical Infrastructure Challenges

One of the foremost challenges is the scalability and reliability of technical infrastructure. Integrating BI tools with Moodle often demands robust server capacity, optimized databases, and secure API endpoints. Aung et al., 2024 highlight the use of distributed computing frameworks such as Hadoop to manage large-scale educational datasets efficiently. However, adopting such infrastructure requires specialized expertise and financial investment. Other technical obstacles include:

- Insufficient logging granularity or data inconsistency
- Performance degradation during ETL (Extract, Transform, Load) processes.
- Difficulty in integrating external systems such as SIS or LRS platforms.

To address these issues, institutions are advised to adopt modular integration strategies and invest in middleware solutions that can mediate between Moodle and BI components.

9.2 Organizational Capacity Development

Beyond technical requirements, successful BI integration hinges on institutional readiness. Froissard et al., 2024 emphasize that developing organizational capacity—including leadership support, cross-functional teams, and clear governance structures—is critical for long term success. Many institutions struggle with siloed data ownership, unclear roles, and lack of institutional vision for analytics. Suggested strategies include:

- Creating cross-disciplinary BI task forces
- Aligning BI initiatives with strategic planning documents
- Establishing data stewardship roles within academic departments

These efforts ensure that BI becomes embedded in the institutional culture rather than remaining a standalone technical project.

9.3 Faculty Training and Adoption Strategies

Faculty resistance and skill gaps are commonly reported barriers. García-Murillo et al., 2023 found that technological acceptance of Moodle's analytics tools is significantly influenced by perceived usefulness and the availability of training. Without targeted support, instructors may ignore or misinterpret BI insights, reducing the system's effectiveness. Best practices include:

- Offering tiered training programs (introductory, intermediate, advanced)
- Embedding analytics into teaching and learning centers' offerings
- Highlighting success stories through faculty champions

Incentivizing adoption and integrating analytics literacy into faculty development plans can foster a more data-informed teaching culture.

9.4 Data Quality and Standardization Issues

Poor data quality undermines the validity of analytics outputs. Moodle data often suffers from inconsistent naming conventions, incomplete logs, or missing metadata. Aitdaoud et al., 2023 emphasize the importance of pre-processing techniques to standardize input for accurate modeling and clustering.

To mitigate these challenges, institutions should:

- Implement automated data validation rules.
- Develop shared data dictionaries and taxonomies.
- Regularly audit datasets for accuracy and completeness

Ensuring high data integrity supports reliable decision-making and enhances user trust in the system.

9.5 Evidence-Based Auditing Approaches

Transparency and accountability are increasingly important in learning analytics. Fernsel et al., 2024 developed a plugin for auditing Moodle's analytics processes, enabling institutions to track data access, modeling decisions, and outcomes. Such auditing capabilities are vital for compliance with privacy regulations and for fostering ethical use of student data.

Recommendations include:

- Embedding audit trails in all analytics workflows
- Requiring justification for high-stakes predictive interventions
- Making model logic and limitations visible to end-users

By integrating evidence-based auditing, institutions can balance innovation with responsibility, ensuring that BI serves both operational efficiency and ethical governance.

10 CONCLUSION

The chapter looked at the effect of introducing business intelligence (BI) architecture into Moodle on the way work is conducted and how education is delivered. Predictive analytics, clustering techniques, recommender systems, and automation are some of the main applications that help make decisions based on data and support individual learning.

Significant achievements in BI can be measured using KPIs, analyses of faculty workloads, and engagement among students. For AI-assisted BI tools to succeed, the institution must be prepared, all faculty must receive proper training, data use should follow ethical guidelines, and the governance practices should be well-developed. If used strategically, BI boosts Moodle's power in teaching, helping learners, and bringing about continuous progress in the institution.

Although this chapter outlines the rules, empirical study and on-going changes are still needed to judge the final results. Overall, strategic use of BI favors equal learning opportunities, encourages new educational ideas, and allows for lasting progress with digital technology in e-learning.

REFERENCES

Abdillah, Y. A., et al. (2024). Design and development of interactive Moodle using design thinking to support online learning. – DOI: DOI: 10.21831/elinvo.v9i2.75255

Aitdaoud, M., Namir, A., & Talbi, M. (2023). New pre-processing approach for clustering learning styles in Moodle LMS. – DOI: DOI: 10.3991/ijet.v18i07.37635

Aung, M. M., et al. (2024). Implementing Hadoop and Moodle integrated student support system. – DOI: DOI: 10.1109/ICAIT65209.2024.10754929

Duch, D., May, M., & George, S. (2024). Enhancing predictive analytics for students' performance in Moodle: Insight from an empirical study. – DOI: DOI: 10.47852/bonviewJDSIS42023777

Fernsel, L., Kalff, Y., & Simbeck, K. (2024). Where is the evidence? A plugin for auditing Moodle's learning analytics. – DOI: DOI: 10.5220/0012689800003693

Firat, M. (2023). Integrating AI applications into learning management systems to enhance e-learning. – DOI: DOI: 10.52911/itall.1244453

Froissard, J.-C., et al. (2024). A learning analytics pilot in Moodle and its impact on developing organisational capacity in a university. – DOI: DOI: 10.14742/apubs.2017.745

García-Murillo, G., Novoa-Hernández, P., & Serrano Rodríguez, R. (2023). On the technological acceptance of Moodle by higher education faculty. – DOI: DOI: 10.3390/bs13050419

Kouvara, T., & Verykios, V. (2024). Discovering the collaborative filtering (CF) recommender system in a Moodle learning environment. – DOI: DOI: 10.12681/icodl.5638

Ouassam, E., Hmina, N., & Bouikhalene, B. (2023). Design of intelligent agent on Moodle to automate the learning assessment process. – DOI: DOI: 10.11591/ijeecs.v31.i3.pp1665-1672

Puspitasari, L. P., Sumaryati, S., & Sudiyanto, S. (2023). Effectiveness of Moodle-based e-learning in enhancing digital literacy. – DOI: DOI: 10.23916/083346011

Souhaib, A., Zakaria, T., & Tarik, T. (2024). Enhancing socio-pedagogical engagement in Moodle through AI-driven personalized learning. – DOI: DOI: 10.14571/brajets.v17.nse4.63-73

Suad, A., Tapalova, O., Berestova, A., & Vlasova, S. (2023). The impact of Moodle learning analytics on students' performance and motivation. – DOI: DOI: 10.29333/iji.2023.16418a

Yunos, N., Muslim, N., Hussain, A. H., Hasim, N. A., Nazri, N. S., & Hamsan, M. H. (2024). Best practice of Moodle implementation for e-learning: A perspective of public university lecturers. – DOI: DOI: 10.62754/joe.v3i5.3899

Chapter 8 Integrating Business Intelligence With QA Processes for Enhanced Software Quality and Operational Efficiency

Harini Shankar
https://orcid.org/0009-0007-6891-8669
Independent Researcher, USA

ABSTRACT

This chapter explores the strategic integration of Business Intelligence (BI) into Quality Assurance (QA) to enhance software quality and operational efficiency. It highlights how BI transforms QA from a reactive process into a proactive, data-driven function that supports real-time decision making, predictive analytics, and continuous improvement. The chapter examines architectural components, technical infrastructure, and implementation roadmaps, while presenting real-world case studies from healthcare, SaaS, and e-commerce sectors. It also addresses organizational challenges such as data silos, tool interoperability, and cultural resistance, offering practical strategies to overcome them. Emphasis is placed on aligning QA metrics with business outcomes, enabling executive-level decision-making through actionable insights. The chapter concludes with a focus on the future of intelligent QA systems, emphasizing the importance of cross-functional collaboration, skill transformation, and the role of BI in driving quality as a core business strategy.

DOI: 10.4018/979-8-3373-2125-7.ch008

1. INTRODUCTION

In today's evolving technological era, data has emerged as a foundational asset in software engineering. It is highly important for organizations to pay attention to speed-to-market as they face increasing pressure to deliver high quality software in a rapidly and reliably. Business Intelligence (BI) has become a critical enabler of operational efficiency and has transformed how enterprises leverage data for decision making. BI has been widely adopted in areas such as sales, marketing, and finance. However, its integration to the Quality Assurance (QA) process remains an emerging trend with significant potential. This chapter explores the emerging intersection of BI and QA, offering insights into how BI architectures can improve overall software quality and drive impactful results. To support this shift in practice, organizations need to rethink their existing processes and seek intelligent, data-driven methods to improve quality.

Traditional QA approaches focused on functionality, performance, and security through structured test processes. As applications grow in complexity leading to accelerated development cycles, QA teams are challenged to not only verify functionality more intelligently. This is where BI supports a shift from reactive to proactive testing methodologies. When BI is embedded into QA processes, organizations can shift from reactive testing into a more proactive approach. Quality management becomes more data driven enabling insights that are predictive, real time monitoring and decision making that is more strategic.

This integration becomes more relevant in the context of modern software development practices that include Agile, DevOps, Continuous Integration/ Continuous deployment where it becomes challenging for traditional QA approaches to keep pace with. Using BI tools, QA related data such as defect rates, test coverage, code quality, cycle time, and customer-reported issues can be aggregated. This enables stakeholders to make informed decisions in a quick and efficient manner. Operational efficiency is not just about cutting costs; it is more about building optimised processes, reducing risks and enhancing customer satisfaction. BI powered QA has become a crucial component in achieving these outcomes.

As illustrated in **Figure 1**, the integration of Business Intelligence (BI) into QA processes enables a shift from reactive to proactive quality practices across modern DevOps pipelines.

In this chapter, we position BI as a strategic enabler of improved software quality and operational efficiency. It also offers a comprehensive roadmap for integrating BI tools and frameworks into QA workflows. We will delve into the architectural aspects, key metrics and case studies demonstrating the tangible benefits of this integration. Additionally, we will address the challenges that organizations can face, such as data in silos, tool interoperability, and skill gaps, and we offer strategies on how to overcome them. This chapter not only discusses technical possibilities but also emphasizes how integrating BI into QA processes can directly contribute towards the operational efficiency. By enabling concepts such as real-time monitoring, predictive insights, and traceable metrics, BI is able to allow enterprises to reduce delays. This improves resource allocation and elevates quality into a measurable business driver.

Figure 1. Overview of how BI-augmented QA processes enable predictive insights and proactive quality strategies in a modern CI/CD pipeline

As organizations are striving for digital excellence, the blend of BI and QA represents the transformation of driving value from data. This is not just understanding what has happened, but in anticipating what needs to happen in each and every stage of the software lifecycle to ensure quality. When organizations leverage modern BI architectures, QA members are able to contribute directly to operational goals. This eventually makes quality not just a checkpoint, rather a driver of business performance.

Through these explorations, readers will gain an in depth understanding of:

- How BI can transform traditional QA into intelligent, insight driven quality engineering
- The architectural components that are needed to integrate BI into QA processes in an efficient manner

- Best practices for deploying BI tools to track, analyze and optimize QA metrics
- The role of predictive analytics and AI to enable proactive quality process
- Operational gains that are realized through improvement in software quality and improved time to market.

As we get through these chapters ahead, We will uncover the strategic advantages of uniting BI and QA and provide practical guidance on how organizations can become ready to elevate their quality practices into the area of data-driven excellence. By doing so, this chapter contributes to the broader theme of this book - "Driving Modern Business Intelligence Architecture for Operational Efficiency". It demonstrates that quality is not just a function, but something that can be measured, managed and optimized in today's data driven world.

Key Takeaways

- QA is evolving from a test execution role into a strategic function aligned with operational efficiency.
- Business Intelligence (BI) offers tools and frameworks to transform QA data into actionable insights.
- There is a growing need to integrate QA data into broader enterprise decision-making systems.

2. Business Intelligence in QA - Strategic Value

The convergence of Business Intelligence (BI) and Quality Assurance (QA) goes beyond just improving reporting or data visualization aspects. It represents a fundamental shift on how we measure, understand and enhance software quality. In the traditional QA approaches, static metrics, test case pass/fail rates and reactive defect analysis are more relied on. These approaches can be valuable; however, they fail to proactively help teams in identifying defects. BI facilitates a shift in QA functions towards a more proactive, strategic function where intelligent data centric mechanisms are able to shed insights earlier and more holistically across the software lifecycle.

Positioning QA as an Upstream Contributor

In a historical sense, QA has been perceived as a gatekeeper. They are tasked with identifying bugs prior to release. In a lot of organizations, QA is involved only towards the end of the development cycle. They often have limited influence over architectural or design decisions. When BI is integrated, QA teams are repositioned from a downstream checkpoint to a more holistic and continuous upstream influencer. With embedded BI tools and practices, QA teams are able to now have access to real time and predictive analytics. These give insights on every phase of development right from planning and coding to deployment and monitoring.

As a result of this evolution, QA's objectives are able to align with wider business goals. With the help of BI dashboards and trend analyses, QA teams are now able to highlight how quality related issues correlate with business KPIs such as customer retention, user feedback and operational cost. Due to this shift, QA becomes an active stakeholder in the enterprise wide decision making and planning process.

Real Time Monitoring and Predictive Quality Metrics

One of the most transformative contributions of using BI in QA is its ability to shift from lagging to more leading indicators. In older QA processes, test failures are identified later in the stage which is mostly after execution. With this new approach of integrating BI, it has become possible to anticipate issues based on development behavior, environment stability issues, or trends on regression. When predictive analytics is powered by BI, it can flag areas that are prone to defects even before testing begins. This enables pre emptive code review or architectural refactoring if needed.

Stakeholders are able to monitor key quality metrics on an ongoing basis using real-time dashboards. For example, it helps engineering leads track defect density based on modules. They are also able to view automation coverage per sprint, or evaluate system performance against established thresholds. It also gives the ability for test managers to observe trends in test execution times, flaky tests, or bottlenecks in the CI CD pipeline. Hence, release quality can now be correlated with customer satisfaction scores. Using these insights, quality engineering is able to align with business outcomes. This ensures QA priorities reflect the organization's priorities.

As illustrated in **Figure 2**, BI dashboards help visualize key metrics across stages of CI/CD, enabling proactive decision-making and continuous quality alignment.

Data-Driven Test Planning and Prioritization

With the help of BI, risk-based testing is also possible. This is a methodology where test effort is distributed based on the risk of each component or feature. Using data from incident logs, customer complaints or performance bottlenecks, QA teams are able to focus testing areas that are more likely prone to impact user experience or compliance. Using this approach, efficiency is maximized by improved ROI and reducing unnecessary overhead.

Operational Efficiency through Continuous Feedback

In software development, operational efficiency is often measured in terms of velocity, throughput, and cost of quality. Using BI, we are able to monitor and improve all three. For example, teams are able to gain insights on higher than average defect escape rates or any code review delayed using automated dashboards. Regression dashboards are able to identify modules that consistently break during integration which can prompt deeper analysis. Using metrics such as cycle times, teams can detect inefficiencies in test case design, environment setup or deployment readiness.

Using these insights, it becomes easier for the implementation of continuous feedback loops. Developers are able to use these early warnings from BI tools to self correct even before issues escalate. Managers are able to allocate resources more effectively. Product owners are able to make informed trade offs between release timelines and risk. Over time, this continuous visibility and feedback fosters an environment of accountability, transparency, and agility. These are the key attributes of a high performing DevOps environment.

Driving Compliance and Audit Readiness

Using custom dashboards, compliance coverage can be demonstrated compliance with regulatory standards. Audit teams can access time stamped evidence of test results, approvals, and anomaly investigations. During compliance audit for example, BI reports are able to provide the documentation and lineage necessary to prove due diligence.

Organizations that use Infrastructure as Code (IaC) practices can now integrate their QA analytics with configuration management and vulnerability scanning tools. Using this approach, organizations can achieve end-to-end traceability based on a business requirement to test. They are also able to create secure production releases which is a key requirement in modern governance, risk, and compliance frameworks.

Figure 2. Example of BI-integrated QA dashboards showing test coverage, regression trends, and defect hotspots in a modern DevOps pipeline

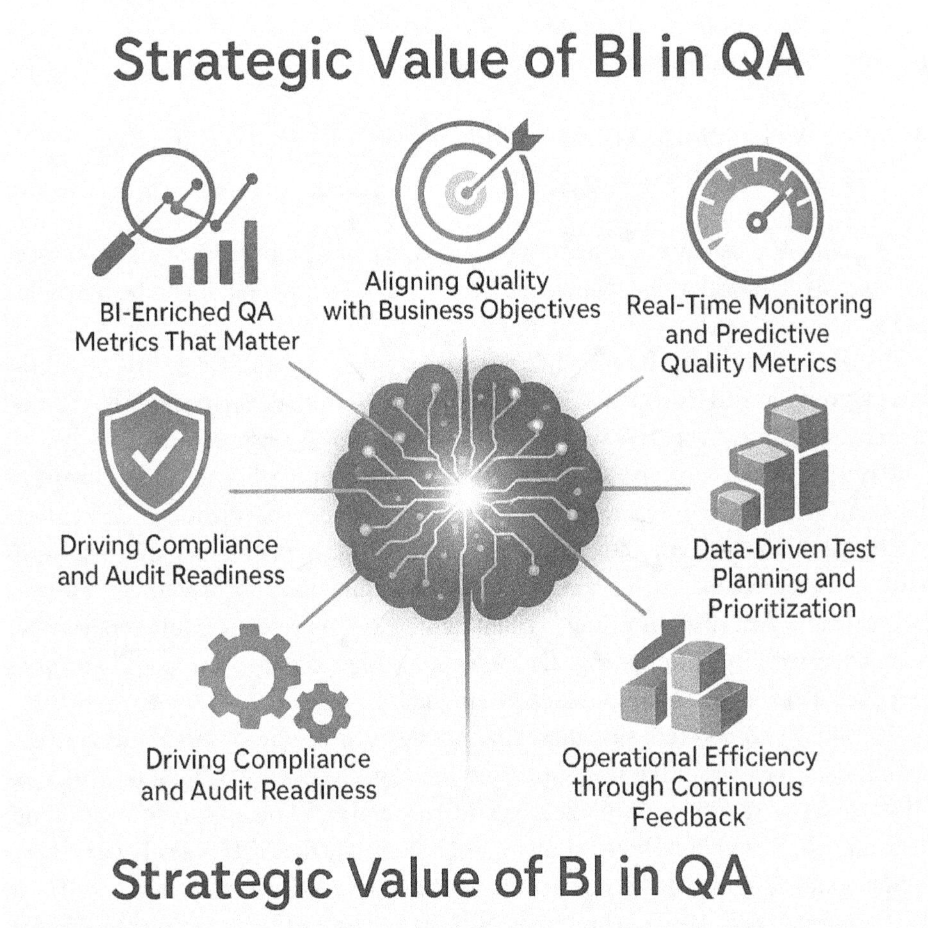

BI Enriched QA Metrics That Matter

Not all QA metrics have the same value. Older metrics such as test case counts, number of defects, or pass fail percentages can often be misleading or lack business context. BI is able to encourage the use of more meaningful metrics that can reflect both engineering health and user impact.

Here are some examples of BI-enriched QA metrics include:

- **Defect Leakage Rate**: Percentage of defects that were missed by QA and were caught in production.
- **Automation ROI**: Time that was saved or defects that were caught due to automated vs manual testing.
- **Test Debt Ratio**: Proportion of outdated or unused test cases in the regression suite.
- **Release Readiness Score**: Score based on test results, bug trends, performance benchmarks, and risk flags.

When metrics such as these are visualized via BI dashboards, decision-makers are able to monitor not just what went wrong, but why and how it can be prevented and what impact they truly had on the business.

The field of Business Intelligence has been studied for strategic decision-making since Davenport and Harris (2007) and Watson (2014) but recent research has started to analyze its transformative impact on DevOps and QA observability.

Mahida (2024) demonstrates how integrating observability into DevOps practices enhances operational resilience and performance optimization, particularly in finance and healthcare industries. Their study highlights the use of dashboards built with Prometheus and Grafana to track CI pipeline stability, test duration trends, and real-time API response times. Thantharate (2023) presents IntelligentMonitor as an observability solution that leverages real-time data collection and analytics to reduce alert fatigue and improve system visibility.

The industry reports confirm these findings by showing how observability converts system data into executive-level strategic insights (Neontri, 2025) and Dynatrace (2024) demonstrates its role in release validation and pipeline optimization. Refonte Learning (2025) explains how Prometheus Grafana and the ELK Stack have become fundamental skills for quality teams that operate under DevOps principles. These works demonstrate that QA functions as a data-intensive strategic practice which drives continuous quality and operational efficiency throughout modern software delivery pipelines.

Key Takeaways

- Early BI research focused on business operations, while recent studies highlight its role in DevOps and QA observability.
- Tools like Prometheus, Grafana, and IntelligentMonitor are redefining how QA teams track system health and performance.
- QA is emerging as a data-intensive practice, yet literature on BI's role in QA remains sparse, indicating a research gap.

3. ARCHITECTURAL OVERVIEW

Organizations are working to make Quality Assurance (QA) more efficient and strategically aligned. This integration of Business Intelligence (BI) into QA practices needs a thoughtful architectural approach. In this section, we will explore the BI architecture and how it intersects with QA systems. We will also discuss the technical infrastructure, integration points and tooling that is needed to transform traditional QA into a more insight driven quality engineering approach.

Modern Business Intelligence Architecture

Modern BI architecture typically consists of four layers:

1. **Data Ingestion Layer** – This layer is responsible for collecting raw data from different sources.
2. **Data Storage Layer** – This includes data lake and warehouses that store structured and unstructured QA data.
3. **Data Processing and Transformation Layer** – This is the layer where ETL (Extract, Transform, Load) or ELT (Extract, Load, Transform) processes clean, prepare, and normalize the data.
4. **Analytics and Presentation Layer** - This layer is powered by BI tools like Power BI and Tableau. This enables visualization, dashboards, predictive analytics, and AI/ML capabilities.

The different layers work together to allow QA teams to use BI effectively. For instance, QA data such as test case execution results, defect logs and metrics can be fed from CICD tools, version control or test automation suites into the ingestion layer. The data is then processed and stored for further usage and analysis.

Intersection of BI and QA Systems

The software delivery pipeline contains multiple essential points where BI and QA intersect.

- **Defect Analytics**: The integration of bug tracking systems like JIRA into BI pipelines enables the analysis of defect trends and severity levels and defect leakage patterns.
- **Visualization of Coverage**: The system aggregates test execution data from Selenium and Cypress tools to display real-time automation coverage across applications.

- **Cycle Time and Velocity**: The build and deployment timestamps from Jenkins or Azure DevOps enable us to track end to end lead time for changes.
- **Release Health Dashboards**: Release Health Dashboards combine QA data with development and operations data for comprehensive analysis.
- **Customer Centric QA**: The integration of customer support ticket feedback with Splunk and Datadog monitoring tool data enhances QA decision-making with user behavior data.

As illustrated in Figure 3, a modern BI-QA architecture includes distinct data layers and integration touchpoints that drive actionable insights across the CI/CD pipeline.

Quality teams can move beyond traditional validation by leveraging this intersection of capabilities. Active product and business outcome influence becomes possible through this approach.

Figure 3. Architectural diagram showcasing the integration of QA data pipelines with BI layers, visualization tools, and observability platforms

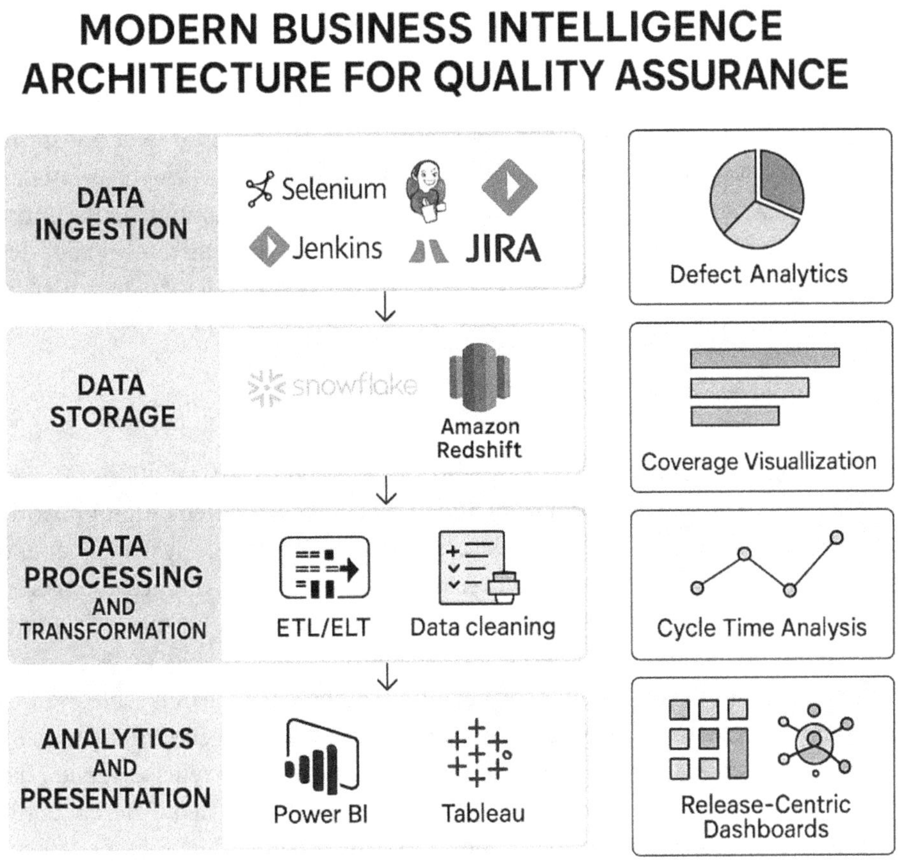

Integration - Technical Infrastructure

A strong technical infrastructure must be established to enable BI and QA collaboration. The following components are the key:

Data Pipelines (ETL/ELT)

ETL (Extract, Transform, Load) and ELT (Extract, Load, Transform) are two key approaches to ingest and prepare QA-related data for business intelligence. When the data needs extensive cleansing before loading—such as transforming inconsistent test logs from Selenium or mapping environment variables to standard names, ETL is used. ELT, on the other hand, is used when the storage layer (like Snowflake) can handle transformations after data is loaded, enabling faster ingestion. For example, using Apache NiFi, QA test execution logs from Selenium and API test results from Postman can be extracted in JSON format. The data is enriched by tagging each test with metadata such as tester ID, build number, and module name. This data is either transformed inline (ETL) or stored first in a warehouse for later transformation (ELT). These structured datasets feed into dashboards showing pass/fail ratios per environment, test flakiness trends, and regression cycle duration across sprints.

The system ingests Selenium test execution results to generate module-level pass/fail ratio calculations. The system can integrate additional metadata elements, including tester identification numbers, test categories, and product release versions.

Data Warehousing

The integration of Quality Assurance (QA) with modern BI solutions often employs a data warehouse platform from Snowflake or Amazon Redshift for historical QA data management. The platforms serve as essential storage systems that allow users to query and analyze large datasets at scale. The design of database schemas determines how data becomes organized for optimal analysis purposes. Fact tables in standard QA data models hold transactional data which includes test case execution logs, defect submissions, and build outcomes. Dimension tables serve to add context to data by storing information about test environments, along with user information, time stamps and application module details and release version data. The database uses bridge tables to establish connections between different entities such as test cases and defects and builds and deployments. This schema structure enables both time-series analysis and categorical insights to generate extensive QA reports which scale within the BI ecosystem.

Semantic Layer

This layer creates business-friendly data definitions and metrics to simplify the understanding of the complex underlying data schema. Power BI's commonly supports the development of measurable elements such as Mean Time to Detect (MTTD), Defect Rejection Rate, Test Automation ROI, and Defect Clustering by Root Cause. Through its well-organized semantic layer structure organizations provide QA stakeholders and leadership with simple meaningful insights that do not require knowledge of technical raw data complexities.

Analytics and Visualization Tools

The implementation of modern BI tools after centralizing QA data enables real time dashboards and advanced analytics. Power BI serves Microsoft-based environments exceptionally well because it offers effortless integration with DevOps platforms. Users find Tableau useful because it offers interactive dashboards with detailed visualizations together with drill-down capabilities. Real-time monitoring through Grafana becomes particularly effective when dealing with time series databases. The BI platforms support three essential use cases: defect density analysis, release readiness score evaluation, and automation ROI calculation. Decision making processes become more informed and aligned because of this development.

Enabling Technologies

Several enabling technologies exist to connect BI functionalities with QA capabilities. TestOps platforms TestRail and Zephyr enable users to access built-in analytics features and create custom dashboards that fulfill enterprise requirements. The integration of Observability tools including Splunk and Datadog enables organizations to monitor test environments and detect anomalies while verifying system behavior under test loads. AI/ML frameworks such as TensorFlow can be used to analyze QA datasets for generating predictive metrics and insights. The AI layer transforms Business Intelligence into a proactive system from its current reactive state.

Key Takeaways

- A modular BI architecture enables seamless integration between QA tools and data pipelines.
- Layered approaches using ETL/ELT workflows help in standardizing and enriching QA metrics.
- Interoperability with CI/CD systems (e.g., Jenkins, GitHub) is critical for real-time observability.

4. IMPLEMENTATION ROADMAP

Integration of Business Intelligence (BI) into Quality Assurance (QA) workflows is more than a simple overlay of reporting tools. It is a strategic shift. This transformation requires structured rollout that begins with readiness that evolves through technical integration and later matures into widespread cultural adoption. This section outlines a phased implementation roadmap that shows how organizations are able to embed BI into their QA processes. This turns quality data into a continuous driver of operational efficiency and informed decision making.

Assessing QA Maturity and BI Readiness

Business Intelligence implementation for Quality Assurance starts with understanding the current position of the organization. The starting point is a comprehensive assessment of regular test execution documentation and availability of test data. This includes assessing how standardized the testing procedures are. The assessment of regular test execution result documentation alongside evaluation of test data availability from manual and automated testing systems in usable formats. Organizations need to establish foundational work when data literacy is low and their data structure is disorganized. The base needs to be established because otherwise efforts may experience stall due to hidden complexities. The diagnostic stage enables organizations to detect both existing technical gaps and necessary skill rebuilding needs.

Identifying Data Sources and Metrics Definition

After readiness is established, the next step is mapping QA data sources metrics definition. Across the software delivery pipeline, quality data is identified. The software delivery pipeline uses test automation tools such as Selenium combined with CI/CD systems including Jenkins and Azure DevOps. The data sources include both defect tracking platforms like JIRA and observability systems like Splunk. BI analysis becomes more significant when this data is unified into a single coherent stream.

The process of deciding which metrics to measure requires equal importance to identifying where the data exists. The traditional QA metrics which measure test case numbers and defect discoveries no longer provide sufficient information. Quality improvement requires metrics that guide improvement in addition to showing quality status. The metrics should include defect leakage rates together with test coverage across business critical modules and time to resolve issues. The goal here is to ensure that the metrics are actionable and aligned with business priorities. The definitions need to involve multiple stakeholders including QA and both BI analysts and engineering leadership to ensure dashboard and insight relevance for the entire organization.

Choosing Tools Aligned to Infrastructure and Goals

Organizations should determine their tools based on their existing infrastructure capacity and their upcoming strategic direction after identifying their data sources and relevant metrics. The correct technical stack depends on whether the organization adopts a cloud-first strategy or a hybrid model or operates from premises. Data pipeline tools such as Apache NiFi, AWS Glue enable the extraction, transformation, and loading (ETL or ELT) of QA data into more centralized repositories. These tools enable standardization of raw test result data and build logs and defect tracking system data for better analysis readiness.

Building Pipelines and Launching Pilot Dashboards

Implementation starts with the proper selection of tools. The actual data pipelines that link test execution systems to CI/CD platforms, and defect trackers with the centralized BI ecosystem get built during this phase. Following this step, data requires cleaning and enrichment with additional metadata which includes test environment and release version information and much more in alignment with defined metrics. The system must reliably handle multiple data formats and periodic updates.

The first phase should include the development of dashboard prototypes instead of immediate full deployment. The main metrics that these dashboards should track include regression stability along with sprint-specific defect patterns and release preparedness indicators. A dashboard tracking automation coverage between sprints helps identify untested critical workflows that maintain low testing frequency. The pilot environment allows users to check data accuracy and test visualization while optimizing metrics before they deploy the initiative at scale. These initiatives should create early wins that support cross-departmental adoption.

Expanding Adoption and Automating Workflows

The implementation scales up after pilot dashboards show their value. The implementation process includes bringing more teams and systems onto the system while developing new dashboards and introducing advanced metrics. The implementation stage requires automation as its main priority. The data pipelines need to operate through scheduled refreshes or events to provide real-time or near-real time updates for dashboard display. The connection of CICD pipelines enables release managers and QA leads to track progress, as dashboards provide real-time visibility into each build's outcome.

BI integration with team routines enables workflow optimization through improved BI implementation. Quality gates within CI pipelines should use BI dashboard metrics to enforce deployment restrictions. The system will stop deployment processes whenever quality targets fail to meet their thresholds. The system enables users to set up notifications that trigger when defect density increases or test execution times lengthen or coverage levels decrease. Through automated insights, developers and testers obtain faster responses which reduce their need for manual oversight during development and testing cycles.

Establishing Governance and Ownership Models

The use of Business Intelligence has deeply penetrated into Quality Assurance workflow processes. The implementation of formal governance structures has become more necessary as a result. The process requires clear identification of data ownership as well as responsibilities for maintaining dashboards and making decisions based on gathered insights. The QA teams should maintain control over test data precision and usefulness while the BI teams handle the technical aspects of data management and presentation.

The integration between Business Intelligence and Quality Assurance functions now requires cross-functional collaboration by nature. DevOps teams must provide data availability together with automation reliability and business stakeholders should interpret metrics through the lens of company objectives. Organizations benefit from forming cross-functional working groups or "QA Intelligence Groups" to review important metrics and track initiative progress and suggest changes. The shared approach supports both responsibility and keeps dashboards from turning into useless isolated tools that fail to affect organizational decisions.

Maintaining Data Quality and Consistency

BI QA integration faces a critical challenge which remains one of the most difficult to handle: maintaining high-quality data. The reliability of dashboards and analytics depends entirely on the quality of their data sources. The quality of QA data directly affects the accuracy of resulting insights because incomplete or mislabeled or outdated data will mislead instead of provide meaningful information. Organizations need to implement data validation methods and naming conventions and pipeline health monitoring to solve this issue. Organizations should build automated systems to check data freshness and schema integrity and duplication as well as implement fallback systems to handle pipeline failures.

The development of metadata dashboards throughout time enables organizations to track their BI infrastructure performance. The dashboard displays metrics which track data update intervals and null field occurrence rates and test result ingestion failure rates. Clear data quality reporting helps stakeholders trust the information and take actions based on what they see.

Key Takeaways

- Successful BI integration starts with defining business-aligned QA metrics.
- Visualization tools (e.g., Power BI, Grafana) allow stakeholders to monitor test effectiveness and release readiness.
- Stakeholder alignment and incremental rollout are key for adoption success.

5. CASE STUDIES AND APPLICATIONS

The theoretical and architectural frameworks of BI integration in QA are critical. However, it is equally important to understand how this approach is applied in real-world implementations. This section outlines case studies from different industries and illustrates how Business Intelligence has been applied to Quality Assurance workflows to address real-world challenges, align QA metrics with business goals, and support continuous improvement.

Case Study 1: Reducing Defect Leakage in a Healthcare Technology Platform

A large Healthcare technology company offering real-time patient analytics solutions was experiencing a rise in production defects that made it to production. Despite having a well-established QA team with advanced automation practices, the company was experiencing an increase in post-release issues that negatively impacted customer trust and compliance.

The company used Power BI to consolidate defect, test coverage, and environment stability data from JIRA and Jenkins into BI dashboards. The company started to analyze historical defect patterns by component along with their relation to release timelines and test coverage metrics. It was revealed that, although automated test execution was high, the coverage of the high-risk business modules was limited.

Based on these findings, the QA team created a new test strategy using risk-based coverage derived from BI defect density heat maps. After only three months, they achieved a 40% reduction in critical production issues, a 25% decrease in defect leakage, and a 20% increase in test coverage across business-critical areas. There was also a 15% improvement in end-user satisfaction scores, as measured by post-release support survey feedback. The company also improved its compliance posture by being able to track defects across sprints and against release checklists, reducing audit preparation time by approximately 30%.

Case Study 2: Enhancing Automation ROI in a SaaS Enterprise

A Software-as-a-Service (SaaS) company focused on marketing analytics needed to quantify the the return on investment (ROI) from its test automation initiatives. The team had a lot of resources invested in tools and frameworks, but the leadership did not think that the investment was worthwhile, especially considering the team's slow test turnaround and the unknown impact on release velocity.

The QA team together with their BI group created several dashboards within Tableau. The data sources included Selenium test suite, GitLab CICD pipelines, and application telemetry systems. The dashboards included information on automation execution times, defect catch rates (automated vs manual), and sprint velocity impact.

The visualization revealed that automated tests in the core modules were catching 80% of regression defects before manual QA even started, saving approximately 3–4 days per sprint. Another dashboard uncovered previously unnoticed duplication—over 30% of manual tests overlapped with existing automated scripts. Using these insights, the team optimized test suites, removed redundancies, and aligned test planning with development priorities.

The overall result was a 20% reduction in QA cycle time, a 35% increase in automation coverage, and a 50% drop in redundant test executions. These metrics provided compelling evidence to support ongoing investment in automation. The company began linking QA outcomes with key business KPIs, such as a 10% improvement in customer onboarding success rate and a 15% faster time-to-market for high-priority features.

Case Study 3: Audit Readiness in a Healthcare Compliance Environment

For a regulated healthcare IT company, it was very important to maintain audit trails for every release cycle. QA had to show the traceability of test execution, defect resolution and security validation across many releases each of which was tied to HIPAA and FDA regulatory mandates.

To address this, the QA and compliance teams implemented a BI solution using Microsoft Power BI and Azure Data Factory. QA results from Zephyr and Azure DevOps were ingested nightly, normalized into a centralized schema, and reported against audit control requirements. Dashboards were developed to show end-to-end traceability from business requirements to final defect resolutions, including time-stamped signoffs, reviewer IDs, and test environment configurations.

During the next compliance audit, regulators were provided real-time access to over 4,500 historical QA records, with zero major findings or escalations. Manual spreadsheet compilation time was reduced by over 85%, cutting audit preparation from two weeks to just two days. The dashboards also helped surface patterns—such as repeated security defects in 3 specific modules over 4 consecutive releases—prompting the integration of static code analysis tools into the CI/CD pipeline.

As a result, the organization saw a 60% drop in repeat security issues within six months and achieved full audit clearance on first submission. The BI-enhanced traceability framework became a standard part of their release process and was extended to other regulatory reporting needs.

Case Study 4: Alignment of QA Metrics with Business Goals in an E-Commerce Platform

An e-commerce company operating seasonal promotions struggled to make QA operations match their rapidly shifting business objectives. The product and marketing teams faced difficulties monitoring quality readiness and release risk levels because QA recorded test execution results and defect closure performance only internally.

To resolve this, the BI team partnered with QA to develop Grafana dashboards that integrated data from TestRail, LoadRunner, and user feedback logs, along with real-time telemetry from production systems. A composite Release Readiness Score was introduced, incorporating test pass rate, defect aging, open blocker counts, and load test benchmarks.

Within one quarter, business stakeholders could view live readiness scores for upcoming promotional campaigns. Marketing teams began to launch campaigns only when readiness exceeded 85%, reducing failed releases during peak traffic events. The dashboards also revealed that two core backend APIs failed load tests in 4 of the last 5 sprints, prompting targeted performance improvements.

These interventions led to a 30% reduction in post-launch incidents, and check-out abandonment during peak sales hours dropped from 9.2% to 5.8%. Engineering teams reported a 25% improvement in test coverage for high-traffic modules, and QA cycle time for seasonal features was shortened by four days per sprint.

With BI-enriched QA visibility, the company transformed QA from a support role to a strategic enabler of business-aligned releases, with metrics now embedded into sprint planning and executive reviews.

Key Takeaways Across Case Studies

These examples illustrate how BI-supported QA processes can help reposition QA as a more strategic contributor. This is applicable across various business environments including finance and SaaS and healthcare and retail. The analysis revealed several essential findings:

- BI dashboards reveal gaps in test coverage and highligh risk allocation.
- Integration with CICD tools can enable continuous monitoring and actionable insights.
- Real-time visualizations supports faster decision-making across departments.
- Traceable, structured QA data simplifies compliance and boosts audit confidence.
- Direct linkage of QA metrics with business outcomes builds executive trust.

These examples demonstrate both technical performance enhancements and new perspectives about how QA functions. The organization now views QA as a business partner who enables reliable user-centric and compliant software delivery instead of a traditional gatekeeping role. Business Intelligence tools extend beyond reporting functions to support data-informed quality management and operational decision-making.

6. CHALLENGES AND HOW TO OVERCOME THEM

Integrating Business Intelligence (BI) into Quality Assurance (QA) presents potential for both strategic and operational improvement. The process presents various challenges. Organizations that pursue this transition experience multiple hurdles which appear in the technical realm alongside organizational aspects and cultural barriers. These challenges require immediate attention, as they can significantly hinder progress. This section examines the primary obstacles that prevent BI QA integration together with effective methods for their successful management.

Figure 4 below visualizes the key challenges that arise during BI integration in QA environments, including data silos, tool fragmentation, and governance gaps.

Figure 4. Common challenges in BI-QA integration including data fragmentation, tool incompatibility, skill gaps, and scalability bottlenecks

Fragmentation and Silos in Data

BI QA integration faces a major obstacle due to the scattered nature of quality-related data. Quality assurance teams currently utilize a combination of defect trackers and test automation suites together with CI/CD pipelines and customer feedback systems for their work. There is no native integration between these systems. QA data resides in disparate systems, often using inconsistent formats and lacking a unified source of truth.

Fragmented data can result in conflicting metrics, redundant analysis efforts, and unreliable dashboard outputs. When a centralized BI tool is implemented, inconsistent data inputs can lead to unreliable insights.

Organizations should establish strong data pipelines together with a standardized data model to overcome this problem. The implementation of ETL/ELT tools including Apache NiFi and cloud native solutions enables flexible data ingestion to standardize and synchronize QA data. The implementation of a semantic layer above the warehouse enables teams to use standardized business definitions for metrics which results in more trustworthy and precise dashboards.

Tool Interoperability and Integration Complexity

The majority of QA and BI tools function without automatic information exchange capabilities. Legacy systems alongside proprietary formats together with the absence of APIs make it challenging to extract and synchronize data. Although contemporary tools offer connectors integration them with BI systems often requires significant development effort.

Integration complexity can delay implementation and limit long-term scalability. In some cases, teams revert to manual data entry or rely on static spreadsheets, limiting the potential benefits of BI automation.

The initial tool selection process should include integration planning to reduce its impact. Select tools which use open standards and have well-documented APIs and receive widespread support in the BI ecosystem whenever possible. Organizations should implement middleware or adapters to connect their existing tools when they need to bridge technical differences. A phased implementation starting with straightforward tools will produce initial results before focusing on more complex integrations that require proper planning.

Lack of QA and BI Collaboration

Business intelligence and data science teams commonly initiate BI initiatives yet QA functions operate under engineering leadership. When there is no intentional alignment between BI and QA integration projects the results fail to provide relevant solutions for testing staff and developers.

Uncoordinated work between teams produces dashboards that show metrics which QA teams find irrelevant alongside insights that business stakeholders cannot use to take action. When responsibilities for data quality and dashboard ownership are unclear, both data reliability and dashboard utility can degrade.

The solution lies in cross-functional governance. Multiple perspectives can be integrated into the decision-making process through the formation of a working group consisting of QA leads, BI architects and product owners and DevOps representatives. The process of regular alignment sessions creates a shared understanding between team members who define priorities and clarify data definitions to verify that displayed metrics align with operational and strategic objectives. BI design participation from QA teams leads to higher adoption rates along with more relevant BI solutions.

Low Data Literacy and Resistance to Change

BI adoption requires more than just technical integration. It demands a cultural shift. QA professionals accustomed to pass/fail reports and Excel logs may struggle to interpret dashboards or grasp predictive metrics. Business stakeholders without knowledge of QA procedures tend to make incorrect interpretations about quality trends which results in decisions that are off-target.

To resolve this issue, we need specific educational measures and capacity building initiatives. QA professionals need to receive training about understanding trend lines and heatmaps and predictive analytics. Workshops for business users can help to clarify QA metrics and their relationship with business outcomes. Introducing BI can be done gradually through starting with familiar metrics and visualizations to make the transition smoother. Early wins should be celebrated while the time savings from BI (e.g., auto-generated reports, flaky test detection)" should be highlighted to transform the view from additional work to beneficial support.

Data Quality and Incomplete Metrics

Centralizing data does not inherently guarantee completeness or accuracy, and assumptions to that effect can hinder effective implementation. In reality, the data collected by QA teams often contains numerous missing values, inconsistent information and outdated data points. Lack of execution logs and inconsistent environment naming and outdated test case mappings can result in metrics that are misleading.

Organizations need to prioritize data quality as an essential factor. The organization should conduct automated data pipeline checks and flag incomplete records while maintaining audit logs for metric calculation. The ideal scenario includes regular data reviews and dashboard validation exercises which are closely linked to release retrospectives for maintaining dashboards' alignment with real-world activities. QA and DevOps workflows should define clear ownership of data quality as a part of their standard operations.

Scalability and Maintenance Burden

As BI integration spreads across different projects and teams, dashboard numbers increase. "Without proper design and governance, BI systems may become complex, inconsistent, and challenging to maintain at scale. The definitions of metrics tend to change resulting in multiple valid "truths" about the same KPI and updates to the data model may cause existing reports to fail.

Organizations require reusable templates along with naming conventions and dashboard standards to achieve successful scalability. BI implementation of requires technical architects to adapt systems and support organizational structure and mindset shifts. Periodic dashboard audits enable the identification of redundant and outdated views.

The implementation of Business Intelligence (BI) in Quality Assurance (QA) brings significant changes but it does not happen without some resistance. The implementation of BI requires technical architects to adapt their systems and teams to change their organizational structures and mentalities. These challenges, while significant, also present opportunities to unify data sources, enhance team insight generation, and reposition quality management as a more integrated component of the software delivery lifecycle

The upcoming chapters will discuss ways to develop this base through innovative approaches and emerging patterns that will sustain the BI-QA collaboration as software development requirements evolve.

Key Takeaways

- Common pitfalls include inconsistent data definitions and resistance to tool adoption.
- BI implementation requires strong collaboration across QA, DevOps, and data engineering teams.
- Tool complexity and skill gaps must be addressed through targeted training.

7. SKILL TRANSFORMATION AND ORGANIZATIONAL READINESS

Integrating Business Intelligence (BI) into Quality Assurance (QA) requires not only technical implementation, but also organizational and workforce transformation. Long-term success depends on people, processes, and culture working in tandem with technology. Organizations must develop their workforce while building improved processes and cultural systems for BI-enhanced QA to achieve success. This part examines changes in QA roles and capabilities along with necessary organizational steps for effective support of this evolution.

Evolving Role of the QA Professional

The conventional QA duties primarily involved creating test cases and running tests and recording defects. BI-driven QA requires professionals to develop skills in data interpretation, strategic contribution, and continuous improvement leadership. The traditional role of testing has evolved from defect gatekeeping to producing valuable insights.

QA professionals are now expected to analyze defect trends, identify potential failure points proactively and validate dashboards for both functional accuracy and business relevance. Modern QA engineers must be proficient in testing tools, BI platforms, data models, and metric-based communication.

Bridging the Skills Gap

The transition demands organizations to handle a natural deficit of capabilities which needs immediate resolution. Most QA team lack deep expertise in data analytics, visualization platforms, and querying structured datasets. Thus, systematic training plays a vital role. Organizations that achieve successful integration of BI with QA provide hands-on training to their QA teams on tools including Power BI, Tableau and SQL. The development of analytical thinking abilities should be encouraged to enable team members to progress from basic checkbox validation to understanding both failure explanations and future release risk positions.

Sustained adoption requires viewing employee training as a strategic investment rather than a discretionary cost. The transition can be supported through workshops together with self-paced learning platforms and mentorship models. The goal is not to transform QA engineers into data scientists but to enhance their ability to use data-driven processes autonomously and confidently.

Cultural Shift Toward Data Driven Quality

The transformation also requires a shift in mindset across the organization. Numerous engineering teams evaluate quality as a post-development assessment process. Data-driven QA transforms quality into an ongoing process which integrates strategic planning at each sprint and build stage and release phase.

This shift typically requires sustained effort and consistent reinforcement over time. The implementation of data usage in everyday QA conversations needs communication along with reinforcement and internal champions who promote these practices. Demonstrating practical use cases-such as early defect detection enabled by BI metrics-can accelerate cultural adoption of data-driven QA practices.

Collaboration Across Teams

BI-QA integration encourages more cross-functional collaboration, reducing siloed team operations. The successful implementation of useful metrics requires BI analysts to collaborate with data engineers and product owners alongside QA engineers for defining metrics and dashboard development and trend interpretation. This calls for new collaboration models.

Organizations that achieve the best results with BI QA integrate their teams through collaborative dashboard reviews across different functions. During sprint reviews, QA team members highlight reduced test coverage, which product managers analyze to determine how it affects customers. Engineering leads can then plan test refactoring, while BI teams help improve how these insights are visualized.

Quality becomes a consistent part of cross functional discussions when QA evolves from a checkpoint function to a overall contributor. Organizations achieve better results by aligning quality discussions with product targets and business objectives, fostering transparent accountability across teams.

Preparing the Organization for Change

Multiple elements make up organizational readiness for BI-QA integration. The evaluation must assess the presence of tools along with the appropriate support systems which enable meaningful utilization of these tools. Technical capabilities of some teams exist but they do not share a unified understanding of important metrics. Other teams possess robust QA abilities yet they have minimal experience with data analytics.

Conducting formal readiness assessments helps organizations identify skill gaps, tool limitations, and organizational barriers to BI-QA integration. Organizations must examine the maturity level of QA processes together with their BI tool availability and staff proficiency with dashboards and analytics. A roadmap emerges from the assessment that includes training needs alongside tool improvements and modifications to roles and leadership support.

The fundamental nature of Business Intelligence integration into QA requires a human-centered transformation. The workforce must use dashboards along with metrics to extract meaningful information that leads to actions. Organizations need to empower their workforce alongside system enablement because success depends on both factors.

Organizations unlock the full value of BI-driven QA by upskilling their QA professionals, fostering cross functional collaboration, and embedding data-informed decision-making into routine processes. This readiness enables quality assurance to advance from its traditional position as a downstream function to become a broad enterprise-wide driver of continuous improvement and strategic insight and innovation.

Key Takeaways

- QA professionals need to upskill in SQL, dashboard tools, and data storytelling.
- Cross-functional data fluency is essential for realizing the full potential of QA-BI integration.
- BI literacy should become a core part of QA career progression frameworks.

8. METRICS THAT INFLUENCE EXECUTIVE DECISION MAKING

When organizations integrate Business Intelligence (BI) with Quality Assurance (QA), the gap between engineering operations and decision-making via data-driven insights is bridged. Executive stakeholders need a strategic summary of software quality data that connects directly to business risk, performance and value rather thanrelying on traditional QA team metrics such as test pass rates and defect counts. This section demonstrates how BI enables QA data modeling to drive executive-level organizational decisions.

Connecting QA to Business Strategy

Executive stakeholders typically avoid asking about the number of test cases executed or the pass rate for a specific build. Executives are primarily concerned with whether upcoming releases align with customer expectations and compliance requirements, and how quality risks may impact strategic goals.

QA metrics need to transform into strategic indicators to fulfill these organizational requirements. QA leaders must transform their reporting style by showing data that reveals product health along with stability and risk levels. Business Intelligence enables the development of user-friendly dashboards that provide both extensive data coverage and accessible insights for non-technical users.

From Operational Numbers to Strategic Indicators

The transformation starts by changing the perspective through which organizations view their metrics. A test case execution report provides limited value when analyzed independently. The combined data about defect resolution time trends together with module risk scores and production stability indicators transforms the story into something significantly stronger.

Executives may not find value in automation coverage as a standalone metric. The impact becomes clearer when automation coverage is displayed as a time-saving element for release cycles and an early detection system of defects along with specific data about cost reductions and time benefits. Linking untested modules to elevated customer complaint volumes provides a quantifiable basis for prioritizing targeted quality improvements.

Decision-making around timelines, resource allocation, and go to market strategies benefits from dashboards which display release readiness scores, quality debt accumulation, and test coverage of high-risk features.

Designing Executive Facing Dashboards

Executive dashboards should distill complex quality data into concise insights aligned with organizational priorities.. The presentation of key quality trends through these dashboards should not need technical interpretation. Thoughtful visualization together with concise narrative summaries proves more effective than dense charts or tables.

A well-designed dashboard demonstrates the general quality improvement during three sprints while highlighting unresolved critical risks. The visualization of production defect leakage trends together with customer satisfaction scores creates an argument for additional QA investment. Strategic decisions about platform migration or budget planning can be influenced by presenting test failure spikes that occur after infrastructure changes.

The most effective dashboards use color and time-based comparisons and weighted indicators to direct attention toward essential areas. Their strength lies in anticipating executive needs and delivering organized, data-driven solutions.

Using QA Data to Drive High Level Conversations

The presentation of QA data which matches executive concerns about customer impact and risk exposure and compliance readiness leads executives to join strategic discussions instead of operational ones. A quality leader who prepares well can demonstrate how delayed test execution in core modules affects marketing campaign performance and how inconsistent automation coverage between teams results in unpredictable release stability.

The relevance of BI dashboards is enhanced when their metrics are explicitly aligned with business goals and KPIs. Security testing gap tracking against industry compliance frameworks enables support for audit readiness discussions through dashboard reporting. The release dashboard provides a link between sprint velocity and defect backlog and customer ticket volume to help organizations make better roadmap priority decisions.

The reporting function of QA transforms into an active advisory role at this point. The organization views QA as a dependable leadership advisor which helps make decisions that affect revenue and user satisfaction and brand reputation.

Evolving KPIs to Reflect Enterprise Priorities

The meaningful influence of QA on executive decision-making requires its essential performance indicators to match enterprise targets. The goal of reducing time to market by 20% requires QA metrics to evaluate whether current test processes speed up or slow down this timeline. Quality Assurance can show how defect patterns affect customer satisfaction when customer retention stands as the main organizational priority.

Quality leaders who link their quality indicators to business KPIs establish a clear path to show their role in achieving organizational targets. The interpretation of metrics such as defect leakage and regression failure rate and automation ROI evolves from technical indicators to business outcome drivers throughout time.

Aligning QA metrics with enterprise KPIs strengthens confidence in quality and justifies continued investment in QA initiatives. Leaders tend to support quality initiatives and testing infrastructure improvements and high-level planning involvement when they witness QA actively tracking product quality relationships with strategic success.

The ability to influence executive decision making represents an advanced stage of Quality Assurance maturity. Through Business Intelligence integration QA teams can deliver their findings both accurately and with strategic direction. Quality data achieves leadership table participation when it is presented through risk analysis and business performance and value assessment.

BI tools will continue to advance until engineering dashboards and executive reports become indistinguishable from each other. The future of QA requires professionals to connect complex technical realities with clear business-aligned stories that deliver compelling narratives. With the support of BI, QA can evolve from a support function to a data-informed discipline that drives strategic decision-making and operational performance.

Key Takeaways

- Executive dashboards should prioritize business-aligned metrics (e.g., release readiness, defect leakage).
- Visualizations must balance granularity and clarity to inform both strategic and operational decisions.
- Unified metrics support evidence-based prioritization and investment in QA initiatives.

9. CONCLUSION

Integrating Business Intelligence (BI) into Quality Assurance (QA) marks a shift from traditional testing methods to a data-centric model that supports continuous improvement and enterprise alignment. The modern business environment demands agility, resilience, and data-driven decision-making, so QA must transform from its current role of execution and defect tracking into a force that drives operational excellence and digital innovation.

Organizations that link Business Intelligence with Quality Assurance gain the power to convert unorganized testing data into a structured intelligence system. The intelligence system provides organizations with real-time product quality insights,highlights emerging risks, identifies optimization opportunities, and reveals direct links to business outcomes.

Elevating QA from a Reactive Function to a Strategic Asset

The traditional view in many legacy environments treated QA as a checkpoint that occurred before release. The testing process involved writing test cases followed by execution and bug reporting yet the results stayed within engineering boundaries. Business Intelligence transforms the entire operational approach. Executives now have access to quality metrics that quantify their impact on release timelines, operational costs, compliance status, and customer satisfaction.

The bridge function of BI enables QA to communicate through business-oriented terminology. Clear visualization of defect trends, test gaps and risk scores alongside business KPIs enables QA leaders to transition from decision support to active decision-making roles.

Data as a Quality Framework, Not Just a Byproduct

A central theme of this chapter has been the recognition that QA is rich in data but often poor in insight. Tests are run, logs are generated, defects are recorded, and regressions are tracked. The lack of a unified data strategy prevents organizations from maximizing their ability to use this information. BI transforms data into strategic tools which include dashboards and predictive models and real-time feedback systems that lead organizational decisions throughout the software development lifecycle.

The acquired intelligence extends beyond internal team boundaries. Executive dashboards enable product owners and business leaders and compliance auditors to view QA data which supports transparency and accountability. Through BI organizations link test results to enterprise KPIs which show quality's direct impact on risk reduction and operational cost management and customer trust. Organizations achieve a more proactive software quality approach by converting their raw QA data into strategic signals.

Building a Culture of Continuous Improvement

The implementation of BI with QA creates a long term cultural transformation as one of its effects. Teams that work in data-rich environments develop introspective abilities and take greater responsibility while adopting iterative approaches. Dashboards serve not only as reporting tools but also as mechanisms for initiating retrospectives and driving actionable improvements. Teams begin to evaluate patterns such as recurring defects and test redundancies, using data to inform more strategic testing decisions. The code base contains specific areas that lack proper testing. This cultural development establishes itself as a permanent part of the organization. The analysis of actual trends and metrics guides retrospectives instead of memory or instinct. Release planning depends on feature completion, defect patterns, user feedback and predicted risk zones. Test strategies evolve through continuous refinement based on achieved outcomes rather than personal intuition.

The established culture extends beyond engineering departments. The quality story provides benefits to all teams including product owners and support staff and compliance officers and marketing teams. The organization benefits from quality measurements which produce reduced churn and better performance metrics and successful product launches.

Business Value Beyond the Engineering Floor

The business alignment of BI-driven QA stands as the main factor which differentiates it from traditional quality management approaches. The traditional QA processes operated without business stakeholder visibility unless they encountered a failure in legacy models. BI enables real-time quality visibility for business stakeholders, in contrast to retrospective, engineer-focused reporting models. Business leaders now obtain direct visibility into quality efforts' impact on timelines and cost and customer satisfaction and compliance through properly designed dashboards and specific metrics.

This alignment enhances trust. Executives now have direct access to real-time readiness indicators and risk scoring and regression impact analysis which link to financial outcomes. The rise of production issues from under-tested modules enables direct financial cost tracking through support expenses. The accelerated cycle times achieved through better automation coverage enable businesses to demonstrate both cost savings and faster time-to-market performance.

The implementation of BI in QA establishes a shared terminology that enables business teams to communicate effectively with engineering teams. The system functions as a unifying element which enables mutual comprehension and expedited decision processes and unified team responsibility.

The Future Belongs to Intelligent QA Systems

Looking ahead, BI enabled QA is not the end, it's the beginning of intelligent quality systems. As artificial intelligence has matured and has become more integrated with DevOps pipelines we will see QA has evolved into a more predictive and autonomous area. For example, these could be systems that decide what tests to run based on the type of code changes or traffic patterns of users or it could be dashboards that don't just report but also prescribe which risks to mitigate before they even surface.

The early implementation of AI-assisted test case generation and anomaly detection in test environments and conversational BI tools which provide dynamic insights to users already exists. These tools will enable QA to monitor software in production with the same level of rigor that they currently use during development through their integration with observability platforms and real user monitoring. The distinction between pre-release and post-release quality will fade into Quality as a Continuous Service.

The future will eliminate the separation between QA teams and BI teams. The future will bring about quality intelligence teams that unite engineers with analysts and product strategists and data scientists to build quality into digital delivery processes across all stages.

Why This Matters Now More Than Ever

The current transition occurs at an essential period for business operations. The digital economy operates at an unprecedented rapid pace. Digital customer expectations demand flawless performance together with fast delivery and absolute security at unprecedented levels. The regulatory environment continues to tighten its oversight particularly within healthcare and finance and education sectors. Quality needs to be proactive in this current situation. The quality needs to be predictive while also being measurable and explainable and strategic.

Organizations can use Business Intelligence to monitor and measure and manage quality with complete clarity. The system removes uncertainty while improving risk control and enables quick recovery from system breakdowns. The system allows software teams to direct their efforts toward delivering outcomes which meet user needs and expectations and deliver expected quality.

Strategic Next Steps

To operationalize BI driven QA, organizations must first evaluate their data maturity, QA processes, and cross-functional collaboration models.Test results must not remain unattended in spreadsheets or logs. Organizations must recognize that quality extends beyond code coverage metrics. Organizations need to identify essential trends for failure prevention and understand how testing data can enhance both software development and strategic decision making.

The first step requires organizations to establish basic capabilities through strong data pipelines and scalable dashboards and cross-functional metrics. Teams need encouragement to transition from basic transactional testing into insight-driven quality engineering. The organization should encourage support for QA professionals to learn data language while BI experts learn quality nuances. The organization should recognize and reward employees who successfully move beyond defect counting to demonstrate meaningful business impact.

Organizations that succeed in the digital era will focus on learning at speed and smart response and safe delivery rather than conducting the most tests. Business Intelligence achieves its power through its integration with Quality Assurance. The future of software quality has arrived and is ready for immediate construction.

The combination of Business Intelligence with Quality Assurance represents a fundamental transformation in organizational software development processes from creation to testing to deployment. Quality assessment needs to measure more than functionality validation because it must evaluate value delivery and risk management and strategic alignment. Enterprises can transition from reactive quality control to proactive quality engineering by converting QA data into real-time actionable intelligence. The transformation enables teams to make better choices while speeding up innovation and guaranteeing their digital products achieve peak excellence standards. Businesses that adopt BI-driven QA will achieve better software delivery while establishing themselves as leaders in data-informed digital transformation for the future.

Key Takeaways

- The convergence of BI, AI, and observability will define next-gen QA practices.
- Predictive analytics and anomaly detection in QA will become increasingly mainstream.
- BI's role in enabling compliance, risk reduction, and platform stability will grow stronger.

REFERENCES

Davenport, T. H., & Harris, J. G. (2007). *Competing on analytics: The new science of winning*. Harvard Business Press.

Dynatrace. (2024). *Enhance DevOps and platform engineering with observability*. https://www.dynatrace.com/news/blog/observability-security-ai-enhance-devops-platform-engineering

Mahida, A. (2024). Integrating observability with DevOps practices in financial services technologies: A study on enhancing software development and operational resilience. *International Journal of Advanced Computer Science and Applications, 15*(7).

Neontri. (2025). *DevOps observability: Transforming data into strategic insights*. https://neontri.com/blog/devops-observability

Refonte Learning. (2025). *Top observability tools DevOps engineers must learn in 2025*. https://www.refontelearning.com/blog/top-observability-tools-devops-engineers-must-learn-in-2025

Watson, H. J. (2014). Tutorial: Big data analytics: Concepts, technologies, and applications. *Communications of the Association for Information Systems*, *34*(1), 1247–1268.

Chapter 9
Integration of Artificial Intelligence and Machine Learning in Business Intelligence: Enhancing Decision Making and Operational Efficiency

Muhammad Usman Tariq
https://orcid.org/0000-0002-7605-3040
Abu Dhabi University, UAE & University College Cork, Ireland

ABSTRACT

Integrating AI and machine learning (ML) in business intelligence (BI) changes industry decision-making and operational efficiency. AI-controlled BI systems allow businesses to analyze large amounts of structured and unstructured data, uncover hidden patterns, and generate predictive knowledge. ML algorithms improve data processing, repeat tasks, and prediction accuracy, allowing companies to make real-time data-controlled decisions. Using Natural Language Processing (NLP) and enhanced analytics, AI-powered BI tools enable intuitive data visualization and self-service analytics, providing users with the knowledge they can implement. This integration optimizes resource allocation and risk management and improves customer experience and competitive advantages. Although AI and ML are being developed, companies must strategically use these technologies to maximize their benefits and maintain an increasingly data-controlled landscape. This chapter will explore the effects, challenges, and future trends of AI and ML on our BI application.

DOI: 10.4018/979-8-3373-2125-7.ch009

INTRODUCTION

Artificial Intelligence (AI) and Machine Learning (ML) have significantly redesigned the business intelligence (BI) landscape and altered the analysis of data, decisions, and optimized operations. Traditionally, BI was strongly based on historical data, manual reporting, and static dashboards to gain insight into business performance. However, the advent of AI and ML has introduced dynamic, predictive, and normative analytics, allowing companies to remain in a highly competitive, data-controlled environment. Traditional BI tools have been developed primarily for structured data from databases, spreadsheets, and corporate systems (Rimon, 2024). However, modern companies generate data from various sources, including social media, IoT devices, email, and video. AI-powered BI platforms can seamlessly integrate and analyze these various data sources, providing a holistic view of your business operations. Natural Language Processing (NLP) allows businesses to extract text-based data from customer reviews, social media, ticket comments, and valuable insights that were previously difficult to quantify. Machine learning algorithms can accurately distinguish historical data patterns and trends to predict future events. For example, AI-powered BI tools can accurately predict customer demand, sales trends, and market changes. Companies can use these findings to make positive decisions. Adjusting inventory, refining marketing strategies, and improving customer loyalty. Predictive analytics allows businesses to proactively use reactive decisions to mitigate risk and use new options. ML algorithms can analyze several scenarios and propose the best strategy based on historical and real-time data. For instance, in supply chain management, AI can recommend the most efficient routes for delivery, minimize transportation costs, and optimize inventory. In marketing, AI can propose personalized campaigns tailored to individual customer preferences, allowing you to maximize conversion rates and customer satisfaction. This level of automation and intelligence allows organizations to make data-controlled decisions with trust and mobility. Traditionally, data cleaning, transformation, and integration have been labor-intensive processes requiring extensive human intervention. The AI-controlled BI platform optimizes these tasks through automated data cleaning, anomaly recognition, and enrichment. Machine learning models can identify errors, inconsistencies, and missing values in data records to ensure high-quality, reliable data for analysis. Additionally, AI improves data management by implementing intelligent data classification, access control, and compliance monitoring, ensuring data security and regulatory compliance. In the past, BI tools have been used primarily by data analysts and IT professionals with expertise in SQL, data modeling, and reporting (El Hajj and Hammoud, 2023).

However, AI-powered BI solutions offer intuitive self-service analytics with a user-friendly interface and queries for natural language. Business users can ask questions in simple language. AI-driven assistants create relevant knowledge, visualizations, and reports in real-time. This democratization of data allows employees from various sectors to use BI for well-discovered decisions without demanding sophisticated technical skills. Traditional BI reports were often created regularly, leading to decision-making delays. The AI-controlled BI platform monitors continuous data flow, recognizes anomalies, and triggers real-time warning messages. For example, AI can identify fraudulent transactions in the financial sector and attract attention to security teams (Mozumder et al., 2024). AI can pursue customer behavior in retail and dynamically adapt pricing strategies based on demand and competitor activity. Real-time analytics improves operational efficiency and responsiveness, allowing businesses to respond to survey results when events occur. Companies can analyze customer behavior, preferences, and history of purchases to provide personalized recommendations, targeted marketing campaigns, and tailor-made interactions. For example, e-commerce platforms use AI-controlled recommendation engines to propose products based on user preferences, sales, and customer satisfaction. AI-run chatbots and virtual assistants provide immediate support, answer questions, and provide solutions to problems without human intervention (Paramesha et al., 2024). This personalization promotes customer loyalty and commitment to customers, ultimately driving sales growth. Companies must be ahead of their competitors by monitoring market trends, consumer moods, and industry development. AI-controlled mood analysis allows companies to assess public opinion about their brands and their competitors and help them refine their strategies accordingly. ML algorithms can pursue competitor prices, product launches, and customer feedback and provide valuable intelligence in your strategic planning. Using AI-powered competitive information allows companies to identify market gaps, distinguish offers, and maintain a competitive advantage (Paramesha et al., 2024). One of the main issues is data protection and security. AI-controlled BI is based on a huge amount of data, and compliance with data protection regulations such as the GDPR and CCPA is essential. Companies must implement robust security measures, encryption protocols, and access controls to protect sensitive information. Furthermore, distortions in AI algorithms are another challenge that companies must meet. The Machine-Learning model is just as good as the trained data, and bias can lead to inaccurate or unfair knowledge. Organizations must ensure data diversity, transparency, and continuous model assessment to reduce the risk of distortion. Employees must embrace data-controlled decision-making and develop analytical skills to use AI-powered BI tools (Tariq, 2025). Companies must invest in training programs and upskilling initiatives to provide employees with knowledge and skills to effectively coordinate with AI-controlled knowledge. Collaboration between data scientists, economic analysts, and domain experts is vital to maximize the potential of AI-powered BI. As for the future, the future of BI will remain to be formed by advances in AI and ML. Estimating technologies such as deep learning, enhanced analytics, and AI-controlled automation further improves BI skills. Deep learning models allow for more accurate predictions and complex data interpretation, and augmented analysis automates production and decision-making processes. Automating AI controls reduces manual data management, reporting, and analytics efforts and allows businesses to focus on strategic initiatives. With AI-controlled BI, companies enable grounded, data-controlled decisions with speed and accuracy, achieving competitive advantages in increasingly dynamic markets (Badmus et al., 2024). Despite challenges such as data protection, bias, and skill gaps, organizations that successfully integrate AI into their BI strategies are well-positioned for growth and innovation. While AI technology is developing, the future of BI promises further increases in efficiency, intelligence, and business transformation.

BACKGROUND

The conversion from traditional business intelligence (BI) to AI manipulation, predictive, and adaptive BI systems represents a paradigm shift that drives progress in artificial intelligence, machine learning, and big data analytics. Traditional BI systems focused primarily on descriptive analytics and historical data to generate static reports, dashboards, and critical performance indicators (KPIs). These systems require considerable human intervention to interpret data, guide knowledge, and make decisions. With exponential data growth and growing complexity in the business environment, businesses recognize the need for intelligent, automated, and adaptable BI systems. This transformation has integrated AI and machine learning into BI, allowing predictive analytics, real decisions, and self-learning skills to improve business size and competitiveness. These systems had problems processing unstructured data, such as text, images, videos, and social media interactions (Saxena et al., 2024). As a result, organizations faced challenges gaining valuable knowledge from various data sources. AI-powered BI systems have overcome this limitation by analyzing structured and unstructured data using augmented procedures such as natural language processing (NLP) and computer vision. This ability expands the scope of BI and lets businesses gain a comprehensive understanding of the business environment. Predictive BI algorithms for machine learning identify patterns in historical data and create data-controlled predictions, unlike traditional BI, which provides retrospective insights (Tariq, 2025).

For example, in the retail industry, forecast BI can predict customer problems, optimize inventory management, and personalize marketing campaigns based on shopping patterns. Healthcare systems can contribute predictive analytics in disease detection, which assesses patient risk and treatment recommendations. Predictive

BI allows businesses to proactively master challenges, optimize operations, and use new opportunities. Traditional BI systems require manual configuration and updates to meet new data sources or develop business requirements. In contrast, adaptive BI systems use machine learning models that automatically improve predictions and recommendations based on new data (Neiroukh et al., 2024). This self learning ability improves decision-making by providing real-time, context-oriented research findings that adapt to a dynamic business environment. For example, adaptive BI can recognize fraudulent transactions in financial services by learning from developing fraud patterns. In contrast, demand forecasts can be dynamically adapted in supply chain management based on external factors such as weather conditions and geopolitical events (Rane et al., 2024). Traditional BI systems were based on batch processes in which data was collected, stored, and analyzed at planning intervals. This approach often leads to delayed discovery, making it tough to respond quickly to new trends and unusually fast. AI-equipped BI systems use real-time streaming analytics to process and analyze generated data. This ability is particularly valuable in industries such as e-commerce, enabling personalized recommendations and targeted ad campaigns through real-time customer behavior analysis. Similarly, monitoring device performance in manufacturing can help predict maintenance requirements and prevent costly downtime (Kothinti, 2024). AugmendedAlytics uses AI-controlled automation to simplify data preparation, analysis, and visualization, reducing reliance on data scientists and technical experts. Users can interact with the BI system using conversation queries by processing natural language. It makes data analytics more accessible to business users (Samara et al., 2024). For example, a marketing manager can ask an AI-driven BI system, "What was the best product in the last quarter?" Get detailed answers using visualizations and implementationable findings. This democratization of data allows employees at all stages of the organization to make decisions to control the data. Traditional BI systems often require on-site infrastructure that limits scalability and flexibility. Cloud-based BI solutions allow us to use, process, and analyze large amounts of data without storing physical infrastructure restrictions. It is particularly advantageous in IoT applications where sensors and network devices generate continuous data flows that require immediate analysis and measurement.

Data quality and governance remain important, as AI models require high-quality, clean, and unbiased data to generate accurate knowledge. Data security assurance and compliance with regulations such as GDPR and CCPA are also crucial to protecting confidential information and maintaining customer trust. Integrating AI-driven BI companies requires investing in qualified talent and change management initiatives to promote a data-controlled culture. Explanatory AI (XAI) becomes more transparent and interpretable and plays an important role in creating AI-controlled knowledge that addresses bias and accountability concerns (Rodriguez and Costa,

2024). AI-driven BI convergence with emerging technologies such as blockchain and quantum computers unlocks new data analytics, security, and decision-making possibilities. As AI evolves, BI systems enable organizations to achieve unprecedented efficiency and innovation, being more intuitive, aggressive, and autonomous. Redefine how organizations analyze data, generate insights, and make decisions. Businesses can use AI, machine learning, and real-world analytics to switch to predictive, normative intelligence beyond descriptive reporting, which improves strategic planning and operational efficiency. Although data quality, governance, and acquisitions pose challenges, the benefits of BI of AI operations dominate well beyond obstacles and positions to succeed in an increasingly data-controlled world. Although technology continues, the role of BI will evolve from passive reporting instruments to intelligent self-learning systems that promote business innovation and competitive advantage (Tariq, 2025).

Business Intelligence Systems (BI) systems traditionally rely on data warehousing, reports, and dashboards to help organizations make their discovery. However, BI has experienced significant changes since artificial intelligence (AI) and machine learning (ML) began. AI and ML improve BI systems by automating data processing, enabling predictive analytics, and detecting hidden data patterns that overlook traditional BI tools. They help companies make data-controlled decisions more efficiently and reduce the time required for manual analysis. AI-powered BI tools can automatically identify trends, recognize anomalies, suggest implementable knowledge, and reduce human bias and error. Natural Language Processing (NLP) also allows business users to interact with BI systems using conversation queries, making data analysis more available to non-technical users. Additionally, ML algorithms continuously learn from data, improving their accuracy and efficiency over time, allowing BI systems to develop as terms of use change. AI also plays a dynamic role in automating data cleaning and preparation. It often leads to time and is prone to human error. AI allows businesses to improve data quality, reduce redundancy, and improve decision-making (Zednik, 2021).

Traditional BI systems focus primarily on descriptive analysis and report on what has happened in the past. However, AI and ML introduce predictive and normative analyses that predict future trends and recommend the optimal action. For example, ML models can predict customer hikes, forecast sales, and optimize supply chains by analyzing historical data and identifying patterns. AI-controlled BI systems allow you to actively attract attention to potential risks and opportunities and act on problems. Furthermore, AI makes real-time analytics easier, enabling businesses to respond swiftly to fluctuations in market situations (Chowdhury, 2024). This ability is particularly advantageous in finance, healthcare, and retail industries. Timely decisions are significant in this industry. Traditional BI tools must combat unstructured data such as email, social media posts, customer reviews, and multimedia content. However, AI-powered BI systems can extract knowledge from such data using NLP, image detection, and mood analysis. For example, mood analysis allows businesses to measure customer opinions and adapt their strategies accordingly. AI can also improve BI systems by activating augmented data visualization techniques, allowing users to understand complex data records better. AI-controlled visualization tools allow you to dynamically adapt diagrams and diagrams based on user preferences, making data exploration more intuitive and beneficial. One of the most critical issues is the data's quality and availability; ML models require a large amount of high-quality data to function effectively. However, many organizations have problems with data silos, inconsistent formats, and incomplete records that can negatively affect AI performance (Rane, 2024). Decreased data quality leads to inaccurate predictions and unreliable discoveries, reducing the effectiveness of BI systems using AI-powered BI systems. Organizations should invest in robust data governance practices to ensure data accuracy, consistency, and accessibility across all departments.

Another major challenge is the complexity of AI implementation. In contrast to traditional BI tools based primarily on predefined queries and reports, AI-controlled BI systems require demanding algorithms, advanced statistical techniques, and continuous model training. Implementing AI and ML in BI requires qualified data scientists and engineers. It can be a hindrance for organizations that lack technical knowledge. Furthermore, the AI model requires constant monitoring and updates to maintain relevance as contract terms and data patterns change (Farayola, 2024). AI-controlled BI systems can generate outdated or misleading knowledge without proper model management. Many AI models and intense learning algorithms act as "black boxes." It means that the decision-making process is not easy to understand. This lack of transparency can make it hard for business users to trust their knowledge of A-generated findings. If the manufacturer doesn't understand how AI has obtained specific recommendations, it can hesitate to respond to the results. To tackle this issue, organizations need to use explanatory AI technologies that provide clear reasons for AI-controlled knowledge. Providing transparency in AI decision-making enables business users to use the BI tools of AI-driven BI tools confidently. AI and ML depend on large amounts of data, including sensitive customer information and unique business data. If this data is not correctly managed, it is vulnerable to virtual threats and unauthorized access (Lokanan and Maddhesia, 2025). Administrations should implement robust security measures such as encryption, access control, and submission with data protection regulations (such as GDPR CCPA).

Furthermore, AI systems must be designed so that distortion leads to unfair or discriminatory decisions. AI distortions can be attributed to historical data patterns or false training processes, leading to biased predictions that can negatively affect a particular user group (Rane et al., 2024). Organizations must ensure AI models are trained on various representative data records to minimize distortion and promote equity. The cost of AI integration is another obstacle for many companies. Implementing AI-controlled BI solutions requires significant technology, infrastructure, and HR investment. Organizations should assess whether the potential benefits of AI-controlled BI dominate implementation costs. Large companies may have the resources to invest in AI, but small businesses can be complex to justify costs. To meet this challenge, cloud-based AI solutions have proven to be a cost-effective alternative to enable businesses to use AI capabilities without a comprehensive local infrastructure. Employees can oppose the acquisition of BI instruments from AI-powered BI instruments. It is because they fear that the effectiveness of AI will be skeptical compared to occupational shifts and skepticism. Organizations should focus on change management strategies such as training programs and user-friendly AI interfaces to promote adoption and ensure that employees view AI as an improvement over an alternative to human decisions. Promoting a culture of data-controlled decision-making and improving employees' AI-related skills can facilitate smoother AI integration.

THE EVOLUTION OF AI IN BUSINESS INTELLIGENCE

The development of artificial intelligence (AI) in business intelligence (BI) has changed the way companies analyze data and make strategic decisions. Traditional BI focused primarily on descriptive analyses in which structured reports and historical data are recorded and presented in dashboards. These reports helped companies understand past trends and performance but rarely provided predictive future outcomes or knowledge that could be implemented in real-time. However, AI-controlled BI revolutionizes this domain by integrating prediction and normative analysis, allowing companies to make more accurate and faster data-controlled decisions (Michael et al., 2024). Traditional BI systems were based on manual processes in which data analysts extracted knowledge with predefined queries and static reports. These systems are often slow and cumbersome, making it tough for companies to respond quickly to changes in market conditions. Meanwhile, AI-controlled BI uses machine learning (ML) algorithms to analyze large amounts of real-time data, identify patterns, and predict future trends. By automating the analytical process, AI reduces human intervention, minimizes errors, and improves decision-making capabilities. Traditional BI data analysts have encouraged data, manually searched for large data records, and identified trends, anomalies, and time-consuming, labor-intensive processes. ML algorithms can process large amounts of structured and unstructured data, recognize patterns, and generate implementable knowledge with minimal human participation. For example, BI tools with ML-driven BI tools can optimize supply chain business activities by recognizing fraudulent transactions at financial institutions, predicting sales trends, and predicting fluctuations in demand. These skills allow businesses to control their data faster and more accurately. With NLP, the BI system can comprehend and process human language, making it simpler for users to interact with natural language queries. Traditional BI users wanted technical knowledge of SQL queries and data visualization tools to extract knowledge. With NLP, even non-technical users can ask, "What was the best-selling product in the last quarter?" Receive instant responses through illustrations, graphics, or summaries (Han et al., 2024).

This AI-controlled conversation interface democratizes data access within an organization, allowing employees to use BI without special training. Instead of spending time writing reports, AI-operated BI Systems can create real-time reports with contextual stories to highlight key trends and possible implementation knowledge. This automation optimizes business operations and allows decision-makers to focus more on strategic initiatives than daily reporting tasks (Young et al., 2022). Additionally, AI-controlled BI tools can analyze customer feedback, social media interactions, and online review moods to measure brand perceptions and identify areas of improvement. Traditional BI systems were limited by stacking, where data was collected, stored, and analyzed at defined intervals. This approach has often led to delays in findings. However, AI-controlled BI uses streaming analysis, manipulated by ML algorithms, to process data after creation, allowing companies to respond to changing conditions quickly. In the e-commerce industry, for example, AI-controlled BI can analyze customer behavior in real-time and personalize product recommendations based on browsers and purchase patterns. Similarly, actual financial sector analysis can recognize and prevent fraud before causing significant damage. Predictive Analytics predicts future trends, but normative analysis continues by recommending the best steps based on historical data and current trends. The AI-controlled BI system analyzes several variables, evaluates different scenarios, and provides implementable recommendations for optimizing business outcomes (Tariq, 2025). For example, AI-driven Bi-Tools can analyze patient data, predict illness, and suggest precautions to improve public health in the healthcare industry. AI-controlled BI can optimize production plans, reduce waste, and improve supply chain efficiency in production. One of the foremost concerns is the quality and availability of the data. The AI and ML models are based on a large amount of high-quality data that generates accurate knowledge. Unpredictable, incomplete, or biased data can lead to false conclusions and bad decisions. Organizations must invest in robust data governance frameworks to ensure data accuracy, consistency, and security.

Additionally, integrating AI into existing BI systems requires considerable investment in infrastructure, training, and change management. Many companies struggle to manage AI-controlled BI platforms with implementing KI and the need for qualified professionals (Hamadaqa et al., 2024). AI-powered BI systems and massive personal and sensitive data analytics raise concerns about data protection and amenability with regulations such as GDPR and CCPA. Organizations must implement strict data protection measures and ethical AI practices when creating AI to ensure transparency, equity, and accountability. Furthermore, reliance on AI for critical business decisions raises concerns about bias and interpretability (Tariq, 2025). Companies need to ensure that the AI model can be described as transparent. It should ensure that stakeholders understand the findings and reasons for recommendations based on the conditions generated by AI. Despite these challenges, the future of BI AI is promising. AI, ML, and NLP advances have further improved BI functionality, making data analysis more intuitive, accessible, and feasible. The convergence of AI-controlled BI further expands the possibilities for real-time analysis and secure data processing through convergence with new technologies such as the Internet of Things (IoT) and blockchain. As businesses increasingly embrace AI-operated BI, they receive a competitive advantage by using data-controlled knowledge to improve innovation, efficiency, and customer experience.

AI-POWERED DATA PROCESSING AND PREDICTIVE ANALYTICS

The increased amount and complexity of data available to businesses requires effective data cleaning and conversion processes to ensure data quality and user-friendliness. Traditional data preparation methods are often labor-intensive and require considerable time and effort from data analysts. Data preparation is more efficient and accurate with Business Intelligence (BI) Analytics. Machine learning models analyze historical data patterns to identify errors and inconsistencies and automatically correct them if possible. For example, AI can standardize various data formats and combine redundant data records to fill in the missing values based on predictive analytics. Businesses can reduce manual effort and improve BI capabilities by automating these processes. AI models can classify and mark data from various sources, such as email, social media, and customer feedback (James et al., 2024). It makes BI tools more accessible. Additionally, AI-powered ECL pipelines (extract, conversion, load) improve data integration and reduce latency for real-time data processing and decision-making. Businesses can generate more accurate knowledge, improving operational efficiency and strategic decision-making by reducing errors and conflicts. Use historical data and algorithms for machine learning to identify predictive model patterns and correlations for predictions of outcomes such as sales, customer behavior, and market fluctuations. Companies use AI models to analyze historical sales data, seasonal trends, and external market factors to predict future revenues (Anozie et al., 2024). These models help businesses adapt to inventory, allocate resources, and improve their pricing strategies. For example, e-commerce companies can use predictive analytics to predict demand hints during the holiday season and optimize their supply chain accordingly.

Customer behavior analysis is another critical application. The AI model analyzes previous interactions, purchases, historical history, and demographic data to predict customer preferences and immigration potential. Companies use this finding to personalize marketing campaigns, recommend products, and improve customer loyalty strategies. For example, subscription-based services can identify customers at risk of cancellation and provide targeted incentives to keep them (Bari & Ara, 2024). AI-powered predictive analytics aggregates data from several sources, including social media, economic metrics, and competitive analytics, to identify emerging trends. Retailers, financial institutions, and health service providers use these findings to actively adapt their strategies. Organizations implementing AI-managed forecasts can minimize risk, optimize performance, and gain a competitive advantage in rapidly developing markets (Kaggwa et al., 2024). Prescriptive analysis of AI control uses machine learning, optimization algorithms, and simulation techniques to provide implementationable recommendations. When optimizing the supply chain, the AI model analyzes inventory levels and analyzes demand forecasting and logistical limits to propose optimal procurement and distribution strategies. For example, systems with AI can recommend the cheapest delivery routes while minimizing delivery delays. The AI model evaluates portfolio power, economic indicators, and investor preferences to recommend asset allocations that amplify returns and, at the same time, lessen risk. Financial institutions also use regulatory analyses to recognize fraud by identifying suspicious transactions and suggesting precautions. The AI model analyzes medical records, treatment outcomes, and real-time patient data to recommend personalized treatment plans. Hospitals use normative analysis to optimize resource allocation, decrease patient waiting times, and improve service delivery. The AI model proposes personalized offers, optimal advertising channels, and campaigns to maximize customer conversion rates (Bauskar, 2024). For example, an AI-controlled marketing platform can recommend the best email and content based on previous campaign performance and customer loyalty. AI control recommendations enable businesses to manage complex challenges and effectively use growth opportunities. Traditional data visualization techniques often require manual effort and technical expertise, limiting access to non-technical users. AI-controlled visualization automatically improves this process by capturing complex datasets' patterns, trends, and anomalies. These tools automatically identify critical performance indicators (KPIs) and generate real-time visual representations of business metrics. For example, AI can analyze sales data, create heat cards highlighting high and low sales production areas, and adapt their strategies accordingly. AI-operated dashboards can generate automated reports and descriptions and summarise plain language trends. This ability enables decision-makers with no technical expertise to quickly understand and respond to insights (Adewumi et al., 2024). For example, AI-powered fraud detection systems use visualization technology to highlight suspicious transactions in financial data, allowing analysts to take precautions.

IMPLEMENTING AI AND ML IN BI ARCHITECTURES

Business Intelligence (BI) framework conditions have evolved significantly, and artificial intelligence (AI) plays a key role in modern analyses. Integrating AI into Bi-infrastructures will improve your ability to derive implementation knowledge, automate processes, and improve decision-making. However, seamless integration requires best practices to ensure efficiency and effectiveness. Understanding the strengths and limitations of existing BI tools, data sources, and workflows can help you identify areas where AI can add maximum value. Organizations must create integrations of AI control characteristics such as predictive analytics, natural language processing (NLP), and automated knowledge. AI models require high-quality, structured, relevant data to provide accurate knowledge. Determining strong guidelines for data management, ensuring data consistency, and implementing data verification techniques can help maintain data integrity (Shittu et al., 2024). Additionally, organizations must use data lakes and stores to concentrate structured and unstructured data to ensure smooth training and preparation rates for AI models. AI-controlled analysis often requires considerable computing power and memory capabilities. Distributed computing, parallel processing, and cloud-based infrastructure can improve scalability. Additionally, organizations must employ modular and flexible architectures to easily integrate AI components without disrupting existing workflows (Adewusi et al., 2024). Employees should be informed of how the findings of AI-generated knowledge are interpreted and whether AI-driven dual tools can be used effectively. Implementing intuitive dashboards and interactive visualizations allows technical and non-technical users to access AI control analytics. Cloud platforms offer unprecedented scalability, flexibility, and computing power, making them ideal for AI control analytics. Using cloud-based AI in BI systems improves data accessibility, reduces infrastructure costs, and enables real-time. Cloud platforms provide scalable storage solutions that allow businesses to collect and analyze large amounts of structured unstructured data. It is particularly advantageous for AI models that require continuous learning from a wide range of data sets (Lo Piano, 2020).

Cloud platforms such as AWS, Microsoft Azure, and Google Cloud offer AI and machine learning services that can be absorbed seamlessly in BI workflows. These services include automated machine learning (Automl), NLP, and Deep Learning models, allowing businesses to improve analytics capabilities without a large internal AI expert. Companies must ensure that cloud providers meet industry standards and regulatory necessities such as GDPR, HIPAA, and SOC2. You can protect sensitive data from cyber threats by implementing robust encryption, access control, and authentication mechanisms. Teams from different locations have real-time access to AI-driven dashboards and reports, increasing decision-making efficiency. Scaling resources on demand also ensures cost optimization, requiring businesses to maintain computing power without expensive on-premises infrastructure. When AI models function efficiently in large BI environments, optimized infrastructure, efficient algorithms, and strategic resource management are required (Arinze et al., 2024). Technologies such as Apache Spark, TensorFlow, and Kubernetes allow businesses to distribute AI workloads to several computer nodes. It is particularly advantageous for AI models that require real-time data analysis and complex calculations. Large BI environments generate a large amount of raw data that requires to be cleaned, transformed, and structured before effectively analyzing AI models. Automated data pipelines and ETL processes (extract, transformation, load) can streamline data preparation and reduce processing time. These techniques simultaneously reduce the complexity of AI models to maintain accuracy. This means that it is more efficient to use in large BI environments. Cloud-based GPU and TPU resources can accelerate AI model training and inference processes.

Organizations must implement continuous model assessment and retraining mechanisms to ensure that AI-controlled knowledge is relevant and accurate. MLOPS (machine learning operations) automates AI model delivery, monitoring, and management, increasing overall system efficiency. AI models should be designed to efficiently interact with data warehouses, visualization tools, and reporting systems, minimizing bottlenecks and improving data flow (Collins et al., 2024). Using APIs and microservices architectures can further promote smooth integration and interoperability. Automl automates various levels of pipelines for machine learning, including data preprocessing, feature selection, model training, and hyperparameter tuning. Developing and delivering AI models requires traditionally specialized knowledge of machine learning, programming languages, and algorithms for statistical methods. Automl eliminates these obstacles by providing an intuitive interface, drag-and-drop functionality, and automatic model selection. Corporate analysts and decision-makers can easily generate AI-driven knowledge (Onesi-Ozigagun et al., 2024). Another important advantage of Automl is that it accelerates the model development process. Creating machine learning models can take time. It requires repeated experiments and fine-tuning. The Automl platform automates this process by running several models in parallel, assessing performance, and selecting the most optimal one. It significantly reduces the time required to deliver AI models in a BI environment. Many Automl platforms provide model prediction explanations highlighting important features affecting the outcome. It allows businesses to understand their knowledge of AI control and build confidence in the recommendations generated by the system. Solutions such as Google Automl, Microsoft Azure Automl, and H2O.AI allow businesses to include AI control analytics in Bi-Workflows without requiring extensive technical changes. These platforms also support real-time model updates, ensuring your AI control knowledge is relevant and up-to-date. It simplifies the delivery of AI models but does not always generate models developed by expert scientists. Additionally, Automl solutions must be monitored carefully to prevent distortions and inaccuracies in the knowledge that AIM is generated. Organizations using this advancement can enable new efficiency, agility, and data-controlled decisions, achieving competitive advantages in today's rapidly changing business environment.

CHALLENGES AND ETHICAL CONSIDERATIONS IN AI-POWERED BI

The distribution of AI-controlled data analytics in Business Intelligence (BI) requires organizations with significant data protection and security risks to be exhibited. AI-powered BI tools process sensitive information, including customer data, financial documents, and unique business knowledge. It raises concerns about unauthorized access, data injuries, and regulatory non-violation. Companies need to ensure that the AI model conforms with strict data protection laws such as the European General Data Protection Ordinance (GDPR), the US California Consumer Privacy Act (CCPA), and other legal regulations of jurisdiction. AI models require large data records for training and optimization. Suppose there are no reasonable protection measures; the chances of data protection violations increase (Ajegbile et al., 2024). Encryption, anonymization, and data masking techniques are essential to reduce these risks. Additionally, organizations can implement robust access control mechanisms to restrict data access to certified staff only. Another challenge is the ethical use of AI in data analysis. AI algorithms can misrecord and process data without explicit user consent, leading to legal and reputable results. Along with precise mechanisms for user consent, transparent data collection and processing practices are essential for maintaining compliance and public trust. In addition, businesses must be up to date with developing data protection regulations to continue to comply with legal requirements. Implementing security solutions from AI-operated will help you recognize anomalies and prevent cyber threats before causing significant damage. AI can improve security, but it must be used responsibly to avoid introducing new weaknesses. The distortions in AI models can be viewed from various sources, including bound training data, algorithm design errors, and implicit distortions in decision-making processes. Many AI models learn from historical data that can reflect existing social or organizational bias (Chowdhury, 2024). If your AI model is trained on biased data records, recommendations can maintain and increase these biases. Companies must regularly audit training data to identify and mitigate distortions. It includes using a variety of representative data records, decorating decoding techniques, and continuing improvements to AI algorithms to improve fairness. Many AI models, especially deep learning systems, act as black boxes, making it tough for administrators to understand how specific decisions are made.

Lack of transparency can lead to doubt in people's knowledge that AI has been generated and limit referrals to organizations. Techniques such as Shapley (Shapley Additive Description) and Lime (Local Interpretable Models - Principle Description) can help make AI control insights more transparent. Furthermore, organizations need to promote a culture of alphabetization of AI, allowing decision-makers to understand the limitations and skills of AI models. By promoting equity and transparency, companies can build trust in BI's knowledge of A-generated BI and improve overall effectiveness. This unwillingness contributes to this fear of postponed work, skepticism about AI reliability, and concerns about the cost of implementation (Mozumder et al., 2024). Overcoming these obstacles requires a strategic approach focused on education, change management, and evidence of the concrete benefits of AI. The main reason for resistance is the fear that AI will replace human work. AI can automate repetitive tasks, but instead of exchanging them, it is designed to increase human decisions. Companies must communicate this message and emphasize how AI can improve employee productivity by focusing on strategic and creative tasks. Delivering AI training and upskills programs helps employees adapt to new technologies and view AI as enablers rather than threats. Many companies have difficulty implementing AI-controlled BI solutions due to a lack of qualified data scientists and AI experts. To improve this, companies can invest in AI education programs, work with AI providers, and use low-code and no-code AI platforms that simplify implementation. Business leaders can hesitate to rely on AI-generated knowledge if they don't fully understand how a model works.

Organizations need to implement a robust verification process to ensure that AI recommendations are correct and align with business goals. Furthermore, evidence of the success of AI applications within an organization can help build trust in technology. Including stakeholders at all levels and addressing concerns through transparent communication can make BI smoother. Organizations must carefully assess costs and potential return on capital (ROI) to justify their AI initiatives. Understanding the financial effects of AI referrals is essential for transparent decision meetings. Additionally, AI integration is necessary to upgrade existing BI infrastructure for computational resources and data management systems. These costs are essential, but the potential benefits of BI AI often outweigh the initial investment. It can lead to improved decision-making, reduced operating costs, and increased sales potential (Hossain et al., 2024). For instance, AI-driven predictive analytics can aid businesses in optimizing their supply chains and improving customer experiences, leading to increased profitability. Metrics such as sales growth, cost reduction, process efficiency, and customer satisfaction can provide quantitative measures of AI value.

CASE STUDIES AND FUTURE TRENDS

Artificial intelligence (AI) has become essential to business intelligence (BI). It provides businesses with valuable knowledge, decision automation, and optimization processes. Several industries use AI in BI to increase efficiency, reduce costs, and improve customer experience. A notable example is Netflix, which uses AI-driven BI to analyze audience preferences, optimize content recommendations, and improve usage (Ahmed et al., 2025). Through advanced machine learning algorithms, Netflix predicts the content users will most likely see, ultimately increasing customer loyalty and satisfaction. For example, IBM Watson Health Ki processes and interprets medical literature, patient files, and clinical data. It provides implementable knowledge to support more accurate diagnosis and creating personalized treatment plans. AI-powered analytics systems help optimize inventory management, predict demand fluctuations, and improve customer experience through personalized recommendations. Amazon improves conversion rates and operational efficiency by assessing customer behavior and purchase history. Similarly, financial institutions such as the JPMorgan Chase AI Control BI Tool recognize fraudulent transactions, automate risk assessments, and use them to improve compliance, making financial processes safer and more efficient. Reducing logistics and operational costs. For example, DHL AI-driven analytics is integrated into logistics operations, enabling real-time tracking, forecasting expectations, and efficient route planning. By analyzing large amounts of supply data, AI helps businesses expect obstacles and data-controlled decisions, increasing efficiency across their supply chain networks. For example, Coca-Cola uses AI-controlled analytics to monitor social media trends, understand consumer moods, and adapt marketing campaigns accordingly. AI algorithms analyze consumer behavior patterns, enable marketers to deliver personalized ads, predict purchase trends, and maximize return on investment (ROI). Similarly, Unilever uses AI to analyze market data, optimize product innovation, and agree to marketing efforts to specific demographic data. For example, American Express

AI-operated Analyzes recognizes fraudulent transactions in real-time, reducing financial losses based on fraud.

Additionally, AI-driven chatbots in banking applications provide immediate customer support, improved user experience, and reduced operational costs. The AI-controlled model allows banks to make more detailed credit decisions by evaluating their customer loans based on historical data and predictive analytics. Such an emerging trend is AI-generated to generate human-like text, images, and data knowledge using AI models. Generated AI revolutionizes BI by automating the production of report reports, creating data-controlled stories, and improving decision-making processes. Companies like Openaai and Google have developed AI-driven tools to generate insights from complex data records and help companies make faster and healthier decisions. Blockchain technology ensures data security, transparency, and immutability and ensures an ideal addition to BI applications. AI-powered BI tools combined with blockchain can improve data integrity, prevent fraud, and improve compliance processes. For example, supply chain companies use blockchain and AI to pursue and verify product collection, ensuring transparency across the supply chain. In contrast to traditional cloud-based AI models, Edge AI processes data locally on devices such as IoT sensors, smartphones, and industrial machines. This approach is handy for manufacturing, where accurate data analysis can optimize the production process and detect devices before they occur. Companies like Siemens and General Electric are already using EDGE AI to improve operational efficiency and reduce downtime in the industrial environment (Mishra et al., 2024). A key prediction is the rise of AI-controlled decision intelligence, where AI systems analyze data and recommend and implement strategic measures. Companies increasingly rely on AI-driven BI tools to automate decision-making processes, reduce human intervention, and improve operational efficiency. Through enhanced analysis, companies can provide natural language questions and receive answers with AI-generated answers. It means that data analysis is accessible to non-technical users. As a result, organizations will democratize data access, letting employees at all levels make data-controlled decisions.

AI-controlled BI is essential in superpersonalization, providing highly adapted experiences based on real-time data analysis. Companies use AI to predict customer preferences, optimize tailor-made marketing reports, and optimize product offers with unprecedented accuracy. This personalization improves customer satisfaction and drives sales growth across various industries. Organizations must implement robust ethical framework conditions, ensure compliance with data protection conditions, and treat potential distortion in AI algorithms. Supervisors can implement stricter AI guidelines in BI to ensure transparency, accountability, and fairness in data-controlled decision-making. With progressions in machine learning, natural language processing, and real-time analytics, BI in AI manipulation continues to improve the industry's efficiency, innovation, and competitiveness. Artificial intelligence (AI) transformatively influences business intelligence (bi), and data revolutionizes how organizations analyze, interpret, and use data. AI-controlled BI has redesigned the decision-making process to increase operational efficiency and allow businesses to get deeper insights from vast data. While BI was traditionally based on static reporting and manual analysis, AI has introduced automation, predictive analytics, and real data processing, significantly improving the accuracy and speed of business knowledge. AI-equipped systems can perform repetitive tasks such as data collection, cleaning, and processing with minimal human intervention. Not only does this automation reduce human error, but it also allows data analysts and managers to focus on strategic decisions rather than mediocre data-related tasks. AI-controlled BI tools use algorithms for machine learning to recognize anomalies, identify trends, and create reports without requiring extensive manual input. As a result, organizations can make faster and more informed decisions based on real data. Traditional BI tools provided descriptive analyses focused primarily on analyzing historical data to understand historical trends. However, AI enables predictive analytics by using algorithms for machine learning to predict future trends and outcomes. AI-powered BI tools can predict customer behavior, market fluctuations, sales trends, and potential risks by analyzing the correlation between historical patterns and real-time data. This predictive ability allows businesses to actively coordinate their strategies, optimize resources, and mitigate risk before escalating critical issues. Previously, companies were based on regular reports from static datasets, leading to knowledge and decision delays (Hosen et al., 2024). AI-controlled BI systems continuously process data in real-time, enabling businesses to respond quickly to changes in market conditions. This ability is critical for finance, e-commerce, and healthcare industries, and timely decisions can have important effects. In finance, for example, AI-driven BI tools can recognize fraudulent transactions in real-time, allowing banks to take action immediately. With e-commerce, AI can analyze customer behavior, personalize real-time recommendations, improve user experience, and increase sales. Traditional BI tools present data in diagrams and graphics, requiring users to interpret information manually. The AI-controlled BI platform uses natural language processing (NLP) and extended analytics to provide more intuitive and interactive knowledge. With NLP, BI tools can understand and generate human explanations of complex data patterns, making findings more accessible to non-technical users. Augmented analysis improves BI by automatically proposing knowledge, identifying correlations, and providing implementationable recommendations based on data patterns. This shift democratized data analytics, allowing corporate managers from various sectors to make data-controlled decisions without needing data science expertise. AI-powered BI systems analyze large amounts of customer data to reveal preferences, behaviors, and trends. In this way, companies can more effectively segment their customers and adapt their marketing and sales strategies accordingly. For example, AI-controlled recommendation engines have become essential in industries such as retail and maintenance, with personalized recommendations driving customer commitment and sales. Using AI in BI allows businesses to improvc customcr cxpcricncc, improvc rctcntion, and maximize sales. With NLG, BI tools can generate a narrative summary of data knowledge and facilitate complex reporting. Conversational analytics run by AI chatbots and virtual assistants allow users to interact with the BI system using natural language queries. Instead of manually searching for knowledge in a dashboard, users can easily ask questions about AI-controlled systems, such as "What was your bestseller product last quarter?" Which factors contributed to the decline in sales last month? "These skills streamline data research and improve access to decision-making.

Organizations deal with sensitive data that must be protected from cyber threats and regulatory violations. AI-powered security analytics can recognize anomalous activities, identify potential threats, and prevent real-time data injury. Additionally, AI-controlled BI tools ensure compliance with industry regulations by automatically monitoring data usage and generating compliance reports. This proactive approach to security and compliance aids businesses in reducing risk and maintaining customer trust. Traditional BI required IT team methods and participation to generate reports and extract knowledge. AI-controlled self-service BI allows employees to easily use AI-generated recommendations to explore data using an intuitive interface and voice commands. This shift reduced reliance on IT teams, accelerated decision-making, and promoted a data-controlled culture within the organization. Data quality remains critical as AI models rely on accurate and comprehensive data records to generate reliable knowledge. Companies must invest in data management and ensure their data sources are clean, structured, and date-to-date. Furthermore, AI-controlled BI requires continuous monitoring and improvement to prevent distortion and inaccuracy in predictive models. Ethical considerations like data security and transparency when finding AI decisions must also be addressed to build participant trust. Another challenge is integrating AI into your existing BI infrastructure. Many organizations work with legacy BI systems that may not be compatible with advanced AI technologies. The transition to AI-controlled BI requires considerable investment in technology, training, and change management. Organizations need to carefully evaluate their strategic roadmap for implementing AI to minimize obstacles to maximize benefits and, at the same time, minimize obstacles. AI improves automation and analysis, but how must humans interpret results, validate knowledge, and make strategic decisions? Organizations must broaden the balance between AI automation and human judgment to ensure business decisions meet broader goals and ethical considerations.

The integration of Artificial Intelligence (AI) and Machine Learning (ML) in Business Intelligence (BI) systems is a transformational process that enables businesses to extract deeper insights, automate decision-making, and improve their data control strategies. However, this process requires careful planning, motivation for infrastructure, and a precisely defined strategy to utilize its possibilities fully. One of the most important considerations is to ensure the quality of your data and follow-up. AI and ML algorithms rely on a large amount of high-quality data to generate accurate predictions and findings. Companies must invest in data cleaning, validation, and governance frameworks to ensure that BI systems receive reliable input. Without this criterion, AI models can achieve misleading or biased results that negatively affect decision-making. Integrating AI into unstructured and unstructured data sources is essential while ensuring data consistency across departments. Companies must assess their needs and determine whether predictive analytics, natural language processing (NLP), computer vision, or other AI control features are required. Model selection should match specific business objectives, such as customer segmentation, sales forecasting, and improved operational efficiency.

Additionally, organizations must decide whether to develop their AI models or use existing AI-as-A-service solutions (AIaaS). While developing internal models offers adaptation, it requires considerable investment in talent and infrastructure. AIaaS completed usage solutions can be used with minimal effort. AI and ML should be embedded in existing BI workflows rather than as separate systems. Companies must assess current BI tools like dashboards and reporting platforms to determine how AI-controlled knowledge improves their decision-making processes. Unestimated integrations allow business users to access AI-driven recommendations in the familiar BI environment. It also includes the choice of the right APIs, automation tools, and cloud platforms, allowing for a smooth connection between your AI model and BI software. One of the most essential benefits of AI and ML integration is its ability to automate repetitive tasks such as data preparation, anomaly recognition, and trend analysis. Companies need to identify processes that can be optimized with AI. It reduces human movement and increases efficiency. For example, AI-controlled BI systems can automatically recognize customer behavior patterns and identify unusual trends for further investigation. It reduces the burden on analysts while at the same time providing faster data-controlled responses to business challenges. Scalability is another important factor in AI integration. Enterprises must ensure that their infrastructure meets the increased arithmetic requirements concerning AI and ML workloads. Cloud computing offers a scalable solution that businesses can use to expand AI capabilities in hardware without significant backup investments. In addition, companies should consider edge computing solutions for real-time analytics, especially in industries such as manufacturing and retail. Fast decisions are critical in this industry. AI-controlled BI systems must be flexible to meet future growth and development of business requirements. For data protection regulations such as the GDPR and CCPA, companies must ensure that the AI model handles customer data responsibly. AI-controlled BI must be transparent with an explanatory model that allows stakeholders to understand decision-making. The hindrances in AI modcls arc another challenge companies must tackle by implementing fairness checks and assurance of diverse data representations. Organizations must determine ethical AI guidelines and governance frames to maintain confidence and compliance with legal requirements.

Many employees can oppose changes in AI control; which fear job changes and lack of technical expertise. Organizations should invest in AI alphabetization programs to help employees understand the benefits of AI-improved BI systems. Providing training and support allows business users to interact with AI-controlled knowledge safely. Furthermore, promoting a data control culture where AI is considered more an enabler than a threat encourages employees to embrace new technologies. AI and ML models rely on large data records, making them attractive destinations for cyber threats. Organizations must implement robust security measures such as encryption, access control, and anomalous recognition mechanisms to prevent unauthorized access to sensitive business data. Regular audits and monitoring of AI models can help you recognize and mitigate security risks before they become significant threats. In addition, companies need to consider the ethical implications of AI decision-making and ensure that AI systems match the company's values (Pokala, 2024). While traditional BI systems are based on historical data analysis, AI and ML allow for predictive and normative analyses that predict future trends and recommend feasible steps. Companies can use AI to make positive decisions. Optimize the offer chain in response to adapting pricing strategies based on real-time market conditions or fluctuations in demand. This agility provides a competitive advantage by enabling businesses to respond effectively to the changing business environment. While traditional BI dashboards show static reports primarily, AI-controlled BI can generate dynamic, interactive visualizations that provide deeper insights. With NLP-powered BI tools, users can ask questions in natural language and get answers with AI-generated answers. It makes the analysis more accessible to non-technical users. Organizations need to use AI-controlled story-counting techniques to present data in ways that improve decision-making and drive business effectiveness. AI models require continuous monitoring and improvement to ensure accuracy and relevance. Companies need to implement a feedback loop that allows users to provide AI with entries into the knowledge generated. It means that the model output improves over time. Regular retraining of AI models with updated data will help you continue to align with developing business trends and challenges. Companies must establish dedicated AI teams responsible for model maintenance, performance assessment, and innovation.

CONCLUSION

AI-powered business intelligence (BI) will develop quickly. However, future research and development may be essential to improve skills, accuracy, and user-friendliness. An important area of improvement is improving the interpretability and explanation of AI-controlled BI systems. Many companies are reluctant to trust AI-generated film knowledge fully. Future research should provide a clear explanation of predictions, allowing users to understand how decisions are made and allow them to understand the reliability of AI-controlled BI systems. The efficiency and effectiveness of BI systems can be significantly improved by improving the ability to automatically clean, harmonize, and integrate AI data sources with minimal human intervention. Research into self-learning data pipelines and AI-controlled data governance mechanisms can further improve this process and reduce errors and discrepancies. AI-Operation BI Future BI Systems should be able to adapt the findings to various users based on their roles, expertise, and business requirements. Research into adaptive AI models considering user behavior, industry trends, and historical decision patterns can lead to more relevant and implementable recommendations and improve decision support. Companies increasingly need current findings to respond positively to market changes. Future research should investigate ways to efficiently process, analyze, improve, and reduce latency to generate knowledge.

Furthermore, improving the accuracy and reliability of predictive models, especially in volatile environments, is extremely important. It includes research into research that allows AI models to address uncertainty, recognize anomalies, and include external factors such as economic indicators and geopolitical events. AI models can mislead and immortalize biases in historical data, leading to unfair or suboptimal business decisions. Future research should focus on developing technologies to recognize and correct distortions in BI systems using AI drives. It includes creating an AI framework that features fairness, involvement of various training records, and implementation of AI testing tools to ensure fair decisions. Natural Language Processing (NLP) and conversation AI allow users to interact with BI systems using everyday languages, making insights about access to non-technical users more accessible. Future research must improve AI-controlled BI chatbots and voice assistants to enable deeper, contextual interactions and ask users complex analytical questions without advanced data science knowledge. Research into how IoT data can be used in real-time for dynamic decision-making or how to improve data security and integrity in BI applications is essential. Future research and development of AI-operated BI should focus on making the system more transparent, intelligent, adaptive, ethical, and user-friendly to maximize the effectiveness of business parts in the decision-making process.

REFERENCES

Adewumi, A., Oshioste, E. E., Asuzu, O. F., Ndubuisi, N. L., Awonnuga, K. F., & Daraojimba, O. H. (2024). Business intelligence tools in finance: A review of trends in the USA and Africa. *World Journal of Advanced Research and Reviews, 21*(3), 608–616.

Adewusi, A. O., Okoli, U. I., Adaga, E., Olorunsogo, T., Asuzu, O. F., & Daraojimba, D. O. (2024). Business intelligence in the era of big data: A review of analytical tools and competitive advantage. *Computer Science & IT Research Journal, 5*(2), 415–431.

Ahmed, F., Ahmed, M. R., Kabir, M. A., & Islam, M. M. (2025). Revolutionizing Business Analytics: The Impact of Artificial Intelligence and Machine Learning. *American Journal of Advanced Technology and Engineering Solutions, 1*(01), 147–173.

Ajegbile, M. D., Olaboye, J. A., Maha, C. C., & Tamunobarafiri, G. (2024). Integrating business analytics in healthcare: Enhancing patient outcomes through data-driven decision making. *World J Biol Pharm Health Sci, 19*, 243–250.

Anozie, U. C., Onyenahazi, O. B., Ekeocha, P. C., Adekola, A. D., Ukadike, C. A., & Oloko, O. A. (2024). Advancements in artificial intelligence for omnichannel marketing and customer service: Enhancing predictive analytics, automation, and operational efficiency. *International Journal of Science and Research Archive, 12*(2), 1621–1629.

Arinze, C. A., Izionworu, V. O., Isong, D., Daudu, C. D., & Adefemi, A. (2024). Integrating artificial intelligence into engineering processes for improved efficiency and safety in oil and gas operations. *Open Access Research Journal of Engineering and Technology, 6*(1), 39–51.

Badmus, O., Rajput, S. A., Arogundade, J. B., & Williams, M. (2024). AI-driven business analytics and decision making. *World Journal of Advanced Research and Reviews, 24*(1), 616–633.

Bari, M. D., & Ara, A. (2024). The Impact Of Machine Learning On Prescriptive Analytics For Optimized Business Decision-Making. *Anjuman, The Impact Of Machine Learning On Prescriptive Analytics For Optimized Business Decision-Making (April 15, 2024).*

Bauskar, S. (2024). Business Analytics in Enterprise System Based on Application of Artificial Intelligence. *International Research Journal of Modernization in Engineering Technology and Science.*

Chowdhury, R. H. (2024). Blockchain and AI: Driving the future of data security and business intelligence. *World Journal of Advanced Research and Reviews*, *23*(1), 2559–2570.

Chowdhury, R. H. (2024). The evolution of business operations: Unleashing the potential of Artificial Intelligence, Machine Learning, and Blockchain. *World Journal of Advanced Research and Reviews*, *22*(3), 2135–2147.

Collins, A., Hamza, O., Eweje, A., & Babatunde, G. O. (2024). Integrating 5G core networks with business intelligence platforms: Advancing data-driven decision-making. *International Journal of Multidisciplinary Research and Growth Evaluation*, *5*(1), 1082–1099.

El Hajj, M., & Hammoud, J. (2023). Unveiling the influence of artificial intelligence and machine learning on financial markets: A comprehensive analysis of AI applications in trading, risk management, and financial operations. *Journal of Risk and Financial Management*, *16*(10), 434.

Farayola, O. A. (2024). Revolutionizing banking security: Integrating artificial intelligence, blockchain, and business intelligence for enhanced cybersecurity. *Finance & Accounting Research Journal*, *6*(4), 501–514.

Hamadaqa, M. H. M., Alnajjar, M., Ayyad, M. N., Al-Nakhal, M. A., Abunasser, B. S., & Abu-Naser, S. S. (2024). Leveraging Artificial Intelligence for Strategic Business Decision-Making: Opportunities and Challenges.

Han, X., Xiao, S., Sheng, J., & Zhang, G. (2024). Enhancing efficiency and decision-making in higher education through intelligent commercial integration: Leveraging artificial intelligence. *Journal of the Knowledge Economy*, •••, 1–37.

Hosen, M. S., Islam, R., Naeem, Z., Folorunso, E. O., Chu, T. S., Al Mamun, M. A., & Orunbon, N. O. (2024). Data-driven decision making: Advanced database systems for business intelligence. *Nanotechnology Perceptions*, *20*(3), 687–704.

Hossain, Q., Yasmin, F., Biswas, T. R., & Asha, N. B. (2024). Integration of Big Data Analytics in Management Information Systems for Business Intelligence. *Saudi J Bus Manag Stud*, *9*(9), 192–203.

James, G. G., Oise, G. P., Chukwu, E. G., Michael, N. A., Ekpo, W. F., & Okafor, P. E. (2024). Optimizing business intelligence system using big data and machine learning. *Journal of Information Systems and Informatics*, *6*(2), 1215–1236.

Kaggwa, S., Eleogu, T. F., Okonkwo, F., Farayola, O. A., Uwaoma, P. U., & Akinoso, A. (2024). AI in decision making: Transforming business strategies. *International Journal of Research and Scientific Innovation*, *10*(12), 423–444.

Kothinti, R. R. (2024). Artificial intelligence in healthcare: revolutionizing precision medicine, predictive analytics, and ethical considerations in autonomous diagnostics. *World Journal of Advanced Research and Reviews*, 3394-3406.

Lo Piano, S. (2020). Ethical principles in machine learning and artificial intelligence: Cases from the field and possible ways forward. *Humanities & Social Sciences Communications*, *7*(1), 1–7.

Lokanan, M. E., & Maddhesia, V. (2025). Supply chain fraud prediction with machine learning and artificial intelligence. *International Journal of Production Research*, *63*(1), 286–313.

Michael, C. I., Ipede, O. J., Adejumo, A. D., Adenekan, I. O., Adebayo, D., Ojo, A. S., & Ayodele, P. A. (2024). Data-driven decision making in IT: Leveraging AI and data science for business intelligence. *World Journal of Advanced Research and Reviews*, *23*(1), 472–480.

Mishra, R., Tripathi, P., & Kumar, N. (2024). Future Directions in the Application of Machine Learning and Intelligent Optimization in Business Analytics. In *Intelligent Optimization Techniques for Business Analytics* (pp. 49–76). IGI Global.

Mozumder, M. A. S., Sweet, M. M. R., Nabi, N., Tusher, M. I., Modak, C., & Hasan, M., ... & Prabha10, M. (2024). Revolutionizing Organizational Decision-Making for Banking Sector: A Machine Learning Approach with CNNs in Business Intelligence and Management. *Journal of Business and Management Studies*, *6*(3), 111–118.

Neiroukh, S., Aljuhmani, H. Y., & Alnajdawi, S. (2024, January). In the era of emerging technologies: discovering the impact of artificial intelligence capabilities on timely decision-making and business performance. In *2024 ASU International Conference in Emerging Technologies for Sustainability and Intelligent Systems (ICETSIS)* (pp. 1-6). IEEE.

Onesi-Ozigagun, O., Ololade, Y. J., Eyo-Udo, N. L., & Oluwaseun, D. (2024). Data-driven decision making: Shaping the future of business efficiency and customer engagement. *International Journal of Multidisciplinary Research Updates*, *7*(2), 19–29.

Paramesha, M., Rane, N. L., & Rane, J. (2024). Big data analytics, artificial intelligence, machine learning, internet of things, and blockchain for enhanced business intelligence. *Partners Universal Multidisciplinary Research Journal*, *1*(2), 110–133.

Pokala, P. (2024). The integration and impact of artificial intelligence in modern enterprise resource planning systems: A comprehensive review. *Available at SSRN* 5069295.

Rane, N., Paramesha, M., Choudhary, S., & Rane, J. (2024). Business Intelligence and Business Analytics With Artificial Intelligence and Machine Learning: Trends, Techniques, and Opportunities. *Techniques, and Opportunities (May 17, 2024).*

Rane, N. L., Paramesha, M., Choudhary, S. P., & Rane, J. (2024). Artificial intelligence, machine learning, and deep learning for advanced business strategies: A review. *Partners Universal International Innovation Journal*, *2*(3), 147–171.

Rimon, S. T. H. (2024). Leveraging Artificial Intelligence in Business Analytics for Informed Strategic Decision-Making: Enhancing Operational Efficiency, Market Insights, and Competitive Advantage. *Journal of Artificial Intelligence General science (JAIGS) ISSN: 3006-4023, 6*(1), 600-624.

Rodriguez, P., & Costa, I. (2024). Artificial Intelligence and Machine Learning for Predictive Threat Intelligence in Government Networks. *Advances in Computer Sciences*, *7*(1), 1–10.

Samara, F. Y. A., Taha, A. H. A., Massa, N. M., Jamie, T. N. A., Harara, F. E., Abu-Nasser, B. S., & Abu-Naser, S. S. (2024). The Role of AI in Enhancing Business Decision-Making: Innovations and Implications.

Saxena, T., Tripathi, D. R., & Jain, R. (2024). Evaluating The Opportunities and Risks of Artificial Intelligence In Strategic Management and Business Integration. *International Journal of Innovations in Science, Engineering And Management*, 19-24.

Shittu, R. A., Ehidiamen, A. J., Ojo, O. O., Zouo, S. J. C., Olamijuwon, J., Omowole, B. M., & Olufemi-Phillips, A. Q. (2024). The role of business intelligence tools in improving healthcare patient outcomes and operations. *World Journal of Advanced Research and Reviews*, *24*(2), 1039–1060.

Tariq, M. U. (2025). AI and Work-Life Balance: Transforming Employee Wellbeing in the Modern Workplace. In Ahmed, E., Babar, A., Samad, A., Ahmed, R., & Beydoun, G. (Eds.), *Strengthening Human Relations in Organizations With AI* (pp. 85–110). IGI Global Scientific Publishing., DOI: 10.4018/979-8-3693-6507-6.ch004

Tariq, M. U. (2025). AI-Powered Business Process Automation: Revolutionizing Firm Management. In Derbali, A. (Ed.), *AI, Economic Perspectives, and Firm Business Management* (pp. 199–224). IGI Global Scientific Publishing., DOI: 10.4018/979-8-3693-7357-6.ch010

Tariq, M. U. (2025). Integrating ICT for Enhanced Organizational Resilience: Strategies and Case Studies. In Carvalho, L., Reis, L., Neves de Almeida Baptista Figueiredo, A., & Russo, N. (Eds.), *Leveraging Technology for Organizational Adaptability* (pp. 59–80). IGI Global Scientific Publishing., DOI: 10.4018/979-8-3693-6045-3.ch004

Tariq, M. U. (2025). Navigating Public Administration 5.0: Embracing AI for Smarter Governance. In Wongmahesak, K., Ahmad, J., & Mustanir, A. (Eds.), *Public Governance Practices in the Age of AI* (pp. 167–186). IGI Global Scientific Publishing., DOI: 10.4018/979-8-3693-9286-7.ch008

Tariq, M. U. (2025). Bridging Generations: Digital Transformation and Its Multifaceted Impact Across Societal Sectors. In Anshari, M., Almunawar, M., & Ordóñez de Pablos, P. (Eds.), *Impacts of Digital Technologies Across Generations* (pp. 1–22). IGI Global Scientific Publishing., DOI: 10.4018/979-8-3693-6366-9.ch001

Young, M. M., Himmelreich, J., Honcharov, D., & Soundarajan, S. (2022). Using artificial intelligence to identify administrative errors in unemployment insurance. *Government Information Quarterly*, *39*(4), 101758.

Zednik, C. (2021). Solving the black box problem: A normative framework for explainable artificial intelligence. *Philosophy & Technology*, *34*(2), 265–288.

KEY TERMS AND DEFINITIONS

Artificial Intelligence (AI): Replication of human intelligence in machines for automation

Business Intelligence (BI): Data-driven procedures for informed business decision-making

Machine Learning (ML): Algorithms letting systems learn from data patterns

Chapter 10
Unlocking Efficiency Through BI-Driven Process Automation:
Case Studies From Manufacturing and Logistics

Abdelraouf Ishtaiwi
https://orcid.org/0000-0001-8013-7151
Data Science and Artificial Intelligence, Faculty of Information Technology, University of Petra, Amman, Jordan

Saad Alateef
https://orcid.org/0009-0002-3219-0833
Newcastle University, UK

Mouhammd Alkasassbeh
https://orcid.org/0000-0001-8396-7441
Princess Sumaya University for Technology, Jordan

ABSTRACT

Organizations in manufacturing and logistics seek ways to enhance operational efficiency through data-driven strategies. Business intelligence (BI) supports this goal by integrating data sources, generating analytical insights, and enabling process automation. Researchers have examined BI systems that leverage real-time dashboards, predictive analytics, and connected platforms to reduce operational bottlenecks. This chapter presents theoretical foundations and empirical examples of BI-driven automation in supply chains and factory settings. Case studies highlight improvements in forecasting accuracy, on-time delivery, labor allocation, and

DOI: 10.4018/979-8-3373-2125-7.ch010

overall equipment effectiveness. These findings suggest that BI-enabled workflows contribute to leaner, more responsive operations. This chapter offers managers and practitioners a framework for designing and deploying BI-driven automation initiatives.

1. INTRODUCTION

1.1 Context and Rationale

Organizations rely on data to drive operational decisions that influence cost structures, responsiveness, and competitive positioning. Rapid shifts in market conditions, consumer preferences, and supply chain complexities have prompted decision-makers to integrate new technologies that transform raw data into actionable insights. Business intelligence (BI) systems unite data sources, perform advanced analytics, and present real-time dashboards to support managers with evidence-based decisions. Concurrently, process automation leverages these insights to streamline tasks, optimize resource allocation, and reduce manual bottlenecks.

Manufacturing and logistics sectors frequently adopt BI-driven automation to enhance operational visibility and eliminate inefficiencies. In manufacturing, BI dashboards can connect production lines, forecast demand, and coordinate just-in-time inventory planning. In logistics, BI analytics facilitate route optimization, warehouse streamlining, and demand-driven fulfillment scheduling. By merging analytics with automated workflows, these sectors can unlock higher productivity and faster response to fluctuations.

This chapter investigates how BI systems support process automation to boost efficiency in manufacturing and logistics. The findings apply to operations managers and researchers seeking systematic, data-driven methods for modernizing supply chains and production environments. Although multiple organizations have embraced digital transformation, the specific mechanisms through which BI insights translate into operational gains require further exploration. This chapter addresses that gap by presenting conceptual frameworks, illustrative case studies, and best practices for implementing BI-driven automation.

Decision-making in manufacturing and logistics often involves incomplete information, siloed data, and complex workflows. Manual processes can delay responses to demand variability, unexpected disruptions, or resource shortages. Traditional reporting systems frequently generate historical metrics without enabling forward-looking scenarios. Leaders must thus identify opportunities to integrate predictive analytics with execution systems that adjust operations in real time.

BI-driven process automation offers an approach that combines descriptive, diagnostic, predictive, and prescriptive analytics with workflow orchestration. Although many organizations acknowledge the promise of such systems, challenges in data integration, user adoption, and operational alignment remain. This chapter aims to:

- Present theoretical foundations of BI-driven automation for manufacturers and logistics operations.
- Highlight case studies that document observed efficiency gains, cost savings, and improvements in visibility.
- Provide an analytical perspective on challenges, success factors, and emerging trends in BI-driven process automation.
- Outline guidelines for managers and stakeholders who seek to implement BI solutions in complex operational settings.

The chapter first lays a conceptual foundation for how business-intelligence (BI) tools can support decision-making and drive process automation and then shifts from theory to practical examples. Section 4 reviews the building blocks of BI that enable data-driven decision-making, such as consolidating data from various systems, creating models, applying analytical methods and building reports or dashboards. Section 5 introduces principles for automating manufacturing and logistics, highlighting the role of digital workflows and execution systems. Section 6 brings these threads together into general frameworks that link BI and automation. Section 7 illustrates the frameworks through a series of manufacturing- and logistics-focused case studies. Section 8 then compares the cases to extract overarching lessons, challenges and best-practice responses. Finally, Section 9 concludes by reflecting implications for managers, acknowledging limitations and suggesting avenues for future research

2. CONCEPTUAL FOUNDATIONS OF BUSINESS INTELLIGENCE

2.1 Defining Business Intelligence

Business intelligence consists of technologies and methods for collecting, integrating, analyzing, and presenting business data to support improved decisions. Early BI systems focused on descriptive reporting, emphasizing historical metrics. Later advancements included diagnostic and predictive analytics to explore root causes and forecast future scenarios. Modern BI extends these capabilities through dashboards, self-service tools, and real-time data pipelines. By consolidating information from disparate sources, BI enables managers to detect patterns, spot inefficiencies, and allocate resources more effectively.

2.2 Key Components of BI

BI solutions typically incorporate:

- **Data Integration**: Merging data from multiple sources such as enterprise resource planning (ERP), customer relationship management (CRM), or operational technology (OT) systems.
- **Data Warehousing**: Creating centralized repositories that store structured and unstructured data for historical trend analysis.
- **Analytics and Modeling**: Using statistical, machine learning, or AI-based models to interpret data and generate insights.
- **Reporting and Visualization**: Developing dashboards and reports that present key performance indicators (KPIs) or alerts.
- **User Access and Governance**: Ensuring data security, role-based permissions, and compliance with relevant regulations.

2.3 BI and Decision-Making

BI-driven decisions stem from timely access to accurate data. When decision-makers can review current inventory levels, sales forecasts, or production capacities, they can schedule operations and allocate resources in alignment with organizational goals. Analytics further supports scenario planning, where managers simulate the effects of changing supplier lead times or adjusting production volumes. As Al-Hadad and Zota (2016) observed, BI systems deliver immediate visibility into potential production delays and enable managers to correct processes before they generate losses. Thus, BI elevates strategic and operational decision-making through automated alerts and real-time metrics.

2.4 Challenges in Traditional BI Implementations

Although BI has gained recognition, some organizations encounter problems that hinder its transformative potential. Fragmented data sources may lead to conflicting KPIs or unresolved data quality issues. Disconnected IT architecture limits real-time insights, especially in fast-moving sectors like logistics. Additionally, employees who rely on legacy reporting systems may resist adopting new BI dashboards or self-service analytics tools. These factors can slow adoption and limit ROI. However, modern data platforms, cloud technologies, and advanced analytics engines offer pathways to overcome integration and usability barriers.

3. Process Automation in Manufacturing and Logistics

3.1 Definition of Process Automation

Process automation involves using digital systems to perform tasks or coordinate workflows with minimal manual intervention. In operations, it can cover production line controls, robotic systems, or software scripts that trigger supply orders when inventory reaches critical levels. Automation reduces human errors, accelerates processes, and allows workers to focus on higher-value tasks. In both manufacturing and logistics, automation aligns with Industry 4.0 and Logistics 4.0 principles that emphasize data-driven decisions, connectivity, and advanced analytics.

3.2 Industry 4.0 and Logistics 4.0

Industry 4.0 represents a paradigm shift in manufacturing that integrates cyber-physical systems, IoT devices, and AI-based analytics. Production lines become "smart" when sensors capture machine data and analytics platforms interpret the information in real time. This enables predictive maintenance, adaptive scheduling, and optimized resource utilization. Logistics 4.0 brings similar concepts to transportation, warehousing, and distribution, where companies use tracking, autonomous vehicles, and route optimization. Vicente et al. (2024) reported on a Portuguese logistics provider that adopted Power BI tools to improve daily operational visibility. Users accessed dashboards to identify inefficiencies and make data-driven improvements, reinforcing the value of embedded analytics in Logistics 4.0 contexts.

3.3 Tools and Technologies for Automation

Organizations frequently adopt software platforms that unify enterprise data, orchestrate workflows, and automate tasks. These can include:

- **Robotics Process Automation (RPA)**: Software robots that replicate human interactions with digital systems, reducing manual data entry or routine tasks.
- **Real-Time Monitoring and Control**: Systems that integrate with sensors, programmable logic controllers (PLCs), or IoT devices to collect operational data.

- **Advanced Planning and Scheduling (APS)**: Tools that create production schedules based on real-time demand and capacity constraints.
- **Connected Platforms**: Solutions that link supply chain partners, enabling automated ordering or fulfillment triggers based on inventory thresholds or forecast updates.

3.4 Use Cases in Manufacturing

Manufacturing involves multiple stages: procurement, production, assembly, quality control, and distribution. Automation can streamline each stage by reducing manual interventions. For instance, an advanced planning/BI solution can allocate resources based on daily demand signals, thus avoiding excess inventory and lowering carrying costs. Brandt Group achieved up to one-third reductions in excess inventory by integrating BI-driven demand planning (Logistics Business, 2018). Automation also addresses production scheduling. Papoutsanis SA digitized its soap production lines and improved overall equipment effectiveness (OEE) by 39% (Evocon, 2022). Through real-time monitoring, managers detected downtime patterns and introduced corrective measures quickly.

3.5 Use Cases in Logistics

Logistics entails warehousing, transportation, and last-mile delivery. Automated systems rely on BI to optimize routing and track shipments. UPS's ORION program leveraged telematics data to save over 100 million miles of driving annually (UPS, 2016). By recalculating routes in real time, drivers used fewer miles and consumed less fuel. Similarly, Amazon employs AI-enabled forecasting and dynamic logistics optimization to reduce delivery times (Krause, 2024). Real-time analytics adjust inventory placements in fulfillment centers, so items with rising demand remain closer to end customers. These examples illustrate the efficiency gains from combining BI with process automation in logistics operations.

4. BI-Driven Automation: Integrating Concepts and Frameworks

4.1 Conceptual Framework for BI-Driven Process Automation

BI-driven process automation links data acquisition, analytics, and automated execution in a continuous loop. Figure 1 depicts a simple framework:

Figure 1. BI-Driven Process Automation Framework

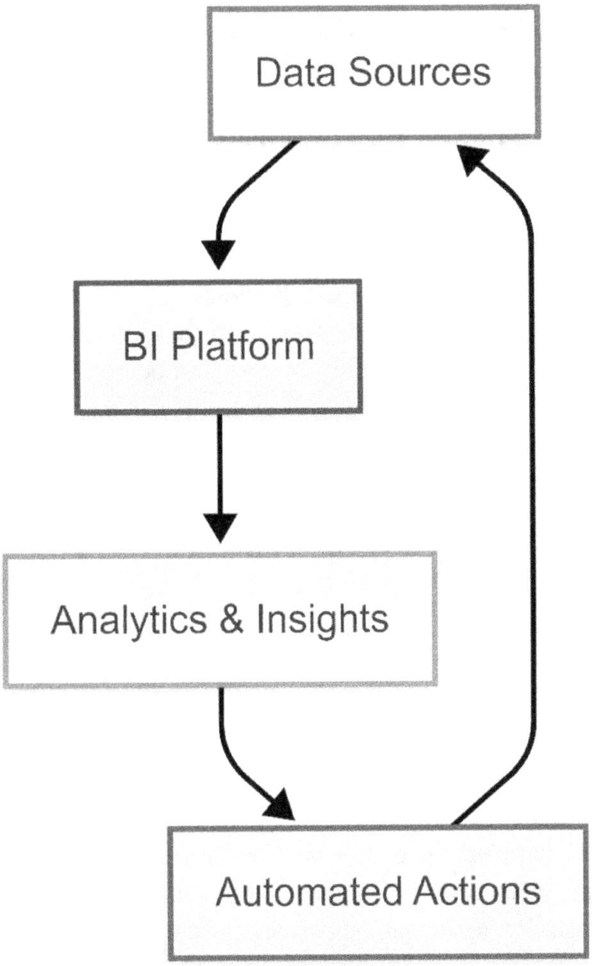

In this framework, data sources feed the BI platform, which applies analytics to identify actionable insights. Automated actions adjust processes or alert managers, closing the loop by feeding new data into the BI system. This cycle continues in real time, promoting agility and transparency.

4.2 Data Integration for Automation

Automation requires consistent data pipelines that merge internal systems (ERP, CRM, production logs) with external sources (supplier portals, market data). Tools like SAP Business One integrate multiple departments and unify data for real-time visibility. BILLY Footwear streamlined order fulfillment by connecting an ERP with shipping software and analytics, thus reducing manual tasks (DC Velocity Staff, 2020). Effective integration ensures that automated triggers—such as reordering raw materials—launch with accurate data rather than inconsistent spreadsheets.

4.3 Predictive Analytics for Optimization

Predictive models support automation by anticipating demand fluctuations, equipment failures, or route delays. These models draw on historical data combined with external factors (e.g., weather, special events). Amazon's AI-enabled forecasting system analyzes diverse data streams to optimize inventory placement (Krause, 2024). Tesco and Carrefour also use real-time dashboards to manage local store inventory, reducing overstock and preventing lost sales. By embedding predictive analytics in operational workflows, managers can adjust production runs or dispatch schedules before constraints arise.

4.4 Operational Metrics Affected by BI-Driven Automation

Organizations often measure the success of BI-driven automation using:

- **Throughput**: Output volume or the number of completed orders in a given time.
- **Lead Time**: Time from order to delivery.
- **OEE**: Aggregate measure of machine availability, performance, and quality.
- **Inventory Turnover**: Speed at which inventory cycles through stock.
- **Fulfillment Accuracy**: Percentage of orders filled without errors.
- **Cost Savings**: Reductions in labor, materials, or overhead.

Carrefour's inventory turnover increased after adopting BI for demand planning (Al-Momani et al., 2025). Papoutsanis SA enhanced OEE by identifying real-time downtime causes (Evocon, 2022). UPS saved significant transport costs through automated route optimization (UPS, 2016). These improvements illustrate the direct impact of BI-driven automation on core operational metrics.

5. Case Studies: Manufacturing and Logistics

This section reviews several cases that demonstrate how BI-driven automation can transform operations in manufacturing and logistics. The examples show diverse strategies, technologies, and outcomes but share a common thread: data-driven approaches improved efficiency and responsiveness. Table 1 summarizes the key characteristics of each case, including industry, BI solution, and reported benefits.

Table 1. Selected Case Studies of BI-Driven Automation

Case Study	Industry	BI Tool(s)	Key Outcomes
Carrefour (Jordan)	Retail/SCM	Real-time dashboards	Higher inventory turnover, accurate demand planning
Portuguese Logistics Provider	Logistics	Power BI, Delphi Method	Improved operational visibility, data-driven optimization
BILLY Footwear	Retail/SME	ERP + ShipStation + BI	Automated order fulfillment, faster processing
Brandt Group	Manufacturing	FuturMaster demand planning	One-third reduction in excess inventory, improved lead time
Italian Leather Goods Company	Manufacturing	Cloud-based workforce mgmt	Increased production efficiency, better labor allocation
Papoutsanis SA	Manufacturing	Evocon OEE system	OEE improvement from ~45% to ~62.5%
Industrial Manufacturer (Infrared)	Manufacturing	Microsoft Power BI	Automated reporting, reduced labor hours, better on-time delivery tracking
Consumer Electronics Manufacturer	Manufacturing	Power BI dashboards	40% increase in resource management efficiency
UPS ORION	Logistics	Advanced route optimization	100 million miles saved annually, $300–$400 million cost savings
Amazon AI-Driven Supply Chain	Logistics	Proprietary AI solutions	Notable inventory turnover improvement, dynamic logistics optimization

5.1 Carrefour Market (Jordan)

Carrefour's Jordan branch sought better demand forecasting and inventory management in a competitive retail environment. Managers implemented BI dashboards that collected sales data in real time, enabling quick response to changing consumer patterns (Al-Momani et al., 2025). The dashboards used predictive analytics to anticipate stock requirements for each store location. As a result, Carrefour's inventory turnover rose, reflecting faster movement of goods. Order fulfillment also became more precise because the system synchronized replenishment schedules with actual demand. Carrefour's experience highlights how large retailers can leverage BI to reduce stockouts, manage seasonal trends, and align procurement with real-time data.

5.2 Portuguese Logistics Provider

A Portuguese logistics provider embraced BI tools through a Power BI implementation to align with Logistics 4.0 initiatives (Vicente et al., 2024). The organization conducted a Delphi study with internal stakeholders to identify the most impactful features. The resulting dashboards visualized daily shipments, warehouse tasks, and route efficiency metrics, allowing staff to detect bottlenecks immediately. Employees used data insights to fine-tune operational processes, leading to improved cargo handling rates and fewer delays. Decision-makers reported greater alignment between different segments of the logistics chain, suggesting that user-friendly BI tools can encourage cross-departmental collaboration.

5.3 BILLY Footwear

BILLY Footwear, a growing retailer, automated its order fulfillment by integrating SAP Business One ERP with a shipping platform and a BI layer (DC Velocity Staff, 2020). The BI module monitored incoming orders and processed them without manual intervention, reducing errors and fulfillment delays. The small team scaled its daily order capacity without increasing headcount. Managers accessed real-time metrics on the volume of shipped orders, shipping costs, and lead times. The automation also provided notifications about potential shipping disruptions or inventory shortages. This case underscores how BI-driven workflows can help small and medium enterprises (SMEs) compete effectively.

5.4 Brandt Group

Brandt Group manufactures home appliances and faced issues with long lead times and overstock. Managers adopted an advanced planning system (FuturMaster) with BI features to automate demand forecasting (Logistics Business, 2018). Data on sales history, production capacity, and supplier lead times fed into the platform. The system generated optimal production plans, reducing excess inventory by nearly one-third. Lead times for parts and products fell from three months to two weeks, since planners no longer relied on spreadsheets and manual scheduling. Brandt applied just-in-time principles, aided by improved forecast accuracy. This illustrates how manufacturers can align production with real-time demand signals and cut inventory costs.

5.5 Italian Leather Goods Manufacturer

An Italian leather goods firm sought to optimize workforce allocation, which was previously handled through manual scheduling. The company adopted a cloud-based workforce management system that integrated BI dashboards with real-time shop-floor data (Pietroni & Marconi, 2023). The system tracked worker availability, skill sets, and line performance, then automatically allocated labor to tasks with immediate needs. Production bottlenecks decreased, and managers gained a single source of information for workforce-related decisions. The digital transformation improved production flow and employee satisfaction, since workers received transparent schedules that accounted for skill matching and shift preferences.

5.6 Papoutsanis SA

Papoutsanis SA installed a real-time OEE analytics platform from Evocon to monitor soap production lines (Evocon, 2022). Before implementation, staff recorded downtime manually, causing delays in root-cause analysis. The new system gathered performance data continuously, visualized it in dashboards, and triggered alerts when machine performance dipped. Managers investigated unplanned downtime patterns more quickly, improving maintenance scheduling. OEE rose from approximately 45% to 62.5%, translating to a 39% relative improvement. Production capacity increased, and the company reduced waste in materials and labor hours. The case shows how real-time BI fosters immediate corrective actions that boost productivity.

5.7 Industrial Manufacturer (Infrared Devices)

An industrial manufacturer specialized in infrared equipment replaced manual data aggregation processes with Microsoft Power BI (BrainSell, 2021). Previously, employees combined data from multiple sources in spreadsheets, which introduced errors and consumed time. The BI platform automated data updates thrice daily, creating near real-time sales and operations dashboards. Managers tracked on-time delivery rates and discovered that many delays were linked to mismatched production sequences. The company resolved these inefficiencies, raising its on-time delivery performance. The manufacturer also reduced the need for manual reporting labor, freeing resources for strategic tasks. This example suggests that BI fosters consistent metrics and continuous improvement.

5.8 Consumer Electronics Manufacturer

A large consumer electronics manufacturer built Power BI dashboards to examine resource allocation across multiple production lines (ACI Infotech, 2025). Planners previously used static Excel reports. After adopting interactive dashboards, they noticed recurring idle time on some assembly lines. The company reallocated labor and machinery based on real-time insights, improving resource management by 40%. The shift to automated data flows also reduced time spent preparing reports, which had been a major administrative burden. By preventing downtime, managers raised throughput without installing new machinery. The case underscores that well-structured BI dashboards can reveal hidden constraints and catalyze better utilization.

5.9 UPS ORION

UPS invested in a decade-long ORION (On-Road Integrated Optimization and Navigation) program to automate driver routing. The initiative integrated telematics, traffic data, and route optimization algorithms with a comprehensive BI framework (UPS, 2016). The resulting system recalculated delivery routes daily, saving over 100 million miles each year. Drivers avoided inefficient paths, and the company cut annual fuel consumption by approximately 10 million gallons. UPS's leadership team noted $300–$400 million in cost savings, illustrating how large-scale logistics operations can leverage BI and optimization to reduce miles driven, fuel use, and emissions. The success of ORION shows the potential for massive efficiency gains when advanced analytics automate operational decisions.

5.10 Amazon's AI-Driven Supply Chain

Amazon invests heavily in AI and BI tools to optimize inventory placement, reduce holding costs, and speed deliveries (Krause, 2024). Data pipelines ingest real-time orders, location data, and external factors to predict demand and reposition stock in nearby fulfillment centers. Warehouse robots and route optimization algorithms work in tandem to expedite picking, packing, and shipping. Amazon improved its inventory turnover and on-time fulfillment rates once it integrated advanced demand forecasting with process automation. Managers can react quickly to demand spikes, shifting capacity across the network. The case reveals how data-driven decision-making can reshape global logistics practices.

6. CROSS-CASE ANALYSIS

6.1 Common Success Factors

The cases share multiplc succcss factors, including:

1. **Accurate and Unified Data**: Each initiative centralized data into a robust BI platform that refreshed frequently. This accurate data foundation supported confident decision-making.
2. **Clear KPIs**: Managers specified target metrics such as inventory turnover, OEE, or route miles, allowing teams to track progress and adapt processes based on factual results.
3. **Real-Time Analytics**: Dashboards or alerts offered timely insights, prompting immediate corrective or preventive actions. Papoutsanis SA exemplified this through real-time OEE monitoring (Evocon, 2022).
4. **User-Friendly Interfaces**: Effective BI tools had intuitive dashboards accessible to non-technical users. BILLY Footwear reported high adoption due to automated order management (DC Velocity Staff, 2020).
5. **Top-Management Support**: Initiatives like UPS's ORION project required executive buy-in to secure resources and encourage organization-wide participation.

6.2 Divergent Contexts and Approaches

Although these cases share themes, each faced unique constraints. Large enterprises like UPS and Amazon could invest in custom AI-driven solutions. SMEs, such as BILLY Footwear, used off-the-shelf ERP and BI platforms. Meanwhile, the Portuguese logistics provider relied on a structured Delphi method to tailor dashboards to stakeholder needs (Vicente et al., 2024). This underscores that organizations can select different BI platforms and automation strategies based on their size, budget, and operational complexity.

6.3 Key Challenges Observed

Common implementation challenges include data integration complexities, resistance to new processes, and the need to maintain data quality. Organizations that manually track performance metrics often struggle with initial data cleansing. Another frequent challenge is scaling pilot projects. A small proof-of-concept might demonstrate promise, but rolling out the solution across multiple sites or global operations requires robust architecture and governance.

6.4 Impacts on Efficiency and Performance

Each case reported substantial efficiency gains, including cost savings, shorter lead times, and improved throughput. Carrefour reported more accurate order fulfillment and better inventory turnover by adopting predictive dashboards (Al-Momani et al., 2025). Brandt Group cut excess inventory by one-third and drastically lowered lead times (Logistics Business, 2018). UPS saved millions of miles, while Papoutsanis SA lifted its OEE by 39%. These examples confirm the ROI potential of BI-driven automation, even if the magnitude depends on organizational readiness and process maturity.

6.5 Trends and Emerging Directions

Several emerging trends appear in these cases:

- **Cloud-Based BI**: Cloud platforms allow real-time data integration from multiple locations.
- **Predictive and Prescriptive Analytics**: Organizations shift from descriptive dashboards toward advanced analytics that recommend actions.
- **IoT Integration**: Equipment sensors supply continuous data for automated triggers in predictive maintenance, scheduling, or logistics planning.
- **Scalability and Flexibility**: BI platforms must adapt to business growth and changing market conditions.
- **Focus on Sustainability**: UPS's ORION project lowered emissions, indicating synergy between efficiency and environmental goals.

7. DISCUSSION OF CRITICAL THEMES

7.1 Human Capital and Skill Development

Even with automation, human expertise remains crucial. Workers interpret BI insights and refine processes. Training staff to read dashboards or run what-if analyses can amplify the impact of technology investments. Without skilled personnel, organizations risk underutilizing advanced BI tools. Some managers resist analytics due to fear of being replaced. Transparent communication about how automation complements human roles helps address this barrier. Deloitte reported that when managers receive user-friendly BI interfaces, they perform tasks more effectively, improving spare parts availability and reducing customer wait times (Vasudevan et al., 204).

7.2 Scalability and Global Supply Chains

Global firms may roll out BI solutions across diverse regions. Cultural and regulatory factors influence how data is collected, shared, and analyzed. Large manufacturers with multiple plants might face complex integration tasks, especial ly when plants use different legacy systems. Amazon's global fulfillment network demonstrates that scaling requires automated data flows, standardized processes, and robust infrastructure (Krause, 2024). Companies must ensure consistent data taxonomies, open communication channels, and a governance model that supports local adaptations without compromising global standards.

7.3 Sustainability and Environmental Impact

Many organizations adopt BI-driven automation to cut costs, but they also realize sustainability benefits. UPS saved fuel and decreased emissions through ORION. DHL used predictive route analytics to lower its carbon footprint by optimizing fleet routing (NumberAnalytics, 2025). Manufacturers that reduce waste or energy consumption often see cost savings and align with sustainability targets. Real-time insights from IoT sensors help operators shut down idle equipment or reuse materials. Managers can showcase these results to stakeholders, reinforcing the link between efficiency and corporate responsibility.

7.4 Security and Ethical Considerations

As organizations automate processes, data security becomes a priority. Logistics and manufacturing data can be sensitive, particularly in defense or aerospace. Deloitte's aerospace OEM aftermarket case highlights the importance of secure data sharing to maintain trust (Vasudevan et al., 2024). Firms must apply encryption, access controls, and compliance frameworks to protect information. Ethical considerations also arise with AI-based decisions that could affect employee workloads or route assignments. Organizations should define guidelines to ensure fairness, transparency, and accountability for automated processes.

7.5 Future Prospects: AI and Autonomous Operations

The BI landscape is evolving toward more autonomous operations. Machine learning models can self-adjust parameters based on changing conditions. In manufacturing, advanced sensors can detect micro-defects and trigger quality rechecks without manual intervention. Tesla's smart factories rely on AI to adapt assembly procedures in real time (DigitalDefynd, 2025). Logistics providers may introduce drone deliveries or driverless trucks guided by real-time analytics. These scenarios hint at a future where decisions occur with limited human input, demanding robust oversight and advanced data governance.

7.6 Managerial and Practical Implications

Managers who oversee manufacturing or logistics operations can harness several insights from the presented cases and frameworks:

1. **Incremental Implementation Strategy**: Rather than attempting a large-scale overhaul, managers can begin with a high-impact pilot, such as an isolated production line or a regional warehouse. Early successes secure support from stakeholders.
2. **KPI Selection and Monitoring**: Identify metrics that matter for each process segment, whether it is OEE for production or route efficiency for logistics. Link these KPIs to financial outcomes to justify investments.
3. **Workforce Engagement**: Involve staff in system design to encourage acceptance. Offer training that demonstrates how BI insights simplify daily tasks and reduce firefighting.
4. **Infrastructure Readiness**: Determine whether on-premises or cloud deployment fits the organization's scale and data security requirements.
5. **Iterative Optimization**: BI projects do not end with deployment. Teams should refine analytics models, incorporate new data streams, and expand automation capabilities as they learn from real-world operations.

8. LIMITATIONS OF BI-DRIVEN AUTOMATION

8.1 Data Dependency

Analytics rely on data completeness and accuracy. If machines or sensors fail to capture events, the BI system cannot detect issues. Firms must invest in robust data collection and maintenance. In logistics, missed GPS signals or delays in updating inventory systems can create blind spots that reduce the effectiveness of automated routing.

8.2 Rapidly Changing Environments

Demand patterns, customer preferences, or regulatory requirements can shift. BI models, especially predictive ones, may become obsolete if not recalibrated.

Continuous data monitoring and model retraining are essential. Overconfidence in static models can erode performance gains.

8.3 Budget Constraints for SMEs

Small enterprises might lack the funds to deploy advanced BI solutions or hire data scientists. While cloud-based tools have lowered entry barriers, some remain expensive. Yet, examples like BILLY Footwear show that SMEs can adopt integrated, cost-effective solutions by leveraging existing ERP platforms and user-friendly BI modules.

8.4 Complex Integration Requirements

Large organizations often have heterogeneous systems. Integrating them can be laborious, requiring specialized skills or third-party vendors. Without careful planning, partial integrations can produce fragmented analytics that fail to capture end-to-end efficiency gains.

9. CONCLUSION AND FUTURE RESEARCH

9.1 Synthesis of Findings

This chapter examined how BI-driven process automation enhances operational efficiency in manufacturing and logistics. The theoretical sections discussed foundational BI concepts, the importance of real-time analytics, and the role of process automation in Industry 4.0 and Logistics 4.0 contexts. The case studies provided evidence that integrating BI dashboards and automated workflows yields measurable improvements, such as increased inventory turnover, reduced lead times, and lower route miles. Cross-case analysis revealed consistent success factors (accurate data, real-time visibility, top-management support) and recurring challenges (data integration, user adoption, scaling).

9.2 Implications for Practice

Managers can leverage BI-driven automation to reduce waste, improve responsiveness, and gain competitive advantages. They should adopt an incremental approach, focusing first on key pain points to demonstrate tangible results. Aligning BI initiatives with strategic objectives and fostering an analytic culture can help sustain engagement. Robust data governance frameworks and continuous monitoring of system performance safeguard the quality of insights.

9.3 Limitations and Recommendations

Although the reported cases show positive outcomes, organizations differ in size, resources, and readiness. Some might struggle with legacy systems or cultural resistance. Future research could compare adoption patterns across industries or explore how machine learning can extend BI capabilities in uncertain environments. Additional work might investigate the interplay between BI-driven automation and emerging trends like blockchain-based supply chain tracking.

9.4 Future Research Directions

- **AI-Enhanced BI**: Evaluate how next-generation analytics platforms use deep learning or reinforcement learning for adaptive scheduling and route planning.
- **Human Factors**: Examine how workforce engagement and skill-building influence the success of BI-driven automation.
- **Hybrid Supply Networks**: Investigate how BI helps coordinate global supply networks that blend in-house production with contract manufacturing.
- **Sustainability Metrics**: Explore standardized ways of measuring the environmental impact of BI-driven automation, including carbon footprint and resource consumption.

BI will continue to evolve, potentially transforming entire industries by linking data, analytics, and automated execution. Decision-makers in manufacturing and logistics can position their organizations for future success by embracing these tools and processes. The case studies presented here illustrate the tangible value of BI-driven automation, as well as the organizational considerations that influence outcomes.

REFERENCES

Al-Hadad, Y., & Zota, R. D. (2016). Implementing business intelligence system – case study. *Database Systems Journal*, *7*(1), 35–44.

Al-Momani, M. M., Awadallah, A., Al-Nassar, B., Ismail, A., Nassoura, M., & Abu-darwish, N. (2025). The role of business intelligence in supply chain optimization: A case study of the Carrefour Market in Jordan. *Data & Metadata*, *4*, 747. Advance online publication. DOI: 10.56294/dm2025747

BrainSell. (2021). Transforming business performance with effective forecasting and data efficiency using Power BI [Case study]. BrainSell. Retrieved August 16, 2025, from https://www.brainsell.com/customer-success/power-bi-manufacturing-case-study/

DigitalDefynd. (2025). 10 ways Tesla is using AI [Case study]. DigitalDefynd Tech Cases. https://digitaldefynd.com/IQ/tesla-using-ai-case-study

Evocon. (2022). Papoutsanis digitizes production with Evocon and increases OEE by 30% [Case study]. Evocon. https://evocon.com/articles/case_study/papoutsanis-digitizes-production-with-evocon-and-increases-oee-by-30

Infotech, A. C. I. (2025). Optimizing resource allocation: Power BI dashboards for manufacturing [Case study]. ACI Infotech. Retrieved August 16, 2025, from https://www.aciinfotech.com/case-studies/power-bi-dashboards-resource-management-efficiency

Krause, C. (2024). Amazon's AI-driven supply chain: A blueprint for the future of global logistics. CDO Times. https://cdotimes.com/2024/08/23/case-study-amazons-ai-driven-supply-chain-a-blueprint-for-the-future-of-global-logistics/

Logistics Business. (2018). Case Study: Demand Management Efficiency for Brandt Group. *Logistics Business Magazine*. https://logisticsbusiness.com/

NumberAnalytics. (2025). Transforming logistics & supply chains with big data insights [Blog post]. NumberAnalytics.com. https://www.numberanalytics.com/blog/transforming-logistics-big-data-insights

Pietroni, G., & Marconi, M. (2023). Data-driven smart manufacturing: Case study of workforce management process in an Italian leather goods company. In Proceedings of the Design Society: International Conference on Engineering Design (ICED 2023) (Vol. 3, pp. 1127–1136). https://doi.org/DOI: 10.1017/pds.2023.113

UPS (United Parcel Service). (2016). ORION logistics optimization project – results overview. UPS Press Release (as reported in BestPractice AI). Retrieved August 17, 2025, from https://www.bestpractice.ai/ai-case-study-best-practice/ups_saves_10_million_gallons_of_fuel_and_%24100_million_per_year_by_optimising_driver_delivery_routes_that_consider_real-time-traffic-and-weather-information-obtained-from-social-media-and-machine-learning

Vasudevan, A., Rassineux, J.-L., & Robertson, P. (2024). Smart operations in the manufacturing sector: Creating a connected aftermarket. Deloitte Insights. https://www.deloitte.com/global/en/Industries/industrial-construction/perspectives/smart-operations-in-the-manufacturing-sector.html

Velocity Staff, D. C. (2020). Shoemaker finds its elves with ERP software. DC Velocity. https://www.dcvelocity.com/articles/48366-shoemaker-finds-its-elves-with-erp-software

Vicente, J. J., Neves, L., & Bernardo, I. (2024). The potential of Logistics 4.0 technologies: A case study through business intelligence framing by applying the Delphi method. *Frontiers in Artificial Intelligence*, *7*, 1469958. Advance online publication. DOI: 10.3389/frai.2024.1469958 PMID: 39484155

Chapter 11
Zero Trust and Predictive Security in Business Intelligence Architectures

Maen Marwan Alzubi
Jadara University, Jordan

Murad Bashabsheh
Jadara University, Jordan

Mohammad Almseidin
https://orcid.org/0000-0002-0782-2168
Tafila Technical University, Jordan

Jamil Al-Sawwa
https://orcid.org/0000-0001-7236-0433
Tafila Technical University, Jordan

Mouhammd Alkasassbeh
https://orcid.org/0000-0001-8396-7441
Princess Sumaya University for Technology, Jordan

Ashraf S Mashaleh
https://orcid.org/0009-0000-5035-7751
Al-Balqa' Applied University, Jordan

ABSTRACT

In recent years, business intelligence architecture has faced mounting challenges in ensuring data confidentiality, integrity, and availability. Traditional perimeter-based security approaches increasingly fail to address sophisticated threats within evolving enterprise environments. To bridge this critical gap, zero trust frameworks combined with predictive security models offer a transformative direction for securing complex business intelligence ecosystems. This chapter explores theoretical foundations of zero trust architecture, predictive analytics, and their synergy in business intelligence contexts. Findings reveal that integrating adaptive authentication, AI-driven anomaly detection, and granular access control enhances resilience against advanced threats. The discussion highlights how predictive models antici-

DOI: 10.4018/979-8-3373-2125-7.ch011

pate breaches, allowing proactive mitigation strategies. The chapter concludes by emphasizing the strategic value of zero trust and predictive security integration for safeguarding data-driven decision-making processes in contemporary enterprises.

1. INTRODUCTION

The evolution of business intelligence systems matches the growing need for immediate data handling combined with predictive analytics together with strategic information acquisition. Modern business reporting structures evolved into dynamic cloud systems that confront traditional security protocols with the accelerated data-flow and large data volumes and varieties (Angle 2024, Aamri 2024). Organizations now use distributed intelligence solutions combined with hybrid cloud architecture and Artificial Intelligence (AI) applications alongside distributed analytics nodes to extract value from complex data datasets (Solanke 2023; Chowdhury 2024). Operational agility becomes possible because of this transformation yet it exposes business intelligence environments to high-level cyber security risks.

According to definitions of AI computers are machines that need human intervention to operate. The activities within AI include perception alongside learning and cognition as well as the understanding of natural language and speech recognition and vision capabilities (Bashabsheh, 2024a). People employ artificial intelligence in diverse situations to duplicate human brain processes which simplify complex operations (Bashabsheh, 2024b). Different academic fields provide unique definitions about the broad extent of artificial intelligence research (Bashabsheh, 2024c). The creation of programs showing intelligent operations represents AI in the eyes of computer scientists who include intelligent planning among those operations (Bashabsheh & Alzubi, 2024).

Multiple entrance points that attackers can exploit appear due to the broadening of data sources incorporating IoT devices together with mobile endpoints as well as third-party integrations. Security attackers nowadays utilize established trust systems among networking elements to conduct their operations (Paul 2023; Korrapati 2023; Al-Sawwa J.& Almseidin M., 2024; Younisse R., 2023; Odeh I., 2022). Current business intelligence systems need security methods which begin without trust and continuously verify while providing access defined by the context and actively defend against impending threats.

Enterprise security in the past relied heavily on perimeter-centric models which base their design on the primary threat origin from outside sources. The models create strict network barriers for the internal environment by assuming safety after user verification and device admission. This premise has broken down because of the current cloud-native and decentralized computing environments as Moresi (2023) and Khan (2023) indicate. Traditional defenses fail to stop malicious insiders and compromised credentials and external attackers who carry out lateral movements which produce breaches with extended undetected detection times until significant damage occurs.

Organizations experience escalating security challenges due to implementation of Software-as-a-Service (SaaS), Platform-as-a-Service (PaaS), and multi-cloud deployments for business intelligence systems (Saleem, Warsi, & Islam, 2023; Giguère, 2024). Existing security models find it difficult to manage attacks that utilize automation together with AI at the speed and magnitude they occur. Security architectures which employ adaptive strength alongside intelligence capabilities and trustless operation need to be developed immediately because they will protect today's dynamic heterogeneous business intelligence environments.

Zero trust architecture (ZTA) constitutes a transformative model that requires ongoing identity checks together with continuous device and environmental parameter assessments before accessing resources (Arora & Tewari, 2023; Sheriffdeen, 2024). Under ZTA principles users must verify access requests since network location no longer stands as a trust indicator for system authorization. The zero trust frameworks effectively stop unauthorized horizontal movements while it decreases possible entry points and protects sensitive information in intricate business intelligence networks.

Predictive security complements zero trust by enabling proactive threat detection and mitigation based on machine learning algorithms, behavioral analytics, and big data processing (Paul, 2023; Tauseef, 2023). Predictive models forecast potential security incidents, identify anomalous behaviors, and recommend preemptive actions, enhancing the resilience of business intelligence systems against evolving threat landscapes. By integrating zero trust principles with predictive analytics, organizations can establish dynamic, self-adaptive defenses aligned with the fluid nature of contemporary business intelligence operations (Loring, 2023; Ajish, 2024).

This chapter examines theoretical underpinnings, integration strategies, challenges, and emerging trends surrounding the deployment of zero trust and predictive security models within business intelligence architectures.

2. THEORETICAL FOUNDATIONS OF ZERO TRUST ARCHITECTURE

2.1 Core Principles of Zero Trust

Zero trust architecture (ZTA) operates on a fundamental assertion: no entity, whether internal or external, should receive automatic trust. Every access request undergoes strict, context-aware validation based on identity, device integrity, location, and behavior (Khan, 2023; Sheriffdeen, 2024). Unlike perimeter-based models, ZTA continuously monitors and assesses trust across the enterprise network, not merely at the point of entry.

Three core principles define zero trust frameworks:

- **Continuous Verification**: Organizations must consistently authenticate users and devices, regardless of their location within or outside traditional network boundaries (Arora & Tewari, 2023).
- **Least Privilege Access**: Entities receive only the minimum necessary permissions required for specific tasks, reducing potential exploitation opportunities (Agoro, Templar, & Tawkoski, 2023).
- **Assumed Breach Mindset**: Security strategies presume that threats already exist inside the network, driving proactive detection and response mechanisms (Ray, 2023).

These principles form the theoretical bedrock of zero trust architectures, enabling more resilient and adaptive business intelligence security frameworks.

2.2 Architectural Components

Zero trust deployment within business intelligence systems integrates several interdependent components to enforce security across diverse environments. **Identity and Access Management (IAM)** governs user and device identities, enforcing adaptive authentication and dynamic authorization based on risk profiles (Arora & Tewari, 2023; Edo et al., 2024). Authentication mechanisms increasingly incorporate machine learning to detect anomalies and flag suspicious access attempts. **Micro-Segmentation** partitions networks into isolated segments, restricting lateral movement and minimizing exposure of critical assets (Moresi, 2023). Micro-segmentation strategies are essential for protecting sensitive business intelligence repositories distributed across hybrid infrastructures. **Policy Engines** dynamically define and enforce access rules based on continuous evaluation of multiple parameters, including device health, behavior analytics, and data sensitivity (Banerjee, Whig, & Parisa, 2024).

Threat Detection and Response Systems leverage AI-driven analytics to monitor network traffic, user behaviors, and system logs for signs of compromise, allowing rapid incident containment (Paul, 2023; Loring, 2023). These components collectively facilitate a scalable and responsive security posture suitable for modern business intelligence architectures. **Table 1** demonstrates the necessary components for zero trust architecture protection of business intelligence systems containing identity management along with micro-segmentation and dynamic policy enforcement and

AI-enhanced threat detection mechanisms. The trustless dynamic environment draws support from its components which adapt proactively to modern security risks.

Table 1. Key Components of Zero Trust Architecture in Business Intelligence Systems

Component	Description	Role in Business Intelligence Security
Identity and Access Management	Verifies user and device authenticity through adaptive mechanisms	Protects sensitive data and controls user privileges
Micro-Segmentation	Divides network assets into isolated security zones	Limits lateral threat propagation across BI systems
Policy Engine	Creates dynamic access rules based on continuous trust evaluation	Enables flexible and context-aware security enforcement
Threat Detection and Response	Utilizes AI to monitor, analyze, and react to potential security events	Ensures timely identification and mitigation of attacks

2.3 Zero Trust for Data-Centric Enterprises

Business intelligence architecture prioritizes data as their primary asset, making data-centric security approaches vital. In a data-centric zero trust model, organizations extend verification beyond users and devices to the data itself, applying policies that govern how data moves, who accesses it, and under what conditions (Aiello, 2024; Edo et al., 2024). Zero trust mandates that data classification, encryption, and real-time monitoring operate seamlessly across business intelligence environments. Sensitive information, including customer records, financial reports, and proprietary analytics models, must remain protected throughout its lifecycle. Dynamic access controls adjust in real time to changes in user behavior, device posture, and environmental risk factors (Saleem, Warsi, & Islam, 2023).

Furthermore, AI-enhanced zero trust models improve decision-making accuracy by integrating predictive analytics into access evaluations. These models forecast potential insider threats or external attacks, enabling preemptive risk mitigation before unauthorized data exfiltration occurs (Joshi, 2024; Tauseef, 2023). By embedding security directly into data workflows, business intelligence systems achieve a stronger, more adaptive defense posture that aligns with the evolving threat landscape.

3. PREDICTIVE SECURITY MODELS

Predictive security refers to proactive mechanisms that anticipate threats before they materialize. These systems analyze historical data, detect anomalies, and forecast potential security breaches using statistical models, machine learning algorithms, and behavioral analysis techniques (Paul, 2023; Tauseef, 2023). Predictive security frameworks move beyond reactive incident response models by identifying early indicators of compromise across enterprise networks.

Within business intelligence architectures, predictive security serves a critical role. These systems ensure that data flows, analytics processes, and decision-making frameworks operate within a protected environment that dynamically adapts to emerging threats (Giguère, 2024; Joel, Chibunna, & Daraojimba, 2024). Predictive models not only mitigate damage but also reduce investigation times, streamline remediation processes, and strengthen compliance with data protection regulations. By embedding predictive security, organizations equip their business intelligence systems with foresight capabilities, enhancing resilience against sophisticated, evolving attacks.

3.1 Predictive Analytics Techniques

Predictive security models leverage a variety of analytical techniques to forecast and prevent breaches. **Machine Learning Algorithms** are at the core of predictive models. Supervised, unsupervised, and reinforcement learning models identify abnormal patterns and predict threat vectors based on historical training datasets (Alweshah, M.,2023; Loring, 2023; Aiello, 2024; Alkasassbeh, M. & Almseidin, M., 2023). **Behavioral Analytics** capture baseline behaviors of users, devices, and systems to detect deviations that may indicate insider threats or external intrusions (Tauseef, 2023; Ray, 2023). Behavioral baselining improves detection accuracy by minimizing false positives and optimizing response prioritization.

Anomaly Detection applies clustering, statistical profiling, and rule-based systems to uncover activities deviating from expected norms (Paul, 2023; Korrapati, 2023). These techniques highlight potentially malicious activities such as unusual data access patterns or unsanctioned system modifications. **Threat Intelligence** Integration combines real-time threat feeds with internal telemetry, enhancing situational awareness and contextualizing predictive alerts (Chowdhury, 2024; Angle, 2024). Building on detection capabilities, **Table 2** presents the major predictive analytics techniques employed for cybersecurity within BI ecosystems. Machine learning, behavioral analytics, anomaly detection, and threat intelligence integration collectively enhance proactive defense mechanisms.

Table 2. Key Predictive Analytics Techniques for Business Intelligence Security

Technique	Description	Application in BI Security
Machine Learning	Models learn from historical attack patterns	Predicts likely future security incidents
Behavioral Analytics	Monitors user and system behavior baselines	Detects deviations suggesting insider threats
Anomaly Detection	Identifies statistically abnormal activities	Flags unauthorized access or unusual system changes
Threat Intelligence	Integrate external threat data with internal monitoring	Enhances predictive accuracy through contextual data

In addition to machine learning and behavioral analytics, fuzzy rule interpolation (FRI) techniques offer valuable enhancements for predictive security models. FRI methods, which generalize decision-making across sparse datasets, improve anomaly detection in cybersecurity contexts where complete training data remains unavailable (Alzubi & Kovacs, 2019; Alzubi, Johanyák, & Kovács, 2019; Alzubi, M.& Almseidin, M, 2024). Recent advances demonstrate that fuzzy inference systems achieve competitive accuracy in detecting network intrusions, phishing attacks, and distributed denial-of-service activities while maintaining computational efficiency (Almseidin et al., 2022; Almseidin et al., 2024).

3.2 Role of Machine Learning in Threat Anticipation

Machine learning transforms static security monitoring into adaptive, dynamic threat anticipation processes. Predictive security platforms utilize machine learning models trained on comprehensive datasets, including authentication logs, network flows, and historical breach incidents (Ajish, 2024; Sheriffdeen, 2024). Supervised learning models classify activities as benign or malicious based on labeled datasets, refining detection precision over time. Unsupervised models identify unknown threats by clustering anomalous behavior without prior classification, essential for addressing novel attack techniques (Paul, 2023; Saleem, Warsi, & Islam, 2023). Reinforcement learning enhances system adaptability, enabling security controls to improve their decision-making through continuous interaction with dynamic environments (Joshi, 2024; Ray, 2023). This approach allows predictive security mechanisms to evolve with changing attack strategies, minimizing the time gap between threat emergence and system defense.

Moreover, federated learning models distributed across edge nodes safeguard sensitive business intelligence data by allowing collaborative model training without centralized data aggregation (Solanke, 2023; Giguère, 2024). This approach strengthens privacy protection while enriching predictive model performance. Predictive security grounded in machine learning accelerates threat recognition, reduces response times, and enhances the integrity of business intelligence operations. A comprehensive understanding of predictive security mechanisms is illustrated in **Figure 1**, which visualizes the sequential data flow from initial data collection through feature extraction, model training, anomaly detection, threat prediction, alert generation, and eventual mitigation.

Figure 1. Predictive Security Data Flow

Figure 1: Predictive Security Data Flow

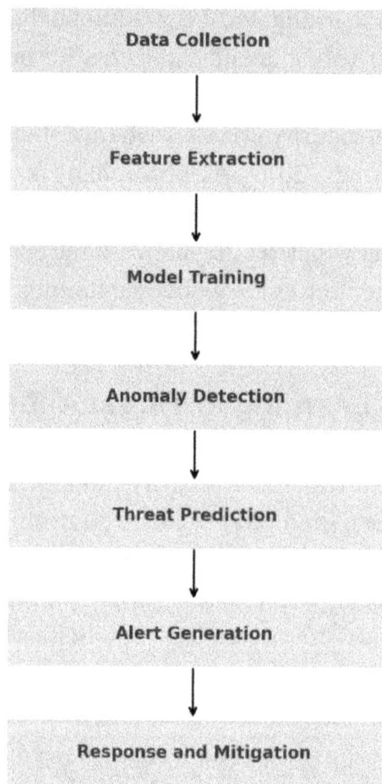

4. INTEGRATION OF ZERO TRUST AND PREDICTIVE SECURITY IN BI SYSTEMS

Integrating zero trust principles with predictive security models requires a carefully structured architectural design that bridges identity management, data protection, and proactive threat mitigation mechanisms. Organizations must embed continuous verification processes into predictive analytics pipelines, ensuring that every transaction, request, and interaction undergoes rigorous evaluation based on contextual risk assessments (Arora & Tewari, 2023; Paul, 2023).

A layered integration approach strengthens security without undermining business intelligence system performance. The integration typically involves:

- Embedding identity-aware proxies and secure access brokers to validate authentication and authorization dynamically (Sheriffdeen, 2024; Agoro, Templar, & Tawkoski, 2023).
- Applying machine learning-driven risk scoring to continuously assess trust levels of users, devices, and sessions.
- Linking real-time telemetry from endpoints, networks, and cloud services into a unified analytics engine capable of predictive insights (Loring, 2023; Ray, 2023).

Predictive models influence zero trust policy decisions dynamically through their synergistic relationship which ensures that access control remains in alignment with changing risk circumstances. Strategies for the integration between zero trust and predictive security systems must be approached through built-in layers. **Table 3** shows how strategic integration layers connect identity-aware access systems with machine learning risk scoring methods which unite telemetry analytics to create resilient business intelligence operations.

Table 3. Strategic Layers for Integrating Zero Trust and Predictive Security

Integration Layer	**Description**	**Role in Business Intelligence Security**
Identity-Aware Access	Verifies every access attempt using dynamic identity validation	Protects sensitive BI resources dynamically
Machine Learning Risk Scoring	Assesses real-time user and device risks based on behavior patterns	Adjusts access permissions proactively
Unified Telemetry Analytics	Aggregates and correlates telemetry across systems	Provides comprehensive visibility for threat prediction

4.1 Identity Management and Adaptive Access Controls

The implementation of zero trust architectures requires identity management as its fundamental aspect when integrated with predictive security methods. The integration of behavioral biometrics with traditional identity frameworks uses contextual risk scoring and continuous authentication models according to Agoro, Templar, & Tawkoski (2023), Edo et al (2024).

The system continuously adjusts user authorization levels by evaluating trustworthiness conditions in real time. A user who attempts to access sensitive data from an unknown device located in an abnormal area will experience intensified verification requirements as well as restricted access permissions and possible denial of all access (Arora & Tewari, 2023; Khan, 2023). The system adjusts access policies through its automated monitoring of authentication patterns and system usage behaviors and environmental factors without requiring human interaction. An automated adaptation process keeps security vulnerabilities from being used and ensures security rules match operational requirements in real time.

A system that implements this method delivers both operational capability and robust security controls which enables continuous availability of business intelligence operations.

4.2 AI-Enhanced Threat Detection

AI plays a crucial role in enhancing threat detection abilities inside zero trust and predictive security systems which function together. AI models extract faint threat alerts that standard rule systems neglect from big datasets combining historical records alongside streaming data and outside threat information (Paul, 2023; Saleem, Warsi, & Islam, 2023). The analytical models powered by deep learning methods detect previously undetected security threats including data breaches as well as fishing attempts and credential stuffing actions and lateral movement mechanics and insider threats (Tauseef, 2023; Chowdhury, 2024). AI threat detection models learn to handle changing attack techniques which deliver reduced false alarms alongside accelerated incident responses.

AI functions within zero trust enforcement controls to trigger automatic policy adjustments through processed threat information. Zero trust systems implement automated protective measures that adjust access controls or require more verification steps and separate suspicious nodes from the network without interrupting business intelligence activities (Joshi, 2024; Giguère, 2024). An integrated framework with this degree of connectivity allows business intelligence systems to implement quick defenses against quickly adapting cyber threats.

The implementation details between zero trust and predictive security appear in **Figure 2**. A secured operational framework connects business intelligence resource access to identity verification followed by risk assessment and trust-level evaluation before undergoing continuous monitoring procedures.

Figure 2. Integration Framework for Zero Trust and Predictive Security

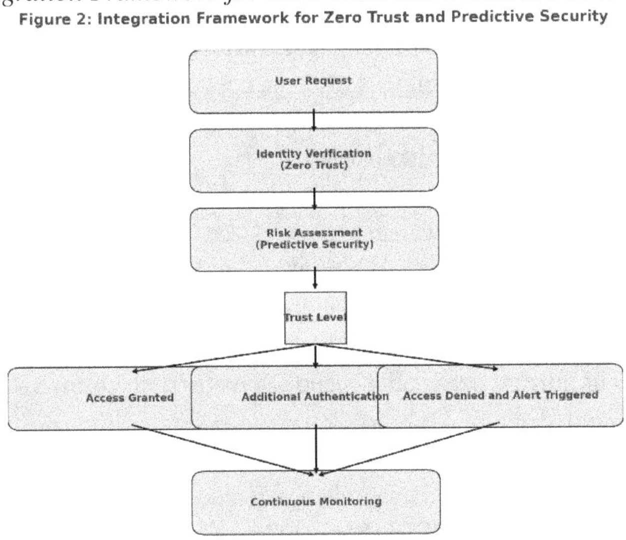

5. IMPLEMENTATION CHALLENGES AND SOLUTIONS

5.1 Organizational Barriers

The implementation of zero trust and predictive security for business intelligence systems faces obstacles due to organizations holding onto past ideas as well as financial limitations and poor cooperation among different departments. Businesses follow perimeter security systems because they have become familiar with them and have already spent their investment costs (Khan, 2023; Aiello, 2024). Moving towards zero trust security demands an organizational transformation focused on unending verification activities as well as decentralized access control and proactive security measures for all operations.

The transition process creates operational distress because various stakeholders have difficulties adjusting to new methods. Business leaders oppose new authentication procedures which limit data repository access because they believe these changes decrease work efficiency (Arora & Tewari 2023; Edo et al. 2024). The effectiveness of expressing predictive security benefits which span from lower breach response expenses to better regulatory compliance remains elusive for some security teams during their efforts to transition despite implementation challenges.

Implementation delays will occur due to organizational inertia especially in digital transformation environments that implement development at a slow pace. The implementation of zero trust and predictive analytics integration needs leadership endorsement and systematic change management along with comprehensive training programs that explain the advantages of these approaches.

5.2 Technological Complexities

The integration of predictive security and zero trust principles into business intelligence systems introduces substantial technological complexity. First, business intelligence architectures often span hybrid environments—on-premises data warehouses, multi-cloud platforms, and third-party analytics engines—complicating enforcement of uniform access policies and telemetry collection (Saleem, Warsi, & Islam, 2023; Sheriffdeen, 2024).

Legacy systems, which may lack APIs or modular interfaces, create integration friction, obstructing real-time data exchange needed for effective risk assessment and threat modeling (Moresi, 2023; Paul, 2023). These systems may also generate inconsistent log formats, requiring significant preprocessing for meaningful predictive analytics.

Moreover, machine learning-based threat detection engines demand significant computational resources and accurate labeled datasets, which are often unavailable or inconsistent across departments (Tauseef, 2023; Korrapati, 2023). Without proper training data and contextual awareness, predictive models risk false positives or blind spots, eroding stakeholder confidence.

Scalability becomes another critical issue. As telemetry volume expands, maintaining low-latency predictive analytics and responsive access controls without degrading BI system performance presents an engineering challenge.

Data scarcity remains a significant hurdle for effective predictive modeling. In cybersecurity applications, fuzzy reasoning approaches mitigate this issue by interpolating predictions from sparse rule bases (Alzubi & and Kovacs, 2020; Alzubi, M.& Almseidin, M., 2024; Alzubi, M. and Kovacs, 2019). Comparative analyses show that interpolative fuzzy models maintain high detection performance even when available labeled cybersecurity data is minimal (Almseidin, M., Alkasassbeh, M., 2022; Almseidin, M.& Alzubi, 2024; Alslman, Y et al., 2024; Almseidin, M., Al-Sawwa, J., 2024).

5.3 Strategies for Smooth Deployment

Overcoming implementation challenges requires a multi-pronged strategy that aligns technological modernization with organizational readiness.

First, a **phased adoption model**—starting with non-critical workflows and gradually expanding to sensitive BI assets—can minimize disruption while demonstrating early value (Giguère, 2024; Ajish, 2024). Second, **cloud-native integration patterns**, such as secure access service edge (SASE) and identity-aware proxies, simplify deployment in distributed environments by offering scalable enforcement points without intrusive architectural overhauls (Solanke, 2023; Edo et al., 2024). These approaches support incremental zero trust layering and real-time predictive telemetry ingestion.

Third, investing in **training datasets**, contextual behavioral profiles, and domain-specific anomaly detection frameworks improves machine learning model reliability and reduces alert fatigue. Enterprises can leverage existing incident records and domain knowledge to fine-tune predictive models and adapt them to sector-specific threat landscapes (Joshi, 2024; Chowdhury, 2024).

Finally, **cross-functional governance models**, involving security, IT, and business stakeholders, foster alignment and reinforce accountability. By embedding security considerations into the business intelligence development lifecycle, organizations enable resilient, adaptable, and user-centered implementation of zero trust and predictive frameworks.

Challenges during implementation demand equally strategic solutions. **Table 4** maps common organizational and technological barriers against corresponding mitigation strategies, providing a practical roadmap for enterprises pursuing zero trust and predictive security adoption.

Table 4. Key Implementation Challenges and Suggested Solutions

Challenge	Description	Proposed Solution
Organizational Resistance	Legacy mindsets, productivity fears	Stakeholder training, phased rollout, leadership engagement
Legacy System Incompatibility	Inconsistent APIs, data formats	Modular middleware, standardized telemetry collection
Inadequate Training Data	Lack of labeled incidents for ML models	Use synthetic datasets, historical breach logs
Model Reliability & Alert Fatigue	False positives erode trust in alerts	Behavioral baselining, sector-specific tuning
Integration Across BI Ecosystem	Diverse platforms and cloud services complicate enforcement	Cloud-native architecture, identity-aware access frameworks

6. CASE STUDIES AND INDUSTRY APPLICATIONS

6.1 Cloud-Based BI Systems

Cloud-based business intelligence systems dominate the enterprise analytics landscape due to their scalability, flexibility, and cost efficiency. However, their reliance on shared infrastructure amplifies security risks, necessitating robust zero trust and predictive security implementations. Studies show that integrating identity-aware proxies and machine learning-driven anomaly detection significantly reduces unauthorized access incidents in cloud BI environments (Saleem, Warsi, & Islam, 2023; Sheriffdeen, 2024).

For instance, retail companies leveraging cloud-native analytics platforms adopted AI-driven zero trust models that continuously evaluated user contexts and adjusted access permissions in real-time (Banerjee, Whig, & Parisa, 2024). These models incorporated predictive analytics to detect credential compromise attempts and lateral movements across multi-tenant cloud ecosystems.

Integrating predictive security tools with cloud-native business intelligence architectures not only mitigated breaches but also improved compliance reporting accuracy, enhancing overall governance (Chowdhury, 2024; Joel, Chibunna, & Daraojimba, 2024).

6.2 Hybrid Business Intelligence Architectures

Enterprises often maintain hybrid business intelligence infrastructures, combining on-premises legacy systems with cloud-based analytics platforms. This duality presents distinct security challenges, including inconsistent access control mechanisms and fragmented visibility across environments (Angle, 2024; Solanke, 2023).

Multiple research examples demonstrate why organizations should implement federated identities together with distributed telemetry monitoring to protect their hybrid BI solutions. The use of machine learning technology in zero trust frameworks by organizations produces superior anomaly identification outcomes and cuts down the time needed to address security incidents (Paul, 2023; Tauseef, 2023).

A technology company used predictive security engines to connect hybrid BI systems with predictive security analytics that automated policy updates through combined user activity monitoring. наявius models from behavioral analytics caught early warning signs of insider dangers through slight alterations in users' querying patterns thus preventing unwanted data transfer (Korrapati 2023 and Edo et al. 2024).

The deployment evidence demonstrates that predictive zero trust solutions need to support various technical structures while maintaining uniform protection rules within dissimilar platforms.

6.3 Industry-Specific Implementations

Some sectors have particular security demands that create distinct zero trust and predictive security usage patterns. The **healthcare** sector needs sophisticated access controls because it requires protection of electronic health records while following HIPAA regulations. Healthcare organizations using zero trust frameworks enhanced by AI-driven anomaly detection lowered their number of unauthorized patient data access incidents according to Edo et al. (2024) and Aiello (2024).

Predictive security models operating within large **financial services** data warehouses enable both fraud detection and the identification of internal misbehavior. Continuous verification in combination with dynamic risk scoring systems effectively reduced breaches while making organizations ready for audits (Paul, 2023, Joshi, 2024).

The combination of zero trust architectures with predictive analytics protected omnichannel BI platforms for **retail operations** from credential theft as well as supply chain manipulation and payment fraud (Banerjee, Whig, & Parisa, 2024; Ray, 2023).

The specific sector applications demonstrate how zero trust and predictive security models can effectively adapt when created to fit different industrial operational requirements as well as regulatory demands. Various industries use these frameworks as practical examples to demonstrate their operation in operational environments. The analysis presented in **Table 5** focuses on specific advantages that zero trust implementations with predictive analytics bring to healthcare, financial services and retail sectors.

Table 5. Sector-Specific Case Study Insights

Industry	Application Area	Observed Benefit
Healthcare	Electronic Health Record Access	Reduced data breaches; improved HIPAA compliance
Financial Services	Transaction Monitoring and Insider Threat Detection	Lowered fraud rates; enhanced regulatory audit readiness
Retail	Customer Data and Omnichannel Analytics	Increased credential security; minimized supply chain manipulation
Technology Enterprises	Hybrid BI Platforms	Faster threat detection; unified visibility across environments

7. CRITICAL ANALYSIS OF EMERGING TRENDS

7.1 AI-Driven Zero Trust Maturity Models

The development of zero trust architecture now depends more heavily on artificial intelligence because this technology helps guide dynamic trust decisions while predicting new security threats and improving security conditions throughout time. Artificial intelligence technologies in maturity models monitor system states together with user behaviors and network irregularities to automatically transform access policies (Ajish, 2024; Sheriffdeen, 2024; Rawashdeh, A., 2024). The predictive capability of AI models assesses dynamic architecture maturity evolution beyond traditional linear developmental stages. Such models first evaluate security risks through segmentation methods and then execute automatic policy application before implementing autonomous self-healing capabilities across business intelligence systems according to Joshi (2024) and Paul (2023).

Studies highlight that organizations implementing AI-guided zero trust maturity assessments experience accelerated incident detection, reduced false positives, and enhanced threat response adaptability (Ray, 2023; Korrapati, 2023). As artificial intelligence capabilities mature, zero trust models will increasingly shift toward predictive, autonomous architecture that adapt in near real-time to evolving threat landscapes and business intelligence operational demands.

7.2 Blockchain Synergies

Blockchain technologies offer complementary capabilities that strengthen zero trust and predictive security models within business intelligence frameworks. Decentralized identity management, tamper-proof audit trails, and smart contract-driven access policies enhance transparency, integrity, and accountability across BI ecosystems (Chowdhury, 2024; de Stefano, 2023). Blockchain-based decentralized identifiers (DIDs) allow business intelligence platforms to verify user and device identities without relying on centralized repositories vulnerable to compromise (de Stefano, 2023; Al Khaldy et al., 2024). Smart contracts enforce policy compliance automatically, mitigating insider threat risks and reducing administrative overhead.

Further, integrating blockchain with predictive security engines improves incident forensics by maintaining immutable, chronological logs of access attempts, security events, and system anomalies (Ray, 2023; Joel, Chibunna, & Daraojimba, 2024). The synergy between zero trust, predictive analytics, and blockchain promotes a decentralized, tamper-resistant, and adaptable security architecture capable of supporting next-generation business intelligence applications.

7.3 Edge Intelligence for Predictive Security

The proliferation of edge computing within business intelligence ecosystems introduces new attack surfaces while enabling localized data processing for performance optimization. Traditional security models struggle to extend comprehensive protection to distributed edge nodes, necessitating the deployment of edge-native zero trust and predictive analytics frameworks (Solanke, 2023; Angle, 2024). Edge intelligence models combine localized anomaly detection, device authentication, and real-time predictive analytics to secure decentralized BI infrastructures (Giguère, 2024; Tauseef, 2023). Machine learning algorithms deployed at edge nodes monitor telemetry, identify deviations from normal behavior, and trigger automated mitigation responses without relying on centralized cloud control planes.

Such distributed security models enhance threat detection accuracy, reduce response latency, and ensure business continuity even during network segmentation or cloud service disruptions (Sheriffdeen, 2024; Edo et al., 2024). Emerging research emphasizes the need to design edge-intelligent zero trust architectures that accommodate heterogeneous device ecosystems, high-velocity telemetry, and resource-constrained environments while maintaining robust predictive security capabilities.

Figure 3 exemplifies the modern trends which support zero trust convergence with predictive security by showing how artificial intelligence-based maturity models join forces with blockchain collaboration and edge computing intelligence to improve future cybersecurity designs for business intelligence infrastructures.

Figure 3. Emerging Trends in Zero Trust and Predictive Security

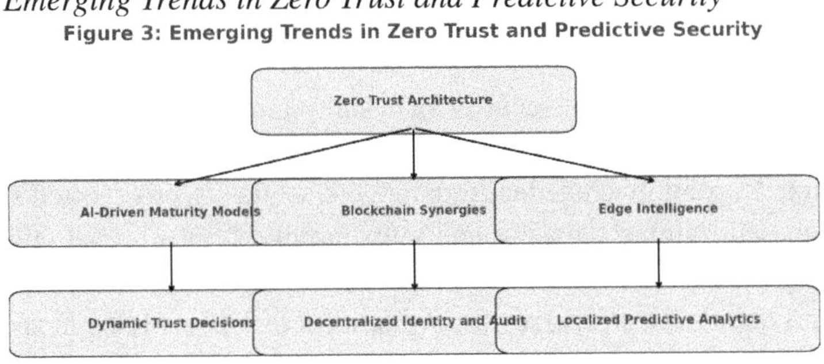

7.4 Fuzzy Reasoning for Predictive Security Enhancement

Predictive security models can use fuzzy logic techniques to solve some of the challenges that business intelligence architectures face with incomplete and diverse data while using conventional machine learning approaches. Fuzzy rule interpolation (FRI) methods allow security systems to decide about anomalies with accurate results from limited datasets (Alzubi & Kovacs, 2019; Almseidin et al., 2024; Almseidin, M., 2020; Almseidin, M., Al-Sawwa, J., 2023).

Research by Al-Kasassbeh et al., (2020) along with other works by Al-Kasassbeh M., Almseidin M., Alkrema, H., Latifee, S., (2022) and several collaboratory research groups (Almseidin et al., 2022; Al-Sawwa et al., 2022; Almseidin, M.& Al-Sawwa, J., 2021, 2022; Shorman, A.R., Alzubi, M., 2025) shows that FRI models detect IoT bot The models demonstrate precise performance for diverse cybersecurity data while requiring minimal resources which permit efficient edge platform deployment (Almseidin et al., 2025; Alslman et al., 2024).

Neural network detection models benefit from fuzzy logic and optimization techniques that use Particle Swarm and Grey Wolf Optimization to deliver better resistance against advanced persistent threats according to Mashaleh et al., 2024 and Almseidin et al., 2024 and Al-Sawwa, J. and Almseidin M., 2022 and Abuzuraiq, 2020. Using fuzzy reasoning methods in predictive security models enhances anomaly identification prowess by creating transparent interpretable frameworks which tighten business intelligence requirements for regulatory standards and operational trust.

8. FUTURE DIRECTIONS AND RESEARCH OPPORTUNITIES

Advancements in predictive security for business intelligence architectures require a focus on improving model precision, adaptability, and resilience against adversarial manipulation. Current machine learning models, while effective, often suffer from data drift, biased training datasets, and vulnerability to adversarial attacks (Paul, 2023; Korrapati, 2023).

Future research must prioritize the development of self-evolving models capable of real-time retraining without compromising performance. Techniques such as continuous learning, federated model updates, and domain-specific feature engineering will play critical roles (Ajish, 2024; Tauseef, 2023). Moreover, integrating explainable AI (XAI) methodologies into predictive security models remains essential. Transparent prediction rationales will enhance trust among cybersecurity teams, improve policy audits, and facilitate regulatory compliance across data-driven industries (Joshi, 2024; Angle, 2024). Enhancing predictive capabilities demands not only technical innovations but also interdisciplinary collaboration between data science, cybersecurity, and business intelligence strategy domains.

While static zero trust models provide significant improvements over traditional perimeter defenses, adaptive zero trust frameworks promise greater resilience and operational efficiency. Future architecture must embrace context-aware dynamic policy orchestration, where authentication and authorization decisions evolve continuously based on environmental conditions and risk scores (Sheriffdeen, 2024; Khan, 2023). Dynamic policy enforcement engines powered by real-time telemetry and predictive analytics will automate security postures without human intervention (Arora & Tewari, 2023; Solanke, 2023). Such capabilities will enable business intelligence systems to self-adjust in response to threat fluctuations, workload changes, or operational disruptions.

Research must explore methods for integrating adaptive access controls with edge intelligence and blockchain-based trust verification to foster a decentralized, autonomous security ecosystem (de Stefano, 2023; Chowdhury, 2024). Building adaptive zero trust architecture will require rethinking identity management, trust scoring algorithms, and policy conflict resolution mechanisms to ensure seamless and secure business intelligence operations.

The convergence of zero trust principles, predictive analytics, and artificial intelligence paves the path toward fully autonomous cybersecurity ecosystems. Future business intelligence architectures will likely rely on self-configuring, self-defending, and self-optimizing security systems capable of operating without continuous human oversight (Giguère, 2024; Loring, 2023).

Autonomous security frameworks will involve autonomous threat hunting, dynamic network segmentation, automated incident response, and continuous compliance monitoring. These capabilities will emerge through the integration of reinforcement learning algorithms, multi-agent security models, and distributed ledger technologies (Joel, Chibunna, & Daraojimba, 2024; Edo et al., 2024). Challenges to autonomous security adoption include governance frameworks, ethical AI deployment, explainability, and managing unintended consequences of autonomous decision-making (Aiello, 2024; Sheriffdeen, 2024). Nonetheless, moving toward autonomous security represents a logical and necessary progression for organizations seeking to safeguard complex, data-intensive business intelligence ecosystems in an increasingly adversarial digital landscape.

9. CONCLUSION

Business intelligence systems experience a complete transformation of their security domain through zero trust architecture integration along with predictive security models. Traditional perimeter-based defenses demonstrate their inadequacy because they cannot manage modern data networks which feature distribution and dynamic characteristics. The zero trust approach provides continuous verification with least privilege access which restricts unauthorized movement through the system. Predictive security improvements these benefits through its ability to detect future threats by analyzing historical data and spotting anomalies as well as making risk predictions through machine learning. Zero trust combined with predictive analytics delivers an adaptive security solution that protects modern complicated business intelligence systems at a high level of context-awareness.

A variety of case studies executed across various BI platforms prove that integrated security models create quantifiable advantages through decreased vulnerability breaches together with swift attack identification and effective regulatory criteria fulfillment. Business intelligence systems develop defense resilience through strategic implementation of combined zero trust solutions along with predictive security features. Businesses need to establish adaptive identity management systems together with threat anticipation capabilities built on machine learning algorithms and distributed trust enforcement functions.

The expected future research concerns improved predictive model transparency, autonomous security architectures, and blockchain and edge intelligence toward the support of decentralized business intelligence ecosystems. Fundamentally embedding predictive zero trust principles into business intelligence frameworks positions organizations to increase their ability to protect sensitive data and sustain regulatory standards and fuel innovation in competitive digital markets facing volatility.

REFERENCES

Abuzuraiq, A., Alkasassbeh, M., & Almseidin, M. 2020, April. Intelligent methods for accurately detecting phishing websites. In *2020 11th International Conference on Information and Communication Systems (ICICS)* (pp. 085-090). IEEE.

Ajish, D. (2024). The significance of artificial intelligence in zero trust technologies: A comprehensive review. *Journal of Electrical Systems and Information Technology*, *11*(1), 30.

Al-Kasassbeh, M., Almseidin, M., Alrfou, K., & Kovacs, S. (2020). Detection of IoT-botnet attacks using fuzzy rule interpolation. *Journal of Intelligent & Fuzzy Systems*, *39*(1), 421–431.

Al-Sawwa, J., & Almseidin, M. (2022). A Spark-Based Artificial Bee Colony Algorithm for Unbalanced Large Data Classification. *Information (Basel)*, *13*(11), 530.

Al-Sawwa, J., Almseidin, M., Alkasassbeh, M., Alemerien, K., & Younisse, R. (2024). Spark-based multi-verse optimizer as wrapper features selection algorithm for phishing attack challenge. *Cluster Computing*, *27*(5), 5799–5814.

Alkasassbeh, M., & Almseidin, M. (2023, July). Machine learning techniques for accurately detecting the DNS tunneling. In *Science and Information Conference* (pp. 352-364). Cham: Springer Nature Switzerland.

Almseidin, M. (2020). *Fuzzy Automaton-based Early Detection Model* (Doctoral dissertation, University of Miskolc, Hungary).

Almseidin, M., Al-Sawwa, J., & Alkasassbeh, M. (2021, July). Anomaly-based intrusion detection system using fuzzy logic. In *2021 International Conference on Information Technology (ICIT)* (pp. 290-295). IEEE.

Almseidin, M., Al-Sawwa, J., & Alkasassbeh, M. (2022). Generating a benchmark cyber multi-step attacks dataset for intrusion detection. *Journal of Intelligent & Fuzzy Systems*, *43*(3), 3679–3694.

Almseidin, M., Al-Sawwa, J., Alkasassbeh, M., & Alweshah, M. (2023). On detecting distributed denial of service attacks using fuzzy inference system. *Cluster Computing*, *26*(2), 1337–1351.

Almseidin, M., Al-Sawwa, J., Alkasassbeh, M., Alzubi, M., & Alrfou, K. (2024). DT-ARO: Decision tree-based artificial rabbits optimization to mitigate IoT botnet exploitation. *Journal of Network and Systems Management*, *32*(1), 14.

Almseidin, M., & Alkasassbeh, M. (2022). An accurate detection approach for IoT botnet attacks using interpolation reasoning method. *Information (Basel)*, *13*(6), 300.

Almseidin, M., Alkasassbeh, M., Alzubi, M., & Al-Sawwa, J. (2022). Cyber-phishing website detection using fuzzy rule interpolation. *Cryptography*, *6*(2), 24.

Almseidin, M., Alzubi, M., Al-Sawwa, J., Alkasassbeh, M., & Alfraheed, M. (2024). A threefold approach for enhancing fuzzy interpolative reasoning: Case study on phishing attack detection using sparse rule bases. *Computers*, *13*(11), 291.

Almseidin, M., Gawanmeh, A., Alzubi, M., Al-Sawwa, J., Mashaleh, A. S., & Alkasassbeh, M. (2025). Hybrid Deep Neural Network Optimization with Particle Swarm and Grey Wolf Algorithms for Sunburst Attack Detection. *Computers*, *14*(3), 107.

Alslman, Y., Alkasassbeh, M., & Almseidin, M. (2024). A robust SNMP-MIB intrusion detection system against adversarial attacks. *Arabian Journal for Science and Engineering*, *49*(3), 4179–4195.

Alweshah, M., Kassaymeh, S., Alkhalaileh, S., Almseidin, M., & Altarawni, I. (2023). An efficient hybrid mine blast algorithm for tackling software fault prediction problem. *Neural Processing Letters*, *55*(8), 10925–10950.

Alzubi, M., Almseidin, M., Lone, M. A., & Kovacs, S. (2019). November. Fuzzy rule interpolation toolbox for the GNU open-source OCTAVE. In 2019 17th International Conference on Emerging eLearning Technologies and Applications (ICETA) (pp. 16-22). IEEE.

Alzubi, M., Johanyák, Z. C., & Kovács, S. (2019). Fuzzy rule interpolation methods and FRI toolbox. arXiv preprint arXiv:1904.12178.

Alzubi, M., Almseidin, M., Alkasassbeh, M., Al-Sawwa, J., & Aldweesh, A. (2024). Comparative analysis of fuzzy rule interpolation techniques across various scenarios using a set of benchmarks (november 2023). *IEEE Access : Practical Innovations, Open Solutions*.

Alzubi, M., Almseidin, M., Kovacs, S., Al-Sawwa, J., & Alkasassbeh, M. (2024). EI-FRI: Extended incircle fuzzy rule interpolation for multidimensional antecedents, multiple fuzzy rules, and extrapolation using total weight measurement and shift ratio. [JRC]. *Journal of Robotics and Control*, *5*(1), 217–227.

Alzubi, M., & Kovacs, S. (2019). Some considerations and a benchmark related to the cnf property of the koczy-hirota fuzzy rule interpolation. arXiv preprint arXiv:1911.05041.

Alzubi, M., & Kovács, S. (2019). Investigating the piece-wise linearity and benchmark related to koczy-hirota fuzzy linear interpolation. arXiv preprint arXiv:1907.01047.

Alzubi, M., & Kovacs, S. (2020). Interpolative fuzzy reasoning method based on the incircle of a generalized triangular fuzzy number. *Journal of Intelligent & Fuzzy Systems*, *39*(1), 709–729.

Angle, M. (2024). Securing the future: Advanced cybersecurity solutions for big data in business intelligence systems.

Arora, S., & Tewari, A. (2023). Zero trust architecture in IAM with AI integration. *International Journal of Scientific Research Archive*, *8*(2), 737–745.

Banerjee, S., Whig, P., & Parisa, S. K. (2024). Cybersecurity in multi-cloud environments for retail: An AI-based threat detection and response framework. *Transactions on Recent Developments in Industrial IoT, 16*(16).

Bashabsheh, M. (2024a). Comprehensive and Simulated Modeling of a Centralized Transport Robot Control System. *International Journal of Advanced Computer Science and Applications*, *15*(5).

Bashabsheh, M. (2024b). Autonomous Robotic Systems with Artificial Intelligence Technology Using a Deep Q Network-Based Approach for Goal-Oriented 2D Arm Control. [JRC]. *Journal of Robotics and Control*, *5*(6), 1872–1887.

Bashabsheh, M. (2024c). Simulation of An Automatic System of Robotics for Artificial Animated Being Manufacturing Using AnyLogic Simulation Software. *International Journal of Electrical and Electronics Engineering*, *11*(5), 129–137. DOI: 10.14445/23488379/ijeee-v11i5p112

Bashabsheh, M., & Alzubi, M. (2024). Integrated simulation model of the spatial distribution of dynamic systems using intelligent cellular automaton. *Panamerican Mathematical Journal*, *34*(3), 29–37. DOI: 10.52783/pmj.v34.i3.1771

Chowdhury, R. H. (2024). Blockchain and AI: Driving the future of data security and business intelligence. *World Journal of Advanced Research and Reviews*, *23*(1), 2559–2570.

de Stefano, A. (2023). Adoption of ZKP in blockchain-based collaborative business intelligence for KPI values sharing.

Edo, O. C., Ang, D., Billakota, P., & Ho, J. C. (2024). A zero trust architecture for health information systems. *Health and Technology*, *14*(1), 189–199.

Giguère, F. (2024). Cyber-resilient big data systems: Strategies for safeguarding business intelligence.

Joel, M. O., Chibunna, U. B., & Daraojimba, A. I. (2024). Artificial intelligence, cybersecurity and blockchain for business intelligence. *International Journal of Multidisciplinary Research and Growth Evaluation*, *5*(1), 1383–1387.

Joshi, H. (2024). Emerging technologies driving zero trust maturity across industries. *IEEE Open Journal of the Computer Society*.

Khan, M. J. (2023). Zero trust architecture: Redefining network security paradigms in the digital age. *World Journal of Advanced Research and Reviews*, *19*(3), 105–116.

Korrapati, R. (2023). Enhancing cybersecurity: Emerging architectures and methodologies for modern threat landscapes. *Available at SSRN* 5139609.

Loring, L. (2023). Dynamic threat mitigation in multi-tenant cloud environments using AI and predictive analytics. *Eastern European Journal for Multidisciplinary Research*, *2*(1), 67–75.

Mashaleh, A. S., Ibrahim, N. F. B., Alauthman, M., Almseidin, M., & Gawanmeh, A. (2024). IoT Smart Devices Risk Assessment Model Using Fuzzy Logic and PSO. *Computers, Materials & Continua*, *78*(2).

Moresi, G. (2023). Zero trust network & zero internet: Defense strategies against the zero day kill chain.

Odeh, I., Alkasassbeh, M., & Almseidin, M. (2022). Diabetic retinopathy detection method using artificial neural network. *International Journal of Bioinformatics Research and Applications*, *18*(4), 300–317.

Paul, F. (2023). The future of cloud security: AI-powered predictive analytics for proactive threat management.

Rawashdeh, A., Alkasassbeh, M., Alauthman, M., & Almseidin, M. (2024). A stacked ensemble approach to identify internet of things network attacks through traffic analysis. *Bulletin of Electrical Engineering and Informatics*, *13*(6), 4316–4326.

Ray, P. P. (2023). Web3: A comprehensive review on background, technologies, applications, zero-trust architectures, challenges and future directions. *Internet of Things and Cyber-Physical Systems*, *3*, 213–248.

Saleem, M., Warsi, M. R., & Islam, S. (2023). Secure information processing for multimedia forensics using zero-trust security model for large scale data analytics in SaaS cloud computing environment. *Journal of Information Security and Applications*, *72*, 103389.

Sheriffdeen, K. (2024). Zero trust architecture: Strengthening cyber defenses with AI-driven policies.

Shorman, A. R., Alzubi, M., Almseidin, M., & Rateb, R. (2025). Adaptive Intrusion Detection for IoT Networks using Artificial Immune System Techniques: A Comparative Study. [JRC]. *Journal of Robotics and Control*, *6*(2), 570–582.

Solanke, A. (2023). Edge computing integration with enterprise cloud systems: Architectural patterns for distributed intelligence. *International Journal of Engineering and Computer Science*, *12*(03).

Tauseef, A. (2023). AI in cybersecurity: Leveraging database innovations for intelligent threat response.

Younisse, R., Alkasassbeh, M., Almseidin, M., & Abdi, H. (2023). An early detection model for kerberoasting attacks and dataset labeling. *Jordanian Journal of Computers and Information Technology*, *9*(1).

Compilation of References

Abbas, T., & Eldred, A. (2025). AI-Powered Stream Processing: Bridging Real-Time Data Pipelines with Advanced Machine Learning Techniques. ResearchGate Journal of AI & Cloud Analytics. http://dx.doi.org/10.13140/RG.2.2.26674.52167

Abdellatif, A. A., Abo-Eleneen, A., Mohamed, A., Erbad, A., Navkar, N. V., & Guizani, M. (2023). Intelligent-slicing: An AI-assisted network slicing framework for 5G-and-beyond networks. *IEEE Transactions on Network and Service Management*, *20*(2), 1024–1039.

Abdillah, Y. A., et al. (2024). Design and development of interactive Moodle using design thinking to support online learning. – DOI: DOI: 10.21831/elinvo.v9i2.75255

Abdiqaxarovich. F. X. (2023). Revitalizing competitiveness: Enhancing the Mechanism for managing industrial enterprise Competitiveness. 36 (2023): Miasto Przyszłości,36(2023).

Abdulkader, R., Ayasrah, F. T. M., Nallagattla, V. R. G., Hiran, K. K., Dadheech, P., Balasubramaniam, V., & Sengan, S. (2023). Optimizing student engagement in edge-based online learning with advanced analytics. *Array (New York, N.Y.)*, *19*, 100301.

Abdullah, H. M., Mohana, N. T., Khan, B. M., Ahmed, S. M., Hossain, M., Islam, K. S., & Ahamed, T. (2023). Present and future scopes and challenges of plant pest and disease (P&D) monitoring: Remote sensing, image processing, and artificial intelligence perspectives. *Remote Sensing Applications: Society and Environment*, *32*, 100996.

Abdulla, M. F. M. H., & Musa, H. (2021). Prioritizing the logistics management factors affecting company performance: Case study of ADNOC. *International Journal of Sustainable Construction Engineering and Technology*, *12*(5). Advance online publication. DOI: 10.30880/ijscet.2021.12.05.007

Abeyratne, D. (2024). Real-Time Streaming Analytics and Latency Minimization in Autonomous Vehicle Big Data Pipelines. *Northern Reviews on Smart Cities, Sustainable Engineering, and Emerging Technologies, 9*(11), 49–62. https://northernreviews.com/index.php/NRSCSET/article/view/2024-11-16/15

Abuzuraiq, A., Alkasassbeh, M., & Almseidin, M. 2020, April. Intelligent methods for accurately detecting phishing websites. In *2020 11th International Conference on Information and Communication Systems (ICICS)* (pp. 085-090). IEEE.

Acharya, A., Singh, S. K., Pereira, V., & Singh, P. (2018). Big Data, knowledge co- Creation and decision-making in the fashion industry. *International Journal of Information Management, 42*, 90–101.

Adewumi, A., Oshioste, E. E., Asuzu, O. F., Ndubuisi, N. L., Awonnuga, K. F., & Daraojimba, O. H. (2024). Business intelligence tools in finance: A review of trends in the USA and Africa. *World Journal of Advanced Research and Reviews, 21*(3), 608–616.

Adewusi, A. O., Okoli, U. I., Adaga, E., Olorunsogo, T., Asuzu, O. F., & Daraojimba, D. O. (2024). Business intelligence in the era of big data: A review of analytical tools and competitive advantage. *Computer Science & IT Research Journal, 5*(2), 415–431.

Adnane, Y. I., & Zerari, M. (2024). Optimizing business intelligence classification rule mining using quantum-inspired genetic algorithm. *IEEE Access : Practical Innovations, Open Solutions.*

Agrawal, V., Mohanty, R. P., Agarwal, S., Dixit, J. K., & Agrawal, A. M. (2022). Analysing critical success factors for sustainable green supply chain management. *Environment, Development and Sustainability*. Advance online publication. DOI: 10.1007/s10668-022-02396-2

Ahi, A. A., Sinkovics, N., Shildibekov, Y., Sinkovics, R. R., & Mehandjiev, N. (2022). Advanced technologies and international business: A multidisciplinary analysis of the literature. *International Business Review, 31*(4), 101967.

Ahmed, F., Ahmed, M. R., Kabir, M. A., & Islam, M. M. (2025). Revolutionizing Business Analytics: The Impact of Artificial Intelligence and Machine Learning. *American Journal of Advanced Technology and Engineering Solutions, 1*(01), 147–173.

Aitdaoud, M., Namir, A., & Talbi, M. (2023). New pre-processing approach for clustering learning styles in Moodle LMS. – DOI: DOI: 10.3991/ijet.v18i07.37635

Ajegbile, M. D., Olaboye, J. A., Maha, C. C., & Tamunobarafiri, G. (2024). Integrating business analytics in healthcare: Enhancing patient outcomes through data-driven decision making. *World J Biol Pharm Health Sci*, *19*, 243–250.

Ajish, D. (2024). The significance of artificial intelligence in zero trust technologies: A comprehensive review. *Journal of Electrical Systems and Information Technology*, *11*(1), 30.

Al Khaldy, M. (2025a). Data Strategy Implementation in Organizations: A Framework for Building Data-Driven Enterprises. *Al-Basaer Journal of Business Research, 1*(2). https://doi.org/10.71202/paper29

Al Khaldy, M. (2025b). The Evolution of Business Intelligence: From Data Warehousing to AI-Driven Analytics. *Al-Basaer Journal of Business Research, 1*(2). https://doi.org/10.71202/paper25

Alaidi, A. H. M., Ramadhan, Z. A., & Alrubaye, J. S., ALRikabi, H. T. S., Mutar, H. A., & Svyd, I. (2025). AI-based monkeypox detection model using Raspberry Pi 5 AI Kit. *Sustainable Engineering and Innovation*, *7*(1), 1–14.

Aleksandrova, Y. (2021). *Predictive analytics implementation in the logistic industry. Journal Name, Volume*. Issue.

Al-Hadad, Y., & Zota, R. D. (2016). Implementing business intelligence system – case study. *Database Systems Journal*, *7*(1), 35–44.

Ali, S. A., Ansari, M., Alam, M., & Rakshit, S. (2023). Federated Learning for Business Intelligence: Predictive Maintenance in Industry 4.0. In AI-Based Data Analytics (pp. 125-140). Auerbach Publications.

Ali, B., Hijjawi, S., Campbell, L. H., Gregory, M. A., & Li, S. (2022). A maturity framework for zero-trust security in multiaccess edge computing. *Security and Communication Networks*, *2022*(1), 3178760.

Aljawarneh, N. M. (2024). The Mediating Role of Organization Agility between Business Intelligence & Innovative Performance. *Journal of Statistics Applications & Probability*, *13*(3), 929–938.

Alkasassbeh, M., & Almseidin, M. (2023, July). Machine learning techniques for accurately detecting the DNS tunneling. In *Science and Information Conference* (pp. 352-364). Cham: Springer Nature Switzerland.

Al-Kasassbeh, M., Almseidin, M., Alrfou, K., & Kovacs, S. (2020). Detection of IoT-botnet attacks using fuzzy rule interpolation. *Journal of Intelligent & Fuzzy Systems*, *39*(1), 421–431.

Allal-Chérif, O., Sim_on-Moya, V., and Ballester, A. C. C. (2021). Intelligent Purchasing: How artificial intelligence can redefine the purchasing function. *Journal of Business Research*, (124), 69–76. DOI: 10.1016/j.jbusres.2020.11.050

Al-Momani, M. M., Awadallah, A., Al-Nassar, B., Ismail, A., Nassoura, M., & Abudarwish, N. (2025). The role of business intelligence in supply chain optimization: A case study of the Carrefour Market in Jordan. *Data & Metadata*, *4*, 747. Advance online publication. DOI: 10.56294/dm2025747

Almseidin, M. (2020). *Fuzzy Automaton-based Early Detection Model* (Doctoral dissertation, University of Miskolc, Hungary).

Almseidin, M., & Alkasassbeh, M. (2022). An accurate detection approach for IoT botnet attacks using interpolation reasoning method. *Information (Basel)*, *13*(6), 300.

Almseidin, M., Alkasassbeh, M., Alzubi, M., & Al-Sawwa, J. (2022). Cyber-phishing website detection using fuzzy rule interpolation. *Cryptography*, *6*(2), 24.

Almseidin, M., Al-Sawwa, J., & Alkasassbeh, M. (2021, July). Anomaly-based intrusion detection system using fuzzy logic. In *2021 International Conference on Information Technology (ICIT)* (pp. 290-295). IEEE.

Almseidin, M., Al-Sawwa, J., & Alkasassbeh, M. (2022). Generating a benchmark cyber multi-step attacks dataset for intrusion detection. *Journal of Intelligent & Fuzzy Systems*, *43*(3), 3679–3694.

Almseidin, M., Al-Sawwa, J., Alkasassbeh, M., & Alweshah, M. (2023). On detecting distributed denial of service attacks using fuzzy inference system. *Cluster Computing*, *26*(2), 1337–1351.

Almseidin, M., Al-Sawwa, J., Alkasassbeh, M., Alzubi, M., & Alrfou, K. (2024). DT-ARO: Decision tree-based artificial rabbits optimization to mitigate IoT botnet exploitation. *Journal of Network and Systems Management*, *32*(1), 14.

Almseidin, M., Alzubi, M., Al-Sawwa, J., Alkasassbeh, M., & Alfraheed, M. (2024). A threefold approach for enhancing fuzzy interpolative reasoning: Case study on phishing attack detection using sparse rule bases. *Computers*, *13*(11), 291.

Almseidin, M., Gawanmeh, A., Alzubi, M., Al-Sawwa, J., Mashaleh, A. S., & Alkasassbeh, M. (2025). Hybrid Deep Neural Network Optimization with Particle Swarm and Grey Wolf Algorithms for Sunburst Attack Detection. *Computers*, *14*(3), 107.

Al-Sawwa, J., & Almseidin, M. (2022). A Spark-Based Artificial Bee Colony Algorithm for Unbalanced Large Data Classification. *Information (Basel)*, *13*(11), 530.

Al-Sawwa, J., Almseidin, M., Alkasassbeh, M., Alemerien, K., & Younisse, R. (2024). Spark-based multi-verse optimizer as wrapper features selection algorithm for phishing attack challenge. *Cluster Computing*, *27*(5), 5799–5814.

Alsayfi, M. S., Dahab, M. Y., Eassa, F. E., Salama, R., Haridi, S., & Al-Ghamdi, A. S. (2022). Securing real-time video surveillance data in vehicular cloud computing: A survey. *IEEE Access : Practical Innovations, Open Solutions*, *10*, 51525–51547.

Alsibhawi, I. A. A., Yahaya, J. B., & Mohamed, H. B. (2023). Business Intelligence Adoption for Small and Medium Enterprises: Conceptual Framework. *Applied Sciences (Basel, Switzerland)*, *13*(7), 4121. DOI: 10.3390/app13074121

Alslman, Y., Alkasassbeh, M., & Almseidin, M. (2024). A robust SNMP-MIB intrusion detection system against adversarial attacks. *Arabian Journal for Science and Engineering*, *49*(3), 4179–4195.

Alweshah, M., Kassaymeh, S., Alkhalaileh, S., Almseidin, M., & Altarawni, I. (2023). An efficient hybrid mine blast algorithm for tackling software fault prediction problem. *Neural Processing Letters*, *55*(8), 10925–10950.

Alzubi, M., & Kovács, S. (2019). Investigating the piece-wise linearity and benchmark related to koczy-hirota fuzzy linear interpolation. arXiv preprint arXiv:1907.01047.

Alzubi, M., & Kovacs, S. (2019). Some considerations and a benchmark related to the cnf property of the koczy-hirota fuzzy rule interpolation. arXiv preprint arXiv:1911.05041.

Alzubi, M., Almseidin, M., Lone, M. A., & Kovacs, S. (2019). November. Fuzzy rule interpolation toolbox for the GNU open-source OCTAVE. In 2019 17th International Conference on Emerging eLearning Technologies and Applications (ICETA) (pp. 16-22). IEEE.

Alzubi, M., Johanyák, Z. C., & Kovács, S. (2019). Fuzzy rule interpolation methods and FRI toolbox. arXiv preprint arXiv:1904.12178.

Alzubi, M., Almseidin, M., Alkasassbeh, M., Al-Sawwa, J., & Aldweesh, A. (2024). Comparative analysis of fuzzy rule interpolation techniques across various scenarios using a set of benchmarks (november 2023). *IEEE Access : Practical Innovations, Open Solutions.*

Alzubi, M., Almseidin, M., Kovacs, S., Al-Sawwa, J., & Alkasassbeh, M. (2024). EI-FRI: Extended incircle fuzzy rule interpolation for multidimensional antecedents, multiple fuzzy rules, and extrapolation using total weight measurement and shift ratio. [JRC]. *Journal of Robotics and Control*, *5*(1), 217–227.

Alzubi, M., & Kovacs, S. (2020). Interpolative fuzzy reasoning method based on the incircle of a generalized triangular fuzzy number. *Journal of Intelligent & Fuzzy Systems*, *39*(1), 709–729.

Anagnostopoulos, I. (2023). Blockchain technology for business intelligence: A secure approach to data governance. *Computers & Security*, *120*, 102975. DOI: 10.1016/j.cose.2022.102975

Anchitaalagammai, J. V., Kavitha, S., Buurvidha, R., Santhiya, T. S., Roopa, M. D., & Sankari, S. S. (2025). Edge Artificial Intelligence for Real-Time Decision Making using NVIDIA Jetson Orin, Google Coral Edge TPU and 6G for Privacy and Scalability. In *2025 International Conference on Visual Analytics and Data Visualization (ICVADV)* (pp. 150-155). IEEE.

Anderson, C., Brown, S., Harman, D., & Dwyer, M. (2024). *Adaptive predictive modeling with online learning: addressing data drift challenges in historical data for distributed inferencing*. Paper presented at the Artificial Intelligence and Machine Learning for Multi-Domain Operations Applications VI.

Anderson, K. (2024). *'The role of edge computing and hybrid clouds in next-generation healthcare. Univ*. Tech. Rep.

Angle, M. (2024). Securing the future: Advanced cybersecurity solutions for big data in business intelligence systems.

Anozie, U. C., Onyenahazi, O. B., Ekeocha, P. C., Adekola, A. D., Ukadike, C. A., & Oloko, O. A. (2024). Advancements in artificial intelligence for omnichannel marketing and customer service: Enhancing predictive analytics, automation, and operational efficiency. *International Journal of Science and Research Archive*, *12*(2), 1621–1629.

Antonini, M. (2021). From Edge Computing to Edge Intelligence: exploring novel design approaches to intelligent IoT applications.

Apostol, E.-S., Truică, C.-O., Pop, F., & Esposito, C. (2021). Change point enhanced anomaly detection for IoT time series data. *Water (Basel)*, *13*(12), 1633.

Aravind raj, K., & Rajan Chinna, P. (2019). A contemporary on recent development activities and challenges in logistics sector in India. International Journal of Innovative Technology and Exploring Engineering, 8(11). https://doi.org/DOI: 10.35940/ijitee.K2209.0981119

Arinze, C. A., Izionworu, V. O., Isong, D., Daudu, C. D., & Adefemi, A. (2024). Integrating artificial intelligence into engineering processes for improved efficiency and safety in oil and gas operations. *Open Access Research Journal of Engineering and Technology*, *6*(1), 39–51.

Arivazhagan, D. (2020). Logistics network in India: Challenges and scope. *International Journal of Scientific and Technology Research*, *9*(2).

Arnott, D., Gibson, M., & Jagielska, I. (2004). Evaluating the intangible benefits of Business intelligence: review & research agenda. The IFIP TC8/WG8.3 International Conference, 1-11. doi:DOI: 10.1.1.94.8550

Arora, S., & Tewari, A. (2023). Zero trust architecture in IAM with AI integration. *International Journal of Scientific Research Archive*, *8*(2), 737–745.

Asim, M., Wang, Y., Wang, K., & Huang, P. Q. (2020). A review on computational intelligence techniques in cloud and edge computing. *IEEE Transactions on Emerging Topics in Computational Intelligence*, *4*(6), 742–763.

Asthana, S., & Bhat, H. (2015). A study of business performance measurement of third-party logistics (3PL) organizations in the Indian logistics industry. [The Journal of Innovations]. *IMS Manthan*, *10*(1). Advance online publication. DOI: 10.18701/imsmanthan.v10i1.5660

Asthana, S., & Dwivedi, A. (2020). Performance measurement of India-based third-party logistics sector: An empirical study of user versus provider perspectives. *Production Planning and Control*, *31*(2–3). Advance online publication. DOI: 10.1080/09537287.2019.1631467

Aung, M. M., et al. (2024). Implementing Hadoop and Moodle integrated student support system. – DOI: DOI: 10.1109/ICAIT65209.2024.10754929

Awan, U., Shamim, S., Khan, Z., Zia, N. U., Shariq, S. M., & Khan, M. N. (2021). Big data analytics capability and decision-making: The role of data-driven insight on circular economy performance. *Technological Forecasting and Social Change*, *168*, 120766.

Azmi, I., Hamid, N. A., Hussin, M. N. M., & Ibrahim, N. I. (2017). Logistics and supply chain management: The importance of integration for business processes. *Journal of Emerging Economies and Islamic Research*, *5*(4). Advance online publication. DOI: 10.24191/jeeir.v5i4.8838

Baars, H., & Kemper, H.-G. (2010). Business intelligence in the cloud? *PACIS 2010 Proceedings*. 145. https://aisel.aisnet.org/pacis2010/145

Badmus, O., Rajput, S. A., Arogundade, J. B., & Williams, M. (2024). AI-driven business analytics and decision making. *World Journal of Advanced Research and Reviews, 24*(1), 616–633.

Bag, S., Pretorius, J. H. C., Gupta, S., and Dwivedi, Y. K. (2021). Role of institutional Pressures and resources in the adoption of big data analytics powered artificial intelligence, sustainable manufacturing practices and circular economy capabilities. Technol. Forecast. Soc. Chang. 163:120420. Doi: . techfore.2020.120420.DOI: 10.1016/j

Bag, S., Gupta, S., Kumar, A., & Sivarajah, U. (2021). An integrated artificial Intelligence framework for knowledge creation and B2B marketing rational decision-making for improving firm performance. *Industrial Marketing Management, 92*(92), 178–189. DOI: 10.1016/j.indmarman.2020.12.001

Balodi, K. C., Jain, R., & Das, R. (2022). Strategy, business model, and innovation at Rivigo: Is Relay-as-a-Service the way forward? *Journal of Information Technology Teaching Cases, 12*(1). Advance online publication. DOI: 10.1177/2043886920986163

Banerjee, S., Whig, P., & Parisa, S. K. (2024). Cybersecurity in multi-cloud environments for retail: An AI-based threat detection and response framework. *Transactions on Recent Developments in Industrial IoT, 16*(16).

Barati, M. (2023). Open Government data programs and information privacy concerns: A literature review. *arXiv preprint arXiv:2312.10096.*

Bari, M. D., & Ara, A. (2024). The Impact Of Machine Learning On Prescriptive Analytics For Optimized Business Decision-Making. *Anjuman, The Impact Of Machine Learning On Prescriptive Analytics For Optimized Business Decision-Making (April 15, 2024).*

Barney, J. B. (1991). Firm resources and sustained competitive advantage. *Journal of Management, 17*(1), 99–120.

Barocas, S., & Selbst, A. D. (2016). Big data's disparate impact. *California Law Review, 104*(3), 671–732.

Bashabsheh, M. (2024a). Comprehensive and Simulated Modeling of a Centralized Transport Robot Control System. *International Journal of Advanced Computer Science and Applications, 15*(5).

Bashabsheh, M. (2024b). Autonomous Robotic Systems with Artificial Intelligence Technology Using a Deep Q Network-Based Approach for Goal-Oriented 2D Arm Control. [JRC]. *Journal of Robotics and Control, 5*(6), 1872–1887.

Bashabsheh, M. (2024c). Simulation of An Automatic System of Robotics for Artificial Animated Being Manufacturing Using AnyLogic Simulation Software. *International Journal of Electrical and Electronics Engineering*, *11*(5), 129–137. DOI: 10.14445/23488379/ijeee-v11i5p112

Bashabsheh, M., & Alzubi, M. (2024). Integrated simulation model of the spatial distribution of dynamic systems using intelligent cellular automaton. *Panamerican Mathematical Journal*, *34*(3), 29–37. DOI: 10.52783/pmj.v34.i3.1771

Batini, C., Cappiello, C., Francalanci, C., & Maurino, A. (2009). Methodologies for data quality assessment and improvement. *ACM Computing Surveys*, *41*(3), 1–52. DOI: 10.1145/1541880.1541883

Bauskar, S. (2024). Business Analytics in Enterprise System Based on Application of Artificial Intelligence. *International Research Journal of Modernization in Engineering Technology and Science.*

Belhadi, A., Mani, V., Kamble, S. S., Khan, S. A. R., & Verma, S. (2021). Artificial Intelligence-driven innovation for enhancing supply chain resilience and performance under the effect of supply chain dynamism: An empirical investigation. *Annals of Operations Research*, **•••**, 1–26. DOI: 10.1007/s10479-021-03956-x

Benito, G. R. G., Cuervo-Cazurra, A., Mudambi, R., Pedersen, T., & Tallman, S. (2022). The future of global strategy. *Global Strategy Journal*, *12*(3), 421–450. DOI: 10.1002/gsj.1464

Berisha, B., Mëziu, E., & Shabani, I. (2022). Big data analytics in Cloud computing: An overview. *Journal of Cloud Computing (Heidelberg, Germany)*, *11*(1). Advance online publication. DOI: 10.1186/s13677-022-00301-w PMID: 35966392

Bharadiya, J. P. (2023). A Comparative Study of Business Intelligence and Artificial Intelligence with Big Data Analytics. *American Journal of Artificial Intelligence*, *7*(1), 24–30. DOI: 10.11648/j.ajai.20230701.14

Bhargava, A., Suhaib, M., & Singholi, A. S. (2024). A review of recent advances, techniques, and control algorithms for automated guided vehicle systems. *Journal of the Brazilian Society of Mechanical Sciences and Engineering*, *46*(7), 419.

Bhaskaran, S. V. (2020). Integrating data quality services (dqs) in big data ecosystems: Challenges, best practices, and opportunities for decision-making. *Journal of Applied Big Data Analytics, Decision-Making, and Predictive Modelling Systems*, *4*(11), 1–12. https://polarpublications.com/index.php/JABADP/article/view/4

Bhattacharyya, S. S., Garlapad, V., & Kulkarni, O. (2021). A study of strategic group mapping and understanding mobility barriers in the Indian logistics industry. *International Journal of Applied Logistics*, *12*(1). Advance online publication. DOI: 10.4018/ijal.286164

Biswas, A., & Wang, H. C. (2023). Autonomous vehicles enabled by the integration of IoT, edge intelligence, 5G, and blockchain. *Sensors (Basel)*, *23*(4), 1963. PMID: 36850560

Bouckaert, G., Peters, B. G., & Verhoest, K. (2016). *Coordination of public sector Organizations*. Palgrave Macmillan.

BrainSell. (2021). Transforming business performance with effective forecasting and data efficiency using Power BI [Case study]. BrainSell. Retrieved August 16, 2025, from https://www.brainsell.com/customer-success/power-bi-manufacturing-case-study/

Brijs, B. (2013). Business analysis for business intelligence.CRC Press. Taylor and Francis Group.

Brynjolfsson, E., & McAfee, A. (2014). *The second machine age: Work, progress, and prosperity in a time of brilliant technologies*. W. W. Norton & Company.

Brynjolfsson, E., & McAfee, A. (2017). *The second machine age: Work, progress, And prosperity in a time of brilliant technologies*. WW Norton & Company.

Brynjolfsson, E., & McElheran, K. (2022). The role of cloud computing in modern business intelligence systems. *Management Science*, *68*(3), 1215–1234. DOI: 10.1287/mnsc.2021.3983

Budhwar, P., Malik, A., De Silva, M. T. T., & Thevisuthan, P. (2022). Artificial Intelligence—Challenges and opportunities for international HRM: A review and research agenda. *International Journal of Human Resource Management*, *33*(6), 1065–1097. DOI: 10.1080/09585192.2022.2035161

Bussa, S. (2023). Enhancing BI tools for improved data visualization and insights. *International Journal of Computer Science and Mobile Computing*, *12*(2), 70–92.

Cao, H., & Wachowicz, M. (2019). An edge-fog-cloud architecture of streaming analytics for Internet of Things applications. *Sensors (Basel)*, *19*(16), 3594. DOI: 10.3390/s19163594 PMID: 31426586

Cao, L. (2022). Decentralized AI: Edge intelligence and smart blockchain, metaverse, web3, and desci. *IEEE Intelligent Systems*, *37*(3), 6–19.

Casino, F., Dasaklis, T. I., & Patsakis, C. (2019). A systematic literature review of blockchain-based applications: Current status, classification and open issues. *Telematics and Informatics*, *36*, 55–81.

Chakraborty, S., Sharma, A., & Vaidya, O. S. (2020). Achieving sustainable operational excellence through IT implementation in Indian logistics sector: An analysis of barriers. *Resources, Conservation and Recycling*, *152*. Advance online publication. DOI: 10.1016/j.resconrec.2019.104506

Chandra, P., & Jain, N. (2007). The logistics sector in India: Overview and challenges. World Scientific Series on 21st Century Business.

Chang, V. (2014). The business intelligence as a service in the cloud. *Future Generation Computer Systems*, *37*, 512–534.

Chang, Z., Liu, S., Xiong, X., Cai, Z., & Tu, G. (2021). A survey of recent advances in edge-computing-powered artificial intelligence of things. *IEEE Internet of Things Journal*, *8*(18), 13849–13875.

Chaudhary, R., Singh, A., Gupta, P., & Verma, S. (2024). Integrating artificial intelligence into business intelligence architectures: A future perspective. *Journal of Business Analytics*, *7*(1), 45–62. DOI: 10.1080/2573234X.2024.1234567

Chaudhry, K., & Dhingra, S. (2021). Modeling the critical success factors for business intelligence implementation: An ISM approach. *International Journal of Business Intelligence Research*, *12*(2), 1–21. DOI: 10.4018/IJBIR.20210701.oa3

Chaudhuri, R., Chatterjee, S., Vrontis, D., & Thrassou, A. (2021). Adoption of Robust business analytics for product innovation and organizational performance: The mediating role of organizational data-driven culture. *Annals of Operations Research*, •••, 1–35. DOI: 10.1007/s10479-021-04407-3

Chaudhuri, S., Dayal, U., & Narasayya, V. (2011). An overview of business intelligence technology. *Communications of the ACM*, *54*(8), 88–98. DOI: 10.1145/1978542.1978562

Chavan, A. (2023). Exploring the Synergy of Cloud and On-Premises Systems-A Case for Hybrid Architectures. *Journal of Computer Science and Technology Studies*, *5*(3), 122–141.

Chawla, N., & Dalal, S. (2021). Edge AI with Wearable IoT: A Review on Leveraging Edge Intelligence in Wearables for Smart Healthcare. Green Internet of Things for Smart Cities, 205-231.

Chen, H., Chiang, R. H. L., & Storey, V. C. (2012). Business Intelligence and Analytics: From Big data to big impact. *Management Information Systems Quarterly*, *36*(4).

Chen, H., Chiang, R. H. L., & Storey, V. C. (2023). Business intelligence and analytics: From big data to AI-driven decision-making. *Management Information Systems Quarterly*, *47*(1), 23–47. DOI: 10.25300/MISQ/2023/16274

Chen, H., Chiang, R. H., & Storey, V. C. (2012). Business intelligence and analytics: From big data to big impact. *Management Information Systems Quarterly*, *36*(4), 1165–1188. DOI: 10.2307/41703503

Chen, Y., & Lin, Z. (2021). Business Intelligence Capabilities and Firm Performance: A Study in China. *International Journal of Information Management*, *57*, 102232.

Chen, Z. (2023). Collaboration among recruiters and artificial intelligence: Removing human prejudices in employment. *Cognition Technology and Work*, *25*(1), 135–149. DOI: 10.1007/s10111-022-00716-0

Choi, J., Yoon, J., Chung, J., Coh, B., & Lee, J. (2020). Social media analytics And business intelligence research: A systematic review. *Information Processing & Management*, *57*, 102279.

Chowdhury, R. H. (2024). Blockchain and AI: Driving the future of data security and business intelligence. *World Journal of Advanced Research and Reviews*, *23*(1), 2559–2570.

Chowdhury, R. H. (2024). The evolution of business operations: Unleashing the potential of Artificial Intelligence, Machine Learning, and Blockchain. *World Journal of Advanced Research and Reviews*, *22*(3), 2135–2147.

Chowdhury, S., Dey, P., Joel-Edgar, S., Bhattacharya, S., Rodriguez-Espindola, O., Abadie, A., & Truong, L. (2023). Unlocking the value of artificial intelligence in human resource management through AI capability framework. *Human Resource Management Review*, *33*(1), 100899. DOI: 10.1016/j.hrmr.2022.100899

Climent, R. C., Haftora, D. M., & Staniewski, M. W. (2024). AI-enabled business Models for competitive advantage. *Journal of Innovation & Knowledge*, *9*, 100532.

Codd, E. F., Codd, S. B., & Salley, C. T. (1993). *Providing OLAP (on-line analytical processing) to user-analysts: An IT mandate. Technical Report*. E.F. Codd and Associates.

Coito, T., Firme, B., Martins, M. S., Vieira, S. M., Figueiredo, J., & Sousa, J. M. (2021). Intelligent sensors for real-Time decision-making. *Automation*, *2*(2), 62–82. https://doi.org/10.3390/automation2020004

Collins, A., Hamza, O., Eweje, A., & Babatunde, G. O. (2024). Integrating 5G core networks with business intelligence platforms: Advancing data-driven decision-making. *International Journal of Multidisciplinary Research and Growth Evaluation, 5*(1), 1082–1099.

Dai, J. (2020). Real-time and accurate object detection on edge device with TensorFlow Lite. []. IOP Publishing.]. *Journal of Physics: Conference Series, 1651*(1), 012114.

Davenport, T. H. (2018). From analytics to artificial intelligence. *Journal of Business Analytics, 1*(2), 73–80. DOI: 10.1080/2573234X.2018.1543535

Davenport, T. H., & Harris, J. G. (2007). *Competing on analytics: The new science of winning*. Harvard Business Press.

Davenport, T. H., & Prusak, L. (1998). *Working Knowledge: How Organisations Manage What They Know*. Harvard Business School Press.

Davenport, T. H., & Ronanki, R. (2018). Artificial intelligence for the real world. *Harvard Business Review, 96*(1), 108–116.

de Stefano, A. (2023). Adoption of ZKP in blockchain-based collaborative business intelligence for KPI values sharing.

Dean, J., & Ghemawat, S. (2008). MapReduce: Simplified data processing on large clusters. *Communications of the ACM, 51*(1), 107–113. DOI: 10.1145/1327452.1327492

Delen, D., & Ram, S. (2018). Research challenges and opportunities in business analytics. *Journal of Business Analytics, 1*(1), 2–12. DOI: 10.1080/2573234X.2018.1507324

Delen, D., & Ram, S. (2022). Predictive analytics for business intelligence: Current trends and future directions. *Decision Support Systems, 164*, 113920. DOI: 10.1016/j.dss.2022.113920

Demchenko, Y., de Laat, C., & Membrey, P. (2023). Scalable business intelligence architectures for distributed data processing. *Journal of Cloud Computing (Heidelberg, Germany), 12*(1), 87–105. DOI: 10.1186/s13677-023-00267-4

Deng, S., Zhao, H., Fang, W., Yin, J., Dustdar, S., & Zomaya, A. Y. (2020). Edge intelligence: The confluence of edge computing and artificial intelligence. *IEEE Internet of Things Journal, 7*(8), 7457–7469.

DigitalDefynd. (2025). 10 ways Tesla is using AI [Case study]. DigitalDefynd Tech Cases. https://digitaldefynd.com/IQ/tesla-using-ai-case-study

Dillon, S. M., Glavas, C., & Mathews, S. (2020). Digitally immersive, international Entrepreneurial experiences. *International Business Review, 29*(6), 101739. DOI: 10.1016/j.ibusrev.2020.101739

Dong, H., Zhang, C., Li, G., & Zhang, H. (2024). Cloud-native databases: A survey. *IEEE Transactions on Knowledge and Data Engineering, 36*(12), 7772–7791.

Duan, S., Wang, D., Ren, J., Lyu, F., Zhang, Y., Wu, H., & Shen, X. (2022). Distributed artificial intelligence empowered by end-edge-cloud computing: A survey. *IEEE Communications Surveys and Tutorials, 25*(1), 591–624.

Dubuc, T., Stahl, F., & Roesch, E. B. (2020). Mapping the big data landscape: Technologies, platforms and paradigms for real-time analytics of data streams. *IEEE Access : Practical Innovations, Open Solutions, 9*, 15351–15374.

Duch, D., May, M., & George, S. (2024). Enhancing predictive analytics for students' performance in Moodle: Insight from an empirical study. – DOI: DOI: 10.47852/bonviewJDSIS42023777

Dunning, J. H. (2019). Explaining global competitiveness: The role of international business theory. In *Global competitiveness* (pp. 25–44). Emerald Publishing Limited.

Dynatrace. (2024). *Enhance DevOps and platform engineering with observability.* https://www.dynatrace.com/news/blog/observability-security-ai-enhance-devops-platform-engineering

Edo, O. C., Ang, D., Billakota, P., & Ho, J. C. (2024). A zero trust architecture for health information systems. *Health and Technology, 14*(1), 189–199.

El Hajj, M., & Hammoud, J. (2023). Unveiling the influence of artificial intelligence and machine learning on financial markets: A comprehensive analysis of AI applications in trading, risk management, and financial operations. *Journal of Risk and Financial Management, 16*(10), 434.

El-Chaarani, H., & El-Abiad, Z. (2018). The impact of technological innovation on bank performance. *Journal of Internet Banking and Commerce, 23*(3). Available at *SSRN*: https://ssrn.com/abstract=3845169

El-Haddadeh, R., Osmani, M., Hindi, N., & Fadlalla, A. (2021). Value creation for Realising the sustainable development goals: Fostering organizational adoption of big data analytics. *Journal of Business Research, 2021*(131), 402–410.

ElMalah, K., & Nasr, M. (2019). Cloud business intelligence. *International Journal of Advanced Networking and Applications, 10*(6), 4120–4124.

Ereth, J., & Baars, H. (2020). *A Capability Approach for Designing Business Intelligence and Analytics Architectures.* Paper presented at the HICSS.

Erik, S., & Emma, L. (2018). Real-Time Analytics with Event-Driven Architectures: Powering Next-Gen Business Intelligence. *International Journal of Trend in Scientific Research and Development*, *2*(4), 3097–3111.

Evocon. (2022). Papoutsanis digitizes production with Evocon and increases OEE by 30% [Case study]. Evocon. https://evocon.com/articles/case_study/papoutsanis-digitizes-production-with-evocon-and-increases-oee-by-30

Fagbohungbe, O., Reza, S. R., Dong, X., & Qian, L. (2021). Efficient privacy preserving edge intelligent computing framework for image classification in IoT. *IEEE Transactions on Emerging Topics in Computational Intelligence*, *6*(4), 941–956.

Farayola, O. A. (2024). Revolutionizing banking security: Integrating artificial intelligence, blockchain, and business intelligence for enhanced cybersecurity. *Finance & Accounting Research Journal*, *6*(4), 501–514.

Fazio, M., Celesti, A., Puliafito, A., & Villari, M. (2015). Big data storage in the cloud for smart environment monitoring. *Procedia Computer Science*, *52*, 500–506. DOI: 10.1016/j.procs.2015.05.023

Fernsel, L., Kalff, Y., & Simbeck, K. (2024). Where is the evidence? A plugin for auditing Moodle's learning analytics. – DOI: DOI: 10.5220/0012689800003693

Firat, M. (2023). Integrating AI applications into learning management systems to enhance e-learning. – DOI: DOI: 10.52911/itall.1244453

Fragkoulis, M., Carbone, P., Kalavri, V., & Katsifodimos, A. (2024). A survey on the evolution of stream processing systems. *The VLDB Journal*, *33*(2), 507–541.

Froissard, J.-C., et al. (2024). A learning analytics pilot in Moodle and its impact on developing organisational capacity in a university. – DOI: DOI: 10.14742/apubs.2017.745

Gandomi, A., & Haider, M. (2022). Beyond the hype: Big data concepts, methods, and analytics. *International Journal of Information Management*, *102*, 102456. DOI: 10.1016/j.ijinfomgt.2020.102456

García-Murillo, G., Novoa-Hernández, P., & Serrano Rodríguez, R. (2023). On the technological acceptance of Moodle by higher education faculty. – DOI: DOI: 10.3390/bs13050419

Garg, V., & Jindal, B. (2023). Resource optimization using predictive virtual machine consolidation approach in cloud environment. *Intelligent Decision Technologies, 17*(2), 471–484. DOI: 10.3233/IDT-220222

Ghasemaghaei, M. (2021). Understanding the impact of big data on firm performance: The necessity of conceptually differentiating among big data characteristics. *International Journal of Information Management, 57*, 102055. DOI: 10.1016/j.ijinfomgt.2019.102055

Giguère, F. (2024). Cyber-resilient big data systems: Strategies for safeguarding business intelligence.

Gomwe, G., Potgieter, M., & Litheko, A. M. (2022). Proposed framework for Innovative business intelligence for competitive advantage in small, medium and micro-organisations in the North West province of South Africa'. *Southern African Journal of Entrepreneurship and Small Business Management, 14*(1), a501. DOI: 10.4102/sajesbm.v14i1.501

Gong, T., Zhu, L., Yu, F. R., & Tang, T. (2023). Edge intelligence in intelligent transportation systems: A survey. *IEEE Transactions on Intelligent Transportation Systems, 24*(9), 8919–8944.

Gong, Y., Yao, H., Wang, J., Wu, D., Zhang, N., & Yu, F. R. (2022). Decentralized edge intelligence-driven network resource orchestration mechanism. *IEEE Network, 37*(2), 270–276.

Grant, R. M. (2019). *Contemporary strategy analysis: Text and cases edition*. John Wiley & Sons.

Güler, K., & Tepecik, A. (2019). Exchange rates change by using economic data. With artificial intelligence and forecasting the crisis. *Procedia Computer Science, 158*, 316–326. DOI: 10.1016/j.procs.201909.057

Günther, W. A., Rezazade Mehrizi, M. H., Huysman, M., & Feldberg, F. (2017). Debating big data: A literature review on realizing value from big data. *The Journal of Strategic Information Systems, 26*(3), 191–209. DOI: 10.1016/j.jsis.2017.07.003

Gupta, M., & Bose, S. (2023). Overcoming adoption barriers in modern BI systems: An empirical study. *The Journal of Strategic Information Systems, 32*(1), 101712. DOI: 10.1016/j.jsis.2023.101712

Gupta, R., Reebadiya, D., & Tanwar, S. (2021). 6G-enabled edge intelligence for ultra-reliable low latency applications: Vision and mission. *Computer Standards & Interfaces, 77*, 103521.

Gupta, R., Reebadiya, D., Tanwar, S., Kumar, N., & Guizani, M. (2021). When blockchain meets edge intelligence: Trusted and security solutions for consumers. *IEEE Network*, *35*(5), 272–278.

Haag, S., Cummings, M., & Philips, A. (2007). *Management Information Systems For the Information Age* (6th ed.). McGraw-Hill/Irwin.

Hai, R., Geisler, S., & Quix, C. (2016). Constance: An intelligent data lake system. *Proceedings of the 2016 International Conference on Management of Data (SIGMOD)* (pp. 2097–2100). https://doi.org/DOI: 10.1145/2882903.2899389

Hai, R., Koutras, C., Quix, C., & Jarke, M. (2021). Data Lakes: A Survey of Functions and Systems. https://doi.org//arXiv.2106.09592DOI: 10.48550

Hamadaqa, M. H. M., Alnajjar, M., Ayyad, M. N., Al-Nakhal, M. A., Abunasser, B. S., & Abu-Naser, S. S. (2024). Leveraging Artificial Intelligence for Strategic Business Decision-Making: Opportunities and Challenges.

Han, X., Xiao, S., Sheng, J., & Zhang, G. (2024). Enhancing efficiency and decision-making in higher education through intelligent commercial integration: Leveraging artificial intelligence. *Journal of the Knowledge Economy*, •••, 1–37.

Hashem, I. A. T., Yaqoob, I., Anuar, N. B., Mokhtar, S., Gani, A., & Ullah Khan, S. (2023). The role of big data in business intelligence: Challenges and opportunities. *Future Generation Computer Systems*, *137*, 321–333. DOI: 10.1016/j.future.2022.12.045

He, W., Zha, S., & Li, L. (2013). Social media competitive analysis and text mining: A case study in the pizza industry. *International Journal of Information Management*, *33*(3), 464–472.

Hofmann, E. (2017). Big data analytics and demand forecasting in supply chains: A conceptual analysis. *International Journal of Logistics Management*, *28*(2), 426–443. DOI: 10.1108/IJLM-04-2016-0109

Hosen, M. S., Islam, R., Naeem, Z., Folorunso, E. O., Chu, T. S., Al Mamun, M. A., & Orunbon, N. O. (2024). Data-driven decision making: Advanced database systems for business intelligence. *Nanotechnology Perceptions*, *20*(3), 687–704.

Hossain, Q., Yasmin, F., Biswas, T. R., & Asha, N. B. (2024). Integration of Big Data Analytics in Management Information Systems for Business Intelligence. *Saudi J Bus Manag Stud*, *9*(9), 192–203.

Huang, M. H., & Rust, R. T. (2022). A Framework for collaborative artificial Intelligence in marketing. *Journal of Retailing*, *98*(2), 209–223. DOI: 10.1016/j.jretai.2021.03.001

Huang, M.-H., & Rust, R. T. (2018). Artificial intelligence in service. *Journal of Service Research*, *21*(2), 155–172. DOI: 10.1177/1094670517752459

Infotech, A. C. I. (2025). Optimizing resource allocation: Power BI dashboards for manufacturing [Case study]. ACI Infotech. Retrieved August 16, 2025, from https://www.aciinfotech.com/case-studies/power-bi-dashboards-resource-management-efficiency

Inmon, W. H. (2002). *Building the data warehouse* (3rd ed.). Wiley.

Isik, Ö., Jones, M. C., & Sidorova, A. (2013). Business intelligence success: The roles of analytics capability and data quality. *Information & Management*, *50*(1), 13–23. DOI: 10.1016/j.im.2012.12.001

James, G. G., Oise, G. P., Chukwu, E. G., Michael, N. A., Ekpo, W. F., & Okafor, P. E. (2024). Optimizing business intelligence system using big data and machine learning. *Journal of Information Systems and Informatics*, *6*(2), 1215–1236.

Jha, R., & Aggarwal, A. (2023). Enhancing predictive analytics in finance with AI-powered BI systems. *Journal of Financial Innovation*, *9*(2), 123–140. DOI: 10.1016/j.jfi.2023.100547

Jia, M., Wu, J., Guo, Q., & Yang, Y. (2024). Service-oriented SAGIN with pervasive intelligence for resource-constrained users. *IEEE Network*, *38*(2), 79–86.

Jiang, F., Jiang, Y., Zhi, H., Dong, Y., Li, H., Ma, S., & Wang, Y. (2017). Artificial intelligence in healthcare: Past, present and future. *Stroke and Vascular Neurology*, *2*(4), 230–243. DOI: 10.1136/svn-2017-000101

Joel, M. O., Chibunna, U. B., & Daraojimba, A. I. (2024). Artificial intelligence, cybersecurity and blockchain for business intelligence. *International Journal of Multidisciplinary Research and Growth Evaluation*, *5*(1), 1383–1387.

Johnson, A. R. (2005). Competitive Intelligence and Knowledge Management: Complementary Partners, Reinforcing Tools. In Rao, M. (Ed.), *Knowledge Management Tools and Techniques: Practitioners and Experts Evaluate KM Solutions* (pp. 302–310). Elsevier Butterworth-Heinemann.

Jordan, M. I., & Mitchell, T. M. (2015). Machine learning: Trends, perspectives, and prospects. *Science*, *349*(6245), 255–260. DOI: 10.1126/science.aaa8415

Joshi, H. (2024). Emerging technologies driving zero trust maturity across industries. *IEEE Open Journal of the Computer Society*.

Kaggwa, S., Eleogu, T. F., Okonkwo, F., Farayola, O. A., Uwaoma, P. U., & Akinoso, A. (2024). AI in decision making: Transforming business strategies. *International Journal of Research and Scientific Innovation*, *10*(12), 423–444.

Kanagarla, K. (2024). Edge computing and analytics for IoT devices: Enhancing real-time decision making in smart environments. *Available at SSRN* 5012466.

Kasem, M., & Hassanein, E. E. (2014). Cloud business intelligence survey. *International Journal of Computer Applications*, *90*(1).

Khalid, A. S., Hassan, N. H., Razak, N. A. A. B., & Baharuden, A. F. (2020). Business intelligence dashboard for driver performance in fleet management. In Proceedings of the 2020 11th International Conference on E-Education, E-Business, E-Management, and E-Learning (pp. 347-351).

Khan, M. J. (2023). Zero trust architecture: Redefining network security paradigms in the digital age. *World Journal of Advanced Research and Reviews*, *19*(3), 105–116.

Kim, G.-S. (2020). The effect of quality management and big data management on customer satisfaction in Korea's public sector. *Sustainability*, *12*(13), 5474. DOI: 10.3390/su12135474

Kitsios, F., & Kamariotou, M. (2025). Artificial Intelligence and Business Strategy Towards Digital Transformation: A Research Agenda. *Sustainability*, *2025*(13), •••. DOI: 10.3390/su13042025

Kola, H. G. (2024). Optimizing ETL Processes for Big Data Applications. *International Journal of Engineering and Management Research*, *14*(5), 99–112.

Kopalle, P. K., Gangwar, M., Kaplan, A., Ramachandran, D., Reinartz, W., & Rindfleisch, A. (2022). Examining artificial intelligence (AI) technologies in marketing via a global lens: Current trends and future research opportunities. *International Journal of Research in Marketing*, *39*(2), 522–540. DOI: 10.1016/j.ijresmar.2021.11.002

Korrapati, R. (2023). Enhancing cybersecurity: Emerging architectures and methodologies for modern threat landscapes. *Available at SSRN* 5139609.

Kothinti, R. R. (2024). Artificial intelligence in healthcare: revolutionizing precision medicine, predictive analytics, and ethical considerations in autonomous diagnostics. *World Journal of Advanced Research and Reviews*, 3394-3406.

Kotler, P., & Keller, K. L. (2016). *Marketing management*. Pearson.

Kouvara, T., & Verykios, V. (2024). Discovering the collaborative filtering (CF) recommender system in a Moodle learning environment. – DOI: DOI: 10.12681/icodl.5638

Krause, C. (2024). Amazon's AI-driven supply chain: A blueprint for the future of global logistics. CDO Times. https://cdotimes.com/2024/08/23/case-study-amazons-ai-driven-supply-chain-a-blueprint-for-the-future-of-global-logistics/

Kruger, J. (2010). A Study Of Strategic Intelligence As A Strategic Management Tool. In *The Long-Term Insurance Industry in South Africa. Master of Commerce.* University of South Africa.

Kuznetsov, S. D., Velikhov, P. E., & Fu, Q. (2023). Real-time analytics: Benefits, limitations, and tradeoffs. *Programming and Computer Software*, *49*(1), 1–25.

Larose, D. T. (2005). *Discovering Knowledge in Data. An Introduction to Data Mining*. John Wiley & Sons, Inc.

Larson, B. (2008). Delivering Business Intelligence with Microsoft SQL Server 2008, New York, McGraw-Hill Osborne Media. Meyer S.R., 2001, Which ETL Tool is Right for You? DM Review Magazine, June 1.

Larson, D., & Chang, V. (2016). A review and future direction of agile, business intelligence, analytics and data science. *International Journal of Information Management*, *36*(5), 700–710. DOI: 10.1016/j.ijinfomgt.2016.04.013

Laudon, K., & Laudon, J. (2014). *Management information systems: managing the digital firm* (13th ed.). Pearson.

LeCun, Y., Bengio, Y., & Hinton, G. (2015). Deep learning. *Nature*, *521*(7553), 436–444. DOI: 10.1038/nature14539

Lee, J.. (2020). The fourth industrial revolution and implications for smart Manufacturing. *Wiley Interdisciplinary Reviews. Data Mining and Knowledge Discovery*, *10*(6), e1388.

Leon, V., Minaidis, P., Lentaris, G., & Soudris, D. (2023). Accelerating AI and computer vision for satellite pose estimation on the intel myriad X embedded SoC. *Microprocessors and Microsystems*, *103*, 104947.

Leventhal, J. (2023). AI-powered predictive analytics in financial decision-making. *Journal of Financial Analytics*, *18*(3), 55–72. DOI: 10.1016/j.jfa.2022.12.045

Li, E., Zhou, Z., & Chen, X. (2018). Edge intelligence: On-demand deep learning model co-inference with device-edge synergy. In *Proceedings of the 2018 workshop on mobile edge communications* (pp. 31-36).

Liebowitz, J. (2006). *Strategic Intelligence: Business Intelligence, Competitive Intelligence and Knowledge Management*. Auerbach Publications.

Li, H., Sun, Y., & Zhao, Y. (2022). Artificial intelligence in business intelligence systems: Enhancing performance and decision-making. *Information & Management, 59*(4), 103567. DOI: 10.1016/j.im.2021.103567

Liu, J., Xiang, J., Jin, Y., Liu, R., Yan, J., & Wang, L. (2021). Boost precision agriculture with unmanned aerial vehicle remote sensing and edge intelligence: A survey. *Remote Sensing*, *13*(21), 4387.

Liu, Y., Peng, M., Shou, G., Chen, Y., & Chen, S. (2020). Toward edge intelligence: Multiaccess edge computing for 5G and Internet of Things. *IEEE Internet of Things Journal*, *7*(8), 6722–6747.

Liu, Y., Wang, W., & Zhang, J. (2021). Smart logistics in China: Role of AI and cloud BI platforms in urban delivery networks. *Transportation Research Part E, Logistics and Transportation Review*, *145*, 102179. DOI: 10.1016/j.tre.2020.102179

Li, W., & Xu, X. (2023). Machine learning applications in business intelligence: A case study approach. *Artificial Intelligence Review*, *56*(4), 2057–2084. DOI: 10.1007/s10462-022-10123-4

Li, Z., Seco, D., & Sánchez Rodríguez, A. E. (2019). Microservice-oriented platform for Internet of big data analytics: A proof of concept. *Sensors (Basel)*, *19*(5), 1134. DOI: 10.3390/s19051134 PMID: 30845687

Li, Z., Xu, P., Chang, X., Yang, L., Zhang, Y., Yao, L., & Chen, X. (2023). When object detection meets knowledge distillation: A survey. *IEEE Transactions on Pattern Analysis and Machine Intelligence*, *45*(8), 10555–10579. PMID: 37028387

Lloyd, J. (2011). *Identifying Key Components of Business Intelligence Systems and Their Role in Managerial Decision Making*. Intel Corporation.

Lo Piano, S. (2020). Ethical principles in machine learning and artificial intelligence: Cases from the field and possible ways forward. *Humanities & Social Sciences Communications*, *7*(1), 1–7.

Logistics Business. (2018). Case Study: Demand Management Efficiency for Brandt Group. *Logistics Business Magazine*. https://logisticsbusiness.com/

Lokanan, M. E., & Maddhesia, V. (2025). Supply chain fraud prediction with machine learning and artificial intelligence. *International Journal of Production Research*, *63*(1), 286–313.

Loring, L. (2023). Dynamic threat mitigation in multi-tenant cloud environments using AI and predictive analytics. *Eastern European Journal for Multidisciplinary Research*, *2*(1), 67–75.

Lou, B., & Wu, L. (2021). AI on drugs: Can artificial intelligence accelerate drug Development? Evidence from a large-scale examination of bio-Pharma firms. *Management Information Systems Quarterly*, *45*, 1451–1482. DOI: 10.25300/MISQ/2021/16565

Lukić, J., Radenković, M., Despotović-Zrakić, M., Labus, A., & Bogdanović, Z. (2016). A hybrid approach to building a multi-dimensional business intelligence system for electricity grid operators. *Utilities Policy*, *41*, 95–106.

Luo, Y., & Zahra, S. A. (2023). Industry 4.0 in international business research. *Journal of International Business Studies*, *54*(3), 403–417. DOI: 10.1057/s41267-022-00577-9

Machireddy, J. R. (2024). Integrating Machine Learning-Driven RPA with Cloud-Based Data Warehousing for Real-Time Analytics and Business Intelligence. *Hong Kong Journal of AI and Medicine*, *4*(1), 98–121.

Madera, C., & Laurent, A. (2016). The next information architecture evolution: The data lake wave. In *Proceedings of the 8th International Conference on Management of Digital Ecosystems (MEDES)* (pp. 174–180). https://doi.org/DOI: 10.1145/3012071.3012077

Mahida, A. (2024). Integrating observability with DevOps practices in financial services technologies: A study on enhancing software development and operational resilience. *International Journal of Advanced Computer Science and Applications*, *15*(7).

Malkoochi, R. (2025). Event-driven fraud detection system: A cloud-native architecture for real-time transaction analysis. *World Journal of Advanced Engineering Technology and Sciences*, *15*(2), 1684–1693. https://doi.org/10.30574/wjaets.2025.15.2.0701

Manchana, R. (2022). The Power of Cloud-Native Solutions for Descriptive Analytics: Unveiling Insights from Data. *Journal of Artificial Intelligence & Cloud Computing. SRC/JAICCE139. http://dx.doi.org/10.47363/JAICC/2022(1)133*

Mashaleh, A. S., Ibrahim, N. F. B., Alauthman, M., Almseidin, M., & Gawanmeh, A. (2024). IoT Smart Devices Risk Assessment Model Using Fuzzy Logic and PSO. *Computers, Materials & Continua*, *78*(2).

Mathrani, S. (2021). Critical business intelligence practices to create meta-knowledge. *International Journal of Business Information Systems*, *36*(1), 1–20.

Ma, Z., Ren, Y., Xiang, X., & Turk, Z. (2020). Data-driven decision-making for equipment maintenance. *Automation in Construction*, *112*, 103103.

Mehmood, E., & Anees, T. (2020). Challenges and solutions for processing real-time big data stream: A systematic literature review. *IEEE Access : Practical Innovations, Open Solutions*, *8*, 119123–119143.

Mendez, J., Bierzynski, K., Cuéllar, M. P., & Morales, D. P. (2022). Edge intelligence: Concepts, architectures, applications, and future directions. [TECS]. *ACM Transactions on Embedded Computing Systems*, *21*(5), 1–41.

Menzies, J., Sabert, B., Hassan, R., & Mensah, P. K. (2024). Artificial intelligence For international business: Its use, challenges, and suggestions for future research and practice. *Thunderbird International Business Review*, *2024*(66), 185–200.

Meribout, M., Baobaid, A., Khaoua, M. O., Tiwari, V. K., & Pena, J. P. (2022). State of art IoT and Edge embedded systems for real-time machine vision applications. *IEEE Access : Practical Innovations, Open Solutions*, *10*, 58287–58301.

Michael, C. I., Ipede, O. J., Adejumo, A. D., Adenekan, I. O., Adebayo, D., Ojo, A. S., & Ayodele, P. A. (2024). Data-driven decision making in IT: Leveraging AI and data science for business intelligence. *World Journal of Advanced Research and Reviews*, *23*(1), 472–480.

Mikalef, P., & Gupta, M. (2021). Artificial intelligence capability: Conceptualization, Measurement calibration and empirical study on its impact on organizational creativity and firm performance. *Information & Management*, *58*, 103434. DOI: 10.1016/j.im.2021.103434

Mishra, R., Tripathi, P., & Kumar, N. (2024). Future Directions in the Application of Machine Learning and Intelligent Optimization in Business Analytics. In *Intelligent Optimization Techniques for Business Analytics* (pp. 49–76). IGI Global.

Mohamed, D. (2020). Data and Business Intelligence Systems for Competitive Advantage: Prospects, challenges, and real-world applications Mercados. *Negocios*, (41), 2020.

Moresi, G. (2023). Zero trust network & zero internet: Defense strategies against the zero day kill chain.

Moscoso-Zea, O., Castro, J., Paredes-Gualtor, J., & Luján-Mora, S. (2019). A hybrid infrastructure of enterprise architecture and business intelligence & analytics for knowledge management in education. *IEEE Access : Practical Innovations, Open Solutions*, *7*, 38778–38788.

Moscoso-Zea, O., Castro, J., Paredes-Gualtor, J., & Luján-Mora, S. (2019). A Hybrid Infrastructure of Enterprise Architecture and Business Intelligence & Analytics for Knowledge Management in Education. *IEEE Access : Practical Innovations, Open Solutions*.

Mozumder, M. A. S., Sweet, M. M. R., Nabi, N., Tusher, M. I., Modak, C., & Hasan, M., ... & Prabha10, M. (2024). Revolutionizing Organizational Decision-Making for Banking Sector: A Machine Learning Approach with CNNs in Business Intelligence and Management. *Journal of Business and Management Studies*, *6*(3), 111–118.

Muchova, M., Paralic, J., & Nagyova, B. (2018). Data analysis of logistics company's data using business intelligence. *Journal Name*, *18*(4), 58–63.

Murphy, C. (2005). *Competitive intelligence: gathering, analysing, and putting it to work*. Gower.

Nain, G., Pattanaik, K. K., & Sharma, G. K. (2022). Towards edge computing in intelligent manufacturing: Past, present and future. *Journal of Manufacturing Systems*, *62*, 588–611.

Naqvi, S. K. H., & Batool, K. (2023). A comparative analysis between general data protection regulations and california consumer privacy act. *Journal of Computer Science. Information Technology and Telecommunication Engineering*, *4*(1), 326–332.

Nasir, M., Muhammad, K., Ullah, A., Ahmad, J., Baik, S. W., & Sajjad, M. (2022). Enabling automation and edge intelligence over resource constraint IoT devices for smart home. *Neurocomputing*, *491*, 494–506.

Neiroukh, S., Aljuhmani, H. Y., & Alnajdawi, S. (2024, January). In the era of emerging technologies: discovering the impact of artificial intelligence capabilities on timely decision-making and business performance. In *2024 ASU International Conference in Emerging Technologies for Sustainability and Intelligent Systems (ICETSIS)* (pp. 1-6). IEEE.

Neontri. (2025). *DevOps observability: Transforming data into strategic insights*. https://neontri.com/blog/devops-observability

Nerella, S., Guan, Z., Siegel, S., Zhang, J., Khezeli, K., Bihorac, A., & Rashidi, P. (2023). AI-enhanced intensive care unit: revolutionizing patient care with pervasive sensing. arXiv preprint arXiv:2303.06252.

Newman, M. E. J. (2010). *Networks. An Introduction*. Oxford University Press.

Ngai, E. W. T., Chau, D. C. K., & Chan, T. L. A. (2011). Information technology, operational, and management competencies for supply chain agility: Findings from case studies. *The Journal of Strategic Information Systems*, *20*(3), 232–249. DOI: 10.1016/j.jsis.2010.11.001

Ngai, E. W. T., Wu, Y., Chau, D. C. K., & Li, X. (2020). Predicting consumer decisions with data mining: The role of sentiment analysis. *Decision Support Systems*, *130*, 113234. DOI: 10.1016/j.dss.2019.113234

NumberAnalytics. (2025). Transforming logistics & supply chains with big data insights [Blog post]. NumberAnalytics.com. https://www.numberanalytics.com/blog/transforming-logistics-big-data-insights

Odeh, I., Alkasassbeh, M., & Almseidin, M. (2022). Diabetic retinopathy detection method using artificial neural network. *International Journal of Bioinformatics Research and Applications*, *18*(4), 300–317.

Olszak C. M., (2014). Business Intelligence and Analytics in Organizations, [in:] M.

Olszak, C. M., & Zurada, J. (2015). Information technology tools for business Intelligence development in organizations. *Polish Journal of Management Studies.*, *12*(1).

Onesi-Ozigagun, O., Ololade, Y. J., Eyo-Udo, N. L., & Oluwaseun, D. (2024). Data-driven decision making: Shaping the future of business efficiency and customer engagement. *International Journal of Multidisciplinary Research Updates*, *7*(2), 19–29.

Ong, I. L., Siew, P. H., & Wong, S. F. (2011). A five-layered business intelligence architecture. *Communications of the IBIMA*, *2011*, 1–11.

Onishi, T., Michaelis, J., & Kanemasa, Y. (2020). *Recovery-conscious adaptive watermark generation for time-order event stream processing*. Paper presented at the 2020 IEEE/ACM Fifth International Conference on Internet-of-Things Design and Implementation (IoTDI).

Otto, B. (2011). Organizing data governance: Findings from the telecommunications industry and consequences for large service providers. *Communications of the Association for Information Systems*, *29*, 45–66. DOI: 10.17705/1CAIS.02903

Ouassam, E., Hmina, N., & Bouikhalene, B. (2023). Design of intelligent agent on Moodle to automate the learning assessment process. – DOI: DOI: 10.11591/ijeecs.v31.i3.pp1665-1672

Pappala, S., Rayudu, M. M., & Faiz, M. S. (2024). The Transformative [*Technology on Industrial Automation, Gaming and Entertainment, Healthcare, and Autonomous Vehicles.*]. *Impact of*, •••, 5G.

Paradza, D., & Daramola, O. (2021). Business Intelligence and Business Value in Organisations: A Systematic Literature Review. *Sustainability*, *13*, 11382. DOI: 10.3390/su132011382

Paramesha, M., Rane, N. L., & Rane, J. (2024). Big data analytics, artificial intelligence, machine learning, internet of things, and blockchain for enhanced business intelligence. *Partners Universal Multidisciplinary Research Journal*, *1*(2), 110–133.

Paul, F. (2023). The future of cloud security: AI-powered predictive analytics for proactive threat management.

Peddireddy, K. (2023). *Streamlining enterprise data processing, reporting and realtime alerting using apache kafka.* Paper presented at the 2023 11th International Symposium on Digital Forensics and Security (ISDFS). https://doi.org/10.1109/ISDFS58141.2023.10131800

Peltonen, E., Ahmad, I., Aral, A., Capobianco, M., Ding, A. Y., Gil-Castiñeira, F., & Yang, T. (2022). The many faces of edge intelligence. *IEEE Access : Practical Innovations, Open Solutions*, *10*, 104769–104782.

Pietroni, G., & Marconi, M. (2023). Data-driven smart manufacturing: Case study of workforce management process in an Italian leather goods company. In Proceedings of the Design Society: International Conference on Engineering Design (ICED 2023) (Vol. 3, pp. 1127–1136). https://doi.org/DOI: 10.1017/pds.2023.113

Pioli, L., de Macedo, D. D., Costa, D. G., & Dantas, M. A. (2024). Intelligent edge-powered data reduction: A systematic literature review. *ACM Computing Surveys*, *56*(9), 1–39.

Pokala, P. (2024). The integration and impact of artificial intelligence in modern enterprise resource planning systems: A comprehensive review. *Available at SSRN* 5069295.

Poojara, S. R., Dehury, C. K., Jakovits, P., & Srirama, S. N. (2022). Serverless data pipeline approaches for IoT data in fog and cloud computing. *Future Generation Computer Systems*, *130*, 91–105.

Popovič, A., Hackney, R., Coelho, P. S., & Jaklič, J. (2012). Towards business intelligence systems success: Effects of maturity and culture on analytical decision making. *Decision Support Systems*, *54*(1), 729–739. DOI: 10.1016/j.dss.2012.08.017

Porambage, P., Okwuibe, J., Liyanage, M., Ylianttila, M., & Taleb, T. (2018). Survey on multi-access edge computing for internet of things realization. *IEEE Communications Surveys and Tutorials*, *20*(4), 2961–2991.

Porter, M. E. (1990). The competitive advantage of nations. *Harvard Business Review*, *68*(2), 73–93.

Porter, M. E. (1991). America's green strategy. *Scientific American*, *264*(4), 96–101.

Poul, S., Gautman, N., & Balint, R. (2003). *Preparing and data mining with Microsoft SQL Server 2000 and Analysis Services*. Addison-Wesley.

Prangon, N. F., & Wu, J. (2024). AI and computing horizons: Cloud and edge in the modern era. *Journal of Sensor and Actuator Networks*, *13*(4), 44.

Puspitasari, L. P., Sumaryati, S., & Sudiyanto, S. (2023). Effectiveness of Moodle-based e-learning in enhancing digital literacy. – DOI: DOI: 10.23916/083346011

Qian, B. (2024). Enabling Efficient ML-based IoT Applications: Edge-Cloud Collaboration for Deployment, Updates, and Optimization. Newcastle University. http://theses.ncl.ac.uk/jspui/handle/10443/6461

Ragazou, K., Passas, I., Garefalakis, A., & Zopounidis, C. (2023). *Business Intelligence model empowering SMEs to make better decisions and enhance their competitive advantage*. Discover Analytics.

Raheja, R. (2020). Enabling kubernetes for distributed ai processing on edge devices (Doctoral dissertation, The University of North Carolina at Charlotte).

Rahman, A. (2011, March). A Five-Layered Business Intelligence Architecture. *Communications of the IBIMA*.

Raisinghani, M. S. (Ed.). (2004). *Business intelligence in the digital economy: opportunities, limitations and risks*. Igi Global.

Rane, N., Paramesha, M., Choudhary, S., & Rane, J. (2024). Business Intelligence and Business Analytics With Artificial Intelligence and Machine Learning: Trends, Techniques, and Opportunities. *Techniques, and Opportunities (May 17, 2024)*.

Rane, N. L., Paramesha, M., Choudhary, S. P., & Rane, J. (2024). Artificial intelligence, machine learning, and deep learning for advanced business strategies: A review. *Partners Universal International Innovation Journal*, *2*(3), 147–171.

Ranjan, J. (2009). Business intelligence: Concepts, components, techniques and benefits. *Journal of Theoretical and Applied Information Technology*, *9*(1), 60–70.

Ranjan, J., & Foropon, C. (2021). Big Data Analytics in Building the Competitive Intelligence of Organizations. *International Journal of Information Management, 56*, 102231.

Ravichandran, P., Machireddy, J. R., & Rachakatla, S. K. (2022). AI-Enhanced data analytics for real-time business intelligence: Applications and challenges. *Journal of AI in Healthcare and Medicine, 2*(2), 168–195.

Rawashdeh, A., Alkasassbeh, M., Alauthman, M., & Almseidin, M. (2024). A stacked ensemble approach to identify internet of things network attacks through traffic analysis. *Bulletin of Electrical Engineering and Informatics, 13*(6), 4316–4326.

Ray, P. P. (2023). Web3: A comprehensive review on background, technologies, applications, zero-trust architectures, challenges and future directions. *Internet of Things and Cyber-Physical Systems, 3*, 213–248.

Refonte Learning. (2025). *Top observability tools DevOps engineers must learn in 2025.* https://www.refontelearning.com/blog/top-observability-tools-devops-engineers-must-learn-in-2025

Rehman, M. H. U., Chang, V., Battol, A., & Wah, T. Y. (2016). Big Data Reduction Framework for value creation in sustainable enterprises. *International Journal of Information Management, 36*, 917–928.

Riad, A. M. and Hassan Q. F. (2008). Service-Oriented Architecture – A New Alternative to Traditional Integration Methods in B2B Applications, Journal of Convergence Information Technologies.

Rimon, S. T. H. (2024). Leveraging Artificial Intelligence in Business Analytics for Informed Strategic Decision-Making: Enhancing Operational Efficiency, Market Insights, and Competitive Advantage. *Journal of Artificial Intelligence General science (JAIGS) ISSN: 3006-4023, 6*(1), 600-624.

Rodriguez, P., & Costa, I. (2024). Artificial Intelligence and Machine Learning for Predictive Threat Intelligence in Government Networks. *Advances in Computer Sciences, 7*(1), 1–10.

Russell, S., & Norvig, P. (2016). *Artificial intelligence: A modern approach* (3rd ed.). Pearson.

Russom, P. (2011). *Big data analytics*. TDWI Best Practices Report, Fourth Quarter. The Data Warehousing Institute (TDWI).

Ryu, C., Lee, J. H., Kim, D. H., Lee, H. S., Kim, Y. S., Han, J. H., & Kim, J. N. (2024). A Comprehensive Survey of TPM for Defense Systems. [TIIS]. *KSII Transactions on Internet and Information Systems*, *18*(7), 1953–1967.

Saleem, M., Warsi, M. R., & Islam, S. (2023). Secure information processing for multimedia forensics using zero-trust security model for large scale data analytics in SaaS cloud computing environment. *Journal of Information Security and Applications*, *72*, 103389.

Salloum, S., Dautov, R., Chen, X., Peng, P. X., & Huang, J. (2016). Big data analytics on Apache Spark. *International Journal of Data Science and Analytics*, *1*(3), 145–164. DOI: 10.1007/s41060-016-0027-9

Samara, F. Y. A., Taha, A. H. A., Massa, N. M., Jamie, T. N. A., Harara, F. E., Abu-Nasser, B. S., & Abu-Naser, S. S. (2024). The Role of AI in Enhancing Business Decision-Making: Innovations and Implications.

Samek, W., Wiegand, T., & Müller, K.-R. (2017). Explainable artificial intelligence: Understanding, visualizing and interpreting deep learning models. https://arxiv.org/abs/1708.08296

Sang, B. (2021). Application of genetic algorithm and BP neural network in supply chain finance under information sharing. *Journal of Computational and Applied Mathematics*, (384), 113170.

Sang, G. M., Xu, L., & De Vrieze, P. (2016). A reference architecture for big data systems. In *Proc. International Conference on Software, Knowledge, Information Management & Applications (SKIMA)* (pp. 1–8). https://doi.org/DOI: 10.1109/SKIMA.2016.7916249

Sankaranarayanan, S. (2025). The Role of Data Engineering in Enabling Real-Time Analytics and Decision-Making Across Heterogeneous Data Sources in Cloud-Native Environments. [IJARC]. *International Journal of Advanced Research in Cyber Security*, *6*(1). https://ijarc.com/index.php/journal/article/view/IJARC.6.1.3

Satheesh, M. K., Samala, N., & Rodriguez, R. V. (2020). Role of AI-induced Chatbot in Enhancing customer relationship management in the banking industry. *ICTACT Journal on Management Studies*, *6*(4), 1320–1323.

Saxena, T., Tripathi, D. R., & Jain, R. (2024). Evaluating The Opportunities and Risks of Artificial Intelligence In Strategic Management and Business Integration. *International Journal of Innovations in Science, Engineering And Management*, 19-24.

Sedlak, B., Pujol, V. C., Donta, P. K., & Dustdar, S. (2023). Controlling data gravity and data friction: From metrics to multidimensional elasticity strategies. In *2023 IEEE International Conference on Software Services Engineering (SSE)* (pp. 43-49). IEEE.

Sengupta, J., Kubendran, R., Neftci, E., & Andreou, A. (2020). High-speed, real-time, spike-based object tracking and path prediction on google edge TPU. In 2020 2nd IEEE International Conference on Artificial Intelligence Circuits and Systems (AICAS) (pp. 134-135). IEEE.

Shafique, M., Marchisio, A., Putra, R. V. W., & Hanif, M. A. (2021). Towards energy-efficient and secure edge AI: A cross-layer framework ICCAD special session paper. In *2021 IEEE/ACM International Conference On Computer Aided Design (ICCAD)* (pp. 1-9). IEEE.

Shankar, V. (2024). Edge AI: A Comprehensive Survey of Technologies, Applications, and Challenges. In 2024 1st International Conference on Advanced Computing and Emerging Technologies (ACET) (pp. 1-6). IEEE.

Sharma, C., & Vaid, A. (2022). Converging SAP, AI, and data analytic for transformative business management. *World J. Adv. Res. Rev*, *14*(3), 736–761.

Sharma, P. (2024). Techniques for Reducing Latency in Cloud-Based Networks: A Comprehensive Study. *Journal of Innovative Technologies*, *7*(1), 1–7.

Sharma, R., Mithas, S., & Kankanhalli, A. (2023). Transforming decision-making with AI-driven business intelligence. *The Journal of Strategic Information Systems*, *32*(3), 101847. DOI: 10.1016/j.jsis.2023.101847

Sheriffdeen, K. (2024). Zero trust architecture: Strengthening cyber defenses with AI-driven policies.

Shittu, R. A., Ehidiamen, A. J., Ojo, O. O., Zouo, S. J. C., Olamijuwon, J., Omowole, B. M., & Olufemi-Phillips, A. Q. (2024). The role of business intelligence tools in improving healthcare patient outcomes and operations. *World Journal of Advanced Research and Reviews*, *24*(2), 1039–1060.

Shorman, A. R., Alzubi, M., Almseidin, M., & Rateb, R. (2025). Adaptive Intrusion Detection for IoT Networks using Artificial Immune System Techniques: A Comparative Study. [JRC]. *Journal of Robotics and Control*, *6*(2), 570–582.

Silitonga, D., Rohmayanti, S. A. A., Aripin, Z., Kuswandi, D., & Sulistyo, A. B. (2024). Edge computing in E-commerce business: Economic impacts and advantages of scalable information systems. *EAI Endorsed Transactions on Scalable Information Systems*, *11*(1), 4375.

Sipola, T., Alatalo, J., Kokkonen, T., & Rantonen, M. (2022). Artificial intelligence in the IoT era: A review of edge AI hardware and software. In *2022 31st Conference of Open Innovations Association (FRUCT)* (pp. 320-331). IEEE.

Sivarajah, U., Kamal, M. M., Irani, Z., & Weerakkody, V. (2017). Critical analysis of big data challenges and analytical methods. *Journal of Business Research, 70*, 263–286. DOI: 10.1016/j.jbusres.2016.08.001

Sodhro, A. H., Pirbhulal, S., & De Albuquerque, V. H. C. (2019). Artificial intelligence-driven mechanism for edge computing-based industrial applications. *IEEE Transactions on Industrial Informatics, 15*(7), 4235–4243.

Sodiya, E. O., Umoga, U. J., Obaigbena, A., Jacks, B. S., Ugwuanyi, E. D., Daraojimba, A. I., & Lottu, O. A. (2024). Current state and prospects of edge computing within the Internet of Things (IoT) ecosystem. *International Journal of Science and Research Archive, 11*(1), 1863–1873.

Solanke, A. (2023). Edge computing integration with enterprise cloud systems: Architectural patterns for distributed intelligence. *International Journal of Engineering and Computer Science, 12*(03).

Solano, M. C., & Cruz, J. C. (2024). Integrating analytics in enterprise systems: A systematic literature review of impacts and innovations. *Administrative Sciences, 14*(7), 138. Advance online publication. DOI: 10.3390/admsci14070138

Soori, M., Arezoo, B., & Dastres, R. (2023). Artificial neural networks in supply Chain management, a review. *Journal of Economy and Technology, 1*, 179–196.

Souhaib, A., Zakaria, T., & Tarik, T. (2024). Enhancing socio-pedagogical engagement in Moodle through AI-driven personalized learning. – DOI: DOI: 10.14571/brajets.v17.nse4.63-73

Sprague, R. H. (1980). A framework for the development of decision support systems. *Management Information Systems Quarterly, 4*(4), 1–26. DOI: 10.2307/248957

Sreemathy, J., Brindha, R., Nagalakshmi, M. S., Suvekha, N., Ragul, N. K., & Praveennandha, M. (2021). *Overview of ETL tools and talend-data integration.* Paper presented at the 2021 7th International Conference on Advanced Computing and Communication Systems (ICACCS).

Sresth, V., Nagavalli, S. P., & Tiwari, S. (2023). Optimizing Data Pipelines in Advanced Cloud Computing: Innovative Approaches to Large-Scale Data Processing, Analytics, and Real-Time Optimization. *International Journal of Research and Analytical Reviews, 10*, 478–496. https://ijrar.org/papers/IJRAR23D3307.pdf

Suad, A., Tapalova, O., Berestova, A., & Vlasova, S. (2023). The impact of Moodle learning analytics on students' performance and motivation. – DOI: DOI: 10.29333/iji.2023.16418a

Sun, Z., Strang, K., & Firmin, S. (2017). Business analytics-based enterprise information systems. *Journal of Computer Information Systems*, *57*(2), 169–178. DOI: 10.1080/08874417.2016.1183977

Tan, P. N., Steinbach, M., & Kumar, V. (2005). *Introduction to Data Mining*. Addison-Wesley.

Tariq, M. U. (2025). AI and Work-Life Balance: Transforming Employee Wellbeing in the Modern Workplace. In Ahmed, E., Babar, A., Samad, A., Ahmed, R., & Beydoun, G. (Eds.), *Strengthening Human Relations in Organizations With AI* (pp. 85–110). IGI Global Scientific Publishing., DOI: 10.4018/979-8-3693-6507-6.ch004

Tariq, M. U. (2025). AI-Powered Business Process Automation: Revolutionizing Firm Management. In Derbali, A. (Ed.), *AI, Economic Perspectives, and Firm Business Management* (pp. 199–224). IGI Global Scientific Publishing., DOI: 10.4018/979-8-3693-7357-6.ch010

Tariq, M. U. (2025). Bridging Generations: Digital Transformation and Its Multifaceted Impact Across Societal Sectors. In Anshari, M., Almunawar, M., & Ordóñez de Pablos, P. (Eds.), *Impacts of Digital Technologies Across Generations* (pp. 1–22). IGI Global Scientific Publishing., DOI: 10.4018/979-8-3693-6366-9.ch001

Tariq, M. U. (2025). Integrating ICT for Enhanced Organizational Resilience: Strategies and Case Studies. In Carvalho, L., Reis, L., Neves de Almeida Baptista Figueiredo, A., & Russo, N. (Eds.), *Leveraging Technology for Organizational Adaptability* (pp. 59–80). IGI Global Scientific Publishing., DOI: 10.4018/979-8-3693-6045-3.ch004

Tariq, M. U. (2025). Navigating Public Administration 5.0: Embracing AI for Smarter Governance. In Wongmahesak, K., Ahmad, J., & Mustanir, A. (Eds.), *Public Governance Practices in the Age of AI* (pp. 167–186). IGI Global Scientific Publishing., DOI: 10.4018/979-8-3693-9286-7.ch008

Tauseef, A. (2023). AI in cybersecurity: Leveraging database innovations for intelligent threat response.

Teece, D. J., Pisano, G., & Shuen, A. (1997). Dynamic capabilities and strategic management. *Strategic Management Journal*, *18*(7), 509–533. DOI: 10.1002/(SICI)1097-0266(199708)18:7<509:AID-SMJ882>3.0.CO;2-Z

Toorajipour, R., Sohrabpour, V., Nazarpour, A., Oghazi, P., & Fischl, M. (2021). Artificial intelligence in supply chain management: A systematic literature review. *Journal of Business Research*, *122*, 502–517.

To, Q.-C., Soto, J., & Markl, V. (2018). A survey of state management in big data processing systems. *The VLDB Journal*, *27*(6), 847–872. https://doi.org/10.1007/s00778-018-0514-9

Tsiu, S. V., Ngobeni, M., Mathabela, L., & Thango, B. A. (2024). Applications and Competitive Advantages of Data Mining and Business Intelligence in SMEs Performance: A Systematic Review. Doi: DOI: 10.20944/preprints202409.0940.v1

Turban, E., Aronson, J. E., Liang, T., & Sharda, R. (2007). *Decision Support And Business Intelligence Systems* (8th ed.). Pearson Prentice Hall.

UPS (United Parcel Service). (2016). ORION logistics optimization project – results overview. UPS Press Release (as reported in BestPractice AI). Retrieved August 17, 2025, from https://www.bestpractice.ai/ai-case-study-best-practice/ups_saves_10_million_gallons_of_fuel_and_%24100_million_per_year_by_optimising_driver_delivery_routes_that_consider_real-time-traffic-and-weather-information-obtained-from-social-media-and-machine-learning

Urblik, L., Kajati, E., Papcun, P., & Zolotová, I. (2024). Containerization in edge intelligence: A review. *Electronics (Basel)*, *13*(7), 1335.

Vasudevan, A., Rassineux, J.-L., & Robertson, P. (2024). Smart operations in the manufacturing sector: Creating a connected aftermarket. Deloitte Insights. https://www.deloitte.com/global/en/Industries/industrial-construction/perspectives/smart-operations-in-the-manufacturing-sector.html

Veber, J. (2012). Operational-economic aspects of cloud computing, [in:] M. Tvrdikova, J. Minster and P. Rozenhal (Eds.), IT for Practice, Ostrava, VSB-TU Economicka Faculta.

Velocity Staff, D. C. (2020). Shoemaker finds its elves with ERP software. DC Velocity. https://www.dcvelocity.com/articles/48366-shoemaker-finds-its-elves-with-erp-software

Vicente, J. J., Neves, L., & Bernardo, I. (2024). The potential of Logistics 4.0 technologies: A case study through business intelligence framing by applying the Delphi method. *Frontiers in Artificial Intelligence*, *7*, 1469958. Advance online publication. DOI: 10.3389/frai.2024.1469958 PMID: 39484155

Villar-Rodriguez, E., Pérez, M. A., Torre-Bastida, A. I., Senderos, C. R., & López-de-Armentia, J. (2023). Edge intelligence secure frameworks: Current state and future challenges. *Computers & Security*, *130*, 103278.

Vizgaitytė, G & Skyrius, R. (2012). Business Intelligence in the Process of Decision Making: Changes and Trends. Network of Scientific Journals from Latin America, the Caribbean, Spain and Portugal Non-profit academic project, developed under the open access initiative.

Vlahovljak, A. (2022). *Business Intelligence*. International Burch University.

Vrontis, D., Christofi, M., Pereira, V., Tarba, S., Makrides, A., & Trichina, E. (2021). Artificial intelligence, robotics, advanced technologies and human resource management: A systematic review. *International Journal of Human Resource Management*, *33*(6), 1237–1266.

Wamba, S. F., Gunasekaran, A., Akter, S., Ren, S. J. F., Dubey, R., & Childe, S. J. (2020). Big data analytics and supply chain performance: A resource-based view. *Information & Management*, *57*(2), 103207. DOI: 10.1016/j.im.2019.103207

Wamba-Taguimdje, S. L., Fosso Wamba, S., Kala Kamdjoug, J. R., & Tchatchouang Wanko, C. E. (2020). Influence of artificial intelligence (AI) on firm performance: The business value of AI-based transformation projects. *Business Process Management Journal*, *26*(7).

Wang, J., Zhang, H., & Liu, P. (2021). Predicting customer churn with AI-driven BI systems: Evidence from telecom. *Expert Systems with Applications*, *173*, 114699. DOI: 10.1016/j.eswa.2021.114699

Wang, Y., Kung, L., & Byrd, T. A. (2023). Big data analytics and business intelligence: A research agenda. *Management Information Systems Quarterly*, *47*(4), 223–252. DOI: 10.25300/MISQ/2023/16288

Wang, Z., Wang, N., Su, X., & Ge, S. (2020). An empirical study on business Analytics affordances enhancing the management of cloud computing data security. *International Journal of Information Management*, *50*, 387–394.

Watson, H. J. (2014). Tutorial: Big data analytics: Concepts, technologies, and applications. *Communications of the Association for Information Systems*, *34*(1), 1247–1268.

Witten, I. H., Frank, E., & Hall, M. (2011). *Data Mining: Practical Machine Learning Tools and Techniques*. Morgan Kaufland.

Wixom, B., & Watson, H. (2010). The BI-based organization. *International Journal of Business Intelligence Research, 1*(1), 13–28. DOI: 10.4018/jbir.2010071702

Wu, Y. H., & Luo, H. (2020). Apply edge intelligence to IoT based home automation. In *17th Int. Conf. on Applied Computing*.

Xiao, L., Zhang, Y., Chen, H., & Li, X. (2023). Artificial intelligence applications in business intelligence: Opportunities and challenges. *Information Systems Frontiers, 25*(2), 345–362. DOI: 10.1007/s10796-022-10345-7

Xidias, E., Zacharia, P., & Nearchou, A. (2022). Intelligent fleet management of autonomous vehicles for city logistics. *Applied Intelligence, 52*(15), 18030–18048.

Xu, R., Nagothu, D., & Chen, Y. (2024). AR-Edge: Autonomous and Resilient Edge Computing Architecture for Smart Cities. In *Edge Computing Architecture-Architecture and Applications for Smart Cities*. IntechOpen.

Xu, D., Li, T., Li, Y., Su, X., Tarkoma, S., Jiang, T., & Hui, P. (2021). Edge intelligence: Empowering intelligence to the edge of network. *Proceedings of the IEEE, 109*(11), 1778–1837.

Yao, M., Ye, D., Yang, G., Shi, H., & Zheng, X. (2021). Are entrepreneurial Capabilities and prior knowledge: The silver bullet for the generation of new digital venture ideas in a digital context? *Journal of Global Information Management, 29*, 1–17. DOI: 10.4018/JGIM.20211101.oa12

Young, M. M., Himmelreich, J., Honcharov, D., & Soundarajan, S. (2022). Using artificial intelligence to identify administrative errors in unemployment insurance. *Government Information Quarterly, 39*(4), 101758.

Younisse, R., Alkasassbeh, M., Almseidin, M., & Abdi, H. (2023). An early detection model for kerberoasting attacks and dataset labeling. *Jordanian Journal of Computers and Information Technology, 9*(1).

Yunos, N., Muslim, N., Hussain, A. H., Hasim, N. A., Nazri, N. S., & Hamsan, M. H. (2024). Best practice of Moodle implementation for e-learning: A perspective of public university lecturers. – DOI: DOI: 10.62754/joe.v3i5.3899

Zagan, E., & Danubianu, M. (2021). Cloud DATA LAKE: The new trend of data storage. In *2021 3rd International Congress on Human-Computer Interaction, Optimization and Robotic Applications (HORA)* (pp. 1-4). IEEE.

Zaharia, M., Chowdhury, M., Franklin, M. J., Shenker, S., & Stoica, I. (2010). Spark: Cluster computing with working sets. In *2nd USENIX workshop on hot topics in cloud computing (HotCloud 10)*.

Zednik, C. (2021). Solving the black box problem: A normative framework for explainable artificial intelligence. *Philosophy & Technology, 34*(2), 265–288.

Zeng, L., Ye, S., Chen, X., Zhang, X., Ren, J., Tang, J., & Shen, X. S. (2025). Edge Graph Intelligence: Reciprocally Empowering Edge Networks with Graph Intelligence. *IEEE Communications Surveys and Tutorials.*

Zhai, Y., Sun, H., & Zhao, X. (2021). The impact of AI-driven BI platforms on operational performance: Evidence from Chinese firms. *Technological Forecasting and Social Change, 168*, 120770. DOI: 10.1016/j.techfore.2021.120770

Zhang, Y., Qian, C., Wu, H., & Chen, X. (2018). IoT-enabled real-time business intelligence: A framework and its applications. *Future Generation Computer Systems, 86*, 124–135. DOI: 10.1016/j.future.2018.03.002

Zhou, L., Wang, J., & Li, M. (2022). Demand forecasting in supply chains using machine learning: A comparative study. *International Journal of Production Economics, 245*, 108–118. DOI: 10.1016/j.ijpe.2021.108118

Zhou, Z., Yu, D., Chen, M., Qiao, Y., Hu, Y., & He, W. (2024). An edge intelligence-based model deployment method for CNC systems. *Journal of Manufacturing Systems, 74*, 716–751.

Zou, Z., Jin, Y., Nevalainen, P., Huan, Y., Heikkonen, J., & Westerlund, T. (2019). Edge and fog computing enabled AI for IoT-an overview. In *2019 IEEE International Conference on Artificial Intelligence Circuits and Systems (AICAS)* (pp. 51-56). IEEE.

About the Contributors

Abdelraouf M. Ishtaiwi is an Associate Professor of Artificial Intelligence and Data Science at the University of Petra, Jordan, with over 22 years of academic and research experience in AI. He earned his Master's and Ph.D. degrees in Artificial Intelligence from Griffith University, Australia, where he focused on heuristic optimization techniques for satisfiability problems. His research expertise spans machine learning, hybrid metaheuristic optimization, associative classification, and AI applications in cybersecurity and emerging technologies like the metaverse. Dr. Ishtaiwi has developed innovative AI algorithms, such as ACRIPPER and hybrid crayfish-DE models, and contributed significantly to areas like phishing detection, blockchain security, and smart IoT defense. As a former Head of the Department of Data Science and AI at Petra University, he led academic reforms and accreditation initiatives. He has also been a visiting scholar at Griffith University and Universitat Pompeu Fabra, reflecting his international academic engagement.

Ahmad Al-Qerem graduated in applied mathematics and M.Sc. in Computer Science at the Jordan University of Science and Technology and Jordan University in 1997 and 2002, respectively. After that, he was appointed as full-time lecturer at the Zarqa University. He was a visiting professor at Princess Sumaya University for Technology (PSUT). He obtained a Ph.D. from Loughborough University, UK. His research interests are in performance and analytical modeling, mobile computing environments, protocol engineering, communication networks, transition to IPv6, machine learning and transaction processing. He has published several papers in various areas of computer science. Currently, he has a full academic post as a full professor at computer science department at Zarqa University-Jordan.

Mohammad Alkhaldy is an accomplished Assistant Professor and researcher specializing in Artificial Intelligence, Data Science, and Business Intelligence, currently serving at the University of Petra in Jordan. With a PhD from the University of Hull (UK), and a strong academic foundation in computer science, he has held various academic and leadership roles across institutions in Jordan, Saudi Arabia, and the UK. Dr. Alkhaldy is recognized for his contributions to cutting-edge research in AI, cybersecurity, blockchain, and digital finance, with numerous peer-reviewed publications and conference presentations. He is also an active member of academic committees and professional societies, playing a vital role in curriculum development, student mentorship, and institutional research strategy. His work reflects a passion for innovation, interdisciplinary collaboration, and empowering students through research and experiential learning.

Mohammad Alauthman is an associate professor and the chair of the Information Security Department at the Faculty of Information Technology, University of Petra in Amman, Jordan. His research focuses on network security, intrusion detection systems, and utilizing artificial intelligence techniques such as machine learning and deep learning for purposes like botnet detection, DDoS mitigation, spam email filtering, IoT security, and network traffic classification. He earned his Ph.D. in computer science, specializing in network security, from Northumbria University in the UK in 2016. Alauthman has received numerous research grants in the field of network security, which have supported his work on advanced intrusion detection systems and the creation of AI-driven security solutions. These grants have facilitated extensive research and collaborations with international experts, leading to projects aimed at strengthening the resilience of network infrastructures against evolving threats and enhancing the precision of threat detection mechanisms.

***

Mohammed Abu-Arqoub is an assistant professor at the Petra University). He earned his B.Sc., M.Sc., and PhD from the University of Saint-Petersburg Electro-Technical University (Russia) in 1990 and 1995, respectively. He has presented numerous papers at world-level scholarly conferences. His research interests include computer simulation and architecture, middleware systems, software and web engineering, education, learning analytics. IoT and AI

Al-E'mari earned her Ph.D. in Cybersecurity from Universiti Sains Malaysia (USM) in 2022. She is the Chair of the Information Security Department and an Assistant Professor at the University of Petra (UoP). With expertise in Blockchain, Deep Learning, and Network Security, she has contributed significantly to cybersecurity research. She previously earned her Bachelor's and Master's in Computer Science from Yarmouk University, Jordan, shaping her strong foundation in security and technology.

Ammar Almomani is a seasoned academic, researcher, and consultant with 20+ years of experience in cybersecurity, AI, and computer science. He holds a Ph.D. in Advanced Internet Security from Universiti Sains Malaysia and has taught over 45 specialized courses. He serves in the IT departments at Al-Balqa Applied University (Jordan) and Higher Colleges of Technology (UAE), contributing to research, curriculum design, and program accreditation (ABET, AACSB). He holds 10 patents (Germany and India) and has published 165+ articles (104 in Scopus), earning global recognition, a UAE Golden Visa, and ranking among the Top 2% of Global Researchers (Stanford & Scopus, 2023–2024). Prof. Almomani also supervises MSc/Ph.D. students internationally, chairs conferences, and engages in industry collaborations. With 113,000+ ResearchGate readers.Prof. Almomani continues to make a significant impact in the fields of cybersecurity,AI and higher education fostering innovation .

Jamil Al-Sawwa is an Assistant Professor of Computer Science at Tafila Technical University, Jordan. He obtained a Ph.D. degree from North Dakota State University, USA, in 2019. His research area of interest includes computational intelligence, Machine Learning, Artificial Intelligence, Big Data Analytics, and Cybersecurity.

Maen Marwan Ali Al-Zubi is currently an Assistant Professor at the Department of Robotics and Artificial Intelligence at JADARA University. He obtained his Ph.D. in AI in 2020 at the University of MISKOLC (Miskolc, Hungary). He also obtained his Master of Computer Information Systems in 2007 at Arab Academy for Banking and Financial Sciences (Amman, Jordan). He did his First Degree in CS in 2004 at Irbid National University (Irbid, Jordan). Dr. Maen Al-Zubi published several papers in international Journals and participated in multi different conferences. He has teaching and technical experience of more than 10 years in the areas of computer science. His research interests are in Fuzzy Systems, Fuzzy rule Interpolation, Image Processing, and machine learning including supervised and unsupervised learning.

Fadi Fataftah is an experienced academic with a PhD in Information Technology and over 15 years of international experience in higher education, research, and industry across Canada, South Africa, Bahrain, and Jordan. He has taught a diverse range of courses in computer science, information technology, and cybersecurity, integrating real-world applications and problem-based learning methodologies. Dr. Fataftah's teaching philosophy emphasizes bridging theoretical concepts with practical skills, preparing students to thrive in dynamic, technology-driven environments. His research interests include cybersecurity, cloud computing, and

IT governance, with contributions to peer-reviewed publications and international conferences. In addition to academia, he has worked in IT support and digital systems administration, further enhancing his practical expertise in the field.

Ala Hamarsheh is an associate professor at the Faculty of Engineering and Information Technology of the Arab American University of Jenin. Dr. Hamarsheh has obtained a PhD in engineering sciences from Vrije Universiteit Brussel (VUB)/ Brussels-Belgium in 2012. He graduated in computer science at the Faculty of Science, Birzeit University, Palestine, in 2000. He obtained an MSc degree in computer science at the Kind Abdullah II School for IT, The University of Jordan, Jordan, in 2003. Dr. Hamarsheh has published numerous papers in international refereed journals and conferences.

Venkateshkumar R is a Senior Manager in Heavy commercial vehicle industry. Experienced operations Manager with a demonstrated history of working in the logistics sector. Skilled in Manufacturing operations, vehicle assembly, Logistics Management and Planning. Strong professional with a DME, B Tech, MBA and have more than 17 years of experience. Research scholar in Hindustan Institute of Technology and Science, India.

Yousef K. Sanjalawe is an Assistant Professor specializing in Cybersecurity and Cloud Computing at the University of Jordan (JU), Jordan. He earned his PhD in Cloud Computing from Universiti Sains Malaysia (USM) in 2020, where his research focused on enhancing cloud service broker selection using optimization algorithms. Dr. Sanjalawe has extensive experience in academia, research, and professional training. He has supervised Ph.D. students in Cybersecurity, Cloud Computing, IoT, Fog Computing, Optimization, and Artificial Intelligence (AI). From 2023 to 2024, he served as the Chair of the Cybersecurity Department at the American University of Madaba (AUM), Jordan, and from 2022 to 2024, he was an Assistant Professor in Cybersecurity at AUM.

Harini Shankar is a seasoned technology leader specializing in automation testing, quality assurance, and software development. Currently serving as a Director of Technology, Harini has been instrumental in transforming the testing landscape for various multi-million large-scale initiatives encompassing numerous micro-applications.She has a proven track record of leveraging cutting edge tools and methodologies, to ensure efficiency, consistency, and high quality outcomes. With a strong background in DevOps and Agile environments, Harini has led and mentored teams of Assurance engineers, enabling them to deliver seamless integration and validation of complex systems.

Ahmad G. Al-Shtayyat is a faculty member in the College of Arts and Sciences at the University of Petra. Al-Shtayyat has extensive experience in e-learning, LMS administration, and IT education. Since 2014, Al-Shtayyat has been working as an LMS administrator specializing in Moodle, where Al-Shtayyat provides training, system customization, and user support. Previously, Al-Shtayyat worked as a lab supervisor in the Faculty of Information Technology at the University of Petra for eight years. Al-Shtayyat's expertise includes programming, web development, and e-learning system management. Al-Shtayyat holds a Master's in Business Administration (E-Business) from Mut'ah University and a B.Sc. in Computer Information Systems from the Arab Academy for Banking and Financial Sciences.

Dennis Amirtharaj is an Associate professor in Hindustan Institute of Technology and Science. Experienced Training Manager with a demonstrated history of working in the hospitality industry. Skilled in Catering, Management, Hospitality Management, Hotel Management, and Hospitality Industry. Strong professional with a B.Sc.,M.T.M.,M.Phil., M.B.A.,Ph.D., focused in Hospitality Administration/Management.

Muhammad Usman Tariq has more than 16+ year's experience in industry and academia. He has authored more than 200+ research articles, 110+ case studies, 130+ book chapters and several books other than 4 patents. He is founder and CEO of The Case HQ, a unique repository for courses, narrative and video case studies. He has been working as a consultant and trainer for industries representing six sigma, quality, health and safety, environmental systems, project management, and information security standards. His work has encompassed sectors in aviation, manufacturing, food, hospitality, education, finance, research, software and transportation. He has diverse and significant experience working with accreditation agencies of ABET, ACBSP, AACSB, WASC, CAA, EFQM and NCEAC. Additionally, Dr. Tariq has operational experience in incubators, research labs, government research projects, private sector startups, program creation and management at various industrial and academic levels. He is Certified Higher Education Teacher from Harvard University, USA, Certified Online Educator from HMBSU, Certified Six Sigma Master Black Belt and has been awarded PFHEA, SFSEDA, SMIEEE, and CMBE.

Index

A

B

C

D

E

F

I

L

M

O

P

Q

R

S

T

Z

www.ingramcontent.com/pod-product-compliance
Lightning Source LLC
LaVergne TN
LVHW080342011026
849161LV00009B/2154